Thomas Dreier / Jan Krämer / Rudi Studer / Christof Weinhardt (Eds.)

Information Management and Market Engineering

Vol. II

AF239740

Studies on eOrganisation and Market Engineering 11

Karlsruher Institut für Technologie

Herausgeber:

Prof. Dr. Christof Weinhardt
Prof. Dr. Thomas Dreier
Prof. Dr. Rudi Studer

Information Management and Market Engineering

Vol. II

Thomas Dreier
Jan Krämer
Rudi Studer
Christof Weinhardt
(Eds.)

Impressum

Karlsruher Institut für Technologie (KIT)
KIT Scientific Publishing
Straße am Forum 2
D-76131 Karlsruhe
www.ksp.kit.edu

KIT Universität des Landes Baden-Württemberg und nationales
Forschungszentrum in der Helmholtz-Gemeinschaft

KIT Scientific Publishing 2010
Print on Demand

ISSN 1862-8893
ISBN 978-3-86644-589-5

Preface

At the Karlsruhe Institute of Technology (KIT), the Graduate School Information Management and Market Engineering (IME) which is financed by the German Research Association (Deutsche Forschungsgemeinschaft, DFG), offers an interdisciplinary doctoral program on the economic, technological and legal design of institutions, services, systems and business models for electronic markets. The expressed aim of the Graduate School is to endow its doctoral students with a profound interdisciplinary understanding of electronic markets and information management that enables them to pursue an outstanding career in academia as well as industry. Since its foundation in April 2004, sixteen graduates have very successfully completed the doctoral program of the Graduate School and went on to become professors themselves or hold key management positions in the industry today, providing proof for the Graduate School's success in achieving its aim.

The research that is conducted in the Graduate School is directly applicable to the large domain of electronic markets and information management and has to steadily keep pace with technological progress. In 2006 the first volume of this book was published, which assembled an overview of the research that was and still is ongoing in the Graduate School. The present and second volume shows the advancements since then, but also points at new research fields that have recently been explored. Altogether, sixteen research papers have been selected, refereed and compiled for this volume. They cover almost all relevant aspects of the field Information Management and Market Engineering and demonstrate the intellectual challenges in this domain.

In short, *Information Management and Market Engineering* comprises the structured, systematic and theoretically founded procedure of analyzing, designing, introducing and also quality assuring of electronic market platforms as well as their legal framework regarding simultaneously their market mechanisms and trading rules, systems, platforms and media, and their business models. This book is structured in four parts, which reflect the different levels of this Market Engineering process.

Electronic markets often generate a tremendous amount of transactional data and, on the other hand, react sensitively to exogenous informational influences. In order to analyze electronic markets, it is therefore indispensable to develop proper methods and tools which facilitate the (i) processing and structuring of this data,

(ii) extraction of the information content of this data, and (iii) analysis of the impact of this information on the market. The research papers in the first part of this book are all concerned with this task of *Market Information Processing and Analysis*.

The second part comprises research papers on the *Design of Market Mechanisms and Systems*. In this core task of the Market Engineering process, new theoretical designs are proposed that are believed to improve the performance of electronic markets. The market design can either influence market behavior directly, for example through appropriate incentive mechanisms, or indirectly, for example through new means of communication or interaction.

The influence of different theoretical designs on actual *Market Interaction and Behavior* is considered in the next level of the Market Engineering process, and exemplified by the research papers in the third part of this volume. In particular the emotional processes of market participants, such as auction fever, are still not fully understood today. Some of the research papers in this part demonstrate how these emotional processes can be measured and evaluate their influence on market behavior and design. The other papers evaluate theoretical market designs on the basis of actually observed market behavior.

Finally, the papers in the fourth part consider various aspects of *Electronic Market Regulation*, i.e. the ongoing normative evaluation of present market designs. More specifically, market regulation seeks to ensure the long run functioning and effectiveness of electronic markets. The regulatory issues that are covered in this part range from the protection of intellectual property rights and personal data to the stimulation and facilitation of information sharing.

However, these different perspectives on Market Engineering and Information Management are not treated separately. Each level of the market analysis is input to and output of the Market Engineering process at the same time, and thereby contributes to the perennial effort of improving market design.

This advancements in Market Engineering and Information Management, which are compiled in this book, have only been possible because the professors and students of the Graduate School have showed great effort and enthusiasm while working for a common goal. In doing so, old-fashioned boundaries between different departments and disciplines were broken-up, making the research and teaching program of the Graduate School truly interdisciplinary. While interdisciplinary research also bears many challenges, this book is ample evidence that it can also provide the researchers with great rewards.

Karlsruhe,   *Thomas Dreier*
October 2010   *Jan Krämer*
                                                                                        Rudi Studer
                                                                                  Christof Weinhardt

Contents

List of Contributors

Marc T. P. Adam
Institute of Information Systems and
Management
Karlsruhe Institute of Technology (KIT)
marc.adam@kit.edu

Helge Backhaus
Institute of Telematics
Karlsruhe Institute of Technology (KIT)
backhaus@tm.uka.de

Klemens Böhm
Institute of Program Structures and Data
Organization
Karlsruhe Institute of Technology (KIT)
klemens.boehm@kit.edu

Caslav Bozic
Institute of Applied Informatics and
Formal Description Methods
Karlsruhe Institute of Technology (KIT)
bozic@kit.edu

Thomas Dreier
Institute of Information and Economic
Law
Karlsruhe Institute of Technology (KIT)
dreier@kit.edu

Karl-Martin Ehrhart
Institute of Economic Theory and
Statistics
Karlsruhe Institute of Technology (KIT)
ehrhart@kit.edu

Andreas Geyer-Schulz
Institute of Information Systems and
Management
Karlsruhe Institute of Technology (KIT)
ags@em.uni-karlsruhe.de

Laura Goebes
Institute for Economic Theory and
Statistics
Karlsruhe Institute of Technology (KIT)
goebes@wiwi.uni-karlsruhe.de

Steffen Hitzemann
Chair of Financial Engineering and
Derivatives
Karlsruhe Institute of Technology (KIT)
hitzemann@kit.edu

Tim Klümper
Institute of Information and Economic
Law
Karlsruhe Institute of Technology (KIT)
kluemper@kit.edu

Jan Krämer
Institute of Information Systems and
Management
Karlsruhe Institute of Technology (KIT)
kraemer@kit.edu

Uta Lösch
Institute of Applied Informatics and
Formal Description Methods
Karlsruhe Institute of Technology (KIT)
uta.loesch@kit.edu

Jens E. Müller
Institute of Information Systems and
Management
Karlsruhe Institute of Technology (KIT)
j.mueller@kit.edu

Kathrin Noack
Institute of Information and Economic
Law
Karlsruhe Institute of Technology (KIT)
kathrin.noack@kit.edu

Ryan Riordan
Institute of Information Systems and
Management
Karlsruhe Institute of Technology (KIT)
ryan.riordan@kit.edu

Detlef Seese
Institute of Applied Informatics and
Formal Description Methods
Karlsruhe Institute of Technology (KIT)
detlef.seese@kit.edu

Stefan Seifert
Institute of Information Systems and
Management
Karlsruhe Institute of Technology (KIT)
stefan.seifert@kit.edu

Sebastian Speiser
Karlsruhe Service Research Institute
Karlsruhe Institute of Technology (KIT)
speiser@kit.edu

Indra Spiecker gen. Döhmann
Institute of Information and Economic
Law
Karlsruhe Institute of Technology (KIT)
spiecker@kit.edu

Christoph Stadtfeld
Institute of Information Systems and
Management
Karlsruhe Institute of Technology (KIT)
stadtfeld@ime.uni-karlsruhe.de

Andreas Storkenmaier
Institute of Information Systems and
Management
Karlsruhe Institute of Technology (KIT)
andreas.storkenmaier@kit.edu

Rudi Studer
Institute of Applied Informatics and
Formal Description Methods
Karlsruhe Institute of Technology (KIT)
rudi.studer@kit.edu

Simone Traub
Institute of Information and Economic
Law
Karlsruhe Institute of Technology (KIT)
simone.traub@kit.edu

Marliese Uhrig-Homburg
Chair of Financial Engineering and
Derivatives
Karlsruhe Institute of Technology (KIT)
uhrig@kit.edu

Karl-Heinz Waldmann
Institute of Operations Research
Karlsruhe Institute of Technology (KIT)
waldmann@wior.uni-karlsruhe.de

Christof Weinhardt
Institute of Information Systems and
Management
Karlsruhe Institute of Technology (KIT)
weinhardt@kit.edu

Lukas Wiewiorra
Institute of Information Systems and
Management
Karlsruhe Institute of Technology (KIT)
wiewiorra@kit.edu

Jing Zhi Yue
Institute of Program Structures and Data
Organization
Karlsruhe Institute of Technology (KIT)
jing.yue@kit.edu

S. Sarah Zhang
Institute of Information Systems and
Management
Karlsruhe Institute of Technology (KIT)
sarah.zhang@kit.edu

Martina Zitterbart
Institute of Telematics
Karlsruhe Institute of Technology (KIT)
zit@tm.uka.de

Part I

Market Information Processing and Analysis

New Event Detection in Financial News Analysis

Uta Lösch[1], Rudi Studer[1], and Christof Weinhardt[2]

[1] Institute of Applied Informatics and Formal Description Methods, KIT
   {uta.loesch, rudi.studer}@kit.edu
[2] Institute of Information Systems and Management, KIT
   weinhardt@kit.edu

Summary. Traders in financial markets commonly have to face an information overload, which is partly due to a continuously arriving stream of news which contains information on events which may influence the markets. In this paper, we present a news processing framework which allows to collect news from various sources and to present them to the user in an aggregated form. An important aspect of this framework is a *New Event Detection* component, which is responsible for recognizing new events and for clustering news dealing with the same event. The design of this component will be studied in more detail: a general framework for New Event Detection will be presented which can be configured to implement a broad variety of concrete systems, including most state-of-the-art systems along with a detailed study of the state of the art in this field.

1 Introduction

Traders and investors in financial markets are confronted with the problem that too much information is available from various, heterogenuous sources like newswires, forums, blogs, and collaborative tools. In order to make accurate trading decisions, traders have to be supported in finding and assessing relevant information efficiently such that they can react to new information in a timely manner.

In contrast to other domains, information and especially the possibility to make profit based on it are extremely transient in financial markets. In fact, it is doubted whether there is at all a possibility of profiting from having information that others do not have: The *Efficient Market Hypothesis* (Fama (1970)) states that it should not be possible to outperform the market, as the stock prices always reflect all the information which is currently available. However, the Efficient Market Hypothesis is a theoretical model which has been doubted by behavioural economists over the last years. Still, it seems intuitive that chances of profiting from new information are the higher the faster it is reacted upon after its publication.

User support in this context may include:

- *Collection of news from various sources:* News are published on a multitude of web sites, which not only include news sites such as Financial Times, Reuters, or the Wall Street Journal, but also personal and collaborative websites, especially blogs, and message boards. Support in the collection of news can be provided by crawling a set of relevant sites for new information.

- *Clustering/aggregation of news:* The same events will be reported by several sources, and the same source may publish several messages on the same event. The goal is to identify clusters of news which report on the same event. This is particularly important as traders are especially interested in events that they have not read about before.
- *Ranking of news:* Once, the news have been aggregated, they should be ranked such that those which are most important to the trader are made more prominent. Relevance and importance of a piece of information for the user depends on several aspects: Does the information concern some company that the user is interested in? Does the user already know about the event that occured? How much is the information expected to influence the price of stocks held by the user?

A lot of research has already been carried out on these aspects. In the following, we will present a framework for news analysis in a financial context. In the subsequent sections we will then focus on some specific aspects of this framework.

2 A Framework for Financial News Analysis

The goal of analysis of financial news is to help traders make informed trading decisions. Therefore, methods of finding the information that is important for a user in a specific situation are needed. Identifying the important information is carried out in a set of analysis steps, which are presented in Figure 1.

Given input data, which consists of textual – news – data on the one hand and of stock data on the other hand, the goal is to predict the further development of the stock market and to assess whether a specific user might be interested in a specific news item that has been published.

The system thus has to combine the numeric stock data and the news data and make predictions based on this combination. In order to make this kind of prediction, preprocessing is needed to obtain suitable representations of the data and to aggregate and filter the data. Useful preprocessing steps for the textual data might include filtering stories that report information that has not been available before or stories that concern topics which the user is interested in.

This kind of process requires many design decisions. The first step is to choose the data on which the system should operate. This means focusing on a specific set of stocks and on a specific set of news sources. Possible news sources include news tickers (e.g. Reuters), news portals (e.g. Google news), blogs, message boards and collaborative tools. For the financial data, some kind of stock data is needed. This can be available in form of order book data, but also as time series of stock prices.

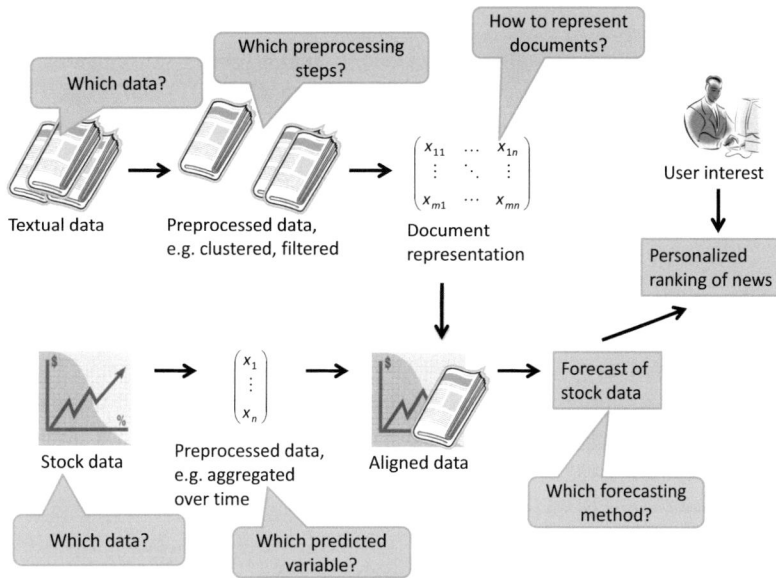

Figure 1: Our financial news analysis framework

After choosing the data, various filtering and aggregation steps may be taken. Depending on the kind of raw data that is available, these may include aggregating order book data to time series or aggregating time series to trends. For the news data, filtering relevant data for the specific application or aggregating news to events (i.e. clustering news such that news in one cluster report on the same event) are some possible preprocessing steps.

Once the data has been preprocessed, it has to be transformed into a representation that is suitable for the prediction task. The classical way of representing text data, is the bag-of-words model – some extensions to that will be presented in Section 3.1.

In the next step, the data has to be aligned, which means that the text is associated with the corresponding part of the stock data. E.g. if we are interested in trends following the publication of the news, the trend that follows each news item has to be identified and a data instance consisting of the representation of the text and the representation of the prediction variable has to be created. The set of all these aligned instances can then be used for learning prediction models on the stock data.

In our research, we focus on the use of New Event Detection as a pre-processing step. New Event Detection focuses on detecting the first story on an event in a stream of news. The motivation for this is, that, as already discussed before, information should only be presented to the user once and as promptly as possible.

A framework for New Event Detection and an overview of previous approaches to the problem will be presented in Section 3. In Section 4 we will detail on the evaluation procedure and corpora in the field before concluding in Section 5.

3 New Event Detection

The problem of New Event Detection (NED) – also known as First-Story Detection (FSD) – is defined in the Topic Detection and Tracking (TDT) challenge Fiscus and Doddington (2002): Given a stream of news arriving in chronological order, a TDT system must group or cluster articles that discuss the same event in the news stream. NED is one of the sub-tasks of TDT and deals with identifying those stories in a news stream which discuss novel news events. The decision whether a text reports on a new event or not is made by considering only documents which have arrived prior to the current document. Thus, the system has to adhere to the temporal constraints of a real-time news stream. A first study on this topic has been done by Allan et al. (1998).

Basically, the problem of New Event Detection can be seen as an outlier detection task. In general, the goal of outlier detection is to find points in a dataset which have a huge distance to the rest of the data. In New Event Detection, if the new document is identified to be different from the older documents, it should be marked as new, otherwise as old. Outlier Detection can be described as a supervised or an unsupervised learning task. The same holds for New Event Detection.

The description of the New Event Detection task as an unsupervised learning task is as an incremental clustering problem. For a stream of training documents $x_1, \ldots, x_n \in \mathcal{D}$, where $\mathcal{D}$ is the document space, and the clusters $y_i \in \mathcal{Y}$, where $\mathcal{Y}$ is the set of clusters that correspond to topics, to which they belong, the goal is to determine a clustering function $c : \mathcal{D} \to \mathcal{Y}$ that accurately clusters the data. In order to achieve an incremental clustering, c has to be defined such that $c(x_i) = \phi(x_i, M_{i-1})$ where M_i is the model after clustering documents $x_1, \ldots, x_i$.

An alternative formulation of the New Event Detection problem is as a classification problem, i.e. as a supervised learning task. For a stream of training documents $x_1, \ldots, x_n \in \mathcal{D}$, the goal is to find a function $f : \mathcal{D} \to \{new, old\}$ that accurately labels the data.

A New Event Detection system has several parameters (see Figure 2). These include the document representation, i.e. the choice of features that define the document space, the similarity measure between documents, and the detection procedure, i.e. the way the output (old, new) is determined for a given document x. These three aspects are interlinked: the similarity measures that are applicable depend on the document representation, each algorithm requires a specific type of input, i.e. it has requirements for the document representations that may be used.

In the following sections, we will present an overview of previous approaches to defining suitable document representations, similarity measures and outlier detection algorithms for New Event Detection.

3.1 Document representation and similarity measure

The classical approach for representing documents in a metric space is the bag-of-words model. In this kind of model, each document is regarded as a set of words.

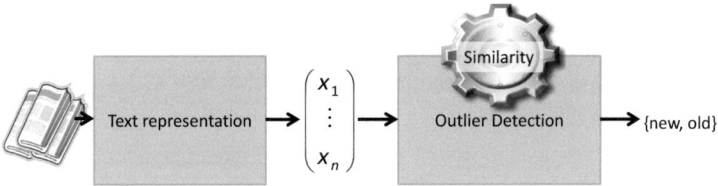

Figure 2: New Event Detection Framework

Each term that occurs in the document set defines a dimension in the document space. Common preprocessing steps are stemming (unifying different forms of the same term, e.g. singular and plural) and stopword removal (eliminating very common words with little meaning, like *and* or *or*). Additional features may be defined; one example is introducing additional features for named entity types (e.g. a feature *company* which has a positive feature weight, if a company name is contained in the text). Other approaches try to combine synonyms in one dimension or to disambiguate between different senses of the same term.

Once the dimensions of the feature space are defined, a weight has to be associated with each dimension. Each document is thus represented as a vector in the document space. There are different approaches for defining the weight of a feature in a document:

- *Boolean weighting.* A feature has weight 1 if the term it represents is present in the text, 0 otherwise: $weight_{wd} = 1$ if term w occurs in document d, $weight_{wd} = 0$ otherwise.
- *Term frequency.* The weight of each feature is determined by the number of times the represented term w is present in the document d:

$$weight_{wd} = \frac{freq_{wd}}{\sum_{k \in T} freq_{kd}}$$

where T is the set of all terms in the document set.
- *Term frequency inverse document frequency (TFIDF).* Term frequency is normalized by document frequency in this approach, where document frequency is the number of documents which contain the term: $weight_{wd} = tf_{wd} * idf_w = \frac{freq_{wd}}{\sum_{k \in T} freq_{w,d}} \log \frac{|D|}{n_w}$ where D is the set of documents and n_w is the set of documents containing w. The idea of this adaptation is that terms that occur in many documents are less meaningful and distinctive than terms which are only contained in a few documents.

Various similarity measures have been defined on bag-of-word vectors. The most prominent one is cosine similarity, which defines the similarity of two documents by the cosine of the angle between the feature vectors of the documents. Thus,

$$sim^{cos}(d_1, d_2) = \frac{d_1 d_2}{||d_1|| ||d_2||} = \frac{\sum_{w \in T} weight_{w,d_1} \sum_{w \in T} weight_{w,d_2}}{\sqrt{\sum_{w \in T} weight_{w,d_1}^2} \sqrt{\sum_{w \in T} weight_{w,d_2}^2}}$$

However, for New Event Detection it seems that the *Hellinger distance* yields better results Brants et al. (2003):

$$sim^{Hellinger}(d_1, d_2) = \sum_{w \in T} \sqrt{\frac{weight_{wd_1}}{\sum_{k \in T} weight_{kd_1}} * \frac{weight_{wd_2}}{\sum_{k \in T} weight_{kd_1}}}$$

Several extensions to these basic models have been considered in New Event Detection. These will be presented in the following paragraphs.

Incremental TFIDF

The TFIDF measure is commonly used in text mining and information retrieval, however, it is not directly applicable in New Event Detection. The problem is that inverse document frequencies (IDF) would have to be recalculated every time a new document is looked at. This recalculation would be by far too expensive. Therefore, an estimate of the overall DF measure is generated based on the documents that have already been published. To increase efficiency, IDF measures are not updated after every document, but only after each k documents. The following incremental IDF measure is obtained for each word w:

$$df_t(w) = df_{t-1}(w) + df_{D_t}(w) \tag{1}$$

where D_t represents the set of documents received at time t, $df_{D_t}(w)$ is the number of documents in D_t in which w occurs and $df_t(w)$ is the number of documents in which w occurs before time t (Brants et al. (2003), citeyang1998.

Time decay models

News on a specific event usually occur close in time. This means that if a message that is similar to a previous one, is released long after release of the earlier message, the probability of the two texts reporting on the same event is small. Therefore, many approaches adapt the similarity of two documents over time. That means that the similarity of two documents is smaller if more time has passed between their publication. There are different approaches for this kind of decay:

The simplest model is that of using a time window, which has e.g. been used by Yang et al. (1999):

$$sim^{win}(d_1, d_2) = \begin{cases} sim(d_1, d_2) & age < m \\ 0 & else \end{cases}$$

Thereby, age is the period that has passed between publication of d_1 and publication of d_2 and m is the size of the time window.

An alternative time decay model is a linear model as proposed by Yang et al. (1998). In their model, time decay is modeled as:

$$sim^{lin}(d_1, d_2) = (1 - \frac{age}{m}) * sim(d_1, d_2)$$

An exponential model has been proposed by Franz et al. (2001):

$$sim^{exp}(d_1, d_2) = sim(d_1, d_2)(1 + 2^{-age/halftime})$$

However, time-decay models do not necessarily improve performance. E.g., Brants et al. (2003) have reported that time-decay did not improve their results.

Source-specific TFIDF model

Another aspect to be considered is the specific writing style of different news providers. To address this, Brants et al. (2003) have studied the use of a specific IDF weight for each news source. The intuition behind that approach is that news stories by the same provider are written using a specific set of words and a specific style. Therefore, terms which might be used to distinguish between two events in one source may just be common terms in another source. The IDF weights for each source are updated using incremental IDF, but instead of using all documents only those issued by a specific source are considered.

Obviously, the similarity measure has to be adapted to this source-specific model. The intuition is that documents that are issued by the same source are per se more similar among each other than two documents issued from a different source. Therefore, the average similarity of documents from the regarded sources is used to normalize the actual similarity between a set of documents. Additionally, Brants et al. argue that it makes a difference whether a story is on a broad topic with many documents or on a narrow and specific topic: therefore, the average similarity of documents on the considered topic is subtracted from the original similarity value. We thus obtain the overall similarity measure:

$$sim^{sourceSpecific}(d_1, d_2) = (sim(d_1, d_2) - \overline{sim}(d_2)) - E_{s_1,s_2}$$

with d_n the new document, $\overline{sim}(d_n)$ the average similarity of d_n to all previous documents and $E_{s_i s_n}$ the average similarity of two stories on the same event issued by the source s_i of d_i and the source s_n of d_n respectively.

Combined document representations

Named entities are an important part of news and seem helpful in discriminating between different events. Therefore, various authors have tried to use named entities as special features in New Event Detection. The assumption is that named entities contain much of the information on an important event.

Kumaran and Allan (2004) have studied a text representation consisting of three vectors: the classical term vector, a second vector containing only the named entities and one vector containing only the non-named entities terms. For the actual classification they use the vector consisting of all terms. Additionally they could show that depending on the topic category in which the document falls, the vector of named entities resp. the vector of non-named entities are useful as additional evidence for whether a story reports on a new event or not.

Zhang et al. (2007) have shown that depending on the topic class in which a news item falls, different named entity types are useful for discriminating between events. According to their results, location name is the most useful term type for the three classes Natural Disasters, Violence or War, and Finances. In contrast to that, person names are very useful for discriminating between Elections, Legal/Criminal Cases, Science and Discovery. For Scandals/Hearings, date is the most important information. Legal/Criminal Cases and Finance topics have high correlation with money terms, while Science and Discovery have high correlation with percentage terms. The influence of non-name terms does not depend on the class to which a news item belongs. They thus adapt the weights of a term dependent on whether it is a named entity and on the class to which the news item belongs.

Makkonen et al. (2002) have taken a similar approach as Pons-Porrata et al. (2002) concerning document representation. However, they have introduced two additional subvectors - one representing *locations* and one representing *proper names*. Each document is thus represented by four vectors.

A new similarity measure is deviced on this document representation. They adapt the measures that rely on the intersection of the occurrence of features by a ranking which depends on the position of a feature in the considered document. The idea is that in news, the earlier some information is mentioned, the more important it is. The overall similarity measure is calculated as a weighted sum over the four individual similarities.

Pons-Porrata et al. (2002) have proposed to introduce a second feature vector for each document. The features of the first vector are terms weighted using term frequency. The second vector's features are mentions of dates or time intervals that are automatically extracted from the texts. These features, too, are weighted according to the frequency of occurrence in the text.

Similarity is measured using cosine similarity on the term vectors. For the time entities vectors of d_i and d_j distance is defined as the pair of time entities (t_i, t_j) with $t_i \in d_i$ and $t_j \in d_j$, for which the time interval between t_i and t_j is minimal. The overall similarity is then defined using a threshold on the time distance. If the distance between the time vectors exceeds a certain threshold, the overall similarity between the two documents is 0, if the distance is below the threshold, similarity is defined as the similarity of term vectors. For example, if document d_i contains the date 6th July, 2010 and document d_j contains the dates 05th July, 2010 and 27th June, 2009, then the time distance between these two documents is one day, as this is the minimal distance between time entities mentioned in the two documents.

Event frequencies

Texts on the same kind of event will probably share some common vocabulary. The expectation thus is that events on a similar topic are more likely to be confused than events of different types. The idea for overcoming this problem is to give less weight to topic-specific vocabulary and has been proposed by Brants et al. (2003). The event frequency of a term is defined as:

$$ef(w) = \max_{r \in ROI} ef(r, w)$$

where $ef(r, w)$ is the number of events in rule of interpretation ROI (rules of interpretation, i.e topic categories) that contain w. Inverse event frequencies are used to adapt the feature weights.

Lexical chains

Stokes and Carthy (2001b) have analyzed the idea of representing documents by the terms that best describe the story of the text. They propose to obtain such a representation using lexical chains. Chains of semantically related terms are formed using WordNet. Each term in the text is processed in the order of appearance in the text. It is then checked whether the current term is related to the currently built lexical chain. If this is not the case, the current chain is closed and a new one is started. In the end all the lexical chains consisting of more than one term are merged together. This set of terms is used to complement the traditional term frequency vector.

However, the lexical chains alone are not sufficient for obtaining a satisfying result. Therefore, Stokes and Carthy (2001a) combine lexical chains with a second document vector which contains all the named entities occuring in the text. This additional representation is useful as WordNet is not capable of making relations between proper nouns and other nouns in its taxonomy.

3.2 Learning algorithms

As explained above, the scenario of New Event Detection requires an outlier detection algorithm, more specifically an incremental outlier detection algorithm. It has already been explained that outlier detection can be formulated as a supervised or an unsupervised learning problem. In New Event Detection, some training data is available, that may be used for tuning the learning component.

Most systems formalize New Event Detection as a clustering problem: Each news item may either report on a known event and thus belong to an existing cluster or it may form a new cluster and thus report on a new event. Two properties of the New Event Detection problem heavily restrict the choice of clustering algorithm: The first is that the problem is an incremental one, which requires each document to be clustered before the next ones are known, and the second one is that the number of clusters is not fixed. Therefore, all algorithms that take the number of clusters as parameter can not be applied in New Event Detection.

Single-pass clustering

The most prominent algorithm for New Event Detection problem is *Single-pass clustering*, which has been proposed by Papka and Allan (1998). The algorithm proceeds as follows: For each new document the nearest cluster is searched. If the similarity of the document to this cluster exceeds a threshold θ the document is clustered with the nearest cluster, otherwise it will form a new cluster. This algorithm is closely related to *Nearest-Neighbour-Classification*, in the sense that if the method for defining the nearest cluster is chosen such that only the closest document is considered, we obtain 1-nearest-neighbour-classification.

Single-pass clustering is not very adaptive: the definition of the nearest cluster has to be chosen: single-link, average-link, or complete-link. Based on the linking strategy and an initial set of documents the optimal parameter value for the threshold θ has to be learned.

Incremental β_0-Compact Algorithm

Pons-Porrata et al. (2002) have proposed to reallocate documents between clusters upon the arrival of new documents. The idea is to use the maximum-similarity graph of all documents for finding the clusters. A cluster is formed by a set of nodes which are connected among each other, but not to other documents in the graph of maximum similarity.

For a new document d_n the similarity to all previous documents d_i is determined and for each document the information on the nearest document is updated. Using the information on the most similar document, the graph of maximum similarities can be constructed. It is defined over all documents, and contains an edge (d_i, d_j) if the most similar document for d_i is d_j. Clusters are extracted from this graph by searching for sets of nodes which are connected among each other but not to other nodes outside the set.

Support Vector Machines

Support Vector Machines have been proposed for solving the New Event Detection problem modeled as a classification problem. The idea is to find a hyper-ball with minimal diameter which contains all the training data (i.e. the texts that already have been published). Thus, the following objective has to be minimized:

$$F(R, \mathbf{c}, \xi_i) = R^2 + C \sum_{i=1}^{N} \xi_i$$

subject to the constraints

$$0 \leq \xi_i$$
$$(\mathbf{x_i} - \mathbf{c})^\top (\mathbf{x_i} - \mathbf{c}) \leq R^2 + \xi_i$$

where $\mathbf{c}$ is the center of the hyperball, R is its radius, and the ξ_i are slack variables that measure how far the data point is from the hyperball's surface.

A text is classified as novel if its distance from the center of the hyper-ball exceeds a certain threshold. As in classical SVMs, kernel functions may be used for calculating similarities, thus projecting the data into a high-dimensional feature space and determining the hyper-ball there. A detailed description of the optimization problem can be found in Zhang et al. (2004). At first glance the use of SVMs may seem very inefficient in the context of New Event Detection. However, retraining only becomes necessary when a text is classified as being novel - therefore, less training effort than one might expect is needed.

Kernel Regression

Zhang et al. (2004) have used *Kernel Regression* for solving New Event Detection. In Kernel regression the predicted variable is calculated as a weighted average of the available data where the weights are determined using a kernel function. The estimation can thus be phrased as $r(y, x_1, \ldots, x_N) = \sum_{i=1}^{N} w_i(y)s(x_i, y)$ where K is a kernel, $w_i(y)$ is given by $w_i(y) = \frac{K(x_i,y)}{\sum_{j=1}^{N} K(x_j,y)}$ (Nadaraya-Watson kernel estimator).

Probabilistic model

Apart from the methods that have been presented in the previous paragraphs, probabilistic methods have been studied as alternative models for New Event Detection. Zhang et al. (2005) have used language models and stochastic processes as their approach to the problem. The development of clusters is modeled using a *Dirichlet process* and a multinominal language model is used for modeling the clusters themselves. The probability of a document x_i being part of a cluster C_j is thus:

$$p(C_j|x_i) = \frac{p(C_j)p(x_i|C_j)}{\sum_{k=1}^{m+1} p(C_k)p(x_i|C_k)}$$

where the prior probabilities of each cluster are determined by

$$p(c_n = C_j) = \frac{card(C_j)}{\lambda + \sum_{k=1}^{m} card(C_k)} \quad (j = 1, \ldots, m) \tag{2}$$

$$p(c_n = C_{m+1}) = \frac{\lambda}{\lambda + \sum_{k=1}^{m} card(C_k)} \tag{3}$$

with $C_1, \ldots, C_m$ being the clusters obtained by processing $x_1, \ldots, x_{n-1}$, C_{m+1} being a possible new cluster whose probability of being generated depends on the parameter λ, $card(C_j)$ describing the number of documents that have been clustered into C_j, and

$$p(x_i|C_j) = \int p(\theta^{(C_j)}|C_j)p(x_i|\theta^{(C_j)})d\theta^{(C_j)}$$

$p(x_i|C)$ decribes the probability of a document x_i being generated by cluster C_j. θ^{C_j} is the parameter vector of cluster C_j.

Zhang and Li (2009) have proposed an alternative probabilistic model which is based on an incremental version of probabilistic latent semantic analysis (IPLSA). The idea of probabilistic latent semantic analysis is to introduce concepts, which are variables linking terms to documents and to estimate the parameters $P(w|z)$ and $P(z|d)$ in a way to describe the available data as good as possible, where w are the words occuring in the dataset, d are the documents in the dataset and z are the latent concepts. Zhang et al. have proposed an incremental version of this algorithm, which allows to add documents to the model in an online manner.

3.3 Complexity and efficiency

The basic New Event Detection approach which uses Single-pass Clustering with single linkage and a bag-of-words model with TFIDF weights has quadratic complexity in the number of documents, as each document is compared to all the previous documents. This complexity results in very low processing speed, leading to systems that are not able to analyze data streams in a real-time manner.

To the best of our knowledge, little work has been done to improve processing speed of New Event Detection systems. The most important approach to improving run-time efficiency is reducing the number of comparisons. Zhang et al. (2007) have used indexing-trees for the search for the most similar document. The idea is to reduce the number of necessary comparisons from linear to logarithmic in the number of documents. Their approach consists in building hierarchical clusters of documents such that the search for the closest document can be done by performing a search in this tree.

The time-decay models presented in Section 3.1 are a possibility of reducing the number of documents with which each document has to be compared.

Further methods for reducing the number of comparisons and the complexity of each comparison have been proposed by Luo et al. (2007). Additionally to a sliding window in which news are considered for comparison, in their approach only the first story for each event is considered for comparison, thus significantly reducing the number of documents to be considered. Additionally, only the terms which are the most important ones for a document, i.e. those with the highest feature weights are used for similarity calculation. Luo et al. could show that it is sufficient to use the top 100 features for comparison. For a further speed-up, the similarity between two documents is only calculated if there is an overlap in the top 10 features of both documents - otherwise the documents are considered to be reporting on different events.

A further improvement that Luo et al. proposed is parallelizing the New Event Detection process by splitting the set of candidate documents into several subsets and by processing each subset on a different machine. If one of the machines returns a classification of the document as reporting on a new event, the document is classified as new, otherwise as old.

4 Evaluation and performance

4.1 Corpora

Five TDT corpora have been developed and are maintained by the Linguistic Data Consortium[1]. These corpora vary in size, the number and kind of sources they use, and in language Cieri et al. (2002)

The *TDT Pilot study corpus* was used in the pilot study, it consists of textual news from newswires (Reuters) and transcriptions of broadcast news speech (CNN). All news are available in English. The corpus covers one year of data – from July 1, 1994 to June 30, 1995, and consists of approximately 16000 stories. On these, a total of 25 events were defined, which defines a subset of the events covered in the data.

TDT-2 consists of English and Chinese news, both in textual as well as in audio form. Data was collected from nine sources over a period of six months from January 1998 to June 1998. Transcripts of the audio data and translations of the Chinese data are available. The corpus consists of a total of approximately 53600 Englisch and 18800 Chinese stories. A total of 200 events were defined on the English data, 20 of them have also been annotated on the Chinese data. This corpus was used for the TDT evaluations in the year 1998.

TDT-3 was used in the evaluations from 1999 to 2001. It contains news collected from October to December 1998 in English, Chinese and Arabic. 120 topics have been annotated for the English and the Chinese data, only a subset of them has been annotated in Arabic.

The *TDT-4* corpus was used for the official evaluations in 2002 and 2003. It also contains English, Chinese and Arabic data. In this corpus a total of 80 topics have been annotated in each language. The corpus consists of data that has been collected between October 2000 to January 2001.

The last corpus that was developed was *TDT-5*, the corpus which has been used for the 2004 evaluation. It contains English, Chinese and Arabic data that has been published between April and September 2003. A total of 250 topics have been annotated on this corpus, 25% of which are annotated in all three languages, the rest is annotated in only one language, distributed equally across languages.

4.2 Evaluation measure

The goal of New Event detection is to mark the first story on an event as new, all the other stories are to be marked as old. Therefore, the system may make different mistakes:

---

[1] http://www.ldc.upenn.edu/

	tagged as new	tagged as old
real new	true positive (TP)	false negative (FN)
real old	false positive (FP)	true negative (TN)

The first kind of mistake occurs when a message that should be tagged as new is tagged as old. In that case we talk of a *miss*. In the second case, where a message that does not report on a new event, is tagged as new by the system, we talk of *false alarms*. The *miss rate* is defined as $\frac{FN}{TP+FN}$. The *false alarm rate* is defined as $\frac{FP}{FP+TN}$.

There is a trade-off between these two kinds of errors (similar to the trade-off between precision and recall in classical IR systems), which depends on the threshold of how big the distance between two news may be before they are not considered to report on the same event anymore.

In the official TDT evaluations, the overall performance of a system is therefore calculated as a weighted average between its miss rate P_M and its false alarm rate P_{FA}:

$$C_{DET} = C_M * P_M * P_{target} + C_{FA} * P_{FA} * P_{non-target}$$

Here, C_M and C_{FA} describe the cost of a miss resp. a false alarm. As false alarms are much more likely to occur, their cost is set lower than the cost of a miss. Therefore, in the official evaluations $C_M = 1$ and $C_{FA} = 0.1$. P_{target} and $P_{non-target}$ describe a priori probabilities for a document being new (resp. old). In the evaluations, $P_{target} = 0.02$ and $P_{non-target} = 1 - P_{target} = 0.98$.

This measure is then normalized using the following formula:

$$(C_{DET})_{norm} = \frac{C_{DET}}{min(C_{miss} * P_{target}, C_{FA} * P_{non-target})}$$

Additional measures that are reported as result of some evaluations are the usual Information Retrieval measures *precision* and *recall*. *Precision* is defined as $\frac{TP}{TP+FP}$, *recall* is defined as $\frac{TP}{TP+FN}$. These two measures are often combined into a single one, the so-called *F1-measure*, which is defined as $\frac{2*Recall*Precision}{Recall+Precision}$.

4.3 Overview of results

In Table 1 we present an overview of the results that have been achieved by the presented New Event Detection systems. In most papers only a subset of the evaluation measures that were defined in 4.2 are presented. Combined with the different corpora that were used by the different authors, this makes a comparison of the systems difficult.

Discussion of performance

As discussed above, New Event Detection systems consist of three components: document representation, similarity measure and outlier detection. All the presented systems try to optimize the overall performance and change more than one of the

Authors	Corpus	$(C_{DET})_{norm}$	Recall	Precision	Miss	F/A	F1
Papka and Al-lan (1998)	TDT	0.4315	0.64	0.5	0.36	0.0146	0.56
Yang et al. (1999)	TDT	0.5926	0.5	0.37	0.5	0.0189	0.42
Makkonen et al. (2002)	3958 Finnish news from single source	–	0.812	0.627	–	–	0.708
Pons-Porrata et al. (2002)	452 Spanish newspaper articles	0.0074	–	–	–	–	0.7037
Brants et al. (2003)	TDT-2, TDT-3, for evaluation TDT-4	0.5303	–	–	0.4167	0.0226	–
Kumaran and Allan (2004)	TDT-2, TDT-3, for evaluation TDT-4	0.5144	–	–	–	–	–
Zhang et al. (2005)	TDT3	0.6901	–	–	0.5789	0.0227	–
Zhang et al. (2004), Nearest Neighbor	TDT-3	0.6890	–	–	–	–	–
Zhang et al. (2004), Linear SVM	TDT-3	0.7452	–	–	–	–	–
Zhang et al. (2004), RBF SVM	TDT-3	0.7546	–	–	–	–	–
Zhang et al. (2007)	TDT-2, TDT-3	0.5089	–	–	–	–	–
Luo et al. (2007)	TDT-5	0.758	–	–	–	–	–
Zhang and Li (2009)	TDT-4 (only on-topic)	0.1275	0.88	0.85	0.12	0.00157	0.86

Table 1: Overview of evaluation results for the presented approaches

components (or one component in more than one way). Therefore, the influence of a single change is often not known. However, some conclusions are possible.

Looking at the document representation, what seems to help is the separate consideration of named entities and other terms. The reduction of the numbers of features as proposed by Luo et al. (2007) and Zhang and Li (2009) not only seems to increase efficiency but also performance of the New Event Detection systems.

Regarding the similarity measure, Brants et al. (2003) have shown that the Hellinger similarity outperforms the cosine similarity. The use of time-decay approaches is strongly discussed: while some authors (e.g. Zhang and Li (2009) and Yang et al. (1999) report improvements, Brants et al. (2003) reports that no improvements where possible by this means. Models that distinguish between different news sources for calculating similarities (Brants et al. (2003), Zhang et al. (2007)) seem to outperform models that do not make this distinction.

Zhang et al. (2004) have shown that the single-pass clustering approach outperforms Support Vector Machines and Kernel Regression. They argue that kernel methods seem to perform quite poorly in unsupervised learning tasks with a high number of features. The authors' explanation for this phenomenon is the lack of information on which features are important in the learning task (in contrast to supervised learning tasks where this kind of information can be derived). An interesting alternative approach is the IPLSA method that has been proposed by Zhang and Li (2009) and which clearly outperforms the other systems. Here, learning is based on an incremental maximum likelihood estimation of the probability of a word w occuring in document d.

5 Conclusion

In this paper we have presented a framework for stock price analysis and prediction based on news that are published. We have presented the idea of using New Event Detection as a pre-processing step in this context – the motivation being that New Event Detection should be essential for enabling accurate predictions (as "old" information is already reflected in the prices).

The problem of New Event Detection has been studied extensively in the literature. Different algorithms, different text representations and different similarity measures have been applied to the problem. Still, the problem remains hard and state-of-the-art systems still have high error rates in their predictions.

Therefore, we think that this problem is still interesting for further analyses. In our work we focus on refining the document representation and suitable similarity measures for New Event Detection. We use OpenCalais[2] to obtain annotations of named entities and events in the documents. As explained above, named entities have been used before in New Event Detection. Using event annotations, i.e. relations between the entities mentioned in a document, is however going beyond the state of the art.

As the text annotations are obtained in an automatic manner, they can not be assumed to be correct and complete. Additionally, only a limited number of event types can be annotated by OpenCalais. Therefore, it is likely that a combined document representation that relies on both the annotations and the bag-of-words yields better results.

Concerning the use of event annotations as document features, it is not clear what the most promising way of using them is. We are evaluating different methods: Either each concrete relation can be used as a feature. Alternatively, relation type and the involved entities can be regarded separately. The latter may better reflect the similarity between the annotated events. OpenCalais annotations are represented as graphs. Therefore, a third alternative is to calculate similarities between document

---

[2] http://www.opencalais.com

annotations as graph similarities instead of extracting features from the graphs, which are then used for similarity calculation.

References

Allan, J., R. Papka, and V. Lavrenko (1998): "On-line new event detection and tracking," in: *SIGIR '98: Proceedings of the 21st Annual International ACM SIGIR Conference on Research and Development in Information Retrieval*, ACM, New York, NY, USA, pp. 37–45.

Brants, T., F. Chen, and A. Farahat (2003): "A System for new event detection," in: *SIGIR '03: Proceedings of the 26th Annual International ACM SIGIR Conference on Research and Development in Information Retrieval*, ACM, New York, NY, USA, pp. 330–337.

Cieri, C., S. Strassel, D. Graff, N. Martey, K. Rennert, and M. Liberman (2002): *Corpora for topic detection and tracking*, Kluwer Academic Publishers, Norwell, MA, USA, pp. 33–66.

Fama, E. (1970): "Efficient Capital Markets: A Review of Theory and Empirical Work," *Journal of Finance*, 25, pp. 383–417.

Fiscus, J. G. and G. R. Doddington (2002): *Topic detection and tracking evaluation overview*, Kluwer Academic Publishers, Norwell, MA, USA, pp. 17–31.

Franz, M., A. Ittycheriah, J. S. McCarley, and T. Ward (2001): "First story detection: Combining similarity and novelty-based approaches," .

Kumaran, G. and J. Allan (2004): "Text classification and named entities for new event detection," in: *SIGIR '04: Proceedings of the 27th Annual International ACM SIGIR Conference on Research and Development in Information Retrieval*, ACM, New York, NY, USA, pp. 297–304.

Luo, G., C. Tang, and P. S. Yu (2007): "Resource-adaptive real-time new event detection," in: *SIGMOD '07: Proceedings of the 2007 ACM SIGMOD International Conference on Management of Data*, ACM, New York, NY, USA, pp. 497–508.

Makkonen, J., H. Ahonen-Myka, and M. Salmenkivi (2002): "Applying Semantic Classes in Event Detection and Tracking," in: R. Sangal and S. M. Bendre (eds.), *Proceedings of International Conference on Natural Language Process*, pp. 175–183.

Papka, R. and J. Allan (1998): "On-Line New Event Detection using Single Pass Clustering," working paper, University of Massachusetts, Amherst, MA, USA.

Pons-Porrata, A., R. B. Llavori, and J. Ruíz-Shulcloper (2002): "Detecting Events and Topics by Using Temporal References," in: *IBERAMIA 2002: Proceedings of the 8th Ibero-American Conference on Artificial Intelligence*, Springer-Verlag, London, UK, pp. 11–20.

Stokes, N. and J. Carthy (2001a): "Combining Semantic and Syntactic Document Classifiers to Improve First Story Detection," in: *24th Annual International ACM SIGIR Conference on Research and Development in Information Retrieval (SIGIR2001)*, pp. 424–425.

Stokes, N. and J. Carthy (2001b): "First story detection using a composite document representation," in: *HLT '01: Proceedings of the 1st International Conference on Human Language Technology Research*, Association for Computational Linguistics, Morristown, NJ, USA, pp. 1–8.

Yang, Y., J. Carbonell, R. Brown, T. Pierce, B. T. Archibald, and X. Liu (1999): "Learning approaches for detecting and tracking news events," *IEEE Intelligent Systems*, 14(4), pp. 32–43.

Yang, Y., T. Pierce, and J. Carbonell (1998): "A study on retrospective and on-line event detection," in: *Proceedings of SIGIR-98, 21st ACM International Conference on Research and Development in Information Retrieval*, Melbourne, AU, pp. 28–36.

Zhang, J., Z. Ghahramani, and Y. Yang (2005): "A Probabilistic Model for Online Document Clustering with Application to Novelty Detection," in: L. Saul and Y. Weiss (eds.), *Proceedings of the 17th Conference on Advances in Neural Information Processing Systems*, pp. 1617–1624.

Zhang, J., Y. Yang, and J. Carbonell (2004): "New Event Detection with nearest Neighbor, Support Vector Machines, and Kernel Regression," working paper CMU-CS-04-118, CMU.

Zhang, K., J. Zi, and L. G. Wu (2007): "New event detection based on indexing-tree and named entity," in: *SIGIR '07: Proceedings of the 30th annual international ACM SIGIR conference on Research and development in information retrieval*, ACM, New York, NY, USA, pp. 215–222.

Zhang, X. and Z. Li (2009): "Online New Event Detection Based on IPLSA," *Advanced Data Mining and Applications*, pp. 397–408.

Towards a Benchmarking Framework
for Financial Text Mining

Caslav Bozic[1], Ryan Riordan[2], Detlef Seese[1], and Christof Weinhardt[2]

[1] Institute of Applied Informatics and Formal Description Methods, KIT
   {bozic, detlef.seese}@kit.edu
[2] Institute of Information Systems and Management, KIT
   {ryan.riordan, weinhardt}@kit.edu

Summary. Different data mining methods for financial texts and various sentiment measures are described in the existing literature, without common benchmarks for comparing these approaches. The framework proposed in this paper and the corresponding implemented system facilitate combining more sources of financial data into comprehensive integral dataset. The use of the dataset is then illustrated by analyzing the candidate measures by estimating parameters of regression on different returns and other financial indicators that can be defined using system's novel data transformation approach.

1 Introduction

Different data mining methods for financial texts are described in the literature, and systems that apply these particular methods have been implemented. For an evaluation of the proposed methods authors use different approaches, some of them incorporating assumptions that do not conform to real financial markets' conditions. This paper presents the current status of a project attempting to offer a possibility to compare performance of these systems by offering a framework, a base dataset, and an implementation of the system according to design science guidelines from Hevner et al. (2004).

The research is a part of the project FINDS (Financial News and Data Services) initiated within Information Management and Market Engineering Graduate School at the Karlsruhe Institute of Technology. Project FINDS has the goal to conduct innovative research on the analysis of quantitative and qualitative information related to financial markets and to provide services that can help both researchers in financial field, and also professional traders (Bozic, 2009).

The paper is organized as follows: in section 2 we give an overview of the existing literature in the field. Section 3 describes data sources for the comprehensive research set, preprocessing methods used on data and gets the reader acquainted with the dataset by presenting some descriptive statistics. Section 4 illustrates the usage of the framework and the system by comparing four sentiment measures. Section 5 concludes the paper and describes the ideas for future research.

2 Related Work

Many researchers have studied how published news influence market reactions. The methodologies used range from a fairly simple content analysis using classical statistical tools, to complex machine-learning methods. The approaches vary from an engineering approach which focuses on implementation and proving economic relevance, to chiefly theoretical approaches whose goal is to describe underlying economic phenomena.

Mittermayer and Knolmayer (2006a) compare eight text-mining systems, including their own. Since more technical performance criteria are often missing, it is not possible to draw clear conclusions about relative performance. Wüthrich et al. (1998) classify news articles published overnight on web portals into three categories depending on their influence on the one of five equity indices: Dow Jones, Nikkei, FTSE, Hang Seng, and Straits Times. With this system they attempt to forecast the trend of the index daily value one day ahead. They use Naïve Bayes, Nearest Neighbour and Neural Net classifier, and a hand-crafted underlying dictionary. Lavrenko et al. (2000) use Naïve Bayes classifier to classify news articles from Yahoo!Finance into five groups, according to the influence on particular U.S. stocks. The features were determined automatically and the forecast horizon was from five to ten hours. Gidófalvi and Elkan (2003) use again naïve Bayes classifier with three categories to recognize articles which have bigger positive or negative influence on constituents of Dow Jones index. With features defined using mutual information measure they work on ten minutes aggregated intraday data. Fung, Yu, and Lam (2003) partially use commercially available text mining systems to predict a price trend for intraday market movements of some of the stocks listed on the Hong Kong Stock Exchange. For classification purposes they use support vector machines. Finally, Mittermayer and Knolmayer (2006b) propose a high frequency forecast system that classifies press releases of publicly traded companies in the U.S. using a dictionary that combines automatically selected features and a hand-crafted thesaurus. For classification the authors use the polynomial version of SVM.

While most of the works focus on predicting price trends of single stock or index, there are works that aim at determining influence of news releases to volatility. Thomas (2003) improves risk-return profile by exiting the market in case of news that are predicting high volatility, while Schulz, Spiliopoulou, and Winkler (2003) attempt to classify press releases of German public companies according their influence on volatility of stock prices.

Another group of publications not included in the survey by Mittermayer and Knolmayer (2006a) contains works that do not primary attempt to prove economical relevance of published text by evaluating specifically tailored trading strategies, but rather to find statistically relevant relations between financial indicators and sentiment extracted from the text.

Antweiler and Frank (2004) use Naïve Bayes and SVM classifiers to classify messages posted to Yahoo!Finance and Raging Bull and determine their sentiment.

They do not find statistically significant correlation with stock prices, but they find sentiment and volume of messages significantly correlated to trade volumes and volatility. In their methodological paper Das and Chen (2007) offer a variety of classifiers, as well as composed sentiment measure as a result of voting among classifiers. In the illustrative example they analyze Yahoo stock boards and stock prices of 8 technology companies, but they do not find clear evidence that the sentiment index can be predictive for stock prices.

There are two pivotal articles published in the Journal of Finance. Tetlock (2007) observes Wall Street Journal's column "Abreast of the Market", uses content analysis software General Inquirer together with Principal Component Analysis approach and finds that high pessimism in published media predicts downward pressure on market prices. Authors of Tetlock, Saar-Tsechansky, and Macskassy (2008) succeeded to find that rate of negative words in news stories about certain company predicts low earnings of the company.

If we observe text mining methodologies as a transformations that assign numerical value to every textual string, we can refer to that numerical value as sentiment index. All publications from the former group have at least implicit statements about the predictive power of the specific sentiment index on e.g. returns or volatility. Following the evaluation approach from the latter group of publication, we aim at providing financial text mining research community with a framework and a tool that can be used for proving their statements using statistical significance criteria.

3 Data

3.1 Data Sources

We use Thomson Reuters TickHistory data and the output from the Reuters NewsScope Sentiment Engine as a source dataset. These data sources are convenient because they provide access to trading data over period of more than 10 years, and extensive amount of sentiment data related to financial news stories.

Data constituting the output of the Reuters NewsScope Sentiment Engine represents the author's sentiment measure for every English-language news item published via NewsScope in years 2003-2008. The measure classifies a news item into one of three categories: positive, negative, or neutral. The probability of the news item falling into each of the categories is also given.

Thomson Reuters TickHistory data is available through the DataScope platform. We use daily data for the period equivalent to the NewsScope Sentiment Engine dataset. This provides us with data on opening and closing prices for the particular product, bid and ask, as well as volume data. Other types of data about companies coming from this source are the total amount of shares, used for calculating market capitalization, and paid dividends, that can be used for adjusting the returns. Additionally, it is the source of the data about daily values of the MSCI Indices for individual countries, as well as MCSI World Index.

Field Name	Description	Source
ric	Reuters Instrument Code	TH
d	Date	TH
Open	Opening daily price	TH
High	Maximal price within the day	TH
Low	Minimal price within the day	TH
vol	Daily trading volume	TH
Last	Closing daily price	TH
Bid	Average bid	TH
Ask	Average ask	TH
spread	Average spread	TH
cc	Close to close daily return of the equity	D
oc	Open to close daily return of the equity	D
oo	Open to open daily return of the equity	D
co	Close to open daily return of the equity	D
cnt	Number of news items mentioning company	RNSE
pnaccnt	Number of news stories mentioning company	RNSE
nsent_pos	Number of positive news items mentioning company	RNSE
nsent_neut	Number of neutral news items mentioning company	RNSE
nsent_neg	Number of negative news items mentioning company	RNSE
avgsent	Average sentiment	RNSE
asent_pos	Average probability that news items are positive	RNSE
asent_neut	Average probability that news items are neutral	RNSE
asent_neg	Average probability that news items are negative	RNSE
net_sent	Net sentiment: asent_pos - asent_neg	D
net_sent_std	Standard deviation of net sentiment	D
ric_market	Abbreviation of company's home market	TH
country	Country	D
icc	Close to close daily return of the country index	D
ioc	Open to close daily return of the country index	D
ioo	Open to open daily return of the country index	D
ico	Close to open daily return of the country index	D
cnt_country	Number of news items related to country	RNSE
avgsent_item	Average sentiment (country level)	RNSE
eccc	Excess daily close to close return w/r to country index	D
ecoc	Excess daily open to close return w/r to country index	D
ecco	Excess daily close to open return w/r to country index	D
ecoo	Excess daily open to open return w/r to country index	D

Table 1: Main fields and sources (TH - TickHistory,
RNSE - Sentiment Engine, D - derived)

Reuters NewsScope Sentiment Engine data has two main properties - the timestamp of the news item publishing, and the related company mentioned in the news item. It is preprocessed in a way that the records are aggregated on the level of each company, and also calendar day - according to local time in force at the location of company's home market. In that way we get an average sentiment for a company for each day in 6 years period. The sentiments are expressed by different calculated values. The first aggregated sentiment measure is average sentiment class - where the classes are represented by values 1, 0, and -1 for positive, neutral, and negative class, respectively. Further measures are average probabilities that each news item falls into positive, negative or neutral class. As the Reuters sentiment index used for the evaluation later we adopted a deducted value defined as average probability of positive class minus average probability of negative class within one day.

From the data on daily prices we derive data on different returns: namely close-to-open, close-to-close, open-to-open, and open-to close returns. This is done considering only days with trades for particular equity or index. The generic way of defining calculated fields derived from source data is described in later section. The calculated returns are adjusted for paid dividends by increasing the price of share on the trading day following the dividend payment by the amount of dividends paid per share.

3.2 Descriptive Statistics

Reuters NewsScope Sentiment Engine data consists of author's sentiment measures of English-language news items published through Reuters NewsScope in the period from 2003 to 2006 inclusive. Each record represents a unique mention of the specific company, with a possibility of one news item relating to more than one company. In our dataset there are 6,127,190 records about 10,665 different companies. Figure 1 shows the top twenty companies with greatest number of records related to that company. According to Reuters news production process, several news items can make one single news story, e.g. short alert item is published immediately, and after some time extension of the same story is published as a new item, or in the case of corrections. In the available data average number of news items per story is 1.995, saying that in average two items make one news story.

Increase in data volume over the years is obvious and yearly record number doubles over the period of 6 years, as shown on Figure 2. Besides, on the same figure, one can follow increase in the partial volume of records related to different home markets. The information about a company's home market is an integral part of the Reuters code uniquely identifying each instrument. Figure 2 separately shows data about the ten markets with greatest changes over the years. It can be seen that the fraction of the two biggest US markets, NYSE and NASDAQ, in the total data volume has grown from something over 40% to little less than 60% in this 6 years period.

Each news item can have multiple tags called topic codes, and topic codes are grouped into categories. One of the categories represents countries, and can be used

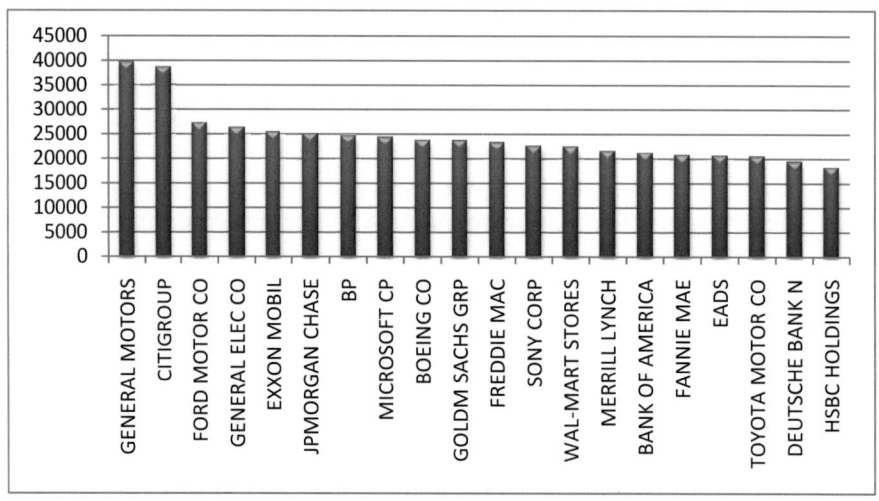

Figure 1: Top twenty companies by number of records

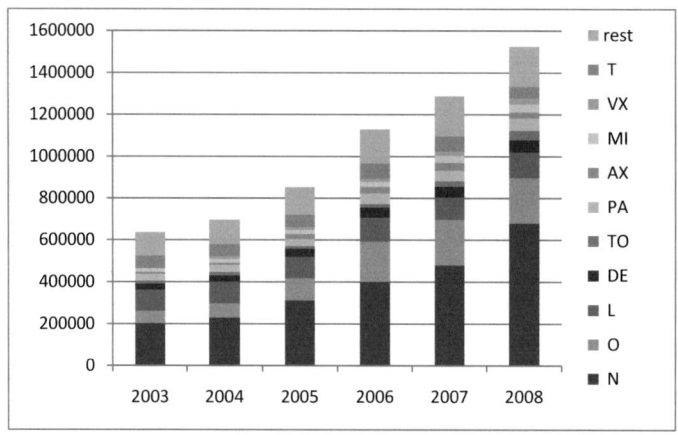

Figure 2: Data volume change over years

for determining what country is mentioned in the particular news item. Using this author tagging feature, average sentiment per country can be calculated. The Figure 3 is showing counties with greatest and lowest average sentiment, when country tags with less than 1000 mentions are excluded.

During the week, only 2.19% of all news items are published on weekends. Figure 4 shows the distribution of records per days of week. Our dataset comprises of data spanning 2192 days in total, considering GMT time zone, and there are even 13 companies that are mentioned at least once in more than 80% of all days, as shown in Table 2. One more interesting property of the data is noticeable sentiment decrease for news items published on Saturdays, as shown on Figure 5.

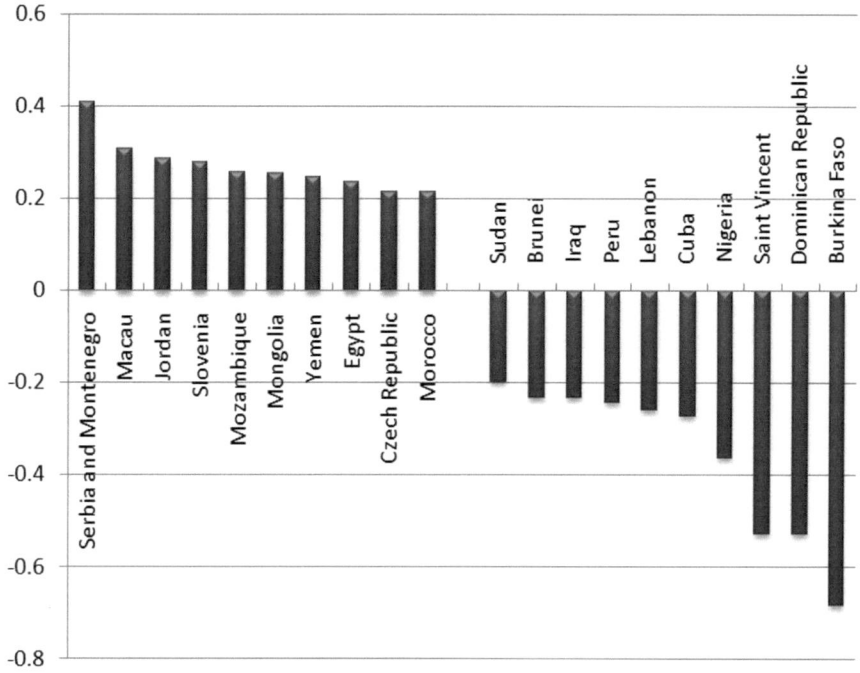

Figure 3: Best and worst average sentiment for countries with over 1000 mentions

Company	Days with news	Percent
GENERAL ELEC CO	1911	87.18
SONY CORP	1891	86.27
CITIGROUP	1863	84.99
BP	1851	84.44
WALT DISNEY CO	1841	83.99
GENERAL MOTORS	1837	83.8
EXXON MOBIL	1822	83.12
WAL-MART STORES	1802	82.21
BOEING CO	1798	82.03
MICROSOFT CP	1792	81.75
HSBC HOLDINGS	1791	81.71
GOLDM SACHS GRP	1782	81.3
FORD MOTOR CO	1754	80.02
EADS	1752	79.93
TOYOTA MOTOR CO	1729	78.88
DEUTSCHE BANK N	1729	78.88
VOLKSWAGEN AG	1720	78.47
VODAFONE GROUP	1711	78.06
CHEVRON	1704	77.74
TOTAL FINA	1693	77.24

Table 2: The 20 companies mentioned on most days

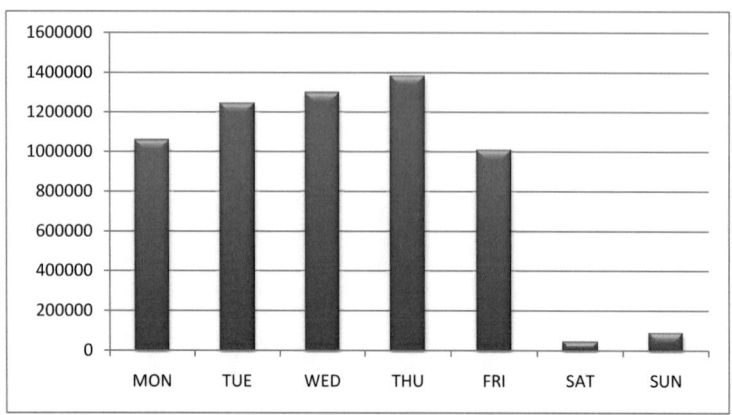

Figure 4: Number of records per days of week

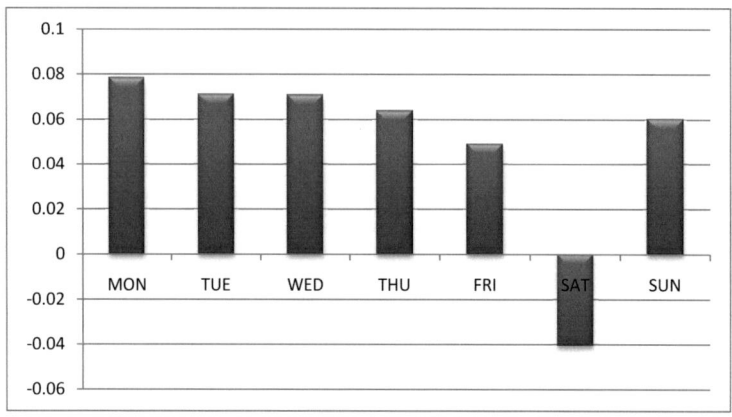

Figure 5: Average sentiment per days of week

3.3 Preprocessing

To enable easy extending of the existing dataset, generic interfacing is one of the system's features. It is generic in that aspect that it allows any format of the DataScope platform output to be loaded into the system automatically. New source to be added is placed in a comma separated values (CSV) file. The procedure of generic load then starts, making new data source available for the next steps of preprocessing. The names of the new columns that can be later used for referencing are extracted from header row of the comma separated input file. The necessary type transformations on the added data are conducted by means of metadata dictionary, which holds datatypes and formats related to the column names. In this way new data is transformed into the representation that can be used as input of the successive steps.

As our goal is to explore dependencies of various indicators and sentiment measures, another feature of the system is a novel approach to defining calculated indicators. Any of the columns from the source datasets can be used as a base for calculations. Besides full range of arithmetic operators, lagging operators can be defined and used as well. The definition of the calculated fields is given in the notation of simple grammar we defined. The definition is saved in control file, which is parsed and used for code generation. It produces PL/SQL code that applied to the source datasets produces additional datasets containing calculated fields.

Final result is a clean dataset with derived fields that were not part of the source datasets, designed for particular benchmarking purpose. The overview of the data flow can be seen on Figure 6.

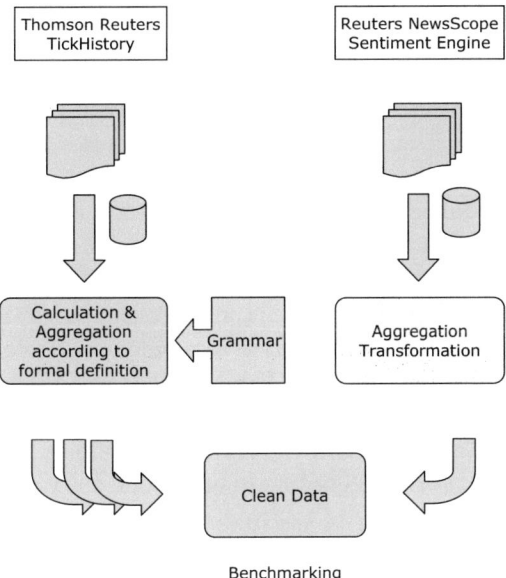

Figure 6: Overview of the Preprocessing system

4 First Results

As an illustration of framework application we performed comparison of four sentiment measures. Three of them are produced using classifiers that are implemented in the scope of FINDS Project. The first one is using Bayes-Fisher filter, second Support Vector Machines, while third implements artificial Neural Networks methodology. The classifiers are trained on high frequency intraday data on trades, aggregated to 1 minute average prices. The news items are grouped into classes depending on their influence on the price movements. Observing the period of two hours immediately following news item publication, we determine class of the news item. If the price stabilized on the level higher than the level at the moment of news item publication, news item was classified as positive. If the price stabilized on lower level, news item was classified as negative. If the price stabilization couldn't be observed, news item is considered neutral. More details about classifier implementation can be found in Pfrommer et al. (2010). Training period was first nine months of 2003, and news stories about five big technology companies (SAP, Oracle, Microsoft, IBM, and Apple) were used.

The last three months of 2003 represent the evaluation period, with total of 729 news stories analyzed. The process of news transformation shown on Figure 7 consists of text tokenizing, stemming, and finally text classification using selected methodology. Using the dataset and the framework we calculated parameters for regression of lagged dependent variables against each sentiment measure. The variables were four different daily returns, four daily excess returns, and average daily spread, all lagged up to ten days. The regression formula is given by $id_t = \alpha_{(id,i)} + \beta_{(id,i)} S_{t-i} + \varepsilon_t$ where id represents dependent variable, and i size of the lag. The results are presented in Table 3 and Table 4. The column title determines dependent variable, and the row represents days of lag between sentiment measure S and dependent variable id. Each cell shows two values: estimated coefficient value β first, and then p value according to t-statistics.

The results show that just for 14 variables could be proven statistically relevant dependence on lagged sentiment values. Although RNSE data shows most of the statistically significant results, seven, and all of them have positive coefficients, it is not possible to give clear statement about comparative performance of sentiment measures. This issue possibly arises from the low data volume, causing the statistical dependence not to be observed. To overcome the problem, regression parameter estimation for one of the measures is repeated with greater number of data points. RNSE measure is chosen because of the extensive volume of the data. Table 5 presents the results from regression parameters estimation on data sample including all six years of processed news stories in period 2003 to 2008 for two major U.S. markets contained in the system. All tested dependent variables show statistically significant dependence on sentiment value with lag of at least one day. The increase in number of statistically relevant results shows that greater amount of data offers a possibility to draw more confident conclusions.

Bayes-Fisher

lag	cc		oo		co		oc		spread		eccc		ecoo		ecco		ecoc	
1	-0.00824	0.11	-0.00316	0.54	-0.00641	0.15	-0.00182	0.48	0.00013175	0.45	-0.00646	0.23	-0.00439	0.40	-0.00386	0.43	-0.0026	0.24
2	-0.00212	0.72	-0.00557	0.19	-0.00046567	0.93	-0.00165	0.54	-0.00019337	0.18	-0.0039	0.53	-0.00263	0.47	-0.00252	0.65	-0.00147	0.54
3	-0.00056663	0.91	-0.00466	0.29	-0.00243	0.54	0.00187	0.49	-0.000633	0.01	-0.0028	0.53	-0.00096592	0.79	-0.00301	0.44	0.00029881	0.90
4	-0.00646	0.15	0.0026	0.51	-0.00667	0.10	0.00020725	0.93	-0.0004977	0.07	-0.00357	0.40	0.0008996	0.77	-0.0033	0.40	-0.00020749	0.91
5	-0.00032704	0.94	-0.00013232	0.97	0.00193	0.61	-0.00225	0.32	-0.00019928	0.30	0.00223	0.60	-0.00148	0.64	0.00242	0.51	-0.00016307	0.93
6	0.0034	0.42	-0.00163	0.67	0.0026	0.43	0.00079763	0.73	-0.0005966	0.04	0.00036264	0.92	-0.00081241	0.83	0.00037901	0.89	-0.00000455	1.00
7	0.00139	0.75	0.00642	0.12	-0.00234	0.47	0.00373	0.17	-0.00034695	0.26	0.00326	0.41	0.00584	0.17	-0.00092262	0.73	0.00424	0.11
8	0.00172	0.69	-0.00095658	0.81	0.00291	0.36	-0.00119	0.65	-0.000121	0.54	0.00165	0.68	0.00262	0.50	0.00106	0.70	0.0006209	0.80
9	-0.00343	0.27	-0.0057	0.11	0.00023065	0.93	-0.00366	0.08	-0.0004424	0.01	-0.00181	0.53	-0.00642	0.09	0.00206	0.42	-0.00385	0.05
10	-0.00411	0.19	-0.0038	0.25	-0.00204	0.49	-0.00207	0.21	-0.00007904	0.64	-0.00231	0.41	-0.00619	0.05	-0.00010074	0.97	-0.00218	0.12

SVM

lag	cc		oo		co		oc		spread		eccc		ecoo		ecco		ecoc	
1	0.00102	0.83	-0.00339	0.48	-0.00101	0.81	0.00203	0.40	-0.00003017	0.76	-0.00104	0.85	0.00127	0.81	-0.0027	0.59	0.00169	0.46
2	-0.0033	0.56	-0.00377	0.36	-0.00499	0.31	0.00169	0.52	-0.00004376	0.65	-0.00535	0.38	0.00371	0.30	-0.00637	0.24	0.00105	0.65
3	-0.00325	0.48	-0.00313	0.46	-0.00568	0.14	0.00243	0.36	-0.0000986	0.59	-0.00353	0.43	-0.00149	0.68	-0.00478	0.21	0.00128	0.58
4	-0.00281	0.54	-0.00186	0.64	-0.0045	0.28	0.00169	0.45	-0.00004667	0.83	-0.00236	0.58	-0.00109	0.73	-0.00413	0.30	0.00179	0.34
5	-0.0002228	0.96	-0.00054979	0.89	-0.00288	0.46	0.00266	0.25	0.00000991	0.96	0.00027364	0.95	0.00119	0.72	-0.00215	0.56	0.00239	0.22
6	0.00218	0.62	0.00156	0.69	-0.00253	0.47	0.00471	0.05	-0.00026022	0.41	0.00148	0.72	0.0039	0.35	-0.00121	0.70	0.0027	0.28
7	-0.00014802	0.97	0.0021	0.63	-0.00358	0.29	0.00344	0.22	-0.00000721	0.99	0.0029	0.48	0.00492	0.26	-0.00128	0.66	0.00416	0.13
8	-0.00127	0.78	-0.00473	0.25	-0.00147	0.66	0.00019947	0.94	0.00045594	0.13	0.00114	0.80	-0.00454	0.29	0.00042362	0.89	0.00072089	0.79
9	-0.00316	0.33	-0.00257	0.49	-0.00493	0.09	0.00177	0.42	0.00013967	0.57	-0.00421	0.16	-0.00391	0.31	-0.0043	0.10	0.00008207	0.97
10	-0.00112	0.73	0.0043	0.21	-0.00434	0.16	0.00322	0.06	0.00046503	0.13	-0.0003814	0.90	0.00532	0.12	-0.00334	0.23	0.00297	0.05

Table 3: Parameter estimate and p value for lagged sentiment measures produced by Bayes-Fisher and SVM classifiers

NN

lag	cc		oo		co		oc		spread		eccc		ecoo		ecco		ecoc	
1	0.00089198	0.85	-0.00005062	0.99	-0.00268	0.52	0.00357	0.12	0.0000888	0.65	-0.00134	0.78	0.00256	0.59	-0.0035	0.43	0.00215	0.28
2	-0.00018544	0.97	0.00534	0.16	-0.00272	0.56	0.00253	0.30	-0.00010813	0.53	0.0019	0.73	0.00566	0.08	-0.00043529	0.93	0.00238	0.26
3	0.00143	0.74	-0.00312	0.44	0.00271	0.45	-0.00128	0.60	0.00014492	0.67	0.0011	0.79	-0.00034131	0.92	0.00179	0.61	-0.00067498	0.75
4	0.00027233	0.95	0.00197	0.58	-0.00103	0.78	0.0013	0.52	-0.00032765	0.32	0.00419	0.28	0.00142	0.62	0.00282	0.44	0.00146	0.39
5	0.002	0.62	-0.00018654	0.96	0.00040267	0.91	0.00159	0.43	-0.00022739	0.30	0.00632	0.10	0.00273	0.35	0.00292	0.38	0.00333	0.05
6	-0.0005128	0.89	0.00377	0.27	-0.00178	0.55	0.00126	0.55	-0.00028003	0.44	0.00258	0.43	0.00298	0.37	0.0004823	0.85	0.00216	0.27
7	0.00208	0.61	-0.00218	0.56	0.00162	0.56	0.00045596	0.58	-0.00020352	0.65	0.00236	0.50	-0.00089887	0.81	0.00092307	0.71	0.00145	0.53
8	0.00198	0.61	0.0062015	0.86	-0.00163	0.86	0.00361	0.57	-0.00043306	0.19	0.00094201	0.80	0.00063296	0.86	-0.00207	0.43	0.00304	0.17
9	-0.00206	0.47	-0.00165	0.61	-0.00299	0.61	0.00093048	0.23	-0.00031224	0.24	-0.00176	0.49	-0.00182	0.58	-0.00254	0.25	0.00079024	0.65
10	-0.00188	0.51	-0.00003904	0.99	-0.00258	0.33	0.00069155	0.33	-0.00042125	0.21	-0.00263	0.31	-0.00152	0.61	-0.00235	0.33	-0.00024215	0.85

RNSE Data

lag	cc		oo		co		oc		spread		eccc		ecoo		ecco		ecoc	
1	0.00364	0.22	0.00077126	0.79	0.0031	0.24	0.00053878	0.73	0.00046926	0.04	0.00338	0.24	0.00076688	0.79	0.00302	0.25	0.00036811	0.79
2	0.00346	0.27	0.00081511	0.75	0.00001746	0.99	0.00345	0.03	0.00005651	0.71	0.00376	0.22	0.00047186	0.84	0.00125	0.64	0.00251	0.07
3	-0.00237	0.37	0.00050175	0.87	-0.00287	0.21	0.0005086	0.74	0.00037629	0.10	-0.00106	0.66	0.00098542	0.74	-0.00233	0.27	0.00129	0.35
4	-0.00194	0.52	0.00209	0.48	-0.00107	0.70	-0.0008709	0.55	0.00017053	0.44	-0.00167	0.58	0.00106	0.72	-0.00050783	0.86	-0.00117	0.39
5	0.00703	0.02	0.00419	0.11	0.00322	0.24	0.00382	0.01	-0.00002896	0.87	0.00491	0.11	0.00444	0.07	0.00134	0.63	0.00358	0.01
6	0.004	0.14	0.00366	0.20	-0.00012613	0.96	0.00413	0.01	-0.00010191	0.63	0.0029	0.23	0.00449	0.13	-0.00113	0.58	0.00402	<0.01
7	0.00155	0.61	0.00255	0.65	-0.00003749	0.99	0.00159	0.30	0.00022742	0.31	-0.00065236	0.83	0.00033338	0.89	-0.0019	0.48	0.00127	0.37
8	0.00126	0.65	0.0068839	0.83	0.00103	0.65	0.00023226	0.88	0.00012542	0.54	-0.00027	0.30	-0.00051524	0.86	-0.00202	0.35	-0.00063563	0.65
9	0.0025	0.37	-0.00054481	0.16	0.00162	0.52	0.00087812	0.52	-0.00018352	0.53	0.00208	0.46	-0.0027	0.27	0.00147	0.57	0.00058709	0.65
10	0.00102	0.70	0.00355	0.16	-0.00107	0.64	0.00209	0.13	0.00006798	0.71	-0.00010018	0.97	0.00124	0.60	-0.00204	0.35	0.00194	0.11

Table 4: Parameter estimate and p value for lagged sentiment measures produced by NN classifier and from RNSE data

RNSE Data 2003-2008

lag	cc	*	oo	*	co	*	oc	*	spread	*	ecc	*	eoo	*	eco	*	eoc	*
	0.00192		0.00422		0.00069627		0.00122		-0.00022379	0.0013	0.00159		0.00315		0.00049224		0.00104	
1		*		*		*		*				*		*		0.0003		*
2	0.00079088	*	0.00094752	*	0.00053439	0.0001	0.0002565	0.0323	-0.00018928	0.0061	0.00032129	0.0376	0.00062796	0.0003	0.00018202	0.1377	0.00010481	0.3582
3	0.00054479	0.0023	0.00047096	0.0103	0.00059187	*	-0.00004708	0.6909	-0.00019863	0.0040	0.00013246	0.4290	0.00008823	0.6246	0.00022776	0.0621	-0.00011461	0.3805
4	0.00064604	0.0002	0.00063494	0.0005	0.00053741	*	0.00010863	0.3476	-0.00021883	0.0016	0.00015744	0.3067	0.00014738	0.3837	0.00014664	0.2254	-0.00002051	0.8586
5	0.00022031	0.2161	0.00029927	0.1003	0.00040797	0.0031	-0.00018766	0.1116	-0.00021297	0.0022	-0.00012185	0.4556	-0.0001969	0.2630	0.00012828	0.2879	-0.00028489	0.0234
6	0.00020479	0.2540	0.00048202	0.0086	0.00010578	0.4423	0.00009901	0.4102	-0.00022633	0.0012	-0.0001574	0.3664	0.00003479	0.8518	-0.00011089	0.3569	-0.00006389	0.6492
7	0.00025166	0.1574	0.00029764	0.1007	0.00007658	0.5771	0.00017509	0.1347	-0.00027038	0.0001	0.00019783	0.1838	-0.00008992	0.5809	0.00009277	0.4398	0.0006607	0.5710
8	0.00025473	0.1529	-0.00003164	0.8623	0.00039427	0.0042	-0.00013954	0.2397	-0.00025098	0.0003	0.00001777	0.9207	-0.0001344	0.4789	0.00022777	0.0596	-0.00023761	0.1003
9	0.000172	0.3371	0.00040752	0.0263	0.00011437	0.4064	0.00005763	0.6307	-0.0002348	0.0006	0.00003302	0.8616	0.00015286	0.4349	0.00003762	0.7555	-0.00002812	0.8524
10	0.00037959	0.0329	0.00017503	0.3333	0.00028868	0.0358	0.00009091	0.4365	-0.00024143	0.0006	0.00001263	0.9289	-0.00001409	0.9276	-0.00000507	0.9666	-0.00001812	0.8507
11	0.00032344	0.0748	0.00025458	0.1683	0.00037599	0.0060	-0.00005256	0.6695	-0.00021858	0.0018	-0.00003697	0.8519	-0.00038506	0.0578	0.0003613	0.0026	-0.00040459	0.0120
12	0.00022131	0.2169	0.00044602	0.0147	0.00018089	0.1862	0.00004042	0.7373	-0.00024489	0.0005	-0.00012861	0.4582	0.00015126	0.4126	0.00007943	0.5070	-0.00024499	0.0797
13	0.00041467	0.0187	0.00025657	0.1517	0.00036354	0.0076	0.00005112	0.6588	-0.00024455	0.0006	0.00010797	0.4786	0.00001232	0.9405	0.00016477	0.1667	-0.00007518	0.5089
14	0.00022718	0.2052	0.00050554	0.0055	0.00013618	0.3213	0.00009101	0.4504	-0.00025425	0.0003	0.00009126	0.5439	0.00014853	0.3607	0.00009409	0.4330	-0.00004179	0.7059
15	0.00003822	0.8286	-0.00000295	0.9869	0.00021168	0.1218	-0.00017346	0.1348	-0.00021112	0.0027	-0.00009376	0.5045	-0.00018682	0.2264	0.00017699	0.1395	-0.00029669	0.0023
16	0.00064305	0.0170	0.00029846	0.1048	0.00036374	0.0081	0.00006676	0.5825	-0.00021967	0.0017	0.00010826	0.5107	0.00013612	0.4411	0.00012293	0.3058	-0.00003922	0.7607
17	0.00028462	0.1203	0.00035585	0.0568	0.00025324	0.0647	0.00003138	0.8026	-0.00022816	0.0012	0.00021946	0.2327	0.00002064	0.9153	0.00029143	0.0153	-0.00009058	0.5510
18	0.00027666	0.1236	0.00028981	0.1121	0.00021893	0.1109	0.00005773	0.6304	-0.000231	0.0008	0.00009887	0.5301	0.00022895	0.1790	0.00013912	0.2442	-0.00005783	0.6331
19	0.00016156	0.3694	0.00015372	0.4024	0.00022874	0.0929	-0.00006717	0.5804	-0.00018249	0.0084	-0.00007894	0.6160	-0.00006326	0.7096	0.00008899	0.4579	-0.00017524	0.1478
20	0.00041741	0.0200	0.00028456	0.1162	0.00036731	0.0077	0.00005011	0.6739	-0.0001935	0.0054	0.00000844	0.9614	-0.00001209	0.9465	0.00009293	0.4407	-0.00009454	0.4753

Table 5: Parameter estimate and p value for lagged sentiment measures from RNSE data in period 2003 to 2008 (* p value ¡ 0.0001)

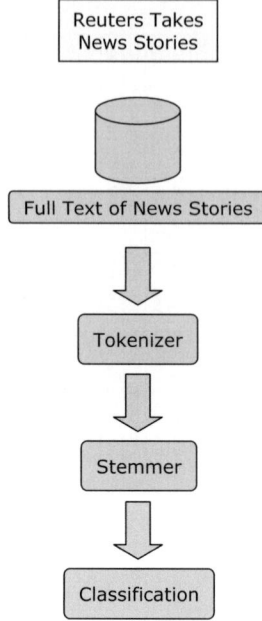

Figure 7: Transformations of news data

5 Conclusion

In an attempt to define a benchmark for performance of sentiment measures for financial texts, we propose the framework and present implementation of the system that enables easy deriving of financial indicators to be used in performance measure. As an illustration we offer a use-case analysis of four different approaches, although not giving any general conclusions about adequacy of particular approaches. It is shown that due to the inadequate data volume conclusions are vague, but the increase in the volume of analyzed data offers us a possibility to draw more robust conclusions.

Some of the future directions of the research would be extending the source base, including Compustat data on market capitalization and earnings of companies, and also extending calculated dataset, to offer wider variety of indicators which could be compared against candidate sentiment measure. More sophisticated statistical analysis should be performed on the final dataset to be able to give more decisive statements about general adequacy of text mining approaches in financial news. These could include using panel regression to control for inter-firm dependencies and applying significance test that would account for possible heteroscedasticity in the data.

References

Antweiler, W. and M. Z. Frank (2004): "Is All That Talk Just Noise? The Information Content of InternetStock Message Boards," *The Journal of Finance*, 59(3), pp. 1259–1294.

Bozic, C. (2009): "FINDS - Integrative services," in: *Computer Systems and Applications, 2009. AICCSA 2009. IEEE/ACS International Conference on*, pp. 61–62.

Das, S. and M. Chen (2007): "Yahoo! for Amazon: Sentiment extraction from small talk on the web," *Management Science*, 53(9), pp. 1375–1388.

Fung, G. P. C., J. X. Yu, and W. Lam (2003): "Stock prediction: Integrating text mining approach using real-time news," in: *Computational Intelligence for Financial Engineering, 2003. Proceedings. 2003 IEEE International Conference on*, pp. 395 – 402.

Gidófalvi, G. and C. Elkan (2003): "Using news articles to predict stock price movements," *Department of Computer Science and Engineering, University of California, San Diego*.

Hevner, A. R., S. T. March, J. Park, and S. Ram (2004): "Design Science in Information Systems Research," *MIS Quarterly*, 28(1), pp. 75–105.

Lavrenko, V., M. Schmill, D. Lawrie, P. Ogilvie, D. Jensen, and J. Allan (2000): "Mining of Concurrent Text and Time-Series," in: *Sixth ACM SIGKDD International Conference on Knowledge Discovery and Data Mining*.

Mittermayer, M. and G. Knolmayer (2006a): "Text mining systems for market response to news: A survey," *Institute of Informations Systems, University of Bern*.

Mittermayer, M.-A. and G. F. Knolmayer (2006b): "NewsCATS: A News Categorization and Trading System," *Data Mining, IEEE International Conference on*, 0, pp. 1002–1007.

Pfrommer, J., C. Hubschneider, and S. Wenzel (2010): "Sentiment Analysis on Stock News using Historical Data and Machine Learning Algorithms," Term Paper, Karlsruhe Institute of Technology (KIT).

Schulz, A., M. Spiliopoulou, and K. Winkler (2003): "Kursrelevanzprognose von Ad-hoc-Meldungen: Text Mining wider die Informationsüberlastung im Mobile Banking," *Wirtschaftsinformatik*, 2, pp. 181–200.

Tetlock, P. (2007): "Giving Content to Investor Sentiment: The Role of Media in the Stock Market," *Journal of Finance*, 62(3).

Tetlock, P., M. Saar-Tsechansky, and S. Macskassy (2008): "More Than Words: Quantifying Language to Measure Firms' Fundamentals," *Journal of Finance*, 63(3), pp. 1437–1467.

Thomas, J. (2003): *News and trading rules*, Ph.D. thesis, Carnegie Mellon University.

Wüthrich, B., D. Permunetilleke, S. Leung, V. Cho, J. Zhang, and W. Lam (1998): "Daily prediction of major stock indices from textual www data," *1998 IEEE International Conference on Systems, Man, and Cybernetics*.

The Impact of Economic News on Information and Liquidity in Electronic Futures Trading

Andreas Storkenmaier[1], Ryan Riordan[1], Christof Weinhardt[1], and Rudi Studer[2]

[1] Institute of Information Systems and Management, KIT
{andreas.storkenmaier,ryan.riordan,weinhardt}@kit.edu
[2] Institute of Applied Informatics and Formal Description Methods, KIT
rudi.studer@kit.edu

Summary. In this paper we analyze the effect of the release of U.S. unemployment numbers on information, liquidity, and trading activity in German Bund Futures. Our sample comprises the years 2000 to 2009 of Eurex traded futures. We find that liquidity and trading activity is lower pre-announcement associated with high adverse selection costs. Liquidity recovers and adverse selection stays on a slightly higher level than normal within thirty minutes after announcements. Trading activity drastically increases and stays on a high level during the first thirty minutes after announcements. Our findings are consistent with existing empirical literature. We find that the Euro-Bund Futures market is a highly liquid and efficient market that incorporates public information fast. Private information arises through varying information processing and gathering capabilities of market participants.

During the last decades, futures trading on government bonds has risen to constitute a major part of trading in financial instruments. This paper analyzes how information asymmetry and liquidity develops around U.S. unemployment rate announcements in trading of German Bund Futures. Bund Futures belong to Europe's most traded securities. With Eurex, we specifically analyze a highly automated electronic market suitable for automated trading. Macroeconomic news are, additionally to official government outlets, also released through news wire networks of Bloomberg, Thomson Reuters, and Dow Jones. Recent evidence from the foreign exchange (FX) market suggests that algorithmic traders also use macroeconomic news as input parameters (Chaboud et al., 2009). Algorithmic traders automatically pull out of the FX market around macroeconomic news announcements to reduce potential adverse selection costs. The role of information and liquidity has long been of interest to market microstructure research. In combination with recent developments in trading systems and market automation the question of information and liquidity around macroeconomic news events in electronic markets is interesting to researchers and practitioners alike.

Our study shows, consistent with existing literature, higher adverse selection costs around macroeconomic news, lower liquidity, and higher trading intensity post announcements. We find that the Euro-Bund Futures market is a highly liquid and efficient market that incorporates public information fast. Private information arises through varying information processing and gathering capabilities of market participants.

The remainder of the paper is structured as follows. Section 1 gives a literature overview, section 2 provides information about Eurex's institutional details and section 3 describes the unemployment and transaction data. Section 4 explains our research design. Section 5 provides the results and section 6 finally concludes.

1 Literature Review

The notion of information in markets, its impact, and its relevance has triggered lots of research in the area of market microstructure during the last forty years. One fundamental model is the Glosten and Milgrom (1985) model which also provides the theoretical foundation for the Madhavan et al. (1997) model used in this paper. The main contribution of the Glosten and Milgrom model is that it shows how bid-ask spreads can emerge independently from exogenous transaction costs and that private information is impounded into prices through order flow. Liquidity suppliers revise their expectations about an asset's value depending on whether trades are buys or sells. Since liquidity suppliers try to safeguard themselves against informed traders the amount of private information is reflected through the adverse selection component in the spread.

This paper does not analyze general aspects of information and liquidity in German Bund futures trading but concentrates on the effects in trading around macroeconomic news announcements. In equity markets private information fundamentally consists of information about future cash flows. However, there should not be substantial private information about future cash flows of government bonds. From a theoretical point of view there are models that analyze effects before and after anticipated announcements. Kim and Verrecchia (1991) formulate a model which explains private information prior to an anticipated announcement such as earnings announcements. Traders acquire costly private information to trade in advance of a public announcement. Kim and Verrecchia (1994) introduce a model with the notion that different traders have different capabilities to interpret earnings announcements. This might lead to an increase in adverse selection costs associated with a reduction in liquidity. However, according to their model trading volume might still increase despite a decrease in liquidity around earnings announcements. In short, their paper "suggests a model of trade in which financial accounting disclosures simultaneoulsy induce increased information asymmetry, less liquidity, and more trading volume" (Kim and Verrecchia, 1994). Economic news indicators are similar to earnings announcements in that there should be no other prior direct private information source and the information contained in the news might be interpreted differently by different market participants. Kim and Verrecchia (1997) provide an extension of their 1994 model in which they incorporate the effects of pre-announcement anticipation and private information as well as post-announcement public event-period information.

Additional to theoretical models researchers have conducted empirical studies on the effects of news announcements on information. Krinsky and Lee (1996) provide empirical evidence for Kim and Verrecchia (1994). They find that the adverse selection component of the spread increases around earnings announcements. They also attribute this effect to temporary information advantages of informed investors and information advantages of public information processors. Niessen (2007) researches into the effect of media coverage on macroeconomic news processing in the futures market on government bonds. Her paper provides evidence that there is macroeconomic information processing prior to economic indicator releases induced through media coverage. Higher pre-announcement media coverage increases investor attention and leads to stronger post-announcement market reactions. Vega (2006) studies how stock prices react to media coverage. She finds a connection between media coverage and post-announcement stock price changes. The paper explains a post-announcement drift with different information market participants receive. In a recent paper, Evans and Lyons (2008) investigate the effect of macroeconomic news on foreign exchange markets. They analyze a broad spectrum of macroeconomic news and study the direct influence on prices through order flow. They find that after the announcement of macro economic news there is more information impounded into the market through order flow than during normal times. This finding translates into higher adverse selection after macro news than normal and is not consistent with the hypothesis that public information is directly impounded into the market and directly causes price changes. The paper closest to our study is Green (2004). He studies U.S. government bond trading around macroeconomic news releases. The results show higher adverse selection costs around macroeconomic news releases as a result of private information impounded through the order flow. Andersen et al. (2007) analyze different futures markets with respect to the release of macroeconomic information. They find quick significant responses also in non-U.S. government bond futures markets. This finding indicates a quick and thus efficient price discovery process.

There exists also literature on the effect of liquidity, volatility, and trading intensity around pulic information releases in securites markets. Mitchell and Mulherin (1994) study the effect of publicly reported information by Dow Jones on securities market activity. They find positive relations between the number of news stories and volume and volatility in equity markets. Fleming and Remolona (1999) find a reduction in trading volume and sharp price reactions with higher volatility after the publication of macroeconomic news in the U.S. Treasury market. In their study the quoted spread increases around macroeconomic news announcements and then slowly reverts to normal. They also find highly significant cross-market linkages between trading venues in different countries. Hess et al. (2008) focus their analysis on the liquidity provision around macrocenomic news announcements in the German Bund Futures market. They measure liquidity supply through the quoted spread and volume at the best bid and ask. However, they lack order book data to analyze liquidity at order book levels beyond the best bid and ask. In their paper, they find that bid and ask volume decreases around macroeconomic news announcements while the quoted spread increases. In another analysis of liquidity in equity markets Lee et al. (1993) find lower liquidity around earnings announcements.

2 Institutional Details

We analyze trading at Eurex[1], a joint-venture of Deutsche Boerse AG and SIX Swiss Exchange. Eurex is a pure derivatives exchange that offers a wide range of products based on interest rates, equities, volatilities, and options, but for instance also weather derivatives. Eurex is built as an electronic public limit order book. Most products are matched based on price-time priority, only money market futures are matched through pro rata matching. Orders are executed against quotes with the best prices first. If prices of quotes are equal, orders are first executed against quotes with a lower timestamp i.e. which have been in the book the longest. The trading day at Eurex lasts typically from 7h30 a.m. to 10h00 p.m. CET (Central European Time) depending on the product and consists of a pre-trading, trading, and post-trading phase. Trading hours have changed several times between the years 2000 and 2009. Since we only consider data between 1h00 p.m. and 4h00 p.m., which have always been within normal trading hours, those changes are not relevant for our analysis. Normal trading refers to the continuous trading period with price-time priority based matching in the public limit order book. Nowadays, Eurex is based on a version of the Xetra system which features low exchange system latencies in the magnitude of milliseconds.[2]

Euro-Bund Futures are fixed income derivatives on German federal bonds[3]. They are based on bonds with a remaining term of 8.5 to 10.5 years and a coupon of 6%. The standardized contract value is 100,000 Euros. A delivery obligation might be met with German federal bonds with a minimum issue amount of 5bn Euros. The minimum tick size is 0.01 percentage points (pts) which is equivalent to a value of 10 Euros. Bund Futures are traded with the delivery months March, June, September, and December. Three Bund Futures trade at the same time, the futures with the

---

[1] http://www.eurexchange.com.

[2] Eurex features different order types. Market orders are directly executed whereas stop orders create market orders when a pre-specified stop price is reached. Market orders contain no limit price and both normal market orders and stop orders are not visible in the order book. Stop orders are not available for options traded at Eurex. There are several flags to influence the behavior of limit orders. Good-for-Day flagged orders are not persistent over night, Good-till-Cancelled orders can stay in the order book up to one year, and Good-till-Date limit orders can stay in the book until some pre-defined date. Immediate-or-Cancel limit orders are filled immediately. If such an order cannot be filled, partly or completely, then the whole order or parts of the order are cancelled. The executed part of an Immediate-or-Cancel limit order is essentially a marketable limit order.

[3] http://www.eurexchange.com/trading/products/INT/FIX/FGBL_en.html.

three nearest delivery months. We incorporate the future with the nearest delivery month in our analysis.

3 Data

3.1 Unemployment Data

We retrieve U.S. unemployment data from the official data bases of the U.S. Bureau of Labor Statistics[4]. The relevant data are released monthly with the Employment Situation Report, always at 8:30 a.m. ET (Eastern Time). The monthly release analyzes the previous month's employment situation, i.e. the report released in October describes the employment situation in September. The United States Department of Labor does not release employment information prior to the official release date. The official report is accessible via Internet at exactly 8:30 a.m. ET, the information is also disseminated through Reuters or Bloomberg systems. We are interested in the exact date of a report release and check these data with the Employment Situation Report. We also re-check the exact release times. The reports are mostly released on Fridays. However, sometimes release dates deviate due to public holidays. Depending on the year and differences in daylight savings time, U.S. unemployment data is released at either 1h30 p.m., 2h30 p.m., or 3h30 p.m. CET.

3.2 Transaction Data

We use transaction and order data retrieved from the Reuters DataScope Tick History archive through SIRCA[5]. The DataScope Tick History archive provides trade and quote and order book data for a wide range of instruments for all major exchanges worldwide.

We retrieve data for Euro-Bund Futures from 1st January 2000 to 30th June 2009. Our analysis comprises the future with the closest maturity date. To construct a time series we roll over to the next future on the last trading day of the current future. We do not use the last trading day of a future since trading already ends at 12h30 p.m. CET on those days for this particular future. Through rolling over we construct a time series that consists of thirty-nine different contracts over eight and a half years. We retrieve both trade and quote and order book data for our analysis. Trade and quote data includes price and volume for transactions as well as best bid and best ask including associated volumes. Order book entries feature bid and ask as well as associated volumes up to twenty levels into the order book. All trades, quotes, and order book entries are timestamped to the millisecond. All prices are reported in percentage points (pts) to a contract value of EUR 100,000.

---

[4] http://www.bls.gov.
[5] Securities Industry Research Centre of Asia Pacific (SIRCA), http://www.sirca.org.au, We thank SIRCA for providing access to the Thomson Reuters DataScope Tick History archive.

As explained in the previous section, U.S. unemployment data arrives in the middle of the Eurex trading day. For each month we cut the daily transaction data to thirty minute time intervals around that month's unemployment news announcement time. For example, if in February the unemployment numbers arrive at 2h30 p.m. CET then only trade and quote and order book data from 2h00 p.m. to 3h00 p.m. are included in the time series for February. If in a month the unemployment numbers arrive at 1h30 p.m. CET then data from 1h00 p.m. to 2h00 p.m. are included in that month's time series. Such an approach minimizes time-of-day effects and compares data from announcement days with appropriate data from other days. We also exclude any non-continuous trading from the transaction data time series. Altogether the final time series comprises 4,917,372 trades with an average price of 116.06 pts.

4 Research Design

4.1 Information

We measure information impounded through order flow with an extended MRR model introduced by Madhavan et al. (1997). We extend the model in the spirit of Green (2004) to include variables for different intervals around a macroeconomic news event. The MRR model is a common market microstructure model to approximate the adverse selection component of the bid-ask spread, the information revealed through trades. When informed traders trade, prices tend to follow their trades which constitutes a risk for market participants that post limit orders. The adverse selection component measures the part of the bid-ask spread that is required as a compensation for liquidity suppliers risk of losing against informed traders. Hence, the adverse selection component of the bid-ask spread can be interpreted as private information that is impounded into prices through the order flow. The MRR model estimates an adverse selection component and an inventory and order processing cost component of the bid-ask spread.

The MRR model is only based on the trade process and analyzes transaction price changes and their relation to the trade direction of orderflow. We use the common Lee and Ready (1991) algorithm to sign trades with contemporaneous quotes as proposed by Bessembinder (2003).

Let x_i be the trade direction, 1 for a market buy order and -1 for a market sell order at time i and p_i denotes the transaction price. Specifically, i denotes a single observation in the trade process. Then the original Madhavan et al. (1997) model formulates the following relation:

$$p_i - p_{i-1} = (\phi + \theta)x_i - (\phi + \rho\theta)x_{i-1} + \epsilon_i. \tag{1}$$

Let ρ be the first-order autocorrelation, θ denotes the asymmetric information component, and ϕ captures inventory and order processing costs. The fundamental concept to measure private information is that only the deviation from expected order flow comprises information. Expected order flow ρx_{i-1} is based on order flow autocorrelation ρ. θ measures "the degree of information asymmetry or the so-called permanent impact of the order flow innovation" (Madhavan et al., 1997). Beliefs about asset values might change through new public information without trade or through information impounded by the order flow. The change in belief is positively correlated with order flow innovation. Inventory and order processing costs represent the transitory effect of order flow on prices. Bid and ask quotes that reflect the inventory and order processing cost component are ex post rational independent of the trade direction. Accordingly, ϕ is not dependent on the trade process' autocorrelation ρ. The MRR model assumes a fixed order size and does not consider volume. Madhavan et al. (1997) address this issue and find that trade direction is better suited to analyze their model than signed volume.

To analyze information around economic news events we extend the original MRR model based on Green (2004). We introduce several dummy variables for different intervals around an economic news event. Dummy variables allow to distinguish ten minute intervals within thirty minute time periods before and after an economic news event from observations not close to the economic news events under consideration. A dummy variable takes 1 if the observation is within the time period asigned to this variable and else 0. Let i denote single observations in the trade process and $n \in \{1, \ldots, 7\}$ denotes the different intervals around macroeconomic news where $n = 1$ indicates observations on non-announcement days then $D_{n,i}$ represents the dummy variable. Then the following model that allows for changes in the bid-ask spread components around macroeconomic news announcements emerges:

$$p_i - p_{i-1} = \sum_{n=1}^{7} [(\phi_n + \theta_n) x_i D_{n,i} - (\phi_n + \rho_n \theta_n) x_{i-1} D_{n,i-1}] + \epsilon_i. \qquad (2)$$

Madhavan et al. (1997) use absolute price changes to estimate the model. To support the interpretation of results we use relative price changes in basis points to estimate equation 2. However, results are robust to using absolute or relative price changes. The model is estimated using the generalized methods of moments (GMM) with the Newey and West (1987) procedure as proposed in the original paper by Madhavan et al. (1997). The Newey-West procedure is robust to autocorrelation and heteroskedasticity. Let r_i denote the relative price change which is calculated as $r_i = 10,000 \times \ln (p_i / p_{i-1})$ then the model can be estimated as:

$$u_i = r_i + \sum_{n=1}^{7} [-(\phi_n + \theta_n) x_i D_{n,i} + (\phi_n + \rho_n \theta_n) x_{i-1} D_{n,i-1}]. \qquad (3)$$

using the following implied moment conditions that exactly identify the constant α and the parameter vector $\beta = (\theta_n, \phi_n, \rho_n)$ with $n \in \{1, ..., 7\}$:

$$E \begin{pmatrix} x_i x_{i-1} D_{1,i-1} - \left(x_{i-1} D_{1,i-1}\right)^2 \rho_1 \\ \vdots \\ x_i x_{i-1} D_{7,i-1} - \left(x_{i-1} D_{7,i-1}\right)^2 \rho_7 \\ u_i - \alpha \\ \left(u_i - \alpha\right) x_{i-1} D_{1,i-1} \\ \vdots \\ \left(u_i - \alpha\right) x_{i-1} D_{7,i-1} \\ \left(u_i - \alpha\right) x_i D_{1,i} \\ \vdots \\ \left(u_i - \alpha\right) x_i D_{7,i} \end{pmatrix} = 0. \tag{4}$$

Equations one to seven in the moment conditions represent the autocorrelation of the trade direction indicator. Equations eight to twenty-two represent the ordinary least square (OLS) normal conditions. Finally, the estimation of equation 3 gives results for private information (θ), the inventory and order processing cost or cost of supplying liquidity (ϕ), and the autocorrelation of order flow (ρ) for each single interval.

To assess the model's statistical significance we apply likelihood ratio tests as in Green (2004). These tests compare the GMM criterion function of the unrestricted model with restricted models. Since model implied spreads are solely based on the order flow they do not necessarily need to be exactly the same as data based quoted spreads. However, they should be roughly similar in their order of magnitude.

4.2 Trading Intensity and Liquidity

To measure trading intensity we calculate the number of trades per minute and transform the trade point process into a process with one observation per minute. For the dummy variable definition we resort to the MRR information model definition of dummy variables and use exactly the same. The no-announcement day dummy variable does not need to be included, it is the basis of comparison and coefficients capture the difference to no-announcement days. Let l denote the minutes in the data and tm_l denotes trades per minute then the following model is used to assess trading intensity around economic news announcements.

$$tm_l = a + t_1 D_{1,l} + t_2 D_{2,l} + t_3 D_{3,l} + t_4 D_{4,l} + t_5 D_{5,l} + t_6 D_{6,l} + e_l. \tag{5}$$

The intercept a captures the number of trades per minute when there is no news announcement thus there is no dummy variable for those time periods. To estimate equation 5 and all future time-series regressions we again use GMM with the Newey-West procedure based on five lags.

Liquidity is measured based on three different measures: quoted half spread, the volume at the best bid and ask, and the volume to depth level three to account for more than just best bid and ask. All liquidity measures are based on a quote-to-quote process which in the case of depth also includes changes in the book away from the best bid and ask. Let a_i denote the best ask and b_i the best bid at time i then the quoted half spreads (qs_i) based on Bessembinder and Kaufman (1997) are calculated as follows in basis points:

$$qs_i = \left(\frac{a_i - b_i}{(a_i + b_i)/2} \right) /2 \times 10,000. \tag{6}$$

Quoted spreads, however, only capture liquidity up to a small trade size at which orders start to sweep the order book. To further analyze liquidity we consider volume at the best bid and ask (depth0) and volume to depth level three (depth3) based on order book data both measured in available volume in points of contract prices. Let again be a_i the best ask, b_i the best bid, an_i the number of futures available at the ask, and bn_i the number of futures available at the bid then volume at the best bid and ask (depth0) (ev_i) is calculated as

$$ev_i = bn_i \times b_i + an_i \times a_i. \tag{7}$$

For estimation purposes we use the natural logarithm of volume at the best bid and ask ($lev_i = \ln ev_i$). However, ev_i only provides information about volume directly at the spread. Order book data allows to analyze available volume deeper in the book and liquidity which is used and needed for larger trades. In combination with the other liquidity measures, depth allows for a much more precise analysis of liquidity than quoted spread alone. Let $a_{i,dl}$ be the ask at time i on depth level dl, $b_{i,dl}$ denotes the bid on depth level dl, $an_{i,dl}$ is the number of futures available on a certain depth level at the ask, and $bn_{i,dl}$ denotes the number of futures at depth level dl on the bid. Then the depth measure for three depth levels d_i (depth3) is calculated as

$$d_i = \sum_{dl=1}^{3} bn_{i,dl} \times b_{i,dl} + \sum_{dl=1}^{3} an_{i,dl} \times a_{i,dl}. \tag{8}$$

As for volume at the best bid and ask we apply the natural logarithm to depth for the estmation ($ld_i = \ln d_i$). The model to estimate the impact on liquidity measures is comparable to the one for trading intensity. The only difference is that the estimation is based on the quote-to-quote process instead of minute data. Let i be the indicator for a single observation and lm_i the liquidity measure under consideration. Using the same definition for dummy variables as for trading intensity, the following model emerges:

$$lm_i = a + m_1 D_{1,i} + m_2 D_{2,i} + m_3 D_{3,i} + m_4 D_{4,i} + m_5 D_{5,i} + m_6 D_{6,i} + e_i. \tag{9}$$

5 Results and Interpretation

Table 1 provides results for the estimated MRR model around macroeconomic news announcements. Statistical significance at the 1% level is indicated through an 'a'. The table shows the estimated spread components for no-announcement periods and ten minute intervals in the thirty minutes pre and post the release of U.S. unemployment information. The adverse selection (θ) component is the component of the spread that arises as a result of private information impounded into the market through order flow and the order processing component (ϕ) represents other costs of supplying liquidity independent the of trade process autocorrelation (ρ). Compared to equity markets it strikes that adverse selection costs only make up a minor part of the spread. However, this is consistent with the fact that private information should be much lower for Bund Futures than for individual firms.

For no-announcement periods the estimation of the spread through the MRR model adds up to 0.3208 basis points, the sum of the adverse selection and order processing components. The no-announcement period average quoted spread calculated from actual quotes is 0.450 basis points. The similarity of estimated spreads and data based spreads indicates that the MRR model is well specified to analyze Bund Futures trading. Table 1 shows that adverse selection costs increase sharply prior to the release of U.S. unemployment information. Thirty to twenty minutes before an announcement adverse selection costs are slightly higher with 0.0797 basis points compared to 0.0680 basis points in no news periods. Then adverse selection costs sharply rise to 0.1597 and 0.1488 in the two ten minute intervals prior to the announcement. In both periods adverse selection costs rise by almost 100% in comparison to normal periods. Directly after an announcement, adverse selection is slightly higher with 0.0761 than normal and seems to slowly revert to normal with 0.0724 basis points during the last ten minute interval.

Although the theoretical models of Kim and Verrecchia (1991, 1994, 1997) operate under some assumptions, they qualitively fit our empirical observations. Economic news releases are similar in nature to earnings announcements. Both forms of news are scheduled and there should not be prior information leakage. Prior to announcements traders who try to trade in advance of public unemployment numbers collect private information. Costly private information gathering as introduced in the Kim and Verrechia models could be the analysis of existing U.S. job market data. As introduced by Kim and Verrecchia prior information gathering is costly and requires benefits from trading in advance of public information. After the announcement there seems to be a period where traders substantially differ in their information processing capabilities and in their evaluation of the U.S. unemployment information. Our results are also consistent with empirical papers (cf. Krinsky and Lee (1996), Niessen (2007), Evans and Lyons (2008), Green (2004)). For further analysis we need to look at trading intensity, liquidity and their relation to information.

Time Interval	Spread Components		
	Adverse Selection θ_n	Order Processing ϕ_n	Autocorrelation ρ_n
No econ news $(n = 1)$			
Coefficient	0.0680^a	0.2528^a	0.4375^a
t-Value	(315.36)	(920.44)	(865.61)
$30 - 20$ min. before news $(n = 2)$			
Coefficient	0.0797^a	0.2284^a	0.3716^a
t-Value	(25.40)	(56.11)	(48.67)
$20 - 10$ min. before news $(n = 3)$			
Coefficient	0.1597^a	0.2434^a	0.3229^a
t-Value	(21.40)	(34.97)	(52.07)
$10 - 0$ min. before news $(n = 4)$			
Coefficient	0.1488^a	0.3061^a	0.3856^a
t-Value	(57.18)	(89.26)	(139.23)
$0 - 10$ min. after news $(n = 5)$			
Coefficient	0.0761^a	0.2581^a	0.4300^a
t-Value	(44.52)	(131.15)	(118.32)
$10 - 20$ min. after news $(n = 6)$			
Coefficient	0.0784^a	0.2325^a	0.3695^a
t-Value	(23.64)	(53.27)	(43.79)
$20 - 30$ min. after news $(n = 7)$			
Coefficient	0.0724^a	0.2563^a	0.4360^a
t-Value	(42.15)	(124.32)	(110.68)

	Likelihood Ratio Tests	
	Statistics	Constraints
LR Test 1 θ_n		
χ^2-value	1168.40	$\theta_1 = \theta_2, \theta_1 = \theta_3, \theta_1 = \theta_4,$
p-value	$< .0001$	$\theta_1 = \theta_5, \theta_1 = \theta_6, \theta_1 = \theta_7$
LR Test 2 θ_n		
χ^2-value	788.49	$\theta_2 = \theta_3, \theta_2 = \theta_4,$
p-value	$< .0001$	$\theta_2 = \theta_5, \theta_2 = \theta_6, \theta_2 = \theta_7$
LR Test 1 ϕ_n		
χ^2-value	307.59	$\phi_1 = \phi_2, \phi_1 = \phi_3, \phi_1 = \phi_4,$
p-value	$< .0001$	$\phi_1 = \phi_5, \phi_1 = \phi_6, \phi_1 = \phi_7$
LR Test 2 ϕ_n		
χ^2-value	287.05	$\phi_2 = \phi_3, \phi_2 = \phi_4,$
p-value	$< .0001$	$\phi_2 = \phi_5, \phi_2 = \phi_6, \phi_2 = \phi_7$
LR Test 1 ρ_n		
χ^2-value	750.24	$\rho_1 = \rho_2, \rho_1 = \rho_3, \rho_1 = \rho_4,$
p-value	$< .0001$	$\rho_1 = \rho_5, \rho_1 = \rho_6, \rho_1 = \rho_7$
LR Test 2 ρ_n		
χ^2-value	342.86	$\rho_2 = \rho_3, \rho_2 = \rho_4,$
p-value	$< .0001$	$\rho_2 = \rho_5, \rho_2 = \rho_6, \rho_2 = \rho_7$

Table 1: MRR Model Results - Information

Table 1 also provides likelihood ratio tests that evaluate the model specification. We test against two restricted models for each value in table 1: the adverse selection cost component, the order processing cost component, and autocorrelation. The first test (LR Test 1) restricts all coefficients such that they cannot vary around announcements and the second (LR Test 2) restricts all coefficents such that they

Time Interval	QSpread in bp	Depth0 in pts	Depth3 in pts	Trades/Min	Volume/Min in pts
Overall					
Mean	0.450	118,055	502,958	33	180,487
StdDev	0.162	98,669	336,348	51	262,642
Min	0.396	207	1,380	0	0
Max	23.772	1,341,411	3,051,869	1,409	5,827,331
No econ news					
Mean	0.447	119,083	507,433	32	173,319
StdDev	0.112	99,042	337,503	47	245,826
Min	0.396	207	1,380	0	0
Max	11.809	1,341,411	3,051,869	1,409	5,158,429
30 − 20 min. bef. news					
Mean	0.451	97,798	410,084	16	86,467
StdDev	0.087	80,739	247,123	14	82,985
Min	0.402	651	30,759	0	0
Max	1.894	717,104	1,261,966	104	574,729
20 − 10 min. bef. news					
Mean	0.455	89,642	369,317	19	99,333
StdDev	0.101	77,423	227,502	24	95,138
Min	0.402	1,137	15,497	0	0
Max	2.805	682,682	1,214,729	309	1,060,851
10 − 0 min. bef. news					
Mean	0.528	63,369	249,590	30	138,826
StdDev	0.509	61,991	168,857	34	141,710
Min	0.402	207	2,615	2	2,480
Max	12.717	704,625	1,080,292	403	2,576,476
0 − 10 min. aft. news					
Mean	0.570	87,115	377,989	154	790,748
StdDev	0.788	77,630	256,907	191	797,614
Min	0.401	232	1,422	14	37,841
Max	23.772	1,078,402	2,169,725	1,327	5,827,331
10 − 20 min. aft. news					
Mean	0.450	116,636	496,078	85	515,903
StdDev	0.102	101,908	326,314	80	425,816
Min	0.402	621	4,224	3	4,343
Max	2.817	955,580	2,073,491	474	3,602,379
20 − 30 min. aft. news					
Mean	0.446	118,260	522,255	73	434,784
StdDev	0.086	99,564	374,364	75	399,885
Min	0.402	831	7,552	2	4,899
Max	3.556	920,757	2,986,006	658	3,424,390

Table 2: Descriptive Statistics - Liquidity and Trading Intensity

cannot vary for different intervals around economic news announcements. The smallest χ^2-value among all measures is 287.05 which rejects the the LR test's null hypothesis of a restricted model that is better specified than the unrestricted with a p-value of less than 0.0001. All coefficients in Table 1 show highly significant t-statistics.

Table 2 provides descriptive statistics for liquidity and trading intensity. On average the quoted spread (*Qspread*) is very low at 0.450 basis points with a volume at the spread (*Depth0*) of 118,055 and 502,958 at three tick size levels into the order book (*Depth3*). A price change of 0.01 represents a value of 10 Euros. Quoted spread, Depth0, and Depth3 reveal a highly liquid market for Bund Futures. The descriptives already indicate a decrease in liquidity prior to unemployment announcements followed by still comparably low liquidity in the first ten minutes after announcements. Then liquidity reverts to normal. Depth0 decreases from 97,798 thirty to twenty minutes before announcements to 63,369 in the ten minutes directly before announcements. The same holds for Depth3 which decreases from 507,433 to 369,317. The quoted spread shows a slightly different pattern. It increases prior to announcements but reaches its high in the ten minute post-announcement period. In combination depth seems to recover directly after announcements but the spread still widens.

Estimation results for quoted spread, the natural logarithm of Depth0, and the natural logarithm of Depth3 are provided in Table 3. Coefficents for all, but the last interval from twenty to thirty minutes after U.S. unemployment announcements, are highly significant with robust t-statistics for non-intercept results between 5.12 and 127.02. The estimation supports the descriptive statistics: a sharp decrease in depth around unemployment announcements with a low prior to announcements and an increase in quoted spreads with a high after announcements. Especially the ten minutes before and after the release of new unemployment numbers are highly statistically signficant as well as economically significant with the largest coefficients of all intervals. Figure 1 shows how Depth0 and Depth3 develop per minute around news announcements. The graph clearly shows that Depth0 and Depth3 reach their low shortly before the announcement and then increase back to normal within thirty minutes. The reduction in liquidity is also consistent with theoretical predictions (cf. Kim and Verrecchia (1991, 1994, 1997)) as well as empirical analyses (Hess et al. (2008), Lee et al. (1993)). Table 3 also provides likelihood tests with the restriction that measures cannot vary for different intervals around U.S. unemployment number releases. The restricted models are all rejected with p-values less than 0.0001. The minimum χ^2-value of all liquidity measures is as high as 1,651 for quoted spreads.

We also measure trading intensity around announcements. Descriptive statistics are provided in Table 2 for trades per minute and volume per minute. The descriptive statistics already indicate that the number of trades and traded volume are significantly lower prior to announcements than normal and significantly higher in post-announcement periods. The normal average number of trades is 32 and average traded volume per minute without news periods is 173,319. In pre-announcement periods, the number of trades per minute is only between 16 and 19 for the periods form thirty minutes before to ten minutes before announcements. The respective numbers for traded volume are 86,467 and 99,333 in comparison to 173,319 in no-announcement periods. Then directly after the U.S. unemployment numbers are released we see a dramatic increase in trading activity up to 154 trades per minute in the first ten minutes after announcements and up to 790,748 traded volume. Even after thirty minutes, trading activity does not revert to normal. The number of

Time Interval	Trading Intensity and Liquidity			
	Trades / Min	Quoted Spread	ln Depth0	ln Depth3
No econ news				
Intercept	32.14^a	0.4471^a	11.3526^a	12.8935^a
t-Value	(129.70)	(6,776.06)	(16,185.30)	(28,588.90)
30 − 20 min. before news				
Coefficient	-15.84^a	0.0040^a	-0.2078^a	-0.1910^a
t-Value	(-19.14)	(6.00)	(-20.12)	(-31.24)
20 − 10 min. before news				
Coefficient	-12.30^a	0.0081^a	-0.2895^a	-0.2985^a
t-Value	(-9.72)	(10.49)	(-30.52)	(-50.72)
10 − 0 min. before news				
Coefficient	-1.43	0.0814^a	-0.6942^a	-0.7256^a
t-Value	(-0.82)	(20.27)	(-73.55)	(-127.02)
0 − 10 min. after news				
Coefficient	122.20^a	0.1229^a	-0.4099^a	-0.3433^a
t-Value	(11.78)	(35.57)	(-59.57)	(-74.29)
10 − 20 min. after news				
Coefficient	53.45^a	0.0025^a	-0.0509^a	-0.0412^a
t-Value	(10.75)	(5.21)	(-7.61)	(-8.92)
20 − 30 min. after news				
Coefficient	41.22^a	-0.0008^b	-0.0108^c	0.0028^c
t-Value	(9.19)	(-2.03)	(-1.65)	(0.0993)
Likelihood Ratio Tests				
	Trades / Min	Quoted Spread	ln Depth0	ln Depth3
χ^2-value	467.02	1651.00	5014.50	12536.00
p-value	< .0001	< .0001	< .0001	< .0001

Table 3: Trading Intensity and Liquidity Model Results

trades is with 73 per minute more than double the normal value of 32 per minute and trading volume still is at 434,784 which is also more than double the normal value of 173,319. Figure 1 depicts the number of trades on a minute-by-minute basis around announcements. The graph shows a huge spike in trading activity directly after announcements.

Table 3 also provides regression estimates for trades per minute around announcements. The estimations confirm the picture painted by the descriptive statistics. Prior to announcements the number of trades per minute is significantly lower. Only the period ten minutes before announcements is not statistically significant since it does not differ much from normal trading activity. However, coming from a very low number of trades per minute we can see an immense and statistically highly significant increase in trading activity after announcements. This increase is still not back to normal levels thirty minutes after announcements.

The increase in trading activity fits the predictions of the Kim and Verrecchia (1994) model. Traders with high information processing capabilities try to use their advantage and trade on public information. Hess et al. (2008) also find an

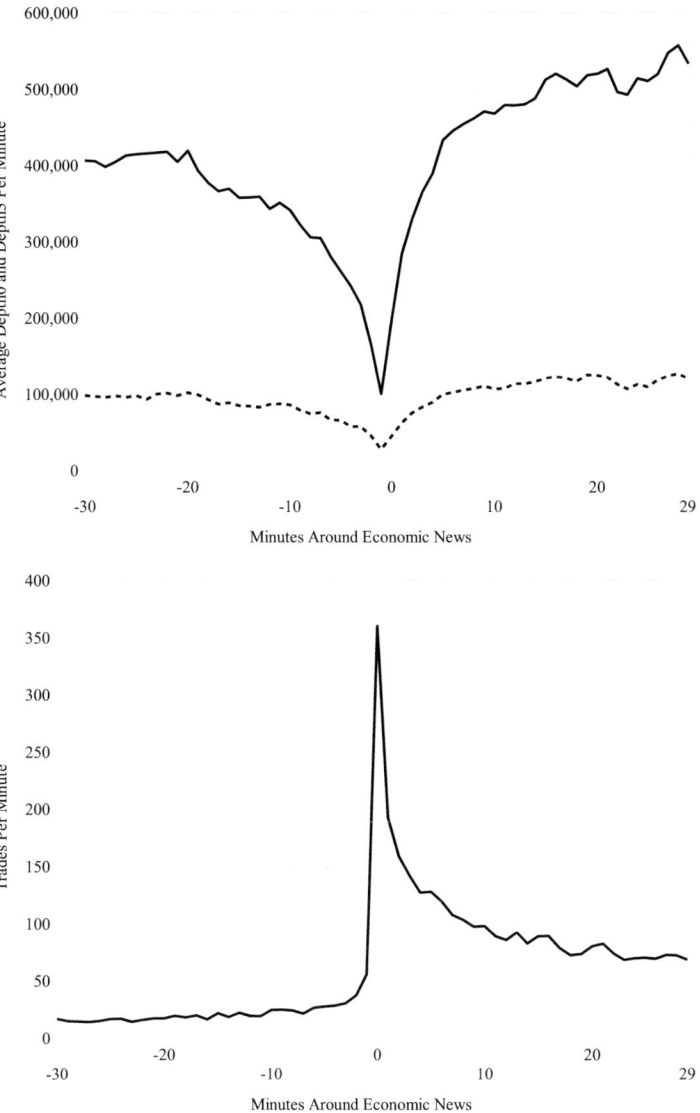

Figure 1: Liquidity and trading intensity around macroeconomic news announcements: The upper graph depicts Depth0 (dashed line) and Depth3 (continuous line) and the lower graph shows trading intensity around announcements measured by the number of trades per minute.

increase in trading volume around the release of U.S. unemployment numbers and Mitchell and Mulherin (1994) find a positive relation between news and volume in equity markets. Fleming and Remolona (1999) find a reduction in trading around macroeconomic news for the U.S. treasury market. They, however, do not study the futures market but directly the underlying U.S. treasury market which has different market characteristics.

Table 3 also provides likelihood ratio test for trading activity with the restriction that measures cannot vary among different intervals around U.S. unemployment number releases. The restricted model is rejected with p-values less than 0.0001. The χ^2-value is 467.02.

The individual results of information, liquidity, and trading intensity are consistent with existing empirical evidence. However, what remains is the relation between all three factors. Before U.S. unemployment numbers are released we find low liquidity and low trading activity but much higher adverse selection costs, i.e. more private information impounded through order flow than normal in the market. Directly after announcements, liquidity slightly recovers until it reverts to normal and trading activity dramatically increases and stays at a high level even thirty minutes after announcements. Adverse selection, however, decreases from its pre announcement high but is still a bit higher than during no-announcement periods. What kind of trading behavior could explain such patterns? Only a few trader with private information trade prior to announcements. Private information derived from in-depth analysis and research is costly and gains from trading in advance of public information need to be high enough to offset the costs of private information gathering. However, such traders seem to see profits from pre-announcement trading since they are not put off by low liquidity. As soon as U.S. unemployment numbers are released we find a strong decrease in adverse selection which is consistent with the fact that this information is now public information. However, adverse selection is still slightly higher than normal. The results for trading activity indicate a "race of public information processing". Massive amounts of traders trade on processed public information but bring considerably less private information into the market than the pre-announcement traders. Overall the fast incorporation of public information is an indication for efficient markets consistent with Andersen et al. (2007).

6 Conclusion

In this paper we analyze the effect of the release of U.S. unemployment numbers and its effect on information, liquidity, and trading activity in German Bund Futures. We find that liquidity and trading activity is lower pre-announcement associated with high adverse selection costs. Liquidity recovers and adverse selection stays on a slightly higher level then normal within thirty minutes after announcements. Trading activity drastically increases and stays on a high level during the first thirty minutes after announcements. Our findings are consistent with existing empirical literature and the theoretical models of Kim and Verrecchia (1991, 1994, 1997). Additionally, the results implicate a significant influence of U.S. unemployment announcements on trading behavior in German Bund futures. The confirms the role of these announcements as an important worldwide economic indicator.

Our results show that Eurex is a highly liquid and efficient market for Bund Futures that incorporates public information fast. Private information arises through varying information processing and gathering capabilities of market participants.

References

Andersen, T. G., T. Bollerslev, F. X. Diebold, and C. Vega (2007): "Real-Time Price Discovery in Global Stock, Bond and Foreign Exchange Markets," *Journal of International Economics*, 73, pp. 251–277.

Bessembinder, H. (2003): "Issues in assessing trade execution costs," *Journal of Financial Markets*, 6(3), pp. 233–257.

Bessembinder, H. and H. Kaufman (1997): "A Cross-exchange Comparison of Execution Costs and Information Flow for NYSE-listed Stocks," *Journal of Financial Economics*, 46(3), pp. 293–319.

Chaboud, A., B. Chiquoine, E. Hjalarsson, and C. Vega (2009): "Rise of the machines: Algorithmic trading in the foreign exchange market," Working Paper, Stanford University.

Evans, M. D. D. and R. K. Lyons (2008): "How Is Macro News Transmitted to Exchange Rates," *Journal of Financial Economics*, 88, pp. 26–50.

Fleming, M. J. and E. M. Remolona (1999): "Price Formation and Liquidity in the U.S. Treasury market: The response to public information," *The Journal of Finance*, 54(5), pp. 1901–1915.

Glosten, L. and P. Milgrom (1985): "Bid, Ask and Transaction Prices in a Specialist Market with Heterogeneously Informed Traders," *Journal of Financial Economics*, 14, pp. 71–100.

Green, T. C. (2004): "Economic News and the Impact of Trading on Bond Prices," *The Journal of Finance*, 59(3), pp. 1201–1233.

Hess, D., A. Kempf, and M. Malinowska (2008): "Liquidity Provision in Periods of High Information Flow," Working Paper.

Kim, O. and R. E. Verrecchia (1991): "Market Reactions to Anticipated Announcements," *Journal of Financial Economics*, 30(2), pp. 273–309.

Kim, O. and R. E. Verrecchia (1994): "Market Liquidity and Volume Around Earnings Announcements," *Journal of Accounting and Economics*, 17, pp. 41–67.

Kim, O. and R. E. Verrecchia (1997): "Pre-Announcement and Event-Period Private Information," *Journal of Accounting and Econmics*, 24, pp. 395–419.

Krinsky, I. and J. Lee (1996): "Earnings Announcements and the Components of the Bid-Ask Spread," *The Journal of Finance*, 51(4), pp. 1523–1535.

Lee, C. and M. Ready (1991): "Inferring Trade Direction from Intraday Data," *The Journal of Finance*, 46(2), pp. 733–746.

Lee, C. M. C., B. Mucklow, and M. J. Ready (1993): "Spreads, Depths, and the Impact of Earnings Information: An Intraday Analysis," *The Review of Financial Studies*, 6(2), pp. 345–374.

Madhavan, A., M. Richardson, and M. Roomans (1997): "Why Do Security Prices Change? A Transaction-Level Analysis of NYSE Stocks," *The Review of Financial Studies*, 10(4), pp. 1035–1064.

Mitchell, M. L. and J. H. Mulherin (1994): "The Impact of Public Information on the Stock Market," *The Journal of Finance*, 49(3), pp. 923–950.

Newey, W. K. and K. D. West (1987): "A Simple, Positive Semi-Definite, Heteroskedasticity and Autocorrelation Consistent Covariance Matrix," *Econometrica*, 55(3), pp. 703–708.

Niessen, A. (2007): "Media Coverage and Macroeconomic Information Processing," SFB 649 Discussion Paper 2007-011.

Vega, C. (2006): "Stock Price Reaction to Public and Private Information," *Journal of Financial Economics*, 82, pp. 103–133.

Market Responses to the Introduction of Interactive Data: The Case of XBRL

S. Sarah Zhang, Christof Weinhardt, and Ryan Riordan

Institute of Information Systems and Managment, KIT
{sarah.zhang, weinhardt, ryan.riordan}@kit.edu

Summary. We examine the introduction of the voluntary filing program of financial reports using XBRL by the Securities and Exchange Commission (SEC) as a quasi-natural experiment to isolate the effects of an improvement in the information environment of program participants. The voluntary SEC XBRL program, generally referred to as Interactive Data, has allowed firms to file annual and quarterly reports using eXtensible Business Reporting Language (XBRL). XBRL is a machine-readable Interactive Data format, designed to improve the financial information environment of a firm and the accessibility of financial information. We study the effects of this event of corporate disclosure on the cost of capital of participating companies and information intermediation of investors following and find statistically significant results for medium-term cost of capital and for information intermediation.

1 Introduction

Over the past two decades, developments in information technology (IT) have facilitated information transparency and investment decisions. This change has translated into easier access to management reporting data and corporate disclosure, for example via the EDGAR (Electronic Data Gathering, Analysis, and Retrieval) system, for investors and regulators alike. In April of 2005, the Securities and Exchange Commission (SEC), the regulating authority in the US, introduced a voluntary filing program (VFP) for the introduction of XBRL (eXtensible Business Reporting Language), or 'Interactive Data' as it is called in the US, designed to make corporate reports more accessible and to reduce costs of data preparation and analysis. XBRL is an innovative XML based format geared towards corporate information disclosure, which has already gained international importance and has been implemented in report management systems by market regulators of several countries. In this paper, which is research in progress, we study how IT innovation facilitates information intermediation and transparency. More specifically, this paper investigates the market effects of the introduction of Interactive Data for companies and investors, and also tries to find interest groups among participating companies for the voluntary participation in this program.

2 Hypothesis Development

For the analysis of market reactions, we extract two hypotheses from related literature of possible effects of voluntary disclosure: (1) reduced cost of equity capital,
and (2) increased information intermediation. The cost of equity capital hypothesis
states that companies increase their level of voluntary disclosure in order to reduce
adverse selection risks for investors, since investors then require lower returns to
offset the information risk they bear. This hypothesis is in line with empirical
evidence of Botosan (1997) and Botosan and Plumlee (2001). Thus, we expect a long-
term effect of Interactive Data reflected in a significantly lower level of cumulative
abnormal returns as an indicator for lower cost of equity capital. This translates
into hypothesis H_1:

> H_1: *The introduction of Interactive Data should lead to decreased cost of equity
> capital of participants.*

Regarding information intermediation, Lang and Lundholm (1996) conjecture
that voluntary disclosure leads to reduced analysts' costs of information acquisition.
As a consequence, the reduction of information acquisition costs ceteris paribus
leads to an increase in the number of analysts covering a specific stock. In our
analysis, the number of available EPS (earnings per share) estimates on a specific
stock serves as a proxy for the number of analysts. Therefore, this proxy is utilized
as an indicator for the conjecture that information intermediation is facilitated
through IT innovation. This reflected in hypothesis H_2:

> H_2: *The number of analysts following should increase with the introduction of
> Interactive Data.*

The SEC's goal by adopting XBRL is to enhance information transparency and
to facilitate investors' report analysis. Decision facilitation may be increased with
XBRL usage as investors can electronically download and analyze reports in a
standardized structure and format with pre-defined semantics and taxonomies
(dictionary of terms). They are able to use information directly from corporate
reports in software applications, which are able to "understand" and "interact" with
this data with little transformation and interpretation.

3 Data and Sample

We use market data from Compustat and Thomson Reuters Tick History[1]. For
the identification of the participating companies, we use the report data from
the 163 participating companies between April 4, 2005 and March 23, 2009 from
the SEC website[2]. We exclude companies, like trust funds and ADRs (American

---

[1] We thank SIRCA for providing access to the Thomson Reuters DataScope Tick History
[2] http://www.sec.gov/spotlight/xbrl/filings-and-feeds.shtml

Panel A: Sample Creation Procedure

Sample	Change	Number of Companies
All filers between April 4, 2005 and March 23, 2009		162
All companies without trust funds	(35)	127
Companies with available RICs	(8)	119
Companies without ADRs	(19)	100
All data available and non pink-sheets	(2)	98
Without Stock splits	(6)	**92**

Panel B: Industry Groups

Industry Group	Industry Group ID	Number of Companies
Materials	1000	8
Consumer Discretionary	2000	8
Consumer Staples	3000	6
Health Care	3500	8
Energy	4000	10
Financials	5000	13
Industrials	6000	14
Information Technology	8000	17
Telecommunication Services	8600	1
Utilities	9000	7
Total Number of Companies		**92**

Panel C: Report Counts

Year Apr-Mar	Number of reports filed	Number of first reports filed
2005/06	27	5
2006/07	105	15
2007/08	192	21
2008/09	254	51
Total Number of Reports	**578**	

Table 1: Event Study Sample Distribution

depository receipts) since we are interested in effects of transparency proxied through Interactive Data on normal stocks, as well as companies with recent mergers, stock splits or other kinds of corporate actions (reverse splits, etc.) around their first reporting with Interactive Data in order to exclude distorting effects in our data. Our final data sample consists of 92 US companies, listed on NASDAQ and NYSE, which filed their first XBRL report between March 2004 and April 2009. The number of reports increased constantly, from 27 reports between April 4, 2005 and March 2006 to 254 reports between April 2008 and March 23, 2009 (cf. Table 1).

From Compustat, we collect data for daily close prices in dollars (*Close*), daily P/E (price/earnings) ratios (*P/E*) and daily market capitalization in millions of dollars (*Market*), as well as daily trading volume (*Volume*) and volatility (*Vola*) as the ratio of the current 10-day average of high-low price difference and the previous one. Annual long-term debt is in millions of dollars (*Debt*), number annual common shares outstanding (*Share*) in millions and annual book value of common equity in millions of dollars (*Book*). The participating companies range from big companies

Variable	Mean	Minimum	Maximum	25th %tile	Median	75th %tile	Std. Dev.
Close	40.245	2.324	357.395	24.599	34.698	47.304	37.822
P/E	16.948	-110.726	202.047	8.424	14.152	18.996	39.003
Market	29816.59	58.19	335446.95	4894.82	10908.59	25577.34	54736.02
Vola	4.4222	0.5485	11.5378	3.5176	4.0556	4.9591	1.8080
Volume	5854	64	69464	1275	2842	5998	10201
Debt	7733.90	0.00	266967.40	429.00	2081.44	6335.20	29504.17
Share	820.87	14.15	10374.50	136.27	323.13	761.57	1669.59
Book	9055.60	-516.08	110542.00	1033.27	4584.90	10176.80	15935.95

Table 2: Company Descriptives

like General Electric and Microsoft to smaller companies like Bowne & Co. and ICUI Medical, Inc. They belong to ten different industry groups, with Information Technology, Energy, Financials and Industrials representing the largest group of participating companies.

Additionally, we cluster our sample into groups. First, we include all sample firms into our analysis. Second, we only analyze those industry groups which have 10 or more participating companies in the voluntary interactive data program. And third, we analyze all companies that belong to industry groups with less than 10 participating companies. Panel B of Table 1 provides an overview of companies' industry groups. The industry groups with 10 or more participating companies comprise of Energy, Financials, Industrials, and Information Technology.

4 Methodology

4.1 Event Study

We use an event-study methodology as described in MacKinlay (1997). Event studies are a commonly used instrument in finance literature to identify and measure the impact of the announcement of new, value-changing information on stock returns. We fit a market model to measure abnormal stock returns during the event windows in order to test for differences in the distribution of abnormal returns. The null hypothesis for these tests is that the event has no impact on the distribution of returns.

We set the filing of the first Interactive Data report as Day 0 for each participating company, and measure the OLS model coefficients during the estimation period (day -211 to -11) in order to compute expected returns and thereby cost of equity capital. The prediction errors during different event periods (day -10 to +2, day -10 to +10, and day -10 to +30) can be interpreted as the abnormal returns during these periods, i.e. the difference of realized and expected returns, more precisely $AR_{it} = R_{it} - E[R_{it}|X_t]$. The event windows are relatively short in order to avoid other possible events that might influence stock prices. We further sum up daily abnormal returns to cumulative abnormal returns, $CAR_i(t_1, t_2) = \sum_{t_1}^{t_2} AR_{it}$, in order to measure the aggregate effects of the event. As recommended in Patell (1976) and in Boehmer et al. (1991), the analysis is based on robust standard test statistics to measure the statistical significance of standardized CARs.

We use the market model in order to calculate expected returns and cost of capital. We follow the standard event-study methodology, which compares the difference of abnormal returns before and after the event.

The statistical market model is a basic model which "relates the return of any security to the return of the market portfolio" defined as in FFJR (cf. Fama et al., 1969):

$$R_{it} = \alpha_i + \beta_i R_{mt} + \epsilon_{it} \tag{1}$$

with R_{it} and R_{mt} being the return in period t of security i and of the market portfolio respectively.

4.2 Information Intermediation

In order to analyze the impact of XBRL on information intermediation, we use the monthly number of EPS forecasts as a proxy for the number of analysts interested in the specific company. We aggregate the number of all monthly estimates from I/B/E/S (Institutional Brokers' Estimate System) (*NEst*) and perform a panel regression on this data by using a dummy variable before and after the introduction of XBRL. Let *m* denote months and *i* the cross section, then the following panel regression emerges

$$NEst_{i,m} = \alpha_i + \delta XBRL_{i,m} + \epsilon_{i,m} \tag{2}$$

We use robust standard errors by Arellano (1987).

5 Results and Interpretation

5.1 Cost of Capital

Our hypothesis that the SEC's voluntary filing program decreases the cost of capital is derived from literature. Again, we cluster our results by industry groups. We analyze the largest industry groups participating in the VFP, which are Information Technology, Energy, Industrials, and Financials, separately from the rest. We assume stronger motives for these industry groups to participate in the program and therefore that the participation might have a stronger effect than on companies of other industry groups.

For a window of 30 days, the event analysis reveals a significant impact for the ITEFI group. For this subsection, we obtain negative coefficients, which are significant at the 5% level. The results are robust against different estimation periods. This provides support for hypothesis H_1, i.e. a reduction in the cost of

Impact of XBRL on CAR

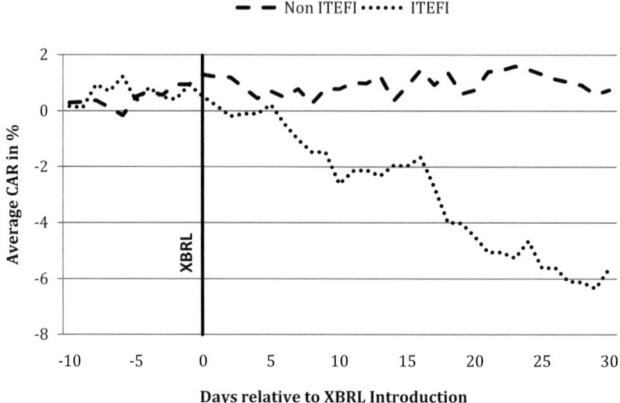

Figure 1: Impact of XBRL on CAR

capital through voluntary XBRL filing. However, the results are not significant for the Non-ITEFI group, which leads to the conclusion that the largest participating industry groups experience a stronger negative effect on their cost of capital than other industry groups. Looking at the 2 day event window, we can observe that firms do not show positive short term abnormal returns. We take the first filing with XBRL as our event date since we do not have information on firms' announcement dates for their participation in the SEC's voluntary XBRL filing program.

In future research, we have to further investigate the results for cost of capital with other models and robustness checks so that we can draw more robust conclusions.

5.2 Information Intermediation

As shown in Table 3, we find an increase in analyst counts consistently over all industry groups, which supports our hypothesis of an increase in information intermediation through XBRL. However the p-value is below 5% for firms which do not belong to the industry groups Energy, Information Technology, Financials, and Industrials.

This is consistent with our expectation that the introduction of XBRL enables more analysts to acquire information and therefore increases the supply of analysts covering a stock. Filing through Interactive Data could have had two effects. First, our hypothesis that it increases information intermediation. However, it could also have reduced the number of analysts covering a specific stock since information is more easily retrieved by investors themselves. Our results indicate that this has not been the case and investors still seek analysts' advice. Further analysis to support the robustness of our results can be done by using newsreport counts and analyst counts from other data sources.

IT, Energy, Industrials, Financials	Estimate	Standard Error	t-statistic	p-value
All	1.84939	0.8950	2.07	0.0388
0	1.10823	1.3710	0.81	0.4190
1	2.40571	1.1731	2.05	0.0404

Table 3: Results of Analysts Counts

6 Conclusion

The main focus of this paper was to investigate whether IT innovations can facilitate information intermediation and transparency in markets. Participation in this program qualifies as voluntary disclosure. In April 2009, the SEC made the program compulsory and the program will be implemented through a staggered introduction over three years. However, it is still unclear what the effects of reporting with XBRL are on financial markets. We derive two hypotheses from existing literature. Previous studies suggest that voluntary disclosure reduces the cost of equity capital and increases information intermediation. The introduction of XBRL has turned out to (H_1) decrease costs of capital for the four largest participating industry sectors and (H_2) increase information intermediation of investors. Further, with respect to the results of hypothesis H1, the analysis reveals that specific industry groups have stronger incentives to participate on a voluntary basis and, therefore, experience stronger market reactions, e.g. on their costs of capital. Our results so far raise questions whether voluntary adaption has had other effects than those we analyzed which might justify the decision of early voluntary adoption or whether participation might even have been harmful for participating companies, considering costs involved in early adoption. We preliminarily accept the increased information intermediation hypothesis. Our results show an increase in analyst coverage after reporting with XBRL through the SEC's voluntary filing program, proxied by I/B/E/S estimates counts. We will further use news reports counts as well as other proxies to get more robust results. In conclusion, future research needs to involve more robust checks on liquidity and information intermediation and a deeper analysis of the effects on the cost of equity capital. Further studies might also include an analysis of the mandatory introduction of Interactive Data by the SEC.

References

Arellano, J. (1987): "Computing Robust Standard Errors for Within-groups Estimators," *Oxford Bulletin of Economics and Statistics*, 49(4), pp. 431–434.

Boehmer, E., J. Musumeci, and A. Poulsen (1991): "Event-study methodology under conditions of event-induced variance," *Journal of Financial Economics*, 30, pp. 253–272.

Botosan, C. A. (1997): "Disclosure level and the cost of equity capital," *The Accounting Review*, 73(3), pp. 323–350.

Botosan, C. A. and M. A. Plumlee (2001): "A Re-examination of Disclosure Level and the Expected Cost of Equity Capital," *Journal of Accounting Research*, 40(1), pp. 21–40.

Fama, E. F., L. Fisher, M. C. Jensen, and R. Roll (1969): "The adjustment of stock prices to new information," *International Economic Review*, 10(1), pp. 1–21.

Lang, M. and R. Lundholm (1996): "Corporate disclosure policy and analyst behavior," *The Accounting Review*, 71(4), pp. 467–496.

MacKinlay, A. C. (1997): "Event Studies in Economics and Finance," *Journal of Economic Literature*, 35(1), pp. 13–39.

Patell, J. M. (1976): "Corporate forecasts of earnings per share and stock price behavior," *Journal of Accounting Research*, 14(2), pp. 246–276.

The Impact of the Yearly Emissions Announcement on CO$_2$ Prices: An Event Study

Steffen Hitzemann[1], Marliese Uhrig-Homburg[2], and Karl-Martin Ehrhart[3]

[1] Chair of Financial Engineering and Derivatives
   hitzemann@kit.edu
[2] Chair of Financial Engineering and Derivatives
   uhrig@kit.edu
[3] Institute of Economic Theory and Statistics
   ehrhart@kit.edu

Summary. One of the most important news events in the European carbon market is the yearly announcement of aggregated realized emissions for the previous year. Especially in 2006, this event attracted a lot of attention, when CO$_2$ allowances lost about two thirds of their value in consequence of a big permit surplus that became known. We use standard event study methodology to analyze the impact of the yearly emissions announcement event on CO$_2$ prices for the years 2006 to 2010. We find that the surprise effect caused by this event has considerably declined over the years. Furthermore, the market seems to incorporate information conveyed by such events efficiently and we cannot find clear evidence of prior information leakage. We additionally observe that futures maturing in the same trading period show almost the same reaction to these events according to the cost-of-carry-relationship.

1 Introduction

In January 2005, the European Union Emission Trading System (EU ETS) was introduced, and along with it, a market for tradable permits began to evolve. Since then, European CO$_2$ prices have gone through turbulent phases. The most spectacular price movements occurred in 2006 when permits of the first trading period lost about two thirds of their value in less than three weeks. This collapse was mainly caused by the yearly emissions announcement of the European Commission, which stated that aggregated emissions for 2005 were far below the number of allowances allocated for that year. Surprisingly, the collapse already took place more than two weeks before the official announcement date, scheduled for May 15, and it became known later that this was due to an accidental publication of preliminary emissions data on the European Commission's website.

Due to these occurrences, the yearly emissions announcement event has attracted the attention of traders as well as researchers. However, there is only sparse literature on this topic. Conrad et al. (2009) analyze the market response to decisions on

National Allocation Plans (NAPs). Mansanet-Bataller and Pardo (2007) also focus on NAP events, but take into account the influence of the emissions announcements in 2006 and 2007. Referring to only two events of that type, they are not able to discuss the price impact of these events in detail. Additionally, they take May 15 as the 2006 event day which is inappropriate in our opinion and causes misleading results for that event. Chevallier et al. (2009) analyze changes in investors' risk aversion around the 2006 announcement event.

Still, it is of interest to analyze the influence of this event in detail which is supposed to be the main news event related to the European CO_2 market. Based on an available set of five events now, it is possible to gain first substantiated insights into this topic. This is, to the best of our knowledge, the first study to analyze the influence of the yearly emissions announcement event on European CO_2 prices in detail. We use standard event study methodology to calculate abnormal returns and volumes around the event date for the five events from 2006 to 2010. We find that the surprise effect caused by this event, which has been clearly visually observable in 2006, has considerably declined over the years. The market seems to incorporate information conveyed by such events efficiently and we cannot find clear evidence for information leakage prior to an announcement event. Furthermore, futures maturing in the same trading period show almost the same reaction to such an event according to the cost-of-carry-relationship.

The paper is organized as follows. Section 2 gives an overview of the most important regulatory rules of the EU ETS and discusses the impact of emissions announcement events on CO_2 prices. Section 3 describes the emissions announcement events. Section 4 derives our research design. Section 5 presents empirical results. Section 6 concludes.

2 EU Emission Trading System and the Impact of Emissions Announcements

2.1 EU Emission Trading System

In 2005, the EU ETS was launched in order to reduce CO_2 emissions of the EU member states. It was designed as a cap-and-trade system. The main advantage of such a market mechanism compared to other measures is that it is supposed to give companies an economic incentive to use the cheapest abatement opportunities of the economy. The EU ETS is subdivided into different trading periods. First, a trial period (Phase I) from 2005 to 2007 was introduced, followed by the current trading period from 2008 to 2012. The next trading period will be from 2012 to 2020. At the beginning of each trading period, the EU Commission allocates emission permits to the regulated companies according to National Allocation Plans. Each permit, called EU Allowance (EUA), allows for the emission of 1 ton CO_2 during the year the permit is allocated for.

At the end of each year, companies have to cover their emissions by EUAs, whereas additional emissions are penalized. The penalty has been 40 Euro per ton in the trial period and is 100 Euro per ton in the current trading period. Still, the payment of a penalty does not exempt a company from delivering lacking allowances later. The compliance date for allowance delivery is April 30 of each year. As the allocation of new permits takes place each year at the end of February and as permits from different years within the same trading period are not distinguishable, allowances allocated for the following year can in fact be used for compliance as well ("borrowing"). Thus, borrowing within a trading period is implicitly allowed, but it is not allowed between two different trading periods. The opposite of borrowing, i.e. the usage of current allowances for the following year ("banking"), is allowed within a trading period, again because permits of the same trading period are identical. Contrary, banking has not been allowed between the trial period and the current period because the trial period was intended to be separated from the following trading periods. From this trading period on, banking is allowed between trading periods as well. Since allowances can be banked and borrowed from one year to another within a trading period, one can consider a whole trading period as one market and penalties are in fact only paid at the end of a trading period.[1]

In addition to EUAs, standard EUA derivatives are traded on several exchanges across Europe, most importantly futures contracts expiring in December of each year with an underlying allowance of the same year.[2] Currently, the futures with the latest maturity date expire in December 2014. That means that there are futures expiring in the next trading period, although the underlying allowances are not allocated yet and thus are not tradable. The December futures contract next to maturity is usually traded with higher liquidity than the EUAs themselves. Furthermore, there are European-style options written on the different futures with maturity dates few days before the underlying futures expire.

2.2 Influence of Emissions Announcements on Permit Prices

As emission permits are used to cover realized emissions and to avoid paying penalties at the end of a trading period, the (expected) scarcity of permits heavily depends on the expected overall emissions belonging to that trading period. Therefore, this parameter is the main influencing factor of CO$_2$ permit prices.[3] The expected overall emissions for a specific trading period are made up of the known realized emissions[4] and the expected emissions up to the end of the trading

---

[1] This simplification cannot be made if there is a significant probability that allowances allocated for the current and the following year are completely needed to cover emissions of the current year because borrowing from later years is not allowed. However, in realistic scenarios this is very improbable.

[2] Recently, futures with expiry in March, June, and September of each year are traded as well.

[3] There are also other influencing factors that are not fixed, such as allowance allocations in the far future or the amount of transferable allowances from connected trading systems, like the Clean Development Mechanism.

[4] Clearly, realized emissions are known once they have been published on an announcement event.

period. If the whole trading period that is considered lies in the future, the realized emissions part does not exist. An emissions announcement event, on the one hand, has the effect that realized emissions are exactly known for one additional year, but as it gives an indication about the current emission rate of the economy, it also affects the expected emissions in the future. Let us distinguish between the first part, which we will call *information about realized emissions*, and the second part, the *indication about future emissions*.

A change of the information about realized emissions clearly affects the expected allowance scarcity for the related trading period, which is the current trading period unless we are in the first year of a new trading period. The indication about future emissions may influence the expected emissions for the current and all future trading periods. Precise effects depend on how these expectations evolve. For example, if they show a mean-reverting behavior to a predefined trend, the indication about future emissions will mainly affect the current trading period and will have only little impact on a trading period in the far future.

Additionally, the allowance scarcity of one trading period might be forwarded to the following period, depending on whether banking is allowed or not. When banking is prohibited, as it was the case in the trial period, the amount of realized emissions during the related period has an impact on the permit scarcity in all following trading periods if the current market is short due to the obligation to deliver lacking allowances later, but is irrelevant if the market is long. In contrast, if banking is allowed, realized emissions always influence permit scarcity in following trading periods, independent of the current market being long or short.

This means that both types of information conveyed by announcement events should influence permit prices of all trading periods when banking is allowed, and that should also be the case when banking is not allowed, but the market of the related trading period is short. In these cases it is not possible to separate both types of information from each other and to identify the dominant one. Contrary to that, if the market of a trading period is known to be long and banking is not allowed, the information about realized emissions should not affect permit prices of the following trading periods, so that only the indication about future emissions should have an impact on those prices.

3 Emissions Announcement Events

The available set of realized emissions announcement events consists of those observed between 2006 and 2010 which we will call EA2006, EA2007, EA2008, EA2009, and EA2010. An overview of these events and related data is shown in Table 1[5]. The first release of verified emissions data took place in 2006 and the official announcement date was planned to be on May 15. However, as the European

---

[5] We refer to data from the first official press release after an emissions announcement. In 2006, this data includes emissions from Austria, Belgium, Czech Republic, Denmark, Estonia, Finland, France, Germany, Greece, Hungary, Ireland, Italy, Latvia, Lithuania, Netherlands, Portugal, Slovak

Table 1: Data related to emissions announcement events from 2006 to 2010: the event date, the compliance year related to the announcement and the associated trading period, the number of permits allocated for the compliance year (in millions) and the emissions realized in that year (in million tons). Data source: EUROPA Press Releases (2006, 2007, 2008, 2009, 2010).

Event	Date	Compliance Year	Trading Period	Permits Allocated	Emissions Realized
EA2006	Apr 25, 2006	2005	2005-2007	1,903	1,785
EA2007	Apr 2, 2007	2006	2005-2007	2,152	2,027
EA2008	Apr 2, 2008	2007	2005-2007	2,152	2,050
EA2009	Apr 1, 2009	2008	2008-2012	1,909	2,060
EA2010	Apr 1, 2010	2009	2008-2012	1,967	1,873

Commission confirmed later, some figures had been published accidentally on the European Commission's website. So already on April 25 it became known that the emissions of the Czech Republic had been 15 % below the quotas and that the emissions of the Netherlands had been 8 % lower than the quotas. Thus, we take April 25 as the event date. Its impact cannot be clearly separated from the information events on April 26, when realized emissions data from France, Estonia, and Spain became public. Spain was the first country for which it became known that emissions exceeded the quota. However, the news on April 25 and 26 clearly indicated that the total 2005 emissions were considerably below the cap. Until May 12 the realized emissions of all other participating states became public, adding up to a surplus of about 118 million tons of allowed CO$_2$ emissions. Since banking was allowed within the trading period from 2005 to 2007, and since emissions were not expected to rise dramatically, the whole trading period was considered to be long of allowances from that time on.

Accordingly, the announcement of realized 2006 emissions on April 2, 2007 was of little importance for the trading period from 2005 to 2007. Contrary to that, it was of interest in terms of providing an indication about future emissions for the following trading period (2008 to 2012), for which most of the allocation plans had been released up to this date, setting the cap much tighter for that trading period. The realized 2006 emissions were about 125 million tons below the quotas.

The announcement of realized 2007 emissions on April 2, 2008 was of even less importance for the first trading period (which the emissions were actually belonging to), because it had terminated at the end of 2007. Hardly worth mentioning, realized emissions in this year were about 102 million tons lower than the quotas.

On April 1, 2009, realized 2008 emissions data (i.e. belonging to the current trading period from 2008 to 2012), was released. For the first time, it occurred that realized emissions exceeded the quotas for one year. For this year, the market

---

Republic, Slovenia, Spain, Sweden, and the United Kingdom. The 2007 and 2008 data additionally covers Cyprus, Luxembourg, and Poland. In 2009, Malta and Romania are added, and in 2010, Bulgaria, Liechtenstein, and Norway are included as well.

was short by about 151 million tons. Comparing this figure to prior projections as established by a Reuters poll shows that emissions were at the upper end of market expectations.[6]

Realized 2009 emissions, published on April 1, 2010, were 94 million tons lower than the quota, a consequence of the economic downturn. According to estimates of the Reuters poll, this was expected by market participants, and in fact the emissions were again higher than expected on average.[7]

4 Research Design

The magnitude of abnormal performance at the time of an emission announcement event provides a measure of the unanticipated impact of this event. We derive hypotheses concerning the behavior of EUA prices around announcement events and apply event study methodology as mean of testing our hypotheses.

4.1 Hypotheses

Bearing in mind the dramatic drop of CO_2 prices on April 25, 2006, when first details of the realized 2005 emissions became known, it is reasonable to conjecture that this event always causes a huge surprise effect. However, in the following years a similarly big surprise was not observable, at least not by visual inspection. To analyze possible surprise effects, we test the following hypothesis.

Hypothesis 1 (H1) *Information regarding emissions of all regulated companies is completely priced into CO_2 prices. The yearly announcement of realized emissions thus does not cause a surprise effect.*

The market crashed on April 25, 2006 although the official announcement date in 2006 was on May 15. As described before, in retrospect it is clear that there was an obvious information leakage caused by the European Commission. Meanwhile, the reporting process has been optimized, so that countries report to the European Commission on March 31 and aggregated figures are published on April 1. Nevertheless, information leakages might still exist on the level of individual countries. To discover possible information leakages, we test H2.

Hypothesis 2 (H2) *The aggregated information about emissions can be kept confidential by the European Commission and countries until the official announcement date. No information will leak out on the days before the official announcement date.*

The collapse on April 25, 2006 was followed by further big losses on the following trading days. Again, in retrospect we know that these were caused by additional

---

[6] Estimates ranged from 100 million tons long (Citi) to 180 million tons short (IDEACarbon), median expectation at 30 million tons short. Biases may arise from divergences in the number of included countries.

[7] Excluding an out-dated estimate of UBS, figures ranged from 190 million tons long (Deutsche Bank) to 60 million tons long (Nomisma Energia), median expectation at 150 million tons long.

information about realized emissions leaking into the market. Anyhow, this price behavior has as well attracted publicity, in this case with respect to market efficiency as formulated in H3.

Hypothesis 3 (H3) *The market reacts to new public information about realized emissions without delay.*

Finally, we have discussed in Section 2 that price reactions to an announcement event should be mainly characterized by the trading period the permit belongs to. Only permits of the current year are tradable, as stated before, but futures are available for permits of other years as well. Prior literature, such as Uhrig-Homburg and Wagner (2009) and Rittler (2009), lends support to the cost-of-carry-relationship between futures belonging to the same trading period. Our hypothesis H4 is that this relationship also holds on a daily basis around the news events considered.

Hypothesis 4 (H4) *Futures belonging to the same trading period react to an announcement event in line with each other.*

4.2 Event Study Methodology

We will analyze our hypotheses by applying standard event study methodology. Our study considers abnormal returns and volumes for a short horizon around the events identified to provide evidence relevant for understanding the role of the yearly emissions announcement event in the EU ETS. A general overview of event study methodology can be found in Binder (1998).

To calculate abnormal returns we choose a mean-adjusted return model according to Brown and Warner (1980, 1985) as a benchmark model. Generally, it is also possible to use market-adjusted returns as proposed in Fama et al. (1969) or certain deviations based on other models (cf. Binder (1998)). As pointed out by Brown and Warner (1980, 1985), the mean-adjusted model is very simple, but the use of more sophisticated models often does not lead to a smaller variance of the abnormal returns.

We apply the mean-adjusted return model to arithmetic daily returns r_t. Given an event at time 0, an estimation window $I_{est} := [t_1, t_2]$ with $t_2 < 0$ is chosen. The mean return $\widehat{r}$ in I_{est} is then calculated as

$$\widehat{r} = \frac{1}{t_2 - t_1} \sum_{t=t_1}^{t_2} r_t. \tag{1}$$

Furthermore, we calculate abnormal (mean-adjusted) returns ar_t in I_{est} and their variance as

$$ar_t = r_t - \widehat{r} \tag{2}$$

and

$$\widehat{\sigma^2}(ar) = \frac{1}{t_2 - t_1 - 1} \sum_{t=t_1}^{t_2} \left(ar_t - \frac{1}{t_2 - t_1} \sum_{s=t_1}^{t_2} ar_s \right)^2, \tag{3}$$

respectively.

Based on $\widehat{r}$ and $\widehat{\sigma^2}(ar)$, we are able to determine standardized abnormal returns in a chosen event window $I_{ev} := [t_3, t_4]$ with $t_2 < t_3 \leq 0, t_4 \geq 0$ as

$$sar_t = \frac{r_t - \widehat{r}}{\widehat{\sigma}(ar)}. \tag{4}$$

To consider the cumulative abnormal return over a certain time window within the event window, we define

$$car_{t,t'} = \sum_{s=t}^{t'} ar_s \tag{5}$$

and standardize by

$$scar_{t,t'} = \frac{car_{t,t'}}{\widehat{\sigma}(ar)\sqrt{t' - t + 1}}. \tag{6}$$

We use a standard one-tailed t-test according to Brown and Warner (1980) with $t_2 - t_1 - 1$ degrees of freedom to test the significance of the (cumulative) standardized abnormal returns under the assumption that the abnormal returns are independent and identically normally distributed. Departures from this assumption and potential biases induced by non-normally distributed abnormal returns are not accounted for in this study.

For the calculation of abnormal volumes, we apply the mean-adjusted model as well. As established by Ajinkya and Jain (1989) and Mai and Tchemeni (1996), it is recommendable to use the logarithm of the traded volume in monetary value[8] rather than the untransformed volumes. Given these daily log-volumes, denoted by v_t, we simply reuse the calculation methodology for the abnormal returns by replacing all rs by v.

To calculate abnormal returns and volumes of the data described in the next section for the days around the announcement events EA2006, EA2007, EA2008, EA2009, and EA2010, we choose an estimation window from 70 to eleven days before each of the events.

4.3 Price and Volume Data

We use price and volume data of futures contracts instead of EUA spot data for two reasons: First, futures are traded with higher liquidity than the EUAs themselves. Second, at every point in time, futures are available for the permits of following years, while the allowances are only traded for the current year (or trading period). Our data set consists of daily EUA futures prices and volumes of all futures contracts

---

[8] To this end, we multiply daily prices by daily volumes. Of course, use of tick-by-tick data would be more accurate to determine the monetary value of trading volumes, but such approach should not lead to markedly different results.

with maturities reaching from December 2005 to December 2012 on all trading days
between April 22, 2005 and May 10, 2010. We use settlement prices from the
European Climate Exchange (ECX), London, which are determined under the ECX
settlement procedure that takes place every day from 4:50 to 5:00 p.m. local time.

In Figure 1, we can observe the price data visually. Most eye-catching is, as

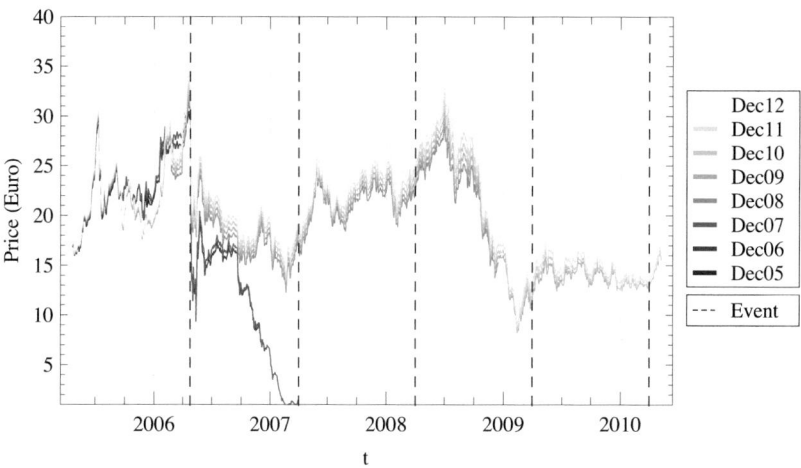

Figure 1: EUA futures prices from April 22, 2005 to May 10, 2010. Prices are settlement
prices determined under the ECX settlement procedure every day from 4:50 to 5:00 p.m.
local time.

described, the collapse of the futures prices belonging to the first trading period
around the emissions announcement in 2006. We also note that the group of
futures belonging to the second trading period strongly decoupled from the futures
belonging to the first trading period at that time, each group, however, trading at
similar prices due to the cost-of-carry-relationship. After that, the former group
recovered and rose up to a high of 29.33 Euros for the December 2008 contract in
July 2008, before the current financial crisis and the related economic downturn
caused another decline to a level between 12 and 16 Euros for the December 2010
contract. The EUA prices remained at that level until today. By visual inspection it
is not clear whether the announcement events after 2006 had a significant influence
on futures prices.

The volume figures of our data set are total traded volumes, which means that
they include screen trading as well as the exchange-for-physical facilities of the ECX.
Volume data is illustrated in Figure 2, where the ten trading days moving average
volumes in the different futures are shown in a "stacked" view, so that the volume
is accumulated. Firstly, it is observable that the total volume traded in EUA futures
has strongly increased from 2005 until today, although the exponentially-looking
increase has halted at the end of 2008. Recently, volumes have soared to a new

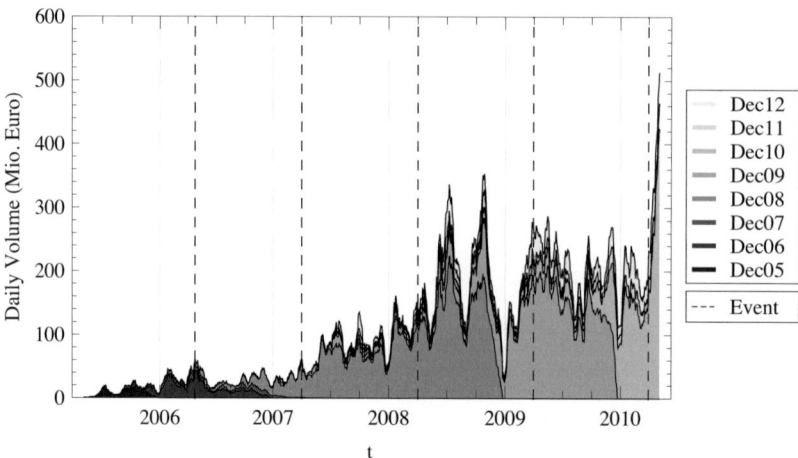

Figure 2: Daily volumes (ten trading days moving average) in EUA futures from April 22, 2005 to May 10, 2010 shown in a "stacked" view, so that the volume is accumulated. Volume data includes screen trading as well as the exchange-for-physical facilities of the ECX.

high. Moreover, we can see that the futures with maturity in December 2008 have been the most liquid EUA futures since the end of 2006, when futures belonging to the first trading period had totally lost their importance. In 2009, as expected, the futures maturing in December 2009 have been traded with the highest liquidity, superseded by the December 2010 futures in 2010.

5 Empirical Results

5.1 Abnormal Returns and Volumes

Abnormal returns and volumes are stated for the three single days before the event day, for the event day itself, and for the two single days after the event day as well as cumulated from seven days before and seven days after (including the event day) the event. Our results include the three futures next to maturity at each of the events.

Table 2 shows abnormal returns and volumes around EA2006. It is clearly observable that there are highly significant negative abnormal returns in the two futures belonging to the first trading period on the event day and the following days. The futures maturing in December 2008, which belong to the second trading period, also show highly significant negative abnormal returns on these days, even though a little less pronounced than the two futures belonging to the first trading period. Looking at volumes, we observe highly significant positive abnormal volumes in the futures maturing in December 2006 on those days as well. Contrary to that, the December 2007 futures do not show any significant abnormal volumes,

Table 2: Abnormal returns and volumes around EA2006 (*,**,*** stand for significance at the 10, 5, 1 per cent level).

days	abnormal returns			abnormal volumes		
	Dec06	Dec07	Dec08	Dec06	Dec07	Dec08
[−7; −1]	−0.011	−0.011	+0.026	+1.734	+6.427	+4.353*
−3	−0.020	−0.022	−0.046**	+0.370	+1.013	+1.314*
−2	−0.011	−0.011	−0.004	−0.304	−0.685	+0.622
−1	−0.000	+0.002	−0.007	+0.005	+0.719	−0.632
0	−0.089***	−0.090***	−0.051**	+1.186**	+0.715	+0.015
+1	−0.266***	−0.271***	−0.256***	+1.518***	+0.856	+1.113
+2	−0.180***	−0.170***	−0.037**	+1.514***	+1.876	+1.952**
[0; +6]	−0.826***	−0.813***	−0.422***	+3.233**	+5.074	+4.785**

suggesting that most trading takes place in the futures of each trading period next to maturity. Accordingly, the December 2008 contract partially shows significant positive abnormal volumes on the days around the event.

Table 3: Abnormal returns and volumes around EA2007 (*,**,*** stand for significance at the 10, 5, 1 per cent level).

days	abnormal returns			abnormal volumes		
	Dec07	Dec08	Dec09	Dec07	Dec08	Dec09
[−7; −1]	+0.412**	+0.071	+0.069	−7.926***	+5.247***	+27.155**
−3	+0.178**	+0.024	+0.022	−1.198*	+0.583	+4.017
−2	+0.157**	+0.010	+0.010	−0.314	+0.868**	+4.833
−1	−0.013	+0.001	+0.002	−1.370⁺	+0.473	+3.655
0	−0.190**	−0.036	−0.035	+0.763	+0.935**	+3.996
+1	−0.102	−0.055**	−0.052*	+0.025	+1.178**	+3.863
+2	−0.031	+0.016	+0.015	−0.921	+1.009**	+3.114
[0; +6]	−0.286	−0.014	−0.013	−19.993***	+1.731	+12.833

Results for EA2007 are shown in Table 3. We see that the futures maturing in December 2007 exhibit significant abnormal returns on most days prior to the event and on the event day. Significant abnormal returns are all positive on the days before the event and negative on the event day. Both of the other futures, which belong to the second trading period, show (weakly) significant negative returns on the day after the event. Regarding abnormal volumes, we observe an increased trading volume around the event in the 2008 and 2009 futures, while volumes in the December 2007 futures are very low in comparison to the estimation window.

Abnormal returns and volumes around EA2008 are stated in Table 4. Here, the only clear observation is a significant positive abnormal return on the event day in all futures considered, which all belong to the second trading period. Moreover, there are weakly significant positive abnormal volumes around the event in the December 2008 futures, especially on the event day.

Table 4: Abnormal returns and volumes around EA2008 (*,**,*** stand for significance at the 10, 5, 1 per cent level).

days	abnormal returns			abnormal volumes		
	Dec08	Dec09	Dec10	Dec08	Dec09	Dec10
[−7; −1]	+0.045	+0.045	+0.043	+1.944*	+1.981	+6.130
−3	−0.022	−0.022	−0.022	−0.020	−0.560	−0.002
−2	+0.024	+0.023	+0.022	+0.154	+0.098	+0.869
−1	+0.011	+0.011	+0.012	+0.153	+0.280	+1.821
0	+0.040**	+0.039**	+0.038**	+0.755*	+0.472	+1.642
+1	+0.002	+0.004	+0.003	+0.528	+0.780	+2.387
+2	−0.007	−0.005	−0.007	−0.003	+0.576	+1.204
[0; +6]	+0.084*	+0.084*	+0.081*	+3.024**	+4.679	+6.848

Table 5: Abnormal returns and volumes around EA2009 (*,**,*** stand for significance at the 10, 5, 1 per cent level).

days	abnormal returns			abnormal volumes		
	Dec09	Dec10	Dec11	Dec09	Dec10	Dec11
[−7; −1]	+0.064	+0.070	+0.066	+4.753**	+10.088***	+17.118*
−3	+0.024	+0.023	+0.026	+0.539	+1.277	+1.811
−2	+0.003	+0.004	+0.003	+0.314	+1.183	+2.475
−1	+0.051	+0.048	+0.044	+0.654	+1.791	+3.177
0	+0.042	+0.037	+0.030	+1.024	+0.613	+2.418
+1	−0.004	−0.005	−0.008	+0.563	+1.068	+2.208
+2	+0.034	+0.035	+0.034	+0.854	+2.068*	+2.956
[0; +6]	+0.150	+0.140	+0.124	+4.613**	+10.313***	+16.280*

Table 5 shows the results for EA2009. Here, we cannot observe any significant abnormal returns within the event window. Only significantly positive abnormal cumulative volumes can be observed around the event.

Table 6: Abnormal returns and volumes around EA2010 (*,**,*** stand for significance at the 10, 5, 1 per cent level).

days	abnormal returns			abnormal volumes		
	Dec10	Dec11	Dec12	Dec10	Dec11	Dec12
[−7; −1]	−0.020	−0.016	−0.016	+0.878	−0.835	+0.411
−3	−0.011	−0.010	−0.009	+0.020	−0.341	+0.396
−2	+0.006	+0.005	+0.007	−0.013	+0.599	+0.509
−1	−0.000	+0.001	−0.001	+0.087	−0.294	+0.335
0	+0.021	+0.020	+0.020	+0.237	−0.299	+0.291
+1	+0.027	+0.027	+0.027	+0.714*	+0.229	+0.745
+2	+0.007	+0.008	+0.009	+0.676	+0.626	+1.182*
[0; +6]	+0.069	+0.069	+0.071	+3.537***	+2.466*	+4.281**

The results for the last event of our set, EA2010, are stated in Table 6. As for EA2009, there are no significant abnormal returns within the event window. Again, partly significant positive abnormal volumes can be observed, but only after the event in this case.

5.2 Interpretation

In light of these results, we can now have a closer look at the hypotheses formulated in Section 4.1.

Hypothesis 1 says that the emissions announcement event does not cause a surprise effect. We have observed highly significant abnormal returns for EA2006 and still significant abnormal returns attributed to EA2007 and EA2008, rejecting H1. For EA2009 and EA2010, however, no significant abnormal returns around the event day are observable. This is noteworthy especially for EA2010, where realized 2009 emissions were announced to be far below the quotas. One may conclude that the surprise effect caused by this event has declined, which might be evidence for an increased capability of the market to anticipate unpublished information about realized emissions and the current emission rate of the economy. Nevertheless there still are increased trading volumes in the relevant futures around the emissions announcements suggesting higher trading activity induced by such an event. While at EA2006 and EA2008, significant positive abnormal volumes roughly correspond to significant abnormal returns on the event day or the days thereafter, at EA2009 and EA2010 mainly the cumulative abnormal volumes over the whole event window are significant. This supports the thesis of the surprise effect caused by the event to have declined.

As discussed in Section 2, in special cases, the allowance prices of different trading periods should be affected by the new information in different ways. In our sample, futures prices from different trading periods are only available for EA2006 and EA2007. Before EA2006, it was not clear that the market of the related trading period had been long, so that the information about realized emissions and the indication about future emissions cannot be separated from each other. On the other hand, it was very clear before EA2007 that there was a huge surplus of allowances belonging to the trial period, and banking into the following trading period was not allowed. This means that, according to our theoretical considerations, abnormal returns in the futures maturing in December 2008 and 2009 around EA2007 are only caused by that share of the information that we call indication about future emissions. As we see, this part can be sufficient to cause a surprise effect.

Hypothesis 2 states that there is no information leakage prior to an announcement event and would be rejected by significant abnormal returns on the days antedating such an event. It is quite obvious that there have been highly significant abnormal returns at EA2006 before May 15 because of information leakages, but these information leakages were obvious. Therefore, we choose April 25 as the event day, as information started to leak on this day. Before that day, there are hardly any significant abnormal returns observable, so there does not seem to have been any additional "hidden" information leakage. Considering EA2007, we observe significant positive abnormal returns in the December 2007 futures prior to the event. This could be construed as evidence for information leakage, but we think that there are other reasons. Firstly, the first trading period market had already collapsed, and the low prices should have attracted speculators previous to the event. Secondly, there has been a significant abnormal return in the opposite direction on the event day, which underpins the conjecture of speculators getting into the market before the event and getting out of it afterwards. Thirdly, the futures belonging to the second trading period do not show any evidence for information leakage, so that it is quite unlikely that such leakage has occurred indeed. The same is valid for EA2008, where no significant abnormal returns prior to the event are observable. On EA2009 and EA2010, there are no abnormal returns at all. Altogether, we are not able to substantiate information leakages previous to the announcement events.

In Hypothesis 3 we have formulated an immediate market reaction to the news published, whereas significant abnormal returns on the days after the event would be evidence to the contrary. On EA2006, such abnormal returns are clearly observable, but again this event is special in that parts of the information were published on every day from April 25 on. Therefore, these abnormal returns are supposed to be a reaction to the new information becoming available. For EA2007, we do not rely on the futures maturing in December 2007 for the reasons described before. However, both of the other futures show significant negative abnormal returns one day after the event day, which, further, are in the same direction as the abnormal returns on the event day. One could take this as evidence for market-inefficiency, which affected futures belonging to the following trading period. Contrary, for EA2008, EA2009, and EA2010 there are no significant abnormal returns after the event day. It is therefore reasonable to conclude that H3 holds true since the market has achieved a more mature state.

Finally, Hypothesis 4 states a similar behavior of futures belonging to the same trading period. We are able to provide support for this hypothesis by comparing the related abnormal returns. Contrary to that, it is interesting to see that futures from different trading periods may behave differently. For example, the abnormal returns after EA2006 are obviously smaller for futures belonging to the second trading period than they are for those belonging to the first trading period. Around EA2007, the behavior of both types of futures differs even more as has been described already. However, due to the small set of relevant events, we are not able to make any statement about the different reaction of futures from different trading periods to an announcement event.

6 Conclusion

The incidents related to the emissions announcement event in 2006 raised several questions regarding the impact of such announcements on CO_2 prices. We formulate these questions in form of hypotheses and analyze them by using standard event study methodology. One finding is that this event has caused a surprise effect in the years 2007 and 2008 which has, however, been much weaker than for the announcement event in 2006. For the events in 2009 and 2010, no surprise effect is observable. Additionally, we cannot find any evidence for information leakage prior to an announcement event. Regarding market efficiency, the market seems to be mature enough now to react immediately and without delay to these events. Furthermore, futures maturing in the same trading period show almost the same reaction to such an event.

Relating to the evolution of this still new market, our results can be interpreted in a very positive way. It is good to see that prices seem to incorporate new information coming from an emissions announcement efficiently. Even before the information is published, the market seems to anticipate it more and more, so that the surprise effect caused by such events has considerably declined. Since we do not detect any information leakages on the days prior to the events, the surprise effect is supposed to diminish due to a better capability of the market in anticipating information about realized emissions and the current emission rate of the economy.

References

Ajinkya, B. B. and P. C. Jain (1989): "The behavior of daily stock market trading volume," *Journal of Accounting and Economics*, 11, pp. 331–359.

Binder, J. J. (1998): "The Event Study Methodology Since 1969," *Review of Quantitative Finance and Accounting*, 11, pp. 111–137.

Brown, S. J. and J. B. Warner (1980): "Measuring Security Price Performance," *Journal of Financial Economics*, 8, pp. 205–258.

Brown, S. J. and J. B. Warner (1985): "Using Daily Returns: The Case of Event Studies," *Journal of Financial Economics*, 14, pp. 3–31.

Chevallier, J., F. Ielpo, and L. Mercier (2009): "Risk aversion and institutional information disclosure on the European carbon market: A case-study of the 2006 compliance event," *Energy Policy*, 37(1), pp. 15–28.

Conrad, C., D. Rittler, and W. Rotfuß (2009): "The European Commission and EUA Prices: A High-Frequency Analysis of the EC's Decisions on Second NAPs," *Working Paper*.

EUROPA Press Releases (2006): "EU emissions trading scheme delivers first verified emissions data for installations," IP/06/612, http://europa.eu/rapid/pressReleasesAction.do?reference=IP/06/612.

EUROPA Press Releases (2007): "Emissions trading: strong compliance in 2006, emissions decoupled from economic growth," IP/07/776, http://europa.eu/rapid/pressReleasesAction.do?reference=IP/07/776.

EUROPA Press Releases (2008): "Emissions trading: 2007 verified emissions from EU ETS businesses," IP/08/787, `http://europa.eu/rapid/pressReleasesAction.do?reference=IP/08/787`.

EUROPA Press Releases (2009): "Emissions trading: EU ETS emissions fall 3 % in 2008," IP/09/794, `http://europa.eu/rapid/pressReleasesAction.do?reference=IP/09/794`.

EUROPA Press Releases (2010): "Emissions trading: EU ETS emissions fall more than 11 % in 2009," IP/10/576, `http://europa.eu/rapid/pressReleasesAction.do?reference=IP/10/576`.

Fama, E. F., L. Fisher, M. C. Jensen, and R. Roll (1969): "The Adjustment Of Stock Prices To New Information," *International Economic Review*, 10.

MacKinlay, A. C. (1997): "Event Studies in Economics and Finance," *Journal of Economic Literature*, 35(1), pp. 13–39.

Mai, H. M. and E. Tchemeni (1996): "Etude d'événement par les volumes: Méthodologies et comparaison," *Working Paper*.

Mansanet-Bataller, M. and A. Pardo (2007): "The Effects of National Allocation Plans on Carbon Markets," *Working Paper*.

Rittler, D. (2009): "Price Discovery, Causality and Volatility Spillovers in European Union Allowances Phase II: A High Frequency Analysis," *Working Paper*.

Uhrig-Homburg, M. and M. Wagner (2009): "Futures Price Dynamics of CO2 Emission Allowances: An Empirical Analysis of the Trial Period," *Journal of Derivatives*, 17(2), pp. 73–88.

Estimating Event-based Exponential Random Graph Models

Christoph Stadtfeld[1], Andreas Geyer-Schulz[1], and Karl-Heinz Waldmann[3]

[1] Institute of Information Systems and Management, KIT
   stadtfeld@ime.uni-karlsruhe.de, ags@em.uni-karlsruhe.de
[2] Institute of Operations Research, KIT
   waldmann@wior.uni-karlsruhe.de

Summary. Communication is often measured as events streams. Events are directed, dyadic and time-stamped interactions. A model is introduced that allows to describe the occurence of new events in a data stream dependent on actor activities and network structures. To illustrate how the model and its estimation works, a straightforward example is given. Some possible applications of the model are proposed.

1 Introduction

Exponential random graph models (ERGMs) are widely used to model structural choices of actor in networks (Wasserman and Pattison (1996); Snijders et al. (2006); Robins et al. (2007); Wang et al. (2009)). Given a static network, its estimates express in how far the network structures that actors are connected with and embedded in differ from some random graph. A similar estimation can be done for binary, static networks that are measured at a small number of discrete points in time as longitudinal data (see Snijders (2001, 2005)). Some new approaches (Butts (2008); Brandes et al. (2009); Zenk and Stadtfeld (2010)) use event data instead. Events are any kind of social, dyadic interaction and are related to certain types of ties in social networks. However, when describing such an event stream with ERGMs, the estimation of optimal parameters is a bit different from the longitudinal data case: Firstly, the model assumes availability of full information, so no guesses about unobserved tie changes have to be made. Secondly, the amount of data which has to be processed is much bigger.

The goal of this paper is to introduce a generic model (that we call event-based ERGM) and illustrate its estimation with some exemplary input data. This idea is explained in several steps: Firstly, in section 2 the underlying event stream format is introduced (subsection 2.1), after this some information about the observed communication network is given (subsection 2.2), then it is explained how events and time change the network (subsection 2.3) using update rules. Based on these basic introductions, a Markov model framework is explained in section 3. A concrete two-parameter model and a related exemplary event stream are defined in section 4. In section 5, the maximum likelihood function of the abstract model is introduced and plotted for the example. The results of the exemplary estimation are provided in secion 6. In section 7 possible applications of event based models are specified. Finally, section 8 summarizes and gives an outlook on future work.

2 Data, Network and Updates

2.1 Event Stream

When analyzing the change in communication networks, the underlying data does not need to be collected at discrete points in time by surveying the actors in a network (as in longitudinal studies). Instead, computer mediated communication data can be used. Dyadic communication interactions are in the following named *events*. Events are defined as directed, dyadic, social interactions.

An event stream Ω is a chronologically ordered finite list of events

$$\Omega = (\omega_1, \omega_2, \ldots, \omega_\nu, \ldots). \tag{1}$$

Events ω_ν are defined as triplets

$$\omega_\nu = (\omega_\nu.sender, \omega_\nu.recipient, \omega_\nu.timestamp)$$
$$= (i_\nu, j_\nu, t_\nu) \tag{2}$$

where the first element is the sender of the event (the person who starts a phone call), the second one the recipient and the third element the timestamp when the event takes place. For each pair of events ω_ν (ν is the index $\in \{1, \ldots, |\Omega|\}$), ω_ϕ holds

$$\nu < \phi \Rightarrow t_\nu \leq t_\phi. \tag{3}$$

The timestamps t_ν have values in $\mathbb{R}^+$. Sender and recipient are elements of the set of actors A. The time between to subsequent events is named

$$\delta_\nu = t_\nu - t_{\nu-1}. \tag{4}$$

2.2 Network

The set of actors A and the communication intensities between them are represented by the stream of events Ω. For each point in time $t \in [t_1, t_{|\Omega|}]$, the communication intensities are represented by a directed, weighted communication network. It is described with a graph X. The nodes of this network are all actors occuring in the data stream as senders or recipients. Ties in this network represent recent communication intensity.

$$X(t) = (x_{kl}(t)), k, l \in \{1, \ldots, |A|\}. \tag{5}$$

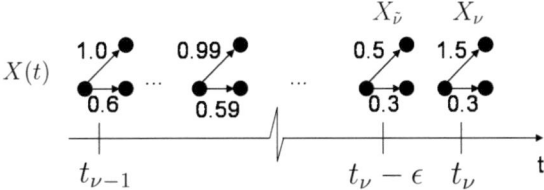

Figure 1: For very short time spans ϵ holds that the adjacency matrices $X(t)$ are stable

is the adjacency matrix of the communication network at time t. It represents the communication intensity $\in \mathbb{R}^+$ until time t between all actors $k, l \in A$. The elements of this matrix are the weights of the directed communication ties.

The value of a directed tie from actor i_ν to j_ν is increased in the network, when event ω_ν takes place. In the time between two events, tie values decay. The network update rules are introduced in section 2.3.

Of specific interest are the two graphs "just before" an event ω_ν, and the graph after the event triggered changes have been realized. These graphs are abbreviated in the following way:

$$X_\nu = (x_{\nu;kl}) := X(t_\nu)$$
$$X_{\tilde{\nu}} = (x_{\tilde{\nu};kl}) := X(t_\nu - \epsilon)$$

The elements of these adjacency matrices are named $x_{\nu;kl}$, where $k, l \in A$ are line and column index of the matrix, and ν stands for the corresponding event. ϵ is a very short time span so that generally holds

$$X(t) \approx X(t + \epsilon) \tag{6}$$

if no events take place in the timespan $\in [t - \epsilon, t]$. In very short time spans, the network is stable, although tie values decay slowly. So, the network states $X_{\tilde{\nu}}$ and X_ν are assumed to be equal, except for an event triggered update of tie $x_{i_\nu j_\nu}$. For events at the same time holds that

$$t_\nu = t_{\nu+1} \Rightarrow X(t_\nu) = X(t_{\nu+1}). \tag{7}$$

Figure 1 shows a network with three nodes at four different point in time: The first three networks represent a decay of tie values. Within the short time span $t_\nu - \epsilon$ to t_ν all ties are stable. Only one tie is updated (increased by 1) because event ω_ν takes place from the lower left to the upper right node.

2.3 Network Update Rules

The occurence of events is influenced by structures in the communication network X. This communication network is changed if events take place and due to a time decay. Informally, a communication event ω_ν leads to the update of the network X.

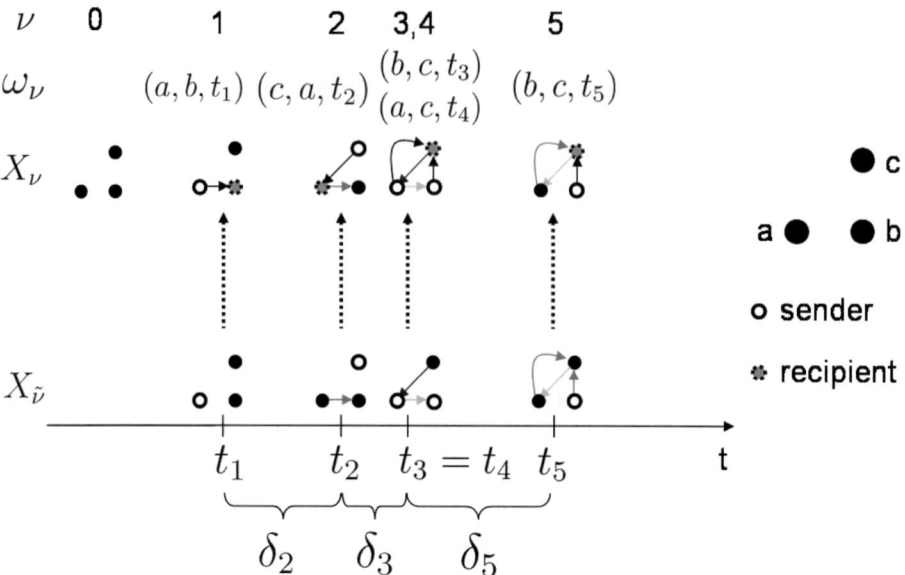

Figure 2: A process with four events. Senders of each event are marked as solid circles, senders as dotted circles. The set of actors is $A = \{a, b, c\}$. The blackness of directed ties represents its value. Tie values decay over time.

This is modelled by increasing the edge weight between i_ν and j_ν by 1 at t_ν. Since X is a continuous time network, inactivity leads to an exponential decay of all edge weights with a defined half-life.

In figure 2 this process is exemplarily sketched for five events $\Omega = \{\omega_1, \ldots \omega_5\}$ on a set of three actors $A = \{a, b, c\}$. This process starts with an empty network X_0 without any ties. $X_{\bar{1}}, \ldots X_{\bar{5}}$ are the state of the networks at the time of the event *before* the communication tie has been updated (in $t_\nu - \epsilon$). Networks $X_1, \ldots, X_5$ are the network states *after* this network update. In the time spans in between ($\delta_2, \ldots, \delta_5$), the tie values decrease dependend on the length of the interval. Time span δ_3, for example, is the shortest one, except for δ_4 which is zero as ω_3 and ω_4 take place at the same time $t_3 = t_4$. Tie values are expressed by the blackness of the directed ties between actors. Over time, new ties get lighter. Events in this example are shown as triplets, like $(i_1, j_2, t_3) = (a, b, t_1)$ in case of the first event ω_1. Senders are marked with a solid, empty circle, recipients of events as dotted, grey circles. The time axis from left to right is continuous, while the indices ν of events ω_ν are discrete.

The update triggered by events is defined as follows: If an event ω_ν takes place, the tie value from actor i_ν to j_ν is increased by 1. This transformation is described by a function $r^{(1)} : X \times \Omega \mapsto X$:

$$r^{(1)}(X_{\tilde{v}}; i_v, j_v) = (x_{v;kl}) = \begin{cases} x_{\tilde{v};kl} + 1 & \text{, if } k = i_v, l = j_v \\ x_{\tilde{v};kl} + 1 & \text{, if } \exists \omega_\phi : k = i_\phi, l = j_\phi, t_\phi = t_v \\ x_{\tilde{v};kl} & \text{, else} \end{cases} \quad (8)$$

In the time between two events, tie values decrease with an exponential decay function $r^{(2)} : X \times \mathbb{R}^+ \mapsto X$. It weakens the ties of a graph, dependent on the time span δ_v between the current and the previous event.

$$r^{(2)}(X_{v-1}, \delta_v; \tau_{\frac{1}{2}}) = (x_{v;kl}) = (x_{v-1;kl}e^{-\theta\delta_v}), \theta = \frac{\ln 2}{\tau_{\frac{1}{2}}} \quad (9)$$

$$\delta_v = t_v - t_{v-1}$$

and a tie half life of $\tau_{\frac{1}{2}}$.

3 Model Framework

Dyadic communication (like phone calls) within communication network structures can be described with a stochastic model. Two decisions about interaction can be modelled as a two-level decision process:

- Every actor has a personal activity rate that determines whether he starts an interaction
- If an actor starts an interaction, the network structures embedding sender and potential communication partners influence the choice of the actual communication partner (recipient)

3.1 Actor activity rate

Informally, the probability for the first decision of an actor i (to become active) in a time span $[t, t + epsilon]$ is

$$P(i \text{ active in } [t, t + \epsilon]) \quad (10)$$

where ϵ is a very short time span so that i is active zero or one time. The points in time when actors start events are determined by a Poisson process with parameters ρ_i for actor $i \in A$. This also means that the time δ^i between events that are started by the same actor i is exponentially distributed with parameter ρ_i (Waldmann and Stocker (2004)):

$$P(\delta^i < \delta; \rho_i) = 1 - e^{-\rho_i\delta} \quad (11)$$

is the probability that actor i starts at least one event in a time span δ. It is assumed to be indendent of the decisions of any other actor to start events. Given a data stream, this actor activity can easily be determined using a maximum likelihood

(ML) estimation. However, this article focuses on the parameter estimation of the second decision in the process about event recipients. So, the estimation of actor rates is not discussed in more detail. More information on the ML estimation of Poisson parameters can be found in Davison (2003)[p.].

3.2 The Choice of Recipients

The second decision of i is the choice of a communication partner (recipient). This decision depends on the state of the communication network $X(t + \delta^i)$ at time $(t + \delta^i) \in [t, t + \epsilon]$. From equation 6 follows that $X(t + \delta^i) \approx X(t)$. Informally, the probability that i contacts j at time span $[t, t + \epsilon]$ is then

$$P(i \text{ contacts } j | X(t)). \tag{12}$$

Since this decision is independent from the first as long as ϵ is very small and the network has not been changed by other actors, the probability for a new communication event between i to j in time span $[t, t + \epsilon]$ is then

$$P(i \text{ active in } [t, t + \epsilon]) P(i \text{ contacts } j | X(t)). \tag{13}$$

The second decision about recipients depends on structures in subgraphs of $X(t + \delta^i)$. How these structures are measured and evaluated in a non-linear regression model is illustrated in the following.

3.3 Network Statistics

The choice of the recipient is based on network structures. For each possible event recipient $k \in A \backslash \{i_v\}$ of an event ω_v, statistics are measured of the subgraphs that surround sender i_v and all possible recipients.

The statistics are represented by a statistics matrix $S_v \in \mathbb{R}_{\geq 0}^{|Q| \times |A|}$ for each event ω_v:

$$S_v = (s_{v;qk}) = \begin{pmatrix} s_{v;11} & \cdots & s_{v;1|A|} \\ \vdots & \ddots & \vdots \\ s_{v;|Q|1} & \cdots & s_{v;|Q||A|} \end{pmatrix} = \left(s_{v;.1} \cdots s_{v;.|A|} \right) \tag{14}$$

$$s_{v;.k} := \begin{pmatrix} s_{v;1k} \\ \vdots \\ s_{v;|Q|k} \end{pmatrix}$$

Q is the set of statistics of the local network embedding sender and recipient of the event. The elements $s_{v;qk}$ of S_v include the q-th statistic for a possibly chosen recipient k in event ω_v. The semicolon is used to avoid confusing the event index v

with the line and column indices $q \in Q$ and $k \in A$. A vector $s_{v;\cdot k}$ includes all $|Q|$ statistics for the potential case that in event ω_v the sender i_v had chosen actor $k \in A$ as recipient. The elements of matrix S_v are results of the evaluation of functions $f_q : X \times A \times A \mapsto \mathbb{R}^+$ that are part of a function $S(X, i)$ for any network state X and a sending actor i:

$$S(X, i) = (s_{qk}) = \left(f_q(r^{(1)}(X, i, k), i, k)\right) \tag{15}$$
$$S_v = (s_{v;qk}) := S(X_{\tilde{v}}, i_v) \tag{16}$$

Under the assumption that k was chosen as the recipient, a subgraph of the potential network $r^{(1)}(X_{\tilde{v}}, i_v, k)$ around sender i_v and potential recipient $k \in A$ is analyzed. Typical examples for communication structures that have an effect on future communication are repeated using of the same communication ties, reciprocal or transitive communication.

The choice of the statistics set Q defines a concrete model. An examplary model with two parameters is introduced in section 4.

3.4 Markov Model

This two-level decision process can be modelled as a Markov process (or continuous-time Markov chain). The state of this process at time t is the state of the communication graph $X(t)$. Poisson transitions can be defined for the occurence of events with each possible sender-recipient combination (i, j) on this graph.

Given a communication data stream, activity of actors and the influence of network structures on recipient choices can ex post be determined. The set of measured structures defines the concrete model. The estimation of the weights of the structures influencing the choice of recipients takes place in a non-linear regression model. It belongs to the class of exponential random graph models. The corresponding probability function for chosing a recipient j_v over any other possible recipient is:

$$p(j_v; S_v, \beta) = \frac{1}{c(S_v, \beta)} exp\left(\beta^T s_{v;\cdot j_v}\right) \tag{17}$$
$$c(S_v, \beta) = \sum_{k \in A \setminus \{i_v\}} exp\left(\beta^T s_{v;\cdot k}\right)$$

$p(j_v; S_v, \beta)$ returns the probability that an event from actor i_v to actor j_v is observed, given that i_v started this event at all. The probability depends on the network statistics in S_v and a vector β that weights statistics in the graph after a new tie has been added. The constant $c(S_v, \beta)$ makes sure that the function is a proper probability distribution by measuring the structures of any other possible recipient decision. Reflexive events are not part of the constant, so sender i_v is excluded from the set of possible recipients.

For very short time spans δ at time t with $X(t + \delta) \approx X(t)$ (see equation 6) holds that the general tendency for certain events can be described with the following Poisson parameter:

$$\lambda(i, j; X(t)) \approx \rho_i p(j; S(X(t), i), \beta) \tag{18}$$

This rate defines transitions in a Markov process and assumes that both decisions in the process are independent. $\lambda(i, j; X(t))$ is a Poisson rate that indirectly defines the probability of the occurence of a new tie from i to j in graph x within short time spans. The subsequent sections focus on the second part of this Markov process rate $\lambda(i, j; X(t))$, which is the probability $p(j; S_v, \beta)$ that defines the choice of recipients. In the following section, exemplary input data for the introduced model are given and a simple dyadic model with two parameters is applied to it.

4 Example

To illustrate the above introduced model framework, a concrete dyadic model is defined, which is later tested on a straightforward data stream with only three events. This exemplary data stream is introduced first.

4.1 Exemplary Data Stream and Initial Network

An examplary event stream Ω with three events is observed:

$$\Omega = \{\omega_1, \omega_2, \omega_3\} \tag{19}$$

These events are defined as triplets like in equation 1. The list of exemplary events can be found in talbe 1. In event ω_1, for example, actor a_4 sends an event to actor a_5 at time 0.

	$\omega_v =$		
v	$\{i_v \in A,$	$j_v \in A,$	$t_v\}$
1	a_4	a_5	0
2	a_1	a_2	100
3	a_2	a_1	200

Table 1: Event stream

This event stream is observed on a set of five actors:

$$A = \{a_1, \ldots, a_5\}.$$

with an initial communication matrix X_0, representing previous unknown communication:

$$X_0 = X_{\bar{1}} = \begin{pmatrix} 0 & 2 & 6 & 0 & 0 \\ 0 & 0 & 0 & 0 & 0 \\ 0 & 2 & 0 & 2 & 0 \\ 0 & 0 & 1 & 0 & 2 \\ 0 & 0 & 0 & 1 & 0 \end{pmatrix} \qquad (20)$$

Elements $x_{\bar{1};kl}$ represent the recent directed communication intensity from actor k to l. Actor a_1, for example, has recently communicated with actor a_2 as the communication matrix returns an intensity of 2. Still, it is lower than the communication intensity from actor a_1 to a_3 which is 6 at time $t = 0$. The diagonal elements are all 0 as there is no reflexive communiation.

4.2 Network Update Rules

The network is changed by the two update rules from section 2.3. Events increase the ties between sender and recipient. In the time between events, there is a steady exponential decay.

$r^{(1)}$ is defined by equation 8. Whenever an event ω_v between actors i_v and j_v takes place, the directed tie from i_v to j_v is increased by 1.

Function $r^{(2)}$ is defined by equation 9 with a half life $\tau_{\frac{1}{2}} = 100$ of 100 time units:

$$X_{\tilde{v}} = r^{(2)}(X_{v-1}, t_v - t_{v-1}, 100) \qquad (21)$$

A tie value of 2, for example, is decreased by 1 (50%) in a time span of length 100 if no event takes place.

4.3 Network Statistics

In this example, we next consider a concrete model. It shall represent in how far actors in this example tend to re-use existing ties and communicate reciprocally. Therefore, the set of statistics is

$$Q = \{\text{re-using of existing ties, reciprocal communication}\}.$$

Note, that this model is a very simple one: In this case, communication choices are only explained with dyadic structures. In more complex models other statistics could be included that also measure multi-node structures or actor attributes. For example, in communication networks often transitivity effects can be observed and therefore should be included in a more precise model that aims on explaining communication choices.

For each event ω_v there are $|A| - 1$ potential recipients $\in A \backslash \{i_v\}$. For each of them, there are two statistics based on the measured structures in the event statistics matrix S_v (see equations 14 and 16). In case of the two given structures the matrix looks as follows:

$$S_v = (s_{v;qk}) \tag{22}$$

$$s_{v;qk} = \begin{cases} f_1(r^{(1)}(X_{\tilde{v}}, i_v, k), i_v, k) & q = 1 \\ f_2(r^{(1)}(X_{\tilde{v}}, i_v, k), i_v, k) & q = 2 \end{cases} \tag{23}$$

$$f_1(X, i, k) = X_{ik} - 1$$
$$f_2(X, i, k) = \min\{X_{ik}, X_{ki}\}$$
$$q \in Q$$
$$i, k \in A$$

Whether existing ties are tended to be re-used is measured by the value of the used tie just before the event takes place. Whether people tend to communicate reciprocally is measured with the weaker of the two in- and outgoing ties between sender and recipient of the event.

The graphs $X_{\bar{1}}$ and X_1 are shown in figure 3 from a global and an ego perspective. The total graph has five actor nodes (indicated by framed numbers) and seven non-zero communication relations. If actor a_4 decides about the recipient based on the given dyadic model, only the decisions to communicate with actors a_3 and a_5 are influenced by dyadic statistics that are not zero. So, these dyadic structures are plotted in a ego network with a_4 as its center in subfigures 3(b) and 3(c).

The corresponding matrix S_1 is shown in equation 24. In can be represented by the statistics vectors $s_{1;\cdot k}$ for all actors $k \in A$.

$$
S_1 = \overbrace{\begin{pmatrix} 0 & 0 & 1 & 0 & 2 \\ 0 & 0 & 2 & 0 & 1 \end{pmatrix}}^{1\,2\,3\,4\,5} \left.\begin{array}{l} \} \text{ Re-using of existing ties } (q=1) \\ \} \text{ Reciprocal communication } (q=2) \end{array}\right. \tag{24}
$$

$$\Rightarrow s_{1;\cdot 3} = \begin{pmatrix} 2 \\ 1 \end{pmatrix}, s_{1;\cdot 5} = \begin{pmatrix} 1 \\ 2 \end{pmatrix}, \forall k \notin \{3, 5\} : s_{1;\cdot k} = \begin{pmatrix} 0 \\ 0 \end{pmatrix}$$

Sender $i_1 = a_4$ choses actor a_5 as recipient. So, the functions f_1 and f_2 in equation 23 return statistics 2 (re-using of existing ties) and 1 (reciprocal communication). Vector $s_{1;\cdot 3}$ it therefore $\begin{pmatrix} 2 \\ 1 \end{pmatrix}$. If a_4 had chosen to communicate with a_3 instead, he had re-used a tie with value 1 and strengthened a dyad with minimum tie value of

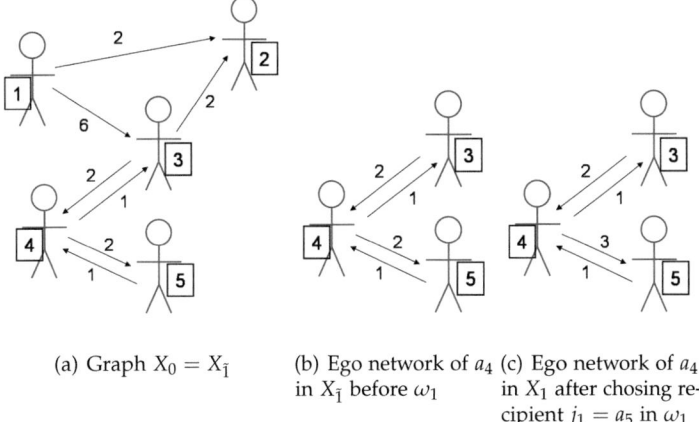

(a) Graph $X_0 = X_{\bar{1}}$

(b) Ego network of a_4 in $X_{\bar{1}}$ before ω_1

(c) Ego network of a_4 in X_1 after chosing recipient $j_1 = a_5$ in ω_1

Figure 3: The graph $X_{\bar{1}}$, the relevant sub graph from an ego perspective of actor 4, and the same ego network after event ω_1

2 then. This explains the values in vector $s_{1;\cdot3}$. All other statistic vectors are zero as they do not measure any dyadic structures.

Because of the exponential decay with tie half-life 100, the tie values in graph $X_{\bar{2}}$ and $X_{\bar{3}}$ before events ω_2 and ω_3 have halved compared to those of the previous event. The time span between these events is 100, which is as long as the half-life of the exponential decay. The corresponding communication networks are shown in figures 4 and 5.

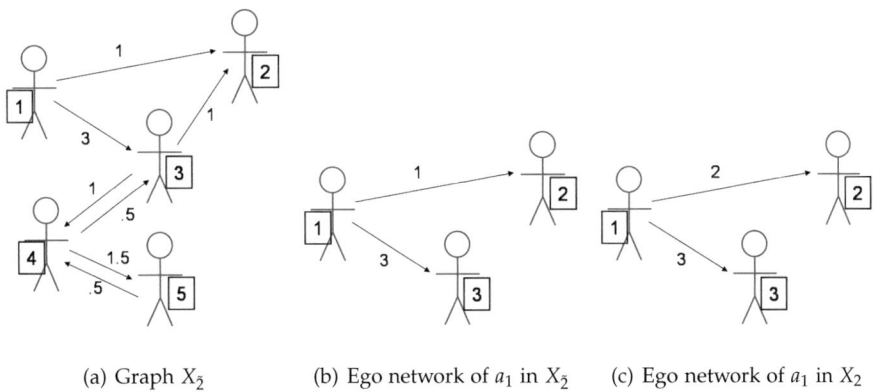

(a) Graph $X_{\bar{2}}$

(b) Ego network of a_1 in $X_{\bar{2}}$

(c) Ego network of a_1 in X_2

Figure 4: The graph $X_{\bar{2}}$, the relevant sub graph from an ego perspective of actor 1, and the same ego network after event ω_2

The statistic matrices and vectors for the second and third decision about recipients are

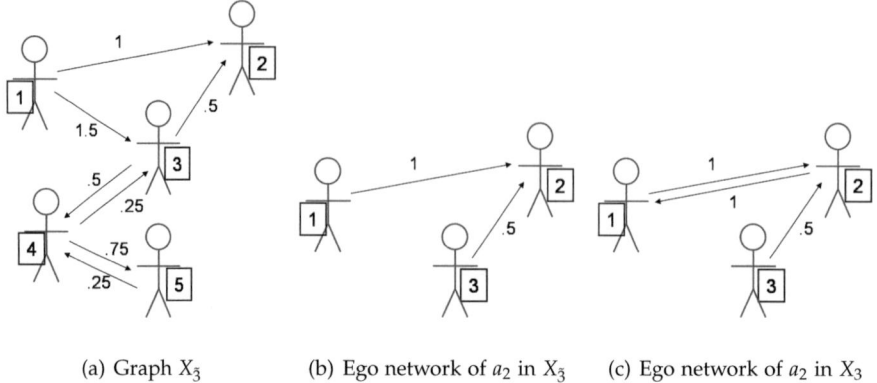

(a) Graph $X_{\tilde{3}}$ (b) Ego network of a_2 in $X_{\tilde{3}}$ (c) Ego network of a_2 in X_3

Figure 5: The graph $X_{\tilde{3}}$, the relevant sub graph from an ego perspective of actor 2, and the same ego network of X_3 after event ω_3

$$S_2 = \begin{pmatrix} 0 & 1 & 3 & 0 & 0 \\ 0 & 0 & 0 & 0 & 0 \end{pmatrix} \tag{25}$$

$$\Rightarrow s_{2;.2} = \begin{pmatrix} 1 \\ 0 \end{pmatrix}, s_{2;.3} = \begin{pmatrix} 3 \\ 0 \end{pmatrix}, \forall k \notin \{2,3\} : s_{1;.k} = \begin{pmatrix} 0 \\ 0 \end{pmatrix} \tag{26}$$

and

$$S_3 = \begin{pmatrix} 0 & 0 & 0 & 0 & 0 \\ 1 & 0 & 0.5 & 0 & 0 \end{pmatrix}. \tag{27}$$

$$\Rightarrow s_{3;.1} = \begin{pmatrix} 0 \\ 1 \end{pmatrix}, s_{3;.3} = \begin{pmatrix} 0 \\ 0.5 \end{pmatrix}, \forall k \notin \{1,3\} : s_{3;.k} = \begin{pmatrix} 0 \\ 0 \end{pmatrix} \tag{28}$$

Based on the observed behavior in the exemplary event stream it can now be figured out, which of the structures explain dynamic behavior in the data set best. The resulting model represents which structures rather increase or decrease communication choices compared to a random choice. This can be concluded from the values in parameter vector β (see equation 17). The optimal estimators $\hat{\beta}$ are found at the maximum of the log likelihood of the observed event stream. In the next section, this likelihood function is introduced generally and plotted for the exemplary two-parameter model and the exemplary data stream.

5 Likelihood

If an event stream is described with a specific model, the unknown part of the second decision is the vector of paramters β that explain whether certain structures (in the example: re-using of existing ties and reciprocal communication) increase or decrease the probability for the choice of recipients compared to random choice of recipients. The network statistics $s_{v;qk}$ can be interpreted as independent variables of a non-linear regression model (see e.g. Myers et al. (2002)). The dependent variable is the choice of a recipient that is described with the probability function in equation 17.

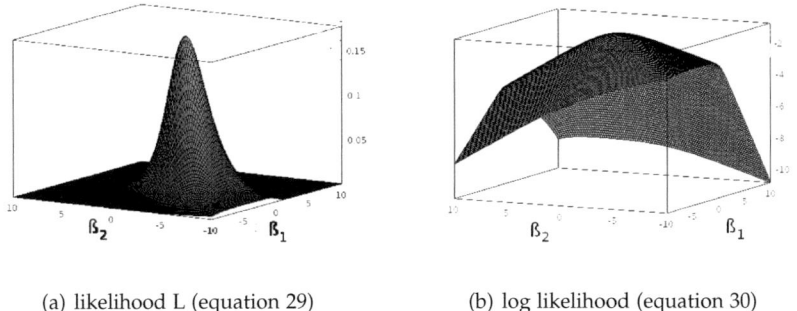

(a) likelihood L (equation 29) (b) log likelihood (equation 30)

Figure 6: Likelihood and log likelihood for different parameters β_1 and β_2 of the example in section 4.

Assuming that all these decisions are independent, the total likelihood for the observed event stream Ω is

$$L(\beta, \Omega) = \prod_{v=1}^{|\Omega|} p(j_v; S_v, \beta). \tag{29}$$

The fact that previous interaction changes the probability of current interaction is assumed to be fully encoded in the underlying network structures. Apart from this, all decisions are independent which follows from the Markov property of the stochastic process. For the example in section 4, a plot of the likelihood dependent on the chosen parameters β_1 (weighting *Re-using of existing ties*) and β_2 (*Reciprocal communication*) is shown in figure 6(a). Clearly, there is an optimal maximum solution for this case. But when estimating the optimum of a maximization problem, it is very helpful to have a (strictly) concave function, so the likelihood function is transformed with the natural logarithm:

$$\log L(\beta, \Omega) = \log \prod_{v=1}^{|\Omega|} p(j_v; S_v, \beta)$$

$$= \sum_{v=1}^{|\Omega|} \log p(j_v; S_v, \beta)$$

$$= \sum_{v=1}^{|\Omega|} \beta^T s \cdot j_v - \sum_{v=1}^{|\Omega|} \log(c(S_v, \beta)) \tag{30}$$

A plot of the log likelihood values dependend on parameters β is given in figure 6(b). The maximum likelihood estimator $\hat{\beta}$ can easily be found by applying a Newton Raphson optimization algorithm.

6 Results of the Example

The estimation of the simple example in section 4 needs four iteration steps with a Newton Raphson algorithm until the additional improvement of estimators is below 10^{-4}. As can be seen in figure 6(a), the estimators are close to zero, the estimation returned the results given in table 2.

$\hat{\beta}_1$	(s.e.)	$\hat{\beta}_2$	(s.e.)
-0.7965	(0.886)	-1.4692	(0.528)

Table 2: Estimation results of the example data in section 4

.

    The estimator of $\hat{\beta}_1$ (*Re-using of existing ties*) is clearly not significant as the standard error is bigger than the absolute value of the parameter. Therefore, it should not be interpreted. Estimator $\hat{\beta}_2$ (*Reciprocal communication*), on the other hand, is significantly negative with a lower standard error. If this effect is measured as part of a sender-recipient-structure, the choice of the corresponding recipient is less likely than chosing a recipient without this structure. Looking on the input data in section 4 it is clear that in the first decision a low statistic for reciprocity is chosen over a high one. However, this effect is weakend by the third decision, where 1 is chosen over 0.5 and other zeros, but as the absolute value of this choice is lower, the general tendency is negative. However, three events are not enough to give any valid statements about communication behavior in a network.

    When aligning the statistics values of the third decision to chosing 1.0 over 0.9 only, $\hat{\beta}_2$ has a even lower parameter value of $-4.464(0.244)$. When observing the third event twice, $\hat{\beta}_1$ gets also lower and then also rather significant value of $\hat{\beta}_1 = -1.7162(0.427)$.

7 Applications

Finding good parameter estimates for event-based exponential random graph models can be useful in many regards. Basically, the parameter vector $\hat{\beta}$ gives an evaluation of network structures that influence decisions about event recipients. The model generally allows a closer look on decision making in networks. As networks can be oberved in various forms and many fields, there is a broad range of possible applications.

In the context of electronic markets, estimated results may describe the environment in which agents in a market interact with others in a certain way. It can be tested whether agents who know each other are likelier to trade.

In the context of information or knowledge management it can be tested whether links between actors and certain entities (like knowledge bases) increase the likelihood of information flow between actors.

In service value networks (SVN), some services are not compatible with others. Events in this context are, for example, the emergence of new interfaces. The introduced model could help to explain whether there are network effects that increase the likelihood for such a product change when observing the SVN market over time. Network effects may represent market concentration or competition between service providers.

In the context of communication theory, the results may help to understand and test sociological theories. Some examples are homophily theories, contagion theories or dependency theories (see Monge and Contractor (2003)) in communication environments.

8 Summary and Outlook

This article aimed on introducing event-based ERGMs, a model to describe choices in communication event streams. The model was illustrated using a simple example and the estimation process was briefly explained. The model can be used to research decision making processes in different environments, some examples for applications were given.

There are still some open, but interesting questions regarding the introduced model. Firstly, a way has to be found to reduce the set of possible recipients without violating statistical assumptions and features of the model. Secondly, further research will focus on how graph dependencies between network structures affect estimates. Also, estimation results may be influenced by general network features like density or degree distributions. These questions will be addressed using simulations. In further work it will be shown that the maximum log likelihood function is concave and in most cases even strictly concave.

References

Brandes, U., J. Lerner, and T. A. B. Snijders (2009): "Networks Evolving Step by Step: Statistical Analysis of Dyadic Event Data," in: *Proceedings of the 2009 International Conference on Advances in Social Network Analysis and Mining (ASONAM 2009)*, IEEE Computer Society, pp. 200 –205.

Butts, C. T. (2008): "A relational event framework for social action," *Sociological Methodology*, 38(1), pp. 155–200.

Davison, A. C. (2003): *Statistical Models*, Cambridge Series in Statistical and Probabilistic Mathematics, Cambridge University Press.

Deuflhard, P. (2004): *Newton Methods for Nonlinear Problems*, number 35 in Springer Series in Computational Mathematics, Springer-Verlag Berlin Heidelberg.

Monge, P. R. and N. S. Contractor (2003): *Theories of Communication Networks*, Oxford University Press.

Myers, R. H., D. C. Montgomery, and G. G. Vining (2002): *Generalized Linear Models*, Wiley Series In Probability And Statistics, John Wiley & Sons, Inc., New York.

Robins, G., T. A. Snijders, W. P., M. Handcock, and P. & Pattison (2007): "Recent developments in exponential random graph (p*) models for social networks," *Social Networks*, 29, pp. 192–215.

Snijders, T. A. (2005): "Models and methods in social network analysis," in: J. S. P. Carrington and S. Wasserman (eds.), *Models for Longitudinal Network Data*, Cambridge University Press, New York.

Snijders, T. A., P. E. Pattison, G. L. Robins, and M. S. Handcock (2006): "New specifications for exponential random graph models," *Sociological Methodology*, pp. 99–153.

Snijders, T. A. B. (2001): "The Statistical Evaluation of Social Network Dynamics," *Sociological Methodology*, 31, pp. 361–395.

Stadtfeld, C. and A. Geyer-Schulz (2010): "Analysing Event Stream Dynamics in Two Mode Networks: An Exploratory Analysis of Private Communication in a Question and Answer Community," *working paper*.

Waldmann, K.-H. and U. Stocker (2004): *Stochastische Modelle: Eine anwendungsorientierte Einführung*, Springer, Berlin.

Wang, P., K. Sharpe, G. L. Robins, and P. E. Pattison (2009): "Exponential Random Graph (p*) Models for Affiliation Networks," *Social Networks*, 31, pp. 12–25.

Wasserman, S. and P. Pattison (1996): "Logit Models and Logistic Regressions for Social Networks: I. An Introduction to Markov Graphs and p*," *Psychometrika*, 61(3), pp. 401–425.

Zenk, L. and C. Stadtfeld (2010): "Dynamic organizations. How to Measure Evolution and Change in Organizations by Analyzing Email Communication," in: *Proceedings of Applications of Social Network Analysis (ASNA), to appear*.

Part II

Design of Market Mechanisms and Systems

A Bonus Mechanism to Stimulate Reciprocity in the Presence of Manipulated Feedback

Jing Zhi Yue[1], Klemens Böhm[1], and Karl-Martin Ehrhart[3]

[1] Institute of Program Structures and Data Organization, KIT
  {jing.yue, klemens.boehm}@kit.edu
[2] Institute of Economic Theory and Statistics, KIT
  ehrhart@kit.edu

Summary. Many online service-oriented interactions rely on reputation systems to facilitate trust and trustworthiness in anonymous transactions. However in the absence of independent verification authorities, *feedback* on interaction outcome could be manipulated. In this work, we constructs a model, which 1) extends symmetric games like prisoner's dilemma by allowing players to elicit feedback; 2) rewards participants having high reputation with *bonus* points. The better reputation a player has, compared to other players, the more bonuses he could gain. In another word, participants have incentives to win higher reputation than others and thus reputation itself turns to be a kind of competitive goods.

Our focus is to investigate what kind of impact has bonus mechanism on participants' cooperation and feedback behavior. In this work we will analyze this game model to find out, under which condition could such a bonus mechanism incentivize cooperation and truthful feedback.

1 Introduction

With the proliferation of a broad range of services on the web like auction platform (eBay, Amazon) or file-sharing (Freenet, Gnutella) or scientific distributed computing (Seti@home, Folding@home), virtual social networks have attracted a lot of attention. Since in many online service-oriented interactions, there are no explicit payments or contracts for the shared service, a widely adopted method is reputation mechanism (Bolton et al., 2007). Much existing literature has confirmed that the publicly available reputation information is an incentive for participants to cooperate, even with unknown interaction partners (D.Engelmann and U.Fischbacher, 2002; Nowak and Sigmund, 1998; I.Seinen and A.Schram, 2006). However the premise of an efficient reputation mechanism is that the reports about participants' behavior in the history are truthful (Jurca and Faltings, 2004).

However in most online communities this premise could not be hold, because in the absence of independent verification authorities the true outcome of an interaction can not be revealed. players' behavior is reported by their co-players. It is difficult to distinguish whether a player is really uncooperative or he is defamed by his co-player. A reputation system could be distorted by strategic reports. To describe this phenomena, in this work we will extend symmetric games like prisoner's dilemma by allowing players to elicit *feedback*, which reports the interaction outcomes. In such surrounding strategic participants could manipulate their submitted feedback.

Furthermore in Internet markets, market competition creates incentives that arguably may enhance or curb the effectiveness of reputation systems. (Bolton et al., 2007) have investigated how different forms of market competition and social reputation networks interact in a series of laboratory online markets. The argument is that information about reputation trumps pricing in the sense that traders usually do not interact with someone with a bad reputation, not even for a substantial price discount.

Based on this observation we argue that reputation has not only indirect influence on pricing, but reputation itself is a kind of competitive goods. High reputation yields a high payoff. For example, on a web portal for hotel reservation, the hotels which have higher reputation, could have better ranking positions and thus attract more tourists. We propose that participants having high reputation will be rewarded by *bonus* points. The better reputation a player has, compared to other players, the more bonuses he could gain. In another word, participants have incentives to win higher reputation than others. Our focus is to investigate what kind of impact has bonus mechanism on participants' cooperation and feedback behavior.

Following we will introduce our model, which enables participants to elicit feedback and participants gain bonus points dependent on their own reputations and the distribution of global reputation. Based on this model, we construct two games and draw analysis, under which condition could such a bonus mechanism yield in equilibrium cooperation and truthful feedback. These two games differ from each other in the available information, one offers no reputation information and the other offers *first-order* information.

2 The Model

At the beginning of a round all M players will be randomly matched into pairs. Two players in a pair have equal roles and make decision simultaneously. In the first stage (*service stage*), players decide whether they want to provide service for the opponent, to cooperate (C) or to defect (D). It costs a player c points for the cooperation, while his opponent gains b ($b > c > 0$) points as profit; otherwise there is no payoff for both. In the second stage (*feedback stage*), players submit feedback on each other to report the opponents' action. Such *feedback* in our setting is either positive (1) or negative (0).

Furthermore players gain *bonus* points from the system as reward. We compute a player's bonus according to his reputation, which is dependent on the feedback submitted in the current round. Player i receives feedback $F_i^n \in \{0, 1\}$ at round n

from his opponent. Hence his reputation at this round is $R_i^n = F_i^n$. The sum of all players' reputations in the n-th round is $R_{total}^n = \sum_{i \in M} R_i^n$. At the end of round n, Player i gains following bonus from the system:

$$Bonus_i^n = \begin{cases} g * \frac{R_i^n}{R_{total}^n} & if\, R_{total}^n > 0 \\ 0 & if\, R_{total}^n = 0 \end{cases} \qquad (1)$$

Parameter g decides the value of assigned bonus. Equation 1 reflects two basic principles for assigning bonus. First, the better reputation has a player, the more bonuses he could gain. Second, the more outstanding is a player's reputation compared to those of other players, the more bonuses he could gain.

Since a negative feedback is a dominant strategy in the subgame of the feedback stage, a rational player is expected to choose this action in the second stage. By taking this prediction into account, a payoff maximizing player decides on playing D on the first stage. Thus there exists a unique symmetric subgame perfect equilibrium (D, 0), which is given by the strategy:" Choose D on the service stage, followed by 0 on the feedback stage, independently of the other player's decision on the first stage."

Based on this analysis we see that players prefer to defect under the belief that the opponent always submits negative feedback. However in the following we want to analyze whether players could be incentivized to cooperate if players change this belief through coordination.

The amount of information available is decisive for players' strategies. Based on this model we analyze games with two information conditions – *no information* and *first-order* information. For *no information* players know nothing about his opponents' behavior in the history. Thus their decision of cooperation or feedback depends only on the action profile of himself and of his opponent in the current round. For *first-order information*, the players know what kind of feedback their opponents submitted and received in the last round.

3 The Game Without Reputation Information

At the decision, whether a player should cooperate in the service stage, he has not only to estimate whether his opponent cooperates but also has to estimate what kind of bonus he could gain. Since there is no reputation information available and it is not possible to observe players' behavior in the history, the estimated feedback outcome is only dependent on the action profile from the service stage. For Player i, we denote his expected bonus as $E_i[Bonus_i|(A_i, A_j)]$. Here (A_i, A_j) stands for the action profile of Player i and Player j in the service stage, $(A_i, A_j) \in \{(C,C), (C,D), (D,C), (D,D)\}$. Furthermore, in a two-player game after each round, it is valid that:

$$Bonus_i = \begin{cases} g & F_i = 1, F_j = 0 \\ \frac{1}{2}g & F_i = F_j = 1 \\ 0 & F_i = 0 \end{cases} \qquad (2)$$

Hence $E_i[Bonus_i|(A_i, A_j)] \in \{0, \frac{1}{2}g, g\}$. The payoff matrix of the game without reputation information could be illustrated in Figure 1.

	C	D
C	$b - c + E_i[Bonus_i|(C,C)],$ $b - c + E_j[Bonus_j|(C,C)]$	$-c + E_i[Bonus_i|(C,D)],$ $b + E_j[Bonus_j|(C,D)]$
D	$b + E_i[Bonus_i|(D,C)],$ $-c + E_j[Bonus_j|(D,C)]$	$E_i[Bonus_i|(D,D)],$ $E_j[Bonus_j|(D,D)]$

Figure 1: Outcome of Game without Reputation Information

Observation 1 *Incentives for (C, C)*

For Player i, if following condition is fulfilled, defecting is strictly dominated by cooperation:

$$\begin{cases} b - c + E_i[Bonus_i|(C,C)] > b + E_i[Bonus_i|(D,C)] \\ -c + E_i[Bonus_i|(C,D)] > E_i[Bonus_i|(D,D)] \end{cases} \qquad (3)$$

In the similar way we know for Player j, if following condition is fulfilled, he always prefers to cooperate rather to defect:

$$\begin{cases} b - c + E_j[Bonus_j|(C,C)] > b + E_j[Bonus_j|(C,D)] \\ -c + E_j[Bonus_j|(D,C)] > E_j[Bonus_j|(D,D)] \end{cases} \qquad (4)$$

Now we can draw the condition, when (C, C) could be one of the dominant strategy combinations. It is:

$$\begin{cases} E_i[Bonus_i|(C,C)] - E_i[Bonus_i|(D,C)] > c \\ E_j[Bonus_j|(C,C)] - E_j[Bonus_j|(C,D)] > c \end{cases} \qquad (5)$$

If following condition is fulfilled, then (C, C) is a unique dominant strategy combination:

$$\begin{cases} E_i[Bonus_i|(C,C)] - E_i[Bonus_i|(D,C)] > c \\ E_i[Bonus_i|(C,D)] - E_i[Bonus_i|(D,D)] > c \\ E_j[Bonus_j|(C,C)] - E_j[Bonus_j|(C,D)] > c \\ E_j[Bonus_j|(D,C)] - E_j[Bonus_j|(D,D)] > c \end{cases} \qquad (6)$$

Symmetric Believes on the Feedback Strategies

In this section, players of a single homogeneous population are involved anony-
mously and symmetrically. A two-player game is "symmetric" if each player has
the same set of actions and each player's evaluation of an outcome depends only on
his action and that of his opponent, not on whether he is Player i or Player j. Player
i has the same expectation on the outcome (A_i, A_j), in which Player i's action is A_i
and his opponent Player j's action is A_j, as Player j expects on the outcome (A_j, A_i),
in which Player j's action is A_i and his opponent's action is A_j. In addition, in this
section we assume that two players have the same belief on the feedback strategy.

Observation 2 *Incentives for (C, C) in a symmetric game with the same belief on feedback
strategy*

Since both players have the same belief on the outcome of feedback stage, which
is only dependent on the action outcome of the first stage, it is valid that:
$E_i[Bonus_i|(C,C)] = E_j[Bonus_j|(C,C)]$ and $E_i[Bonus_i|(D,C)] = E_j[Bonus_j|(C,D)]$.
Further constraints on expected bonus are: $0 \leq E_i[Bonus_i|(A_i, A_j)] + E_j[Bonus_j|(A_i, A_j)] \leq$
g and $E_i[Bonus_i|(A_i, A_j)] \in \{0, \frac{1}{2}g, g\}$. Back to Equation 5 we get the only possible
combination is:

$E_i[Bonus_i|(C,C)] = E_j[Bonus_j|(C,C)] = \frac{1}{2}g$ and
$E_i[Bonus_i|(D,C)] = E_j[Bonus_j|(C,D)] = 0$ and $g > 2c$.

Lemma 1. *Under the condition $g > 2c$, (C, C) is dominant in the first stage if through
coordination, players from a single homogeneous population could agree with following
perception on feedback strategies: both submit positive feedback if both cooperated and they
submit definitely negative feedback if his opponent defected and he himself cooperated.*

Proof. From Observation 1 we know the condition for (C, C) as dominant ac-
tion profile in the first stage is $E_i[Bonus_i|(C,C)] = E_j[Bonus_j|(C,C)] = \frac{1}{2}g$ and
$E_i[Bonus_i|(D,C)] = E_j[Bonus_j|(C,D)] = 0$. Thus we gain constraints on the possible submitted feedback, which leads to (C, C) as dominant action profile. Figure
2 shows the feedback submitted by Player i under different action profiles in the
service stage.

	CC	DC	CD	DD
$i \rightarrow j$	1	0	0	0
	1	0	0	1
	1	1	0	0
	1	1	0	1

Figure 2: Possible Feedback Strategies leading to (C, C) as dominant action profile in the
first stage

The intuition behind above feedback strategies is: if both cooperated, both submit
positive feedback; if the player himself cooperated but his opponent defected, the

opponent receives then negative feedback. The resulted Nash Equilibria of above feedback strategies is either $[(C,C)]$ or $[(C,C),(D,D)]$. Since the payoff for both players under (D,D) is surely smaller than the payoff under (C,C), we could assume that after coordination both players will agree to cooperate in the service stage.

4 The Game with First-Order Information

Now we consider the game with *first-order* information, where players know what kind of feedback their opponents submitted and received in the last round. Intuitively speaking, a player cooperates in the service stage in the hope that his opponent also cooperates and he could gain positive feedback for a higher bonus. But a player prefers to submit negative feedback to the opponent, so that his own reputation could be more outstanding compared to those of others. Thus defaming co-players by submitting negative feedback should be penalized.

Strategy Space

We assume that all players use uniformly the same *Service Trigger (ST)* strategy for the service stage. A player cooperates if his opponent didn't receive or submit any negative feedback in the last round; otherwise he defects. This trigger strategy penalizes not only the player who received negative feedback strictly, but also the players who submitted negative feedback. Under this strict punishment players may tend to avoid negative feedback by submitting untruthful positive feedback.

Therefore in this work we analyze the effect, in which three feedback strategies interact with each other: honest players tell always truth, unconditioned positive players submit always positive feedback and unconditioned negative players submit always negative feedback. We notate these three feedback strategies as *Truth, AllP* and *AllN*. We consider a large, well-mixed population. Among all M players, the number of players of these three feedback strategies (*Truth, AllP, AllN*) are given by r, s and t with $r + s + t = M$.

4.1 Cooperate or Defect

According to the ST strategy, a player cooperates only if the opponent is qualified in the way that he didn't receive or submit negative feedback in the last round. We suppose at round n, there are ω_n percent of the players who are qualitfied to win cooperation, whereby $0 \leq \omega_n \leq 1$.

Observation 3 *Sum of all players' reputations*

If all players follow the prescribed service strategy, it means they cooperate with probability of ω_n at round n. Any player who meets a AllP player, gets always positive feedback, while he always receives negative feedback if he meets a AllN player. Any player who meets a truth telling player, receives positive feedback if he cooperated.

Thus the sum of reputation of all players is $R_{total}^n = r(\frac{r-1}{M} * w_n + \frac{s}{M} * 1) + s(\frac{r}{M} * w_n + \frac{s-1}{M} * 1) + \frac{t}{M}(\frac{r}{M} * w_n + \frac{s}{M} * 1) = \frac{M-1}{M} * (rw_n + s)$.

Assumption 1 *In a stable system, the probability that a player is qualified to win cooperation stays unchanged.*

Observation 4 *Probability of qualified players $w = w_{n-1} = w_n$ in a stable system*

At the beginning of the game each player is qualified to win cooperation, so $w_0 = 1$. A player is qualified for winning cooperation in the next round, if he receives and submits positive feedback at the current round. He receives positive feedback if he cooperates with a qualified opponent according to the prescribed service strategy and his opponent tells truth or if he meets with a AllP player: $Prob_{rec}^n = \frac{s}{M} + \frac{r}{M} * w_{n-1}$. With the same probability he submits positive feedback: $Prob_{sub}^n = Prob_{rec}^n$. So the probability that a player is qualified for winning cooperation is $w_n = Prob_{rec}^n * Prob_{sub}^n = (\frac{s}{M} + \frac{r}{M} * w_{n-1})^2$. According to Assumption 1 ($w_n = w_{n-1}$) and under the constraint $0 \leq w \leq 1$, we get: if $r > 0$, $w = \frac{M^2 - 2rs - M * \sqrt{M^2 - 4rs}}{2r^2}$ or if $r = 0$, $w = (\frac{s}{M})^2$, the probability that a player is qualified to win cooperation stays unchanged.

Lemma 2. *A rational player prefers to cooperate, if all other players follow ST strategy and following condition is fulfilled: if $r > 0$,*
$$g > (M - 1)(\frac{M^2 - M * \sqrt{M^2 - 4rs}}{2r^2})(c - b\delta\frac{M - \sqrt{M^2 - 4rs}}{2M}).$$

Proof. We assume that each player believes that all other players follow the subscribed service strategy. Now we want to discuss under which condition a player prefers to cooperate.

If a player cooperates, it costs him c points and he could gain positive feedback with the probability of $1 - \frac{t}{M}$. According to Observation 3 his expected bonus for this round is $g * \frac{1 - \frac{t}{M}}{\frac{M-1}{M} * (rw + s)}$. He could be free from punishment by his next opponent only if he receives and submits positive feedback in the current round. In an infinitely repeated game with discount factor δ, his expected punishment in the next round is $b\delta[1 - (w * \frac{r}{M} + \frac{s}{M}) * (1 - \frac{t}{M})]$. His expected utility by cooperating is therefore:

$$U_c = -c + g * \frac{1 - \frac{t}{M}}{\frac{M-1}{M} * (rw + s)} - b\delta[1 - (w * \frac{r}{M} + \frac{s}{M}) * (1 - \frac{t}{M})] \qquad (7)$$

If a player defects, he could save the cooperation cost but he could gain positive feedback only when he meets a AllP player. His expected utility by defecting is:

$$U_d = g * \frac{\frac{s}{M}}{\frac{M-1}{M} * (rw + s)} - b\delta[1 - \frac{s}{M} * (w * \frac{r}{M} + \frac{s}{M})] \qquad (8)$$

If $U_c > U_d$, a player prefers to cooperate. So we gain following condition: if $r > 0$,

$$g > \frac{(M-1)(r\omega + s)}{r}[c - b\delta\frac{r(r\omega + s)}{M^2}], \tag{9}$$

whereby $\omega = \frac{M^2 - 2rs - M*\sqrt{M^2 - 4rs}}{2r^2}$.

For long-run players, they have incentives to keep above condition fulfilled so that there are still players, who are willing to cooperate. We see the relationship between bonus parameter g and the number of *Truth* and *AllP* players decides whether rational players prefer to cooperate.

4.2 Dynamic among Feedback Strategies

We consider the effects of three feedback strategies. With U_{Truth}, U_{AllP} and U_{AllN} we denote the expected utility by using these three strategies. Strategy with high utility dominates.

Under the premise that all players follow the *ST* strategy, we could analyze when is a feedback strategy more successful than another. For a truth telling player if he meets another truth telling player, he could gain positive feedback if he cooperates. And he could be free from punishment if both truth telling players cooperate. If this truthful telling player meets a AllP player, he gains certainly positive feedback. He will not be punished if his opponent cooperates and thus he submits positive feedback. However if he meets a AllN player, he could never get positive feedback and he will be surely punished in the next round. Therefore for a truth telling player, his expected utility is:

$$U_{Truth} = \frac{r-1}{M}[g * \frac{\omega}{R_{total}} - b\delta(1 - \omega^2)] + \frac{s}{M}[g * \frac{1}{R_{total}} - b\delta(1 - \omega)] - b\delta\frac{t}{M} \tag{10}$$

Two AllP players meet each other and both get certainly positive feedback and will never be punished. But if he meets a truth telling player, he gets positive feedback only when he cooperates. Similarly he gets also only negative feedback and will be punished by his next opponent if he meets a AllN player. His utility under AllP strategy is:

$$U_{AllP} = \frac{r}{M}[g * \frac{\omega}{R_{total}} - b\delta(1 - \omega)] + \frac{s-1}{M} * g * \frac{1}{R_{total}} - b\delta\frac{t}{M} \tag{11}$$

A AllN player could never escape from punishment. In the similar way we could gain the utility of AllN strategy:

$$U_{AllN} = \frac{r}{M}(g * \frac{\omega}{R_{total}} - b\delta) + \frac{s}{M} * (g * \frac{1}{R_{total}} - b\delta) - b\delta\frac{t-1}{M} \tag{12}$$

By comparing the resulted utility of different feedback strategies, we could see which strategy is more successful. From Lemma 2 we know rational players have incentives to keep opponents to cooperate. For a given bonus parameter g, the number of *Truth* and *AllP* players decide, whether cooperation and truth feedback yield equilibrium. If condition $r > 0$, $g > (M-1)(\frac{M^2 - M*\sqrt{M^2 - 4rs}}{2r^2})(c - b\delta\frac{M-\sqrt{M^2-4rs}}{2M})$, $U_{Truth} > U_{AllP}$ and $U_{Truth} > U_{AllN}$ is fulfilled, rational players will choose to cooperate and to submit truthful feedback.

5 Conclusion

In this work we have constructed a model, which 1) extends symmetric games like prisoner's dilemma by allowing players to elicit feedback; 2) rewards participants having high reputation with *bonus* points. The better reputation a player has, compared to other players, the more bonuses he could gain. In a game without reputation information, a player estimates his received feedback based on the interaction outcome in the service stage, i.e., whether the player himself and his opponent cooperated. According to the analysis in section 3, we know if players play pure strategies, the relationship between bonus parameter g and payoff parameter b and c decides whether cooperation and truth feedback is dominant action combination.

In a game, where *first-order* information is available, we suppose players penalize not only the players received negative feedback strictly, but also the players submitted negative feedback. In addition, we analyze how three possible feedback strategies (telling truth, always positive feedback and always negative feedback) interact with each other. For a given bonus parameter g, we have observed that the number of *Truth* players and *AllP* players decide the outcome of the game. In a stable system, where the number of players who are qualified to win cooperation stays unchanged, players are motivated to keep the number of *Truth* players to fulfill certain threshold so that there are still incentives for players to cooperate.

References

Bolton, G. E., C. Loebbecke, and A. Ockenfels (2007): "How Social Reputation Networks Interact with Competition in Anonymous Online Trading: An Experimental Study," Working Paper Series in Economics 32, University of Cologne, Department of Economics, http://ideas.repec.org/p/kls/series/0032.html.

D.Engelmann and U.Fischbacher (2002): "Indirect Reciprocity and Strategic Reputation Building in an Experimental Helping Game." Technical report 132, Zuerich IEER.

I.Seinen and A.Schram (2006): "Social Status and Group Norms: Indirect Reciprocity in a Repeated Helping Experiment," *European Economic Review*, 50(3).

Jurca, R. and B. Faltings (2004): "Truthful Reputation Information in Electronic Markets without Independent Verification," .

Nowak, M. and K. Sigmund (1998): "Evolution of Indirect Reciprocity by Image Scroing," *European Economic Review*, 393.

Requirements for Formalizing Usage Policies of Web Services

Sebastian Speiser[1], Rudi Studer[1], and Thomas Dreier[2]

[1] Karlsruhe Service Research Institute, KIT
   {speiser, rudi.studer}@kit.edu
[2] Institute of Information and Economic Law, KIT
   dreier@kit.edu

Summary. The availability of functionality and information as Web services fosters the dynamic cooperation of heterogeneous providers in form of service compositions. The standardized interfaces of Web services enable unlimited options to combine services on a technical level. In contrast there is also a business and economical view that may constrain these possibilities. Service and data providers can restrict allowed usages of their resources and link it to obligations, e.g. only non-commercial usage is allowed and requires an attribution of the provider. Such terms and conditions are currently typically available in natural language which makes verifying, if a composition is compliant with the policies of the used services, a tedious task. In order to make it easier for users to adhere to these usage policies, we propose to formalize them. This enables policy-aware tools that can (semi-)automatically check compliance of service compositions. In this paper we analyze the requirements for such a formalization, both from technical view as well as driven by the actual usage restrictions of existing Web services. We propose design decisions for a formal model and show how they fulfill the postulated requirements. Furthermore we outline legal aspects of a system relying on formal usage policies.

1 Introduction

Modern information and communications technology (ICT) enables low-effort integration of services from different providers. This facilitates the dynamic formation of service value networks (SVN), which are compositions of services created in order to fulfill customer needs (Blau et al., 2009b). SVNs are not restricted to use only services from a closed repository, but can foster service offers in open markets, that pose low entry barriers for service providers due to the use of standardized Web service interfaces. Due to changing customer needs and the steady (dis-)appearance of providers and offered services, SVNs are continuously formed and transformed. This can be automated, e.g. by an electronic auction market (Blau et al., 2009a) or decentralized formation algorithms (Speiser et al., 2008). Such automation mechanisms rely on formal descriptions of Web services. There exist several approaches that describe the functionality of services as well as their quality attributes, e.g.

WSMO (Roman et al., 2005) or OWL-S (W3C, 2004a). These approaches however do not cover usage restrictions, which are relevant as not all services and their output data can be freely used for every purpose. For example take a photo community that provides pictures over a Web service interface. The service has the usage policy that a payment of 1 Euro per call has to be paid and that the picture is displayed with an attribution. This is illustrated in Figure 1. Formalized usage policies can be used by a tool to automatically inform the Web service user which requirements his application has to fulfill in order to be compliant with the usage policy of the Web service.

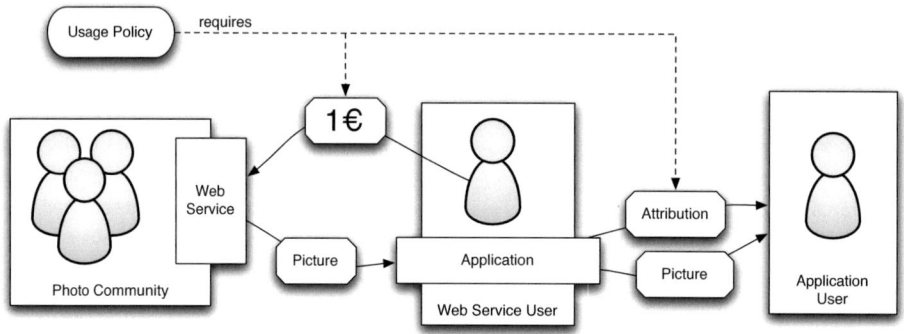

Figure 1: Example for an application adhering to a usage policy

The rest of this paper is structured as follows. In Section 2 we define the scope for Web services and usage restrictions that are treated in this paper and motivate why formalized usage policies are beneficial for Web service applications. Section 3 analyzes the requirements for a corresponding policy language. The analysis treats two different perspectives. First, we analyze which technical properties are required to support usage policies that are compatible to Web service design principles and can be used effectively for service composition. Secondly, we define requirements for the expressivity of the usage policy language, driven by the analysis of the content of actual natural language terms and conditions of existing Web services. We present a number of design decisions for the policy formalism in Section 4 and explain how they support the postulated requirements. In Section 5 we outline legal aspects that are relevant for a system based on formalized usage restrictions. Finally we discuss related work in Section 6 and conclude in Section 7.

2 Web Services and Usage Restrictions

Web services are broadly used for different tasks such as giving programmatic access to Web applications, providing standardized interfaces for information sources, or enabling the creation of lightweight mashup applications. Furthermore Web services are the most commonly used technology to implement service-oriented architectures

(SOA). Correspondingly there exist numerous definitions of Web services, that cover a wide range of aspects. We do not rely on a narrow definition of Web services, that dictates the adherence to specific standards (e.g. WSDL and SOAP). Instead we accept that depending on the used architecture or application environment, different technologies can be appropriate. We consider as Web services all components that fulfill the following requirements:

- **Self-contained:** the functionality of the Web service is independent of other services and can be used in different applications and processes.
- **Interoperable:** no or minimal integration effort is needed to access the service. This is realized by communicating over an interface adhering to a standard Web protocol (e.g. HTTP) and exchanging data represented in a (quasi-)standard format (e.g. XML, JSON).
- **Self-described:** the Web service provides a description of its interface that enables the correct invocation of the service by a client that fulfills the same interoperability requirements.
- **Loosely coupled:** for the Web service, the only relevant property of a system using it, is that it adheres to the published interface of the service.

This rather broad classification abstracts from technical details and includes, depending on the used environment, also technologies like linked data or HTML forms. For more detailed information on these requirements and more aspects, that are not relevant in our context, we refer the reader to Erl (2007).

Descriptions of Web services are not only helpful for the invocation but also for the selection of services. Users select services based on the net value they expect from the service consumption (Ng, 2007, p. 23ff). The net value is given by subtracting the costs from the experienced gross value. Both can only be determined after consumption, as the actual service is only co-created at the time of consumption. Therefore users have to rely on value estimations that are based on experience or service descriptions.

Description of services that can be used for service selection have to be more extensive than in the above definition of the requirement "self-described". The most obvious parts of a description influencing service selection are about the functionality of the service and its price. However costs of a service have not to be restricted to payments and value gained from the functionality can be influenced by the non-functional properties (NFPs) of the service. NFPs cover a wide range of issues, such as quality of service (QoS), limited liabilities, usage restrictions of the service or its output data, privacy terms or obligations, e.g. to attribute the provider of a used service in the corresponding application.

Service selection can be split into two operations: discovery and ranking. Discovery filters from a set of services (e.g. retrieved from a repository or by crawling the Internet) those that match the user's request (Sycara et al., 2003). Ranking sorts this list according to preferences given by the user, see e.g. Lamparter (2007). Furthermore several services can be combined to form a service composition with combined functionality and properties that can be determined from the service descriptions. Another desired operation is to check if the use of a service in a composition is compliant with the restrictions and conditions stated in its NFP descriptions. Validating a composition means checking if all service uses are compliant and the desired functionality is achieved.

Performing these operations manually can be a cumbersome and time-consuming task. This is in contrast to the principles of dynamic service selection and frequent transformation of applications, business processes and service compositions, that are propagated by popular Web service scenarios, such as SOA or mashups. Formalized service descriptions help to perform discovery, ranking, composition and validation (semi-)automatically. Current approaches to formal service descriptions mainly concentrate on functionality and quality of service. These aspects are often sufficient for service users to build running systems and therefore other properties such as usage restrictions and obligations are easily ignored. We call these properties usage terms and define them as follows:

*The **usage terms** of a Web service restrict the invocation of the service and the utilization of its output data based on the usage context, including purpose, time, location, identity of the user, as well as structure and non-functional properties of the composition in which the service or its output data is used. Furthermore the usage terms can optionally link obligations, including attributions and payments, to the service or data usage.*

In this paper we analyze the requirements for usage policies, i.e. the formalization of usage terms, that can be used to consider them for (semi-)automatic discovery, ranking, composition and validation. Our main goals are:

- Make it easier to adhere to usage terms than to break them. Tools can help the user to build and check for compliance. However we do not want to enforce usage policies technically, e.g. by using digital rights management (DRM). Such approaches are based on cryptography and work only in trusted computing environments. This contrasts our notion of open markets, where everybody can participate. Furthermore DRM only allows predefined actions, which hinders new and innovative data and service usages.

- Support providers to make their services and data broadly available in open markets, without giving up their rights and commercial interests. This has both advantages for users, who can access more services and for providers, who reach a larger customer base.

Currently usage terms are defined in natural language documents, depending on the relation between provider and user. This ranges from individually negotiated contracts to terms and conditions published on the provider's homepage. We are especially interested in the latter case, where a provider offers his service under certain conditions and the user can decide whether to accept or not. The reason for this decision is that individual contracts are negotiated in a way that the desired usage scenario is compliant to the contracts.

3 Requirements for Formalizing Usage Policies

Web services are typically not directly invoked by end users but as part of applications. These applications provide the context in which the service and its output data is used. The context can be of different types from simple user interface wrappers, over dynamic Web pages and service compositions to business processes. The context however is not only defined by the technical description of the application but also includes aspects such as the purpose of the service invocation and the intended usage context of the application. As an example for the last statement, consider a Web service which provides confidential data that is displayed by a dynamic Web page. This usage is only compliant, if the access to the Web page is restricted in the same way as for the service.

The usage context regards the usage of a service and its output data as an isolated event. Usage terms however can also regulate repeated service usages, e.g. impose a limit on the number of service invocations per day, or obligate the user to pay a price based on the total number of service usages. Repeated usage situations describe multiple occurrences of usages, which can be of different types (e.g. commercial or academic usage), as well as other actions, such as payments, that are not directly linked to the application, respectively usage context in which a service or its output data is used. We therefore split a usage policy in two parts:

- Usage context policy: a function mapping the set of all possible usage contexts to a hierarchical set of usage types, e.g. compliant usage and non-compliant usage. Compliant usage could have a possible subtype "compliant non-commercial usage" of a specific service.
- Repeated usage situation policy: a function mapping the set of all repeated usage situations, that can refer to the usage types as defined by the usage context policy, to either compliant or non-compliant.

In order to support formalization we need models for usage contexts and repeated service usages, as well as languages for specifying restrictions that form the policies. Additionally we need algorithms that can process the models and languages. In the following we present requirements that have to be fulfilled by the models, languages, policies and algorithms in order to enable usage policy aware applications.

3.1 Technical Requirements

In this section we concentrate on aspects that are independent of the contents of concrete usage policies but are required in order to build applications that support both Web service consumers and providers to be policy compliant, respectively specify policies.

Requirement 1: Interoperability

We defined above that interoperability is a required criterion for Web services, which can be directly transferred as an requirement for usage policies of services. Web services are used in heterogeneous environments across technological boundaries. We therefore require that policies are accessible over standard Web protocols (e.g. HTTP) and can be serialized in a widely understood format (e.g. XML, JSON, RDF). In order to avoid ambiguities, we require that the terms of the policies are uniquely named by using URIs. Furthermore it is desirable that the meaning of usage situation descriptions and policies are not dependent on a reference implementation of used algorithms or the human interpretation of a textual specification. This has to be achieved by basing models and policy languages on a formal logic with well-defined semantics.

Requirement 2: Loose Coupling

The purpose of usage policies is to restrict the situations and applications in which a service can be employed. This means that providers deliberately constrain the reusability requirement of Web services. By referring to the usage context of a service, however also the loose coupling property is violated as a form of collateral damage. While this cannot be completely avoided, it is essential to keep the violation at a minimum. This means that the usage model underlying the policies should be general and abstract enough to support the wide range of possible technical environments in which services could be used, e.g. BPEL processes, dynamic Web pages or lightweight mashups.

Requirement 3: Computational Efficiency

We cannot make the used formalism arbitrarily powerful, as we have to keep it decidable, so that automated reasoning about compliant usages and policy properties is possible. Furthermore, operations such as searching for a service with given policy properties, can involve the evaluation of a large number of policies. Thus we require that reasoning complexity for the policy formalism should be kept at a level, which allows the efficient evaluation of realistic policies.

Supporting this point, we require that it is possible to directly specify properties of usage situations, that cannot or only very costly be determined from the formal model. An example for this includes determining whether a service is called for academic purposes, which cannot be inferred from a technical description of an application, but can be specified very easily by a human user.

Requirement 4: Usability for Web Service Consumer

Above we described a usage policy as a function that classifies a usage situation as either compliant or non-compliant. This is not sufficient for service consumers, who do not only want to know that their current application is non-compliant, but also why this is the case (e.g. missing payment) and how they can fix this (e.g. add a payment of 1 Euro). Thus we require our algorithms to include a justification mechanism for their decisions. In principal, justifications can be embedded with little effort in reasoning algorithms for many logics by saving a history of logical conclusions. However such bare-metal justifications are not easily understandable for service consumers that cannot be expected to be logic specialists. Therefore it is essential that justifications are given in a format that users can utilize.

Requirement 5: Usability for Web Service Provider

Not only the service consumers but also the service providers and policy specifiers will be mostly non-logicians. Therefore it is important that providers are not required to specify their policies directly as logic formulas. Instead they should be able to reuse building blocks which they can configure for their specific offer.

3.2 Content Requirements

In this section we list a number of requirements that are motivated by the contents of actual usage restrictions. Many different terms can be covered by the first content requirement *extendability*, but it is followed by others that have to be structurally present in the policy formalism.

Requirement 6: Extendability

Specifications of policies should be able to extend the used vocabulary, terms and attributes. This is required because it cannot be assumed that a standard model can be built that covers all desired aspects of all service providers on the Web. This should include possibilities to define new attributes of operations, e.g. a restriction about the minimal or maximal size which has to be used to display output data of a service, this is required by YouTube[1], respectively Google Maps[2]. Another example is the inclusion of flexible authentication requirements. While for company internal services it may be possible to use a centralized, identity-based system, it may be more appropriate for a service provided between independent partners to rely on a credential-based authentication scheme (see e.g. Agarwal and Sprick (2005)).

   In the following we will discuss requirements that cannot be covered by introducing new operations and attributes.

Requirement 7: Restrictions on other Policies

Providers can also impose constraints on the policies of applications using their services or data. This is mostly done to prevent third parties from making a profit of cheap or free offers. Examples include the share-alike clause of Creative Commons[3], and the restriction of Google Maps that forbids that applications using this service are only made available for paying users. This can be interpreted as a

---

[1] http://code.google.com/apis/youtube/terms.html

[2] http://http://code.google.com/apis/maps/terms.html

[3] http://creativecommons.org

non-commercial clause, which is also popular by Creative Commons users, even though there is no general consensus what this clause exactly means[4].

Requirement 8: Dependence on Invocation of other Services

In general Web services can be combined with other services in so-called compositions. According to the Web service characteristics *self-contained* and *interoperable* there is no restriction about which other services can be used, as long as they have compatible inputs and outputs. However it is required that usage policies can specify that certain other services must or must not be composed with their described service. Depending on the used composition model this property has to be checked in different ways. For simple dynamic Web pages the composition model can be seen as a set of services, where (non-)containment of (un)desired services has to tested. Complex processes on the other hand require that branching conditions are evaluated in order to determine if two services are always, respectively never invoked together in a process instance.

Policy examples for this requirement include:

- A Web service requires that an external authentication service is successfully called before each invocation.
- An image forbids that services with the purpose "advertisement" are used in an application displaying the image. This is another partial interpretation of a non-commercial clause.
- Amazon.com Product Advertising API[5] can only be used for applications, whose main purpose is generating sales of products and services on the Amazon site.

Requirement 9: Counting and Arithmetic Operations

This requirement concerns the language of repeated usage policies. Usage restrictions can contain quantifiers on the number of allowed invocations of services. Furthermore counts of certain usage types have to be added, multiplied with cost per call prices, compared to discount levels, etc. in order to calculate the total amount that has to be payed for service usage in a specific time period.

Examples for this requirement are:

- Usage terms of Amazon Simple Storage Service (S3)[6] that require a payment for each package of thousand service calls.
- eBay API license agreement[7] which imposes a limit on the number of calls that users are allowed to make.

---

[4] Creative Commons has commissioned a study about the understanding of commercial vs. non-commercial use. An interim report can be found at:
   http://mirrors.creativecommons.org/nc-study/NC_Use_Study_Interim_Report_20090501.pdf
[5] https://affiliate-program.amazon.com/gp/advertising/api/detail/agreement.html
[6] http://aws.amazon.com/s3/#pricing, http://aws.amazon.com/agreement/
[7] http://developer.ebay.com/join/licenses/individual/,
   http://developer.ebay.com/join/pricing/

Requirement 10: Notion of Time

The previously introduced limits on the number of service calls as well as the complex payment terms usually refer to a time period. Thus it is essential that the repeated usage policy component is able to relate the occurrence of service usages to time points and intervals.

Examples for time in usage terms are Amazon S3 that is paid monthly and eBay which specifies call frequency limitations on a daily basis.

4 Concepts for a Formal Model

In this section we describe high level design decisions for our formal model for usage policies. We base these decisions on the requirements analysis presented in Section 3.

Decision 1: RDF Model of Usage Contexts

Applications using Web services can be treated as distributed computer programs using message passing. A powerful model for such programs are process calculi. Constraints on such models can be expressed by temporal logic formulas. Agarwal (2007) employs these techniques for Web service discovery. For our purposes, we however do not need this level of detail in modeling usage contexts. The only requirement for expressiveness regarding the structure of a usage situation is *(R8) dependence on invocation of other services*. To fulfill *(R8)*, it is sufficient to have a usage model that specifies if two service invocations are either (i) always executed in combination, or (ii) can be executed in combination. Case (i) is relevant if another service is required to be always executed whenever the regulated service is called. Case (ii) can be used in a negated condition, in order to forbid other services to be used in combination with the regulated service. We propose to model actions, such as service invocations or payments as instances of corresponding classes of an RDF(S) model (W3C, 2004b). Action instances are then linked with properties representing cases (i) and (ii) above that are abstracted from the specific computing model underlying a usage situation. Such a model has the following properties:

- Actions are not modeled with a fixed schema, but can be easily extended by using standard RDF constructs, thus fulfilling *(R6) extendability*.
- Usage contexts are represented on a general and abstract level, that does not have assumptions on the technology underlying a service usage. This fulfills *(R2) loose coupling*.
- RDF(S) is a standard Web format, relying on URIs and providing formal semantics, which supports fulfillment of *(R1) interoperability*.
- The usage of RDF(S) instead of a more expressive ontology language such as OWL has the advantage that complex queries over the model have well-defined

semantics and there exist efficient algorithms for query evaluation. This supports *(R3) computational efficiency*. Queries are suitable for policy specification, as we will discuss in the next paragraph.

Decision 2: Usage Context Policies using SPARQL Queries

We propose to construct policies using SPARQL queries (W3C, 2008) on usage descriptions according to the RDF usage model. The queries can extract instances that fulfill given properties, e.g. return all usage situations that invoke a specific service. By combining several queries, we can reuse previous results to check further properties, e.g. check for each usage situation, if the service invocation is always executed in combination with a payment action. The two basic ways of combining such queries are (i) for each result of query 1, evaluate query 2, and (ii) if query 1 has a result, proceed to query 2, else proceed to query 3. Such combinations lead to directed graphs with queries as nodes and as leafs (nodes that are no queries and have no outgoing edges) we allow the creation of statements that classify instances retrieved by one of the queries as specific usage types. We will define a formal semantics for these query trees and thus fulfill *(R1) interoperability*. By checking all possible paths from the root of a query tree to its leafs, we can check (i) if a certain condition is required for compliance in all paths, or (ii) if it is impossible to reach compliance given a certain condition. These tests enable the fulfillment of *(R7) restrictions on other policies*. In such a model it is also possible to reuse parametrized queries provided by a third party in its own policies. This mechanism can be used to provide standard building blocks, thus fulfilling *(R5) usability for Web service provider*.

Decision 3: Foster User-given Query Groupings and Labels

As mentioned in *(R4) usability for Web service consumers*, we want to have decision justifications that are valuable for a service consumer. Therefore we propose to foster the groupings given by the specifier of the policy, when he splits his usage policy into several SPARQL queries, as described above. We assume that he will typically check a specific aspect in a single query, that the user can fix, if the evaluation fails. An algorithm that regards the policy as a complete logical specification, has to work with heuristics to determine which level of detail for explanations is useful for a service consumer.

Additionally the policy creator has the possibility to label SPARQL queries, using natural language strings with references to variables occurring in the current and previously evaluated queries. These labels can give a high level and easily understandable explanation, why the checked restriction was not fulfilled, and possibly a hint, how it can be fixed.

A similar approach is taken by the policy language AIR (Kagal et al., 2008), but it has currently no formal semantics, therefore violating *(R1) interoperability* and does not support *(R7) restrictions on other policies*.

Open Decision: Repeated Usage Situation Policies

Above we described, how we can split usage policies into a usage context part and a part constraining the repeated usages of services. We have defined that the interface between the two parts is a number of usage events with corresponding usage types and point in time when they occurred. These usage events can also be generated by an estimate in order to forecast the repeated usages, e.g. to know the price for a planned service usage. Currently we have not yet decided on a formalism to represent the aspects of usage policies concerning repeated usage situations. In the following we list two possible approaches that can solve the task:

- Treat the event log as a linear trace of system behavior and define the repeated usage situation policy as restrictions in temporal logics. The *(R10) notion of time* can be introduced by creating artificial events representing relevant time points.
- Treat the event log as a set of data tuples, consisting of usage type and time point. One could then filter events in a specific time frame and then use a query language for counting the tuples and performing arithmetic operations, fulfilling *(R9) counting and arithmetic operations*.

5 Legal Perspective

In this section we regard usage policies from a legal perspective, based on the laws in Germany. The purpose of this section is to point to questions that have to be considered, when formalized usage policies and policy-aware systems are used. Note that it is neither possible nor intended to answer these questions in the scope of this work. Rather we want to give an overview of laws and norms that are relevant for the following questions: (i) what is the legal foundation for usage policies?, (ii) do restrictions on the freedom of contract apply?, (iii) who is liable in case of policy violations?, and (iv) are usage policies protected by intellectual property right?

5.1 What is the legal foundation for usage policies?

Software in general is subject to the German Copyright Act (§69a UrhG) and thus the creator holds the exclusive rights to exploit the software. For software that is created within an employment, the employer is entitled to the exploitation rights according to §69b UrhG. The rights holder can grant third parties rights to exploit the software. This grant can be linked to obligations and usage restrictions. Web service consumers however do not directly use the software providing the service's functionally, but only use its interface. The code implementing the interface is also protected by copyright, but not the specification of the interface (Meyer, 2008, p. 55)(Gangadharan et al., 2008). It has therefore to be examined, if the copyright is applicable as a legal foundation for specifying usage policies.

Data that is obtained from a Web service, can be subject of copyright, if it is a creative work, e.g. a photo. For output data that is no creative work, one has to check, if it can be protected as a database, according to §§87a ff. UrhG. However it has to be reviewed, if the result of a service call is considered as a marginal part of a database, and thus not protected.

Copyright does not have to be registered by a creator, but is given automatically. This means that without an explicit grant of the creator, one is not allowed to exploit his works. Thus an usage policy in this case can be seen as an allowance of usages that would otherwise be forbidden.

Similar is the situation with data that is related to individuals and thus is subject of data protection laws (in Germany "Bundesdatenschutzgesetz"). This protection is also automatically given and usage of such data requires the consent of the concerned individual.

In case that data is not automatically protected, usage policies can be specified, that forbid things that would otherwise be allowed. The foundation for such policies depends on the data to protect. If data can be declared as a trade secret, it is protected by §17 UWG, the German law against unfair competition. Usage policies can in this case be seen as non-disclosure agreements.

Apart from legal foundations, the restriction of service and data usage can also be based on social norms. This can be the case for usage inside a company, or between private persons, e.g. a friend providing personal pictures to another friend via a Web service, and forbidding him to share the pictures or give access to the service to other people.

5.2 Do restrictions on the freedom of contract apply?

Usage policies are formalized contracts (or parts thereof) between a service provider and a service user. In general both parties are free to form the contact as they like, as long as it does not break any laws. However we can think of two sources for restrictions on the freedom of contract, that are explained in the following.

First is the German Civil Code ("bürgerliches Gesetzbuch" BGB) and its regulations on general terms and conditions. We assume that individually negotiated contracts are only established if they allow the intended usage of the service user. Thus formal usage policies are more useful in situations where they are offered to all potential customer on a take-or-leave basis. In such cases it has to be checked if the policy is considered as general terms and conditions (AGB). AGB are subject to a content check according to §307 BGB and §§308 - 309, if the service user is a consumer. The latter can be a blurry notion, if we consider the Web 2.0, where individual users also often act as providers. A similar situation is given with online auctions on eBay[8], where private persons act both as seller and buyers. There have been several judgments in Germany concerning the classification of individuals as consumers or tradesman, that could possibly be relevant in a Web service scenario.

---

[8] http://www.ebay.de

Furthermore AGB have to be presented and pointed to in an appropriate way, according to §305 BGB.

Second is §19 GWB (German Law Against Restraints on Competition), that forbids the misuse of a market dominating position. The prohibition comprises besides others arbitrary pricing and denial of service to other companies.

5.3 Who is liable in case of policy violations?

The obvious answer to this question would be the service user violating the policy. However there may be other parties involved that can make mistakes, which lead to an unintended policy violation by the user. The policy specifier for example can be different from the service provider, e.g. a third party company that provides formalized usage policies as added value services. Similarly the developer of the policy engine can have errors in his software that leads to wrong classifications. In case of mistakes by third parties that lead to policy violations, it is unclear if the user can have recourse. Policy specifiers and engine vendors are certainly interested how far they can rule out liabilities according to law and user acceptance.

5.4 Are usage policies protected by intellectual property right?

This question is important for a potential market for reusable policy clauses. A policy clause can backed by a legal text, having the advantage that it can be checked automatically and has a representation that is suitable for enforcing it through a lawsuit. The creation of such clauses can cause great effort and can only be conducted by lawyers, but can be reused in many situations by many people (cf. the Creative Commons RDF representation (Abelson et al., 2008)). If the clauses can be protected by intellectual property right, its creators can develop business models based on the licensing of rights to use the clauses. If intellectual property rights apply to a legal document does however not depend on the amount of effort that went into its creation. Rather the decision is based on the level of creativity that was required to produce the document. Legal documents have been classified as scientific documents (e.g. in the judgment of the Oberlandesgericht München on October 16th 2007, reference: 29 W 2325/07), for which other criteria of creativity apply than for literature.

6 Related Work

O'Sullivan (2006) presents in his thesis an extensive taxonomy of non-functional properties (NFPs) of services. His results are based on the analysis of classic services and Web services from numerous domains. The taxonomy deals with various categories of NFPs, such as availability, price, discounts and quality. Usage policy related concepts that allow providers e.g. to forbid commercial usage of their service are not considered. The taxonomy itself is not concerned with the specification of service policies but delivers a vocabulary for common aspects of services.

The taxonomy of O'Sullivan was modeled as WSML ontologies and used to represent NFPs in WSMO (Toma and Foxvog, 2006). Originally WSMO supported annotations like creator or title adapted from Dublin Core to describe non-functional properties of ontology elements. With the integration of the O'Sullivan NFP concepts and the extension of WSMO models to include rule-based definitions of NFPs for services, the approach is now able to describe expressive NFP offers in terms of the defined ontologies. The proposed ontologies can serve as a formal vocabulary to model restrictions in our approach.

Web service policy languages can be used to define quality guarantees and also user requirements. For example WS-Policy can specify with assertions which technologies users have to support, e.g. encryption (W3C, 2007). Assertions are defined in different WS-* standards which cover technical domains but no usage rights and restrictions. Furthermore the semantics of language constructs that combine several assertions are not clearly specified and thus can lead to ambiguities.

Formalized usage policies exist for digital objects such as e-books and music files. The RDF serialization of the Creative Commons licenses can be used for automatic determination of associated rights (Abelson et al., 2008). This is used by Google's advanced search[9], where users can specify their desired Creative Commons license and only documents that were annotated correspondingly by their owner are returned. However Creative Commons is mainly suitable for open contents, as the licenses are generally addressed to the public and do not specify rights for single users. Another point is that commercial usage can be allowed but no specific terms (e.g. price) can be expressed. Thus the Creative Commons licenses, can be regarded as a subset of our proposed usage policies. The standard building blocks of our proposed approach are inspired by Creative Commons, and we plan to enable reuse of their existing blocks.

In the area of digital rights management (DRM), there exist several rights expression languages (REL), e.g. ODRL (Iannella, 2002) and XrML (Wang et al., 2002). These are XML based languages that allow more complex right specifications than Creative Commons. In theory existing RELs would be a good basis for service usage policies, however the mentioned RELs include language elements that go far beyond rights expression. They handle encryption, media encodings, user authentication and other domain-specific aspects. These are represented as syntactically defined XML elements and a meaning has to be given in the corresponding standard specifications (e.g. ODRL). Also they are lacking formal semantics which leads to ambiguities in scenarios with heterogeneous providers.

This problem is also recognized by Jamkhedkar et al. who present a DRM architecture that separates rights expression from other aspects (Jamkhedkar and Heileman, 2009). They propose that there is a need for a core REL which is based on

---

[9] http://www.google.com/advanced_search

a logical foundation (Jamkhedkar and Heileman, 2008). We share this thought and have split the usage description model and the formalism for specifying policies. In contrast to our work, Jamdkhedkar et al. do not consider usability and thus employ a complex formalism that also prevents the specification of restrictions on other policies.

Arnab and Hutchison (2007) present LiREL which is a formal REL. They show what the difference to classical access control is and what the resulting requirements for an REL are. LiREL focuses on the expression of rights and requires an external standardized vocabulary for the definition of actions, constraints, etc. This is in contrast to our planned solution which relies on extendable ontologies and ontology mappings rather than trying to build a closed standard vocabulary that covers all domains and has to be used by all providers and users.

Gangadharan et al. (2008) developed an ODRL profile for service licenses (ODRL-S). As a service license they define regulations concerning the use of a service. This is a similar concept to our proposed usage policies, however their approach defines a static vocabulary of actions, including composition or attribution. This regulates the general usage of the service but does not incorporate context information, e.g. this means that generally composition can be forbidden but there is no way to specify that composition is allowed with specific other services or providers. Also the policy does not refer to the output data of services. The lack of clear semantics is inherited from ODRL. The interpretation of licenses relies on information such as: composition is a special case of derivation. This hierarchy is however not modeled formally, so that it has to be implemented manually in every program that reasons about service licenses.

The thesis of Lamparter (2007) presents a policy-based approach for service offers, requests and contracts for Web service markets using ontologies to match different provider vocabularies. The approach models functions ranging over non-functional properties of Web services. The functions are used to compactly represent policies that map configurations of NFPs to numerical values. Users specify their valuation of configurations and providers their prices. The policies are then used to find the optimal configuration with respect to the difference of user valuation and price. Lamparter identifies the allowed use of information returned by services as a relevant NFP. Our approach can be used as a NFP representation in Lamparter's approach and thus enabling a usage policy aware market mechanism.

Accountability in RDF (AIR) is a policy language based on RDF, extended with formulas using quantified variables that can be used as conditions in nested if-then-else rules (Kagal et al., 2008). It supports justifications based on user-given labels, which inspired us to support them in our approach. In fact we evaluated the possibility of using AIR as a general purpose policy language as foundation for our approach and supplement it with usage models. However, currently the semantics of the variables and the rules are not formally defined, and therefore the interpretation of policies is dependent on its existing implementation. This violates the requirement interoperability and makes it unsuitable for extending the language with features that we require, such as introducing restrictions on other policies.

The traditional access control model is the access control matrix, which specifies whether a specific action on a specific object by a specific subject is allowed or not (Lampson, 1971). Most access control approaches like role based access control do not explicitly state the matrix but can be reduced to it. Park and Sandhu (2004) break with this model and present the UCON$_{ABC}$ approach for usage control which not only regulates the access to resources but also their further usage (Park and Sandhu, 2002). Their model includes obligations on the user side and mutable subject and object attributes that have influence on user rights after the initial access to a resource was granted, e.g. an object can only be printed twice. Parker et al. observe that DRM, privacy policies and access control are developed independently despite their similarity and propose the UCON$_{ABC}$ model as a theoretical foundation for the mentioned wide range of application areas (Park and Sandhu, 2004). The model has received broad attention, but views usage control from another perspective as our approach. UCON$_{ABC}$ regulates access requests and the following ongoing usage at the time they occur. In contrast, our proposed solution is able to classify descriptions of usage situations, that can be instantiated many times.

7 Conclusions and Future Work

In this paper we motivated the need for formalized usage policies. We conducted an extensive requirements analysis based both on technical aspects and on the usage restrictions of existing services. The two overarching goals of formal usage policies are: (i) being able to build tools that make it easier for users to adhere to usage restrictions than to break them, and (ii) supporting providers to make their services and data available in open markets, without having to fear that they give up all their rights and commercial interests.

Based on the requirements analysis, we proposed conceptual decisions how the usage policy formalism should be designed. We showed how the proposed solution fulfills the requirements postulated before. Namely the decisions are: (i) develop an RDF model of usage contexts, (ii) design policies as SPARQL queries on this model, and (iii) foster user-given query groupings and labels for policy decision justification. We also presented some initial ideas for the repeated usage situations part of usage policies, but left the decision open for the future.

We gave an comprehensive overview of related works, and showed how they differ from our approach and only partially fulfill our stated requirements.

Furthermore we outlined legal aspects of the proposed solution. We covered questions about the legal foundation, possible legal restrictions on policies, liabilities, and the protection of policy clauses by intellectual property rights.

As future work we plan to develop a usage policy language and engine, based on the design decisions, proposed in this paper. Based thereon we will evaluate our approach by formalizing usage restrictions of existing Web services and testing the usability of policy-aware tools. Thus we can check, if our two main goals are reached, i.e. if service providers can express their interests adequately and if users can adhere to usage restrictions more easily with the help of tools.

References

Abelson, H., B. Adida, M. Linksvayer, and N. Yergler (2008): "ccREL: The Creative Commons Rights Expression Language," working paper, Creative Commons, available at `http://creativecommons.org/projects/ccREL`.

Agarwal, S. (2007): *Formal Description of Web Services for Expressive Matchmaking*, Ph.D. thesis, Universität Karlsruhe (TH), Institut AIFB.

Agarwal, S. and B. Sprick (2005): "Specification of Access Control and Certification Policies for Semantic Web Services," in: *E-Commerce and Web Technologies*, pp. 348–357.

Arnab, A. and A. Hutchison (2007): "Persistent Access Control: A Formal Model for DRM," in: *ACM Workshop on Digital Rights Management*, pp. 41–53.

Blau, B., T. Conte, and C. van Dinther (2009a): "A Multidimensional Procurement Auction for Trading Composite Services," *Issue in the Electronic Commerce Research and Applications Elsevier Journal on: Emerging Economic, Strategic and Technical Issues in Online Auctions and Electronic Market Mechanisms*.

Blau, B., J. Krämer, T. Conte, and C. van Dinther (2009b): "Service Value Networks," in: *Proceedings of the 11th IEEE Conference on Commerce and Enterprise Computing*, Vienna, Austria, pp. 194–201.

Erl, T. (2007): *SOA: Principles of Service Design*, Prentice Hall Press, Upper Saddle River, NJ, USA.

Gangadharan, G. R., V. D'Andrea, and M. Weiss (2008): "Service Licensing Composition and Compatibility Analysis," *Int. J. Cooperative Inf. Syst.*, 17(3), pp. 301–317.

Iannella, R. (2002): "Open Digital Rights Language (ODRL) Version 1.1," W3C Note, available at `http://www.w3.org/TR/odrl/`.

Jamkhedkar, P. A. and G. L. Heileman (2008): "A Formal Conceptual Model for Rights," in: *Digital Rights Management Workshop (DRM)*, pp. 29–38.

Jamkhedkar, P. A. and G. L. Heileman (2009): "Digital Rights Management Architectures," *Comput. Electr. Eng.*, 35(2), pp. 376–394.

Kagal, L., C. Hanson, and D. Weitzner (2008): "Using Dependency Tracking to Provide Explanations for Policy Management," in: *2008 IEEE Workshop on Policies for Distributed Systems and Networks*, pp. 54–61.

Lamparter, S. (2007): *Policy-based Contracting in Semantic Web Service Markets*, Ph.D. thesis, Universität Karlsruhe (TH), Institut AIFB.

Lampson, B. W. (1971): "Protection," in: *Proc. Firth Princeton Symposium on Information Sciences and Systems*, Princeton University, pp. pp. 437–443, reprinted in Operating Systems Review, 8,1, January 1974, pp. 18 – 24.

Meyer, O. (2008): *Aktuelle vertrags- und urheberrechtliche Aspekte der Erstellung, des Vertriebs und der Nutzung von Software*, Ph.D. thesis, University of Karlsruhe.

Ng, I. C. (2007): *The Pricing and Revenue Management of Services: a Strategic Approach*, Routledge Advances in Management and Business Studies.

O'Sullivan, J. (2006): *Towards a Precise Understanding of Service Properties*, Ph.D. thesis, Queensland University of Technology.

Park, J. and R. Sandhu (2002): "Towards Usage Control Models: Beyond Traditional Access Control," in: *ACM Symp. on Access Control Models and Technologies (SACMAT'02)*.

Park, J. and R. Sandhu (2004): "The UCON$_{ABC}$ Usage Control Model," *ACM Trans. Inf. Syst. Secur.*, 7(1), pp. 128–174.

Roman, D., U. Keller, H. Lausen, J. de Bruijn, R. Lara, M. Stollberg, A. Polleres, C. Feier, C. Bussler, and D. Fensel (2005): "Web Service Modeling Ontology," *Applied Ontology*, 1(1), pp. 77–106.

Speiser, S., B. Blau, S. Lamparter, and S. Tai (2008): "Formation of Service Value Networks for Decentralized Service Provisioning," in: *Proceedings of the 6th International Conference on Service Oriented Computing (ICSOC)*.

Sycara, K., M. Paolucci, A. Ankolekar, and N. Srinivasan (2003): "Automated Discovery, Interaction and Composition of Semantic Web Services," *Journal of Web Semantics*, 1, pp. 27–46.

Toma, I. and D. Foxvog (2006): "Non-Functional Properties in Web Services," working paper D28.4 v0.1, WSMO Working Draft.

W3C (2004a): *OWL-S: Semantic Markup for Web Services*, W3C Member Submission, available at `http://www.w3.org/Submission/OWL-S/`.

W3C (2004b): *Resource Description Framework (RDF): Concepts and Abstract Syntax*, W3C Recommendation, available at `http://www.w3.org/TR/rdf-concepts/`.

W3C (2007): *Web Services Policy 1.5 - Framework*, W3C Recommendation, available at `http://www.w3.org/TR/ws-policy/`.

W3C (2008): *SPARQL Query Language for RDF*, W3C Recommendation, available at `http://www.w3.org/TR/rdf-sparql-query/`.

Wang, X., G. Lao, T. Demartini, H. Reddy, M. Nguyen, and E. Valenzuela (2002): "XrML - eXtensible rights Markup Language," in: *ACM workshop on XML security (XMLSEC'02)*.

A Feature-based Application Interface for Future Networks

Helge Backhaus and Martina Zitterbart

Institute of Telematics, KIT
{backhaus, zit}@tm.uka.de

1 Introduction

The Internet is considered to be one of the most important inventions in the history of information technologies since the introduction of letterpress printing. Services like *E-Mail*, file transfers, and the *World Wide Web* have become a part of everyday life. Services traditionally provided by dedicated networks like cable television, telephony, and radio are becoming more and more available via the Internet, through new services such as *VoIP*, *IPtv*, and online radio.

Theoretically it is possible for any two devices to exchange information via the Internet regardless of their current position. In order to enable all kinds of different devices such as cell phones, laptops, or for example cars to communicate with each other, some kind of protocol is needed. In the Internet several protocols define the form of exchanged data, and regulate how this data is exchanged.

Historically a relatively small number of protocols emerged, with *TCP* (transmission control protocol) respectively *UDP* (user datagram protocol) and *IP* (internet protocol) being the most prominent ones. Nearly all applications and services offered via the Internet today are somehow based on these protocols.

Over time the need for several enhancements to this initially simple set of protocols arose. Originally designed to connect stationary devices like desktop PCs, we have to deal with mobility today. There are cell phones and other mobile devices, which change their location and thereby their Internet access point. Another example would be security in general. Security mechanisms are often just tacked on instead of being properly integrated into today's Internet protocol stack. Viruses, worms, phishing, and spyware pose a serious threat for inexperienced Internet users today and we experience a constant arms race between malware developers and security solutions providers.

Many new applications, like social networks, online data storage accessible from everywhere, or online gaming for instance, put further demands on the current Internet architecture, which have become increasingly difficult to meet. This will become even worse in the future. With scenarios like car-2-car communication or pervasive computing on the horizon, there will be all kinds of new devices with online access.

2 Architectural Problems

Today we are facing a multitude of problems within the current Internet architecture, some of which are described in *Why the Internet only just works*[Handley (2006)]. These stem mainly from the fact that the Internet core protocols have not significantly changed since the early nineties. Many changes occurred on the physical layer, considering the introduction of several new wireless standards in the field of mobile devices for instance. Above that however it is basically all *TCP/IP*.

Some problems are more deeply rooted within the Internet architecture and its core protocols.

2.1 Address space exhaustion

In today's Internet a hosts network interface is reachable via an *IPv4* address. Every host participating in an IP-based network like the Internet, needs a unique *IP* address in order to receive and send data packets from or to other hosts in the network. Since the early 1990s it has become apparent, that the Internet will eventually run out of *IP* addresses. This has been delayed by introducing *Classless Inter-Domain Routing* (CIDR) in 1993 and the rise of network address translation (NAT) later on. NAT is used to connect (private) subnetworks with the Internet, by allowing the usage of several private *IP* addresses behind one public *IP* address. This is achieved through rewriting the *IP* address information for incoming or outgoing connections. Today NAT is considered to be rather harmful. It does not solve the address space exhaustion problem but instead just conceals it. Despite all efforts it is still assumed, that *IPv4* addresses will run out in 2012.

With *IPv6* on the horizon and *IPv6* support in most major operating systems, this problem might be solved in the near future. Yet widespread adoption of *IPv6* is still lacking. A study conducted by *Google*[1] in 2008 concluded, that less than one percent of the Internet's hosts was reachable via *IPv6*. This is also a prime example of how rigid the structure of today's Internet is. *IPv6* was first proposed in 1998 over 10 years ago, and thus took a long time to develop and establish. In general it has become elaborate to change core parts of todays's Internet, as most of our infrastructure today is dependent on the Internet. Future network architectures therefore should foster a flexible replacement of different components without compromising the robustness of the Internet itself.

2.2 Mobility

Another problem is lacking support for mobile devices like laptops or mobile phones. Due to their nature those devices are often used to access the Internet on the go via

[1] http://www.ripe.net/ripe/meetings/ripe-57/presentations/thursday.html

wireless connections. Mobility refers to the fact that while communicating, a device can migrate from the reception area of one wireless network to another. The same applies for mobile phones, while moving through different radio cells. In such cases the connection is normally lost for a short time and has to be re-established, often accompanied by an *IP* address change. Today applications are mostly designed to be delay and loss tolerant, to compensate for regular reconnects. On a connection loss applications pretend to still be connected. Data to be sent is cached, while re-establishing the connection in the background, so that the user does not notice any unwanted behavior. With the possibility of support for *VoIP* and *IPtv* on mobile devices, in the future a more transparent, and application independent way of handling handovers is desirable.

2.3 ID/Locator split

Both of the aforementioned issues are part of an additional problem. Even with *IPv6*, an *IP* address always specifies a location and at the same time serves as an unique identifier. In today's Internet this is sufficient, as most applications are designed in a way that a specific resource is expected to be found at a specific location. In the future however, it might be possible to address specific content directly. A circumstance described by the lately coined term *Content centric Networking*[2]. In such a scenario it is conceivable, that an actual resource like an online video or a webpage, may be available on multiple host e.g. locations. Also one host may hold many resources, which should be directly accessible via unique identifiers. Finally it is possible, that one resource changes its location. In all of these cases, specific content should still be available via the same identifier.

A solution to this problem is often called *ID/Locator* split. In the future a new addressing scheme, which offers a dynamic association between an objects identifier and one of its current locations, is very likely. Today this is mainly achieved by search engines like *Google*, as most Internet users rely on them for finding certain resources quickly. Even with *IPv6* there is however no immanent support for an *ID/Locator* split in today's Internet architecture.

3 The Future Internet

One core issue within the scope of Internet development and advancement, aside from fixing current short and long term problems, is to specify and anticipate what the Internet of tomorrow might look like. It is important to assess though, that there exists no such thing as one *Future Internet*. Rather several national and international research initiatives exist, which try to overcome the shortcomings of and improve the current Internet architecture. These are often summarized under the term *Future Internet*. Our understanding is that instead of one network, there will be many different networks in the future, with many heterogenous devices.

---

[2] http://mmlab.snu.ac.kr/courses/2007_advanced_internet/papers/20071010_1.pdf

Currently the Internet operates according to the best-effort paradigm. For a packet switched network this means, incoming data-packets are forwarded as long as there are enough free resources. Theoretically every Internet user is able to utilize the maximum bandwidth provided by his network access. There are however no guarantees regarding the actual provided bandwidth or any delays before a data-packet is delivered. Neither is there a guarantee, that a data-packet reaches its destination at all.

The best-effort paradigm is however mitigated by higher level protocols like *TCP*, which enable reliable delivery of data-packets by retransmitting lost packets. In addition multiple quality of service mechanisms like *IP differentiated services*[3] (DiffServ) or *IP integrated services*[4] (IntServ) exist. None of them was however able to achieve a widespread distribution thus far. Still the need for quality of service support is constantly growing, as more new applications emerge, which could profit from quality of service mechanisms.

Instead of integrating existing or new quality of service approaches into the current Internet architecture, we envision a *Future Internet* consisting of many different networks, specifically suited for single applications or services. One step towards such service tailored networks is to provide an architecture and environment, which allows for easy creation and deployment of new networks. Network virtualization[Schaffrath et al. (2009)][Chowdhury and Boutaba (2010)] is regarded to be one key technology towards achieving this goal, by providing a flexible virtual infrastructure, which abstracts from the underlying physical infrastructure.

On the other hand different protocols are needed to control, how data is exchanged in different networks. Within the scope of the projects *4Ward*[5] and *GLab*[6] a *Node Architecture* was developed, which aims at providing a flexible environment for concurrently running different network architectures, each with its own set of protocols. Also tools were developed, which aid protocol designers with the creation and deployment of new protocols.

4 The Node Architecture

A simplified version of the *Node Architecture* is shown in figure 1. The *Node Architecture* is intended to work on end-nodes. The main goal is to provide a protocol-stack independent framework to connect applications and network interfaces. Instead of being bound to a certain set of protocols, it provides the option to run a multitude of future protocols and applications side-by-side. It hides the actual protocol-stack from the application and provides a generic interface, which connects applications

---

[3] http://tools.ietf.org/html/rfc2474
[4] http://tools.ietf.org/html/rfc1633
[5] http://www.4ward-project.eu
[6] http://www.german-lab.de

to the *Node Architecture*. Thus it becomes possible to exchange complete protocol-stacks, without the need to modify or adapt the application. Applications are hence enabled to communicate via a multitude of protocols and even networks, without detailed knowledge about the underlying network architecture. In the following sections the individual components shown in figure 1 are outlined. A more detailed description of the *Node Architecture* and its concepts is available in [Völker et al. (2009a)].

4.1 Netlets as future protocol containers

Netlets represent the fundamental concept of the *Node Architecture*, as they contain the actual network protocols or even complete protocol stacks. For example today's protocol-stack could be encapsulated by a *Netlet*. At the most basic level a *Netlet* provides a simple send and receive interface for an application on top of the *Netlet* and a network access point beneath the *Netlet*.

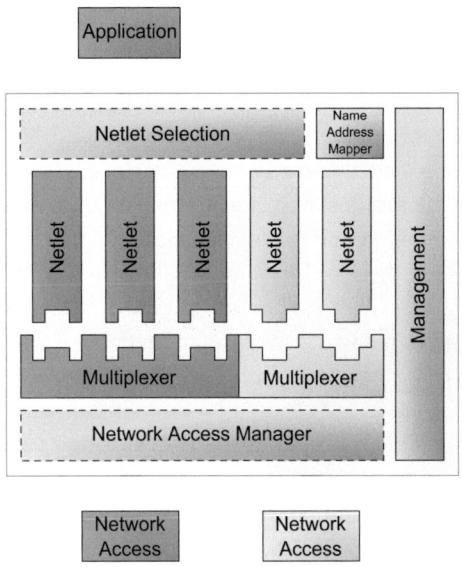

Figure 1: Simpliefied node architecture for flexible protocol selection

As *Netlets* are generic protocol containers. Whether encapsulated protocols are compiled from handwritten code or are e.g. composed from smaller protocol components is of no consideration. Therefore *Netlets* are also able to support different existing protocol composition approaches, like e.g. RNA[Touch et al. (2006a)] or SILO[Touch et al. (2006b)].

Netlets need to share a common understanding about the exchanged data. *Netlets* have to use a common *Protocol Data Unit* (PDU) format. A *PDU* has to contain basic information about a common identifier, in order to match incoming data-packets or streams to their designated *Netlets*. As depicted in figure 1, the *Node Architecture* allows several multiplexers, responsible for matching incoming data-streams and *Netlets*, to run alongside. Each multiplexer is specific to one architecture. Through different multiplexers it is still possible to connect to multiple network architectures at once, each with their own basic *PDU* and addressing scheme. Netlets are always associated with a certain multiplexer and thus certain network architecture.

4.2 Management

The management component of the *Node Architecture* is responsible for gathering and exposing information about the underlying virtual or physical network infrastructure, as well as the specific network architectures. *Netlets* can query the management component or register themselves to be notified, if certain parameters in the underlying network change. *Netlets* are then able to adapt their behavior. Such changes may for example occur, if a smartphone has to switch from HSDPA to GPRS, due to worsend reception conditions. Adaptable parameters in such a case include e.g. different bandwidth usage or longer packet delays.

4.3 Name Address Mapper

Communication between applications and today's *TCP/IP* based protocol stack is normally handled via a standardized socket interface. It fills the gap between the operating systems implementation of the standard communication protocols and the actual applications using them to connect to a network. In order to communicate with another end system, the *IP* address of that system has to be known. Today it is common though, to reach other hosts through human readable names. Therefore applications often need to resolve those human readable names themselves, in order to get the corresponding *IP* addresses, before they can start to communicate with another host. This is done by invoking a lookup service, the *Domain Name System* (DNS), which is responsible for name resolution in today's Internet.

Within the *Node Architecture*, the name address mapper is responsible for name resolution. In the following we distinguish between name, identifier and locator as depicted in figure 2. A name is always in a human readable form like e.g. a URI. An identifier has to be unique within a specific network architecture and identifies a specific resource, e.g. a webpage. It is possible that a name is an identifier at the same time. An identifier could also be in a non-human readable form, e.g. a hash string. In that case several names could be mapped onto the same identifier, e.g. http://www.kit.edu and http://kit.edu are two names, which identify the same resource. The identifier of an resource is needed to get the location of a resource. A resource has at least one location at any moment, but can also have more than one locator at the same time, when it is available at several locations. An address is nothing more than a locator, as its sole purpose is to specify a location.

Within the Node Architecture applications only need a name of a resource instead of its locator or address. The *Node Architecture* handles the lookup of the correct

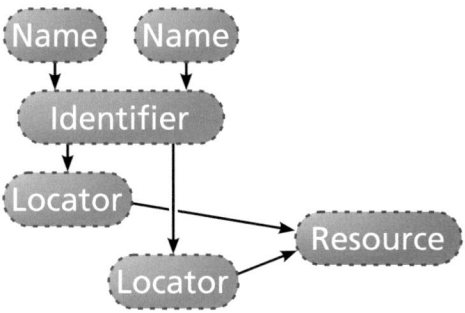

Figure 2: Name, Identifier and Locator in relation to a Resource

locator, by mapping the name onto an identifier and checking in which networks a locator for the identifier is available. With several different networks running concurrently on a host, this enables applications to be network independent, as different networks could feature different addressing schemes. The name address mapper is also responsible for deciding, which locator should be used, when one identifier returns several locators, probably in different networks. For these cases it is possible to define heuristics to decide which locator should be favored.

4.4 Network Accesses

Network accesses provide an interface between the *Node Architecture* and any physical or virtual network infrastructure underneath the *Node Architecture*. A network access abstracts from certain physical media and provides a generic and extensible interface. The *Node Architecture* and *Netlets* therefore are useable in different networks and do not rely on a certain hardware infrastructure. Network accesses can also provide basic information about a network. Properties like packet loss rate or the maximum permitted bandwidth of a network or a link can be obtained. These properties also aid with the *Netlet* selection process.

Network accesses are connected to a suitable multiplexer. This ensures that a network access understands an architecture specific *PDU*. Each Multiplexer can have an arbitrary number of network accesses, as long as the *PDU* format used matches.

5 Netlet description and selection

A great challenge when running many concurrent networks next to each other, each with its own *Netlets*, is selecting a suitable *Netlet* available for a certain task. Also this should happen automatically since users expect to be able to communicate with other users instantly, without having to specify what kind of connection or protocol they want to use.

The *Node Architecture* automates *Netlet* selection where it is possible, even though there will always remain scenarios where user interaction is needed. For example

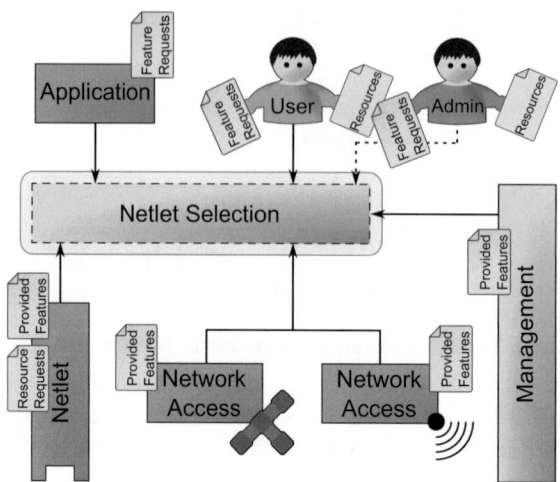

Figure 3: Features and requirements affecting protocol selection

when a certain Netlet's usage is associated with immediate costs for the user. Figure 3 illustrates the role of different *Node Architecture* components during the process of selecting a *Netlet*. Network accesses expose technical properties, like e.g. bandwidth or the support for secure communication. The management component exposes features, which have to be measured. The current packet loss rate or the experienced packet delay to another host for example.

As *Netlets* contain the actual communication protocols, they can provide all kinds of different services. Features like reliable transport, error detection and correction mechanisms, routing, or security are common of today's *TCP/IP* based protocol stack. In the future however Netlets may also have additional features like data privacy, validity of delivered content, or access rights management for certain data.

Applications can state their requirements through feature requests, which a *Netlet* has to meet in order to be a suitable for the users communication needs. These requirements have to be defined by the application's developer. To make the task of defining requirements easier, extensible profiles can be predefined for standard use cases. For application developers, profiles like WWW, distributed file storage, multimedia data, or a generic reliable transport can be defined. Device manufacturers could set up predefined profiles for, e.g., mobile phones, which are tuned for low energy consumption.

Not only applications, but also *Netlets* can have requirements. A *Netlet* might need a certain set of system resources to work properly. For example a *Netlet* could require local disk space to store data or have certain energy consumption demands, which have to be met by e.g. a mobile device.

Furthermore the user can formulate additional requirements as a set of feature requests. These can be defined as a general policy, for a specific application, or per connection. Users could limit the maximum bandwidth an application uses for instance. In the context of social networking, features could include privacy preferences which define how long certain data may remain within a network, or who is allowed to access it. Further features concerning content validity may be possible, e.g., networks that guarantee a trusted source for delivered content instead of just guaranteeing non-manipulated data. If application and user requirements are conflicting with each other, user requirements override application requirements. This can however prevent the usage of certain applications, until the user resolves that conflict.

In rare cases users may have to decide, which resources the *Node Architecture* or a certain (group of) *Netlets* may use. *Netlets* can request resources on a per connection basis. These are handled by default policies for a certain (group of) *Netlets*, as manually deciding on resource consumption per connection would be far too elaborate. Default policies should be defined within the Node Architecture. Operating Systems may feature their own set of extended default policies though. These policies can however be overriden by the user, so that it is possible to accomodate the Node Architecture to personal needs. Also system administrators are enabled to modify these policies, to adjust the *Node Architecture* to their specific communication needs.

The *Netlet* selection component gathers all this data, and tries to determine the best possible *Netlet* for an incoming connection request. A set of features can be derived from application, user, and policy defined requirements. This process is shown in Figure 4. When an application wants to establish a connection, a set of features alone is not sufficient. In most cases, there will be dependencies between at least some if not all features. Therefore, constraints have to be defined too. Features then have to be checked against these constraints. Constraints define functional dependencies between two or more features. They can state simple dependencies, like two features which can never be used together, but also more complex dependencies, like relations between two features.

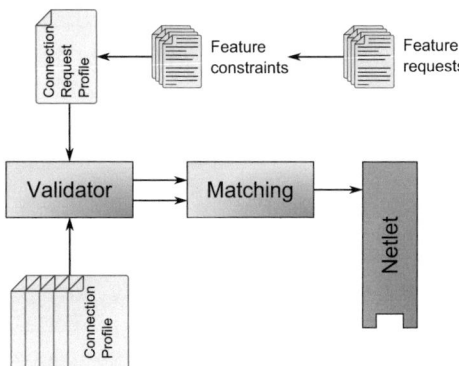

Figure 4: The protocol selection process

Feature constraints and the set of desired features are therefore combined into a Connection Request Profile. This is done with combined user and application requirements. Furthermore, a Connection Profile for each Netlet has to be created. Constraints have to be predefined for every feature combination which has dependencies, and can later be automatically derived from the set of features. Within the Validator, constraints are then applied to the features. If constraints can not be fulfilled, a list of features which do not work together is sent to the application. The application then has to modify its requirements where feasible. Alternatively, the decision which requirements have to be modified can be passed to the user or an error can be shown to inform the user that no connection could be established.

Once all constraints can be fulfilled, a Connection Profile is considered to be valid. Finding the best Netlet available for a Connection Request Profile is then done, by matching the feature-sets of all available Connection Profiles against it. A Netlet, whose Connection Profile overlaps completely with the Connection Request Profile is chosen. If several Netlets fulfill the requirements, additional features can be specified or default behavior, like choosing the first Netlet that fits can be set. If no overlapping Connection Profile can be found, the non-satisfiable features are sent back to the application, and the same process is triggered as with non-satisfiable constraints before.

Connection Profiles are split up into features and feature constraints, to allow for a flexible extension of the system. As constraints are not mandatory, new features can be added without the need to create several constraints alongside of them. It is the responsibility of the application designer then, to define feasible requirements. This allows for features that would otherwise be hard to verify. Also constraints can be added at a later time, to make the verification of application or user requirements easier. Another advantage in relation to performance is, that a given set of features and constraints can be pre-checked for validity and only a few checks or just a matching of features is needed at run time, when a connection should be established. Finally new features and constraints can be negotiated via the Management component and a signaling protocol to adjust application requirements between two or more hosts. Constraints between two features may also be platform specific, and can thus be exchanged independently from existing features.

5.1 Features and feature constraints in RDF

Features are expressed in XML in an RDF-based[W3C Recommendation (2004b)] format, so that they are easy to extend and modify. RDF describes resources via statements. A RDF statements consist of a *subject, predicate, object* triple. Features are identified via a *FeatureName*, which is a unique resource identifier (URI) to avoid ambiguities. The *FeatureName* forms the *subject* part of a RDF statement. Nested within the *subject* are the *predicates* whose actual values are the *objects*. The *Info* predicate provides a human readable explanation of the feature, which can be displayed to the user, if requirements have to be altered. The *ValueComperator* predicate defines how this feature's value has to be compared during the matching phase. At the moment, we allow comparators like *greater*, *smaller*, *equal*, or *none*. The *none* comparator can be used for features, which have no value and just need to be present. A *ValueFormat* predicate sets, whether the predicate *Value* is an integer, float, or per cent value for instance. Figure 5 shows an exemplary definition of three *Quality of Service* features, e.g. *minimal bandwith*, *average packet loss*, and *maximum latency*.

```
<rdf:RDF xmlns:rdf = "http://www.w3.org/1999/02/22-rdf-syntax-ns#"
      xmlns:na = "http://www.kit.edu/nodearch-ns#" >
  <rdf:Description rdf:about = "na://features/QoS/minimalBandwidth"><!-- minimal bandwidth feature -->
    <na:name>"Minimal Bandwidth"</na:name>
    <na:info>Describes the minmum bandwidth needed for a connection.</na:info>
    <na:comparator>greater</na:comparator>
    <na:unit>
      <rdf:Bag>
        <rdf:li>mBit/s</rdf:li>
        <rdf:li>kByte/s</rdf:li>
      </rdf:Bag>
    </na:unit>
  </rdf:Description>
  <rdf:Description rdf:about = "na://features/QoS/averagePacketLoss"><!-- average packet loss feature -->
    <na:name>"Average Packet Loss"</na:name>
    <na:info>Describes...</na:info>
    <na:comparator>average</na:comparator>
    <na:unit>
      <rdf:Bag>
        <rdf:li>perCent</rdf:li>
        <rdf:li>pkt/s</rdf:li>
      </rdf:Bag>
    </na:unit>
  </rdf:Description>
  <rdf:Description rdf:about = "na://features/QoS/maximumLatency"><!-- maximum latency feature -->
    <na:name>"Maximum Latency"</na:name>
    <na:info>Describes...</na:info>
    <na:comparator>smaller</na:comparator>
    <na:unit>ns</na:unit>
  </rdf:Description>
</rdf:RDF>
```

Figure 5: A RDF document defining three Quality of Service features

Feature constraints can be defined in a similar manner. Constraints identify two features by their *FeatureName*. Dependencies between these two features can be formulated with comparators as well. For example the *Value* of the *minimumBandwithFeature* always has to be smaller than or equal to the *Value* of the *maximumBandwithFeature*. Additionally dependencies between features itself can be specified, with *and*, *or*, *xor* relationships.

6 Related Work

Several description languages for application interfaces or web services already exist within the World Wide Web context. Common to many solutions like the Web service Description Language (WSDL)[W3C Recommendation (2001)] is however, that they are tailored to a specific kind or class of service. In order to support platforms like sensor networks for instance, we need a lightweight solution. Our approach does not require a complex syntax or even full-featured XML parser for its properties, which also makes it easily portable to other languages. The Web Ontology Language (OWL)[W3C Recommendation (2004a)] which is also based on RDF, could be used in a lite version. OWL comes with a larger vocabulary and stronger syntax than RDF. Therefore OWL is more powerful in terms of expressiveness. OWL however is more complex to parse and process. We believe that describing services at a basic level is sufficient for protocol selection, as in our context time constraints are also an important factor.

7 Conclusion

This paper described an architecture, which is suited for executing parallel network architectures on a single host. It is designed with flexibility and extensibility in mind. We presented a concept for defining requirements for and features of network protocols and applications in future networks. The solution aims at recreating the straightforward and hassle-free experience users have come to expect from today's Internet, in an environment where several protocols and network architectures are running concurrently. We achieve flexibility by using an RDF-based format, which is portable and can be converted to other formats. Extensibility is supported by a design, which fosters the addition of new features and feature constraints step-by-step.

Current work focuses on the definition and refinement of requirements and features. In a next step means are needed to synchronize protocol selection over several hosts. Therefore some sort of signaling mechanism is needed, to communicate protocol selection decisions to other network users. Also we want to investigate how our approach can aid in finding the best protocol, in cases where several protocols satisfy provided requirements equally well. Therefore we want to build upon a solution initially developed for selecting e.g. security mechanisms[Völker et al. (2009b)] and extend it to incorporate our feature descriptions.

References

Chowdhury, N. M. K. and R. Boutaba (2010): "A survey of network virtualization," *Computer Networks*, 54(5), pp. 862 – 876, http://www.sciencedirect.com/science/article/B6VRG-4XKBYY4-4/2/91ac30e6e1c4d24c53d95798a6148f03.

Handley, M. (2006): "Why the Internet only just works," *BT Technology Journal*, 24(3), pp. 119–129.

Schaffrath, G., C. Werle, P. Papadimitriou, A. Feldmann, R. Bless, A. Greenhalgh, A. Wundsam, M. Kind, O. Maennel, and L. Mathy (2009): "Network virtualization architecture: proposal and initial prototype," in: *VISA '09: Proceedings of the 1st ACM workshop on Virtualized infrastructure systems and architectures*, ACM, New York, NY, USA, pp. 63–72.

Touch, J. D., Y.-S. Wang, and V. Pingali (2006a): "A Recursive Network Architecture," in: *ISI, Tech. Rep.*

Touch, J. D., Y.-S. Wang, and V. Pingali (2006b): "A Recursive Network Architecture," in: *ISI, Tech. Rep.*

Völker, L., D. Martin, I. El Khayat, C. Werle, and M. Zitterbart (2009a): "A Node Architecture for 1000 Future Networks," in: *Proceedings of the International Workshop on the Network of the Future 2009*, IEEE, Dresden, Germany.

Völker, L., D. Martin, C. Werle, M. Zitterbart, and I. El Khayat (2009b): "Selecting Concurrent Network Architectures at Runtime," in: *Proceedings of the IEEE International Conference on Communications (ICC 2009)*, IEEE Computer Society, Dresden, Germany.

W3C Recommendation (2001): "Web Services Description Language (WSDL) 1.1," Available at http://www.w3.org/TR/wsdl.html.

W3C Recommendation (2004a): "OWL Web Ontology Language Semantics and Abstract Syntax," Available at http://www.w3.org/TR/owl-semantics/.

W3C Recommendation (2004b): "Resource Description Framework (RDF): Concepts and Abstract Syntax," Available at http://www.w3.org/TR/rdf-concepts/.

Analysis of Market Interaction and Behavior

Investigating Auction Fever

Marc T. P. Adam[1], Jan Krämer[1], Christof Weinhardt[1], and Karl-Martin Ehrhart[2]

[1] Institute of Information Systems and Management, KIT
{marc.adam, kraemer, weinhardt}@kit.edu
[2] Institute for Economic Theory and Statistics, KIT
ehrhart@wiwi.uni-karlsruhe.de

Summary. Auction fever is a frequently observed phenomenon in traditional and Internet auctions. However, traditional approaches of auction theory often neglect the influence of emotions. In this paper we discuss a unified framework for emotional bidding in auctions and identify challenges for future auction fever research. In particular, we identify interdependent utilities and product characteristics as important influencing factors for auction fever, which have only gained little attention in the literature at this stage. Further, methodological approaches for auction fever research are discussed. While a substantial part of auction fever literature is based on deception of participants, one has to consider fundamental drawbacks of this approach. In contrast, we find that applying physiological measurements in economic laboratory experiments and auctioning real world commodities is a promising (complementary) approach. Further, letting subjects compete with computerized agents seems to be an adequate approach for assessing the importance of interdependent utilities.

1 Introduction

Auctions are nowadays a popular and frequently employed market mechanism in electronic markets. In particular Internet auctions for consumers have turned out to be *"one of the greatest success stories of web-based services"* (Ariely and Simonson, 2003). As the end of 2008, alone the market leader *eBay.com* reported a total number of 86.3 million active users worldwide and net revenues of 5.6 billion US dollars (eBay Inc., 2009). In economic literature, the success of Internet auctions has been largely attributed to reductions of transaction costs, the large number of potential buyers, and the independence of time and space (Ockenfels et al., 2006). However, these characteristics also apply to retail sites as *Amazon.com*. Further, the popularity of Internet auctions seems somewhat counterintuitive from a consumer perspective as several field studies have confirmed that auctions yield on average higher prices compared to fixed price offers on retail sites (e.g. Lucking-Reiley, 1999; Lee et al., 2009a).

1.1 Emotions as a Quality Characteristic of Internet Auctions

An additional explanation for the success of Internet auctions are *hedonic* or *emotional* values bidders derive from auction participation (e.g. Möllenberg, 2004; Stern et al., 2008). While utilitarian value refers to the utility gained from obtaining the desired commodity, hedonic value is gained from perceived entertainment and emotional worth of auction participation. In this regard, Lee et al. (2009b) identify in particular *"thrill of bidding, excitement of winning, stimulation of beating competitors, and enjoyment of finding rare or unusual items"* as sources for hedonic value. This characteristic clearly distinguishes auctions from fixed price offers and may even be understood as a quality characteristic of Internet auctions.

Marketing departments of Internet auction platforms have long understood that emotions plays an important role in attracting consumers. Referring to the competitive nature of auctions, eBay launched an advertisement campaign in 2007 titled *"shop victoriously"* stating that *"it's better when you win it"* (eBay.com, 2007). In the corresponding television commercials, bidding in an eBay auction is compared to sport events such as football matches or dog races. In Germany, eBay even simply advertises directly the immediate emotions bidders experience upon winning an auction (see Figure 1). Similarly, the platform swoopo.com advertises with *"pulse up, price down,"* referring to the actual physiological arousal bidders can experience on their platform. Another indicator for the emotions in auctions and their *"game-like action and bidding frenzy characteristic"* (Stafford and Stern, 2002) is the terminology bidders apply for describing the course of action. Contrary to retail websites, bidders do not just buy commodities, they *win* or *lose* them. Correspondingly, Ariely and Simonson (2003) find in an Internet survey that 76.8% of the respondents perceive other bidders as *"competitors"* and refer to auction outcomes as *"winning"* and *"losing."*

Figure 1: German eBay Advertisement (retrieved from `spiegel.de` on March 19th, 2008)

This general development can be interpreted as a paradigm shift to *"entertainment shopping"* or *"auctainment"* (Glänzer and Schäfers, 2001). Salient evidence for this paradigm shift are emerging sites as *swoopo.com* and *dubli.com*. These sites aim at attracting consumers with new (exciting) auction mechanisms and explicitly advertise themselves as *"entertainment shopping"* and *"fun shopping"* platforms, respectively.

1.2 Engineering Emotions in Auctions

As outlined above, emotions are an important incentive for participation in Internet consumer auctions. This, however, raises another question: what is the impact of emotions on bidding behavior? This question is particularly important for the market engineer of an Internet auction platform (Weinhardt et al., 2003).

A distinguished strand of the literature analyzes auctions theoretically with highly sophisticated analytical models (Vickrey, 1961; McAfee and McMillan, 1987). While these models are undoubtedly an important contribution for the design and understanding of electronic markets, they seldomly include hedonic values of auction participation.[1] However, results from the laboratory and the field indicate that emotions induced during the dynamic process of auctions have an impact on bidding behavior and, subsequently, on market outcome and seller revenue (e.g. Ku et al., 2005; Lee and Malmendier, 2010). Even slight variations in the auction mechanism can lead to large disparities in bidding behavior and this change in behavior is often not (fully) predicted by auction theory.

One phenomenon frequently observed in traditional and Internet auctions which is often referred to an increased emotionality is *"auction fever"* (e.g. Ku et al., 2005; Ehrhart et al., 2008). Under the influence of auction fever, so Murnighan (2002), bidders' *"adrenaline starts to rush, their emotions block their ability to think clearly, and they end up bidding much more than they ever envisioned."* This paper focuses specifically on auction fever. In particular, we identify challenges for future research in the field of auction fever and discuss related methodological approaches.

The remainder of this paper is structured as follows. Section 2 discusses a unified framework for emotional bidding in auctions. Then, Section 3 outlines challenges for future research on auction fever and Section 4 discusses methodological approaches. Section 5 concludes.

2 Emotions in Auctions

2.1 A Unified Framework for Emotional Bidding

Traditional approaches of auction theory neglect the influence of emotions. In order to coherently approach the interaction of cognitive reasoning and emotional processing, Adam et al. (2010) introduce a unified framework for emotional bidding in auctions. The framework is depicted in Figure 2.

The upper part of the framework describes the traditional perspective of auction theory. Auction theory typically describes auctions as non-cooperative games with

---

[1] See Katok and Kwasnica (2008) and Ehrhart et al. (2008) for different approaches.

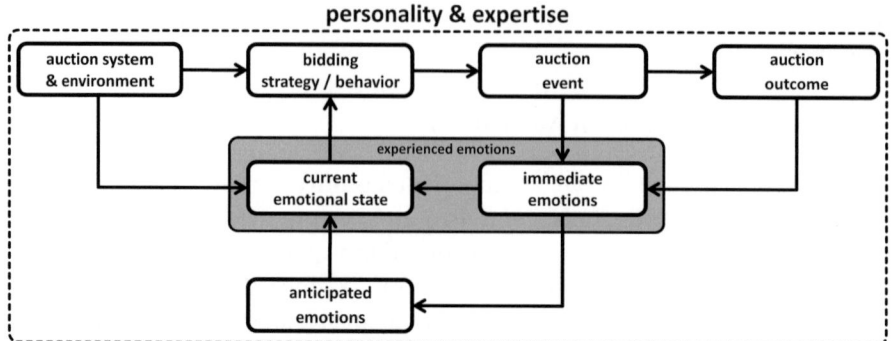

Figure 2: Framework for Emotional Bidding in Auctions

incomplete information (Bayesian games) and provides the auction participants with a strategy in order to maximize their expected payoff (e.g. McAfee and McMillan, 1987; Krishna, 2002). A strategy is defined as a set of rules, which tells a decision maker which action to chose at each instant of the game, given her information set (Rasmusen, 2007). In terms of auctions, a bidding strategy tells a bidder when to place a bid for what amount, and whether to participate in the auction at all. Often a particular auction mechanism implicates a set of one or more optimal (symmetric) bidding strategies. In particular, the rather simple auction mechanisms usually employed on Internet auction platforms have this characteristic. Depending on the particular auction mechanism, the induced bidding strategy results in one or more auction events, which ultimately end in an auction outcome.

The lower part of Figure 2 describes the interaction of the auction mechanism, bidding behavior, auction events, and emotional processing. An emotion can be roughly defined as a subjectively experienced state that can be described qualitatively and is accompanied by changes in feeling, physiology, behavior, and expression (Gerrig and Zimbardo, 2007). As pointed out by Loewenstein (2000), emotions can be distinguished into anticipated and experienced emotions. An anticipated emotion refers to the expected emotional processing in response to a salient future event, e.g. the end of an auction and the anticipated win or loss. In contrast, an experienced emotion refers to the actual emotional processing, which comprises both *immediate emotions* in response to a single stimulus (Loewenstein, 2000) and ongoing current emotional states (Ding et al., 2005).

Immediate emotions are triggered by auction events and the auction outcome. Auction events comprise for instance the placement of new bids, entry of new bidders, becoming the current high bidder, or being outbidden. The auction outcome induces immediate emotions as *"joy of winning"* and *"frustration of losing"* (Delgado et al., 2008). The processing of immediate emotions can be anticipated by bidders throughout the process of an auction. The set of possible immediate emotions is limited by the auction system[2]. Therefore, some auction mechanisms pronounce emotionality stronger than others. For instance, some auction mechanisms only allow for placing a single sealed-bid. These auctions are often referred to as *static* auctions. In contrast, *dynamic* auctions allow bidders for placing multiple bids and observing the behavior of other bidders. As argued by Gimpel (2007), auction fever is particularly a phenomenon of dynamic auctions.

The terms immediate and anticipated emotion refer to momentary *(phasic)* responses to a single stimulus. In contrast, a bidder's current emotional state refers to her ongoing *(tonic)* emotional processing. As outlined by Ariely and Simonson (2003), the current emotional state of a bidder is influenced by the *"frequency and magnitude of anticipated post-auction feelings."* For instance, frequently anticipating the joy of winning and frustration of losing can increase a bidder's tonic level of arousal. But also anticipated and immediate emotions with respect to auction events other than the auction outcome have an impact on a bidder's current emotional state. For instance becoming the current high bidder in an auction and being outbidden have been identified as salient events (Ehrhart et al., 2008). However, as indicated in the framework for emotional bidding, the current emotional state can also be directly affected by the employed auction system. For instance, Malhotra et al. (2008) denote that *"a ticking clock (...) can overwhelm people with the desire to win,"* indicating that a high degree of time pressure in auctions can directly increase the bidders' individual level of arousal.

2.2 Auction Fever

The controversy about auction fever is probably as old as auctions. Apparently, legal scholars already debated in ancient Rome whether auctions were void if the winner was infected by *"bidder's heat"* (Lee and Malmendier, 2010). Based on the framework for emotional bidding, Adam et al. (2010) define auction fever as *"a current emotional state elicited in the course of one or more auctions that distorts a bidder's preselected bidding strategy."* This definition comprises not only overbidding in ascending auctions, but also underbidding in Dutch auctions, repeated bidding, and other changes in the preselected bidding strategy.

The definition is based on the assumption that bidders commit themselves to a bidding strategy before the auction starts.[3] This is in line with the observation of an Internet survey conducted by Ku et al. (2005). The authors report that 82% of the survey respondents set themselves a limit prior to bidding.

---

[2] In this paper, an auction system is well defined by the auction mechanism design and the user interface design.

[3] Note that the preselected bidding strategy does not necessarily need to be derived by means of auction theory. As already observed by Vickrey (1961), some of the bidders may be *"insufficiently sophisticated to discern the equilibrium-point strategy."* In a rather behavioral approach, one can argue that bidders may set themselves a limit by estimating a subjective valuation for the commodity and then heuristically deriving a corresponding bidding strategy (Ariely and Simonson, 2003).

3 Challenges for Auction Fever Research

Auction fever literature identified in particular perceived competition (e.g. Heyman et al., 2004; Ku et al., 2005), previous investments (Ku, 2008; Park et al., 2008), and perceived ownership (Heyman et al., 2004; Wolf et al., 2005) as elicitors of auction fever. Further, in Internet auctions the elicitation of auction fever is mediated through the user interface design of the auction system. In this section, two main challenges for future auction fever research are identified, which have only gained little focus in the literature at this stage. In particular, we will focus on the role of interdependencies in bidders' utility functions and product characteristics of the auctioned commodities.

3.1 Interdependent Utilities in Auctions

Time pressure, social facilitation, and rivalry have been identified as the main influencing factors for the degree of competition bidders perceive in auctions (e.g Ku et al., 2005; Malhotra et al., 2008). In the following we focus specifically on social facilitation and rivalry.

Social Facilitation and Rivalry

The literature on social facilitation distinguishes two major paradigms: *audience effects* and *co-action effects* (cf. Zajonc, 1965). *Audience effects* refer to the influence passive spectators have on human behavior. In the context of auctions, audience effect are elicited by individuals who observe the course of bidding but are not actively participating. For instance, this may be an audience watching a charity auction or the media attention on spectrum license auctions. On the other hand, *co-action effects* refer to the influence the presence of other individuals has, who are also engaged in the same activity (cf. Zajonc, 1965). In a live auction, for instance, co-action effects are elicited by the presence of other bidders who are bidding on the same item and bidders who are merely observing the current auction and actually waiting for a specific item following up.

It is important to highlight that audience and co-action effects already occur without strategic interaction. Accordingly, social facilitation only refers to the sheer presence of other individuals, i.e. the awareness of being observed by passive observers and other bidders. In contrast, the concept of rivalry addresses the fact that bidders are actually competing for obtaining the very same good. Therefore, strategic interaction is a necessary condition for rivalry. Rivalry is an inherent characteristic of live and Internet auctions, as *"each bidder competes against others who want the same item"* (Stern and Stafford, 2006).

Interdependencies in Bidders' Utility Functions

The degree of rivalry increases *ceteris paribus* with the number of bidders in an auction (Heyman et al., 2004).[4] However, rivalry can also get more intense, when a bidder's utility does not only depend on her own individual monetary gains and losses, but also on the utilities of other bidders. This concept of utility is usually referred to as *"interdependent utilities"* (e.g. Schall, 1972; Bault et al., 2008). For instance, subjects may develop personal rivalries with other individuals and perceive feelings of envy or gloating (Smith et al., 1996). In the context of auctions, the literature has identified in particular *"spitefulness"* and (nonmonetary) *"joy of winning"* as sources for such interdependencies.

A bidder is spiteful, if she derives an additional negative utility when her opponent wins an auction. This negative utility depends on the monetary profit of the competitor (cf. Morgan et al., 2003). Morgan et al. (2003) show that symmetric equilibrium bidding becomes more aggressive in various auctions, if bidders are spiteful. Therefore, if an agent's utility depends on the outcomes of other agents, it can be a (rational) best response to place higher bids. In contrast, a bidder experiences a nonmonetary joy of winning if she derives an additional positive utility from the *"uniqueness of being first"* in the social competition of an auction (Ku et al., 2005). Morgan et al. (2003) refer to this nonmonetary component as the *"love of winning."* Although there is not much evidence for love of winning in the literature (e.g. Andreoni et al., 2007; Delgado et al., 2008), most of these studies investigate sealed-bid auctions. However, there is strong indication to conjecture that love of winning, and its anticipation, is strongly intertwined with auction fever. As outlined above, auction fever is frequently described as a phenomenon only occurring in dynamic auctions (e.g. Gimpel, 2007; Haruvy and Popkowski Leszczyc, 2009).

Immediate emotions induced by the auction outcome are depicted in Figure 3. Assume a single unit auction, in which the auction outcome reveals which bidder obtains the commodity for sale and how much she has to pay for it. If a bidder *wins* the auction, she may experience a *"joy of winning"* (Goeree and Offerman, 2003). This joy does not only comprise her utility from monetary payoffs, but also the utility from winning the social competition inherent in an auction, i.e. the love of winning. However, the winner of the auction may at the same time also suffer from *"winner regret."* For instance, in a first-price sealed-bid auction, the winner of the auction may still have won the auction by placing a lower bid and, thus, won the auction with a higher monetary payoff (Engelbrecht-Wiggans, 1989). In contrast, if the bidder *loses* the auction, she can experience *"loser regret"* from the missed opportunity of achieving a monetary payoff and from losing the social competition (Filiz-Ozbay and Ozbay, 2007). If bidders anticipate joy of winning and loser regret

---

[4] Recall that an increasing number of bidders decreases the expected payoff of each bidder (Vickrey, 1961).

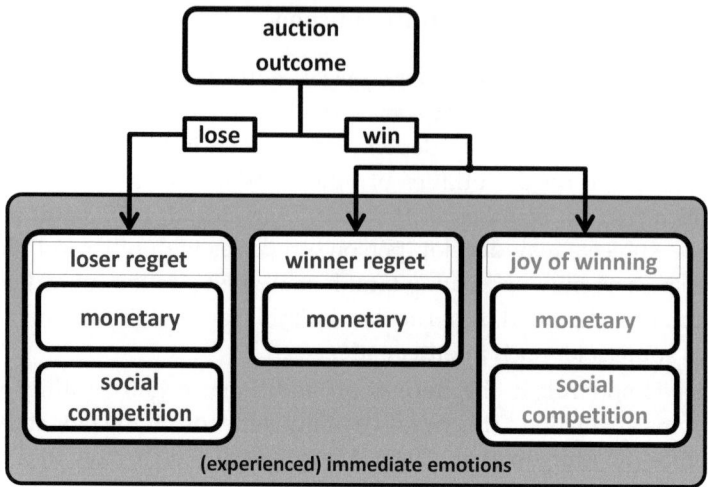

Figure 3: Immediate Emotions Induced by the Auction Outcome
(As depicted in Adam et al. (2010))

regarding the social competition and reflect these anticipated emotions in their bidding behavior, then their utilities comprise interdepencies.

Head-to-Head Battles

Bidders' utility functions which exhibit such interdependencies can result in *"head-to-head battles"* (Ku et al., 2008) among a small (sub-)group of bidders. In a survey among bidders from live auctions, Johns and Zaichkowsky (2003) observe a U-shaped dependency between the number of bidders and the degree of rivalry. In auctions with only two active bidders, the authors state that *"the bidding war was more personal."* However, when an auction attracted a large number of active bidders, there is a *"race to bid on and win the item."* Ku et al. (2005) argue that rivalry is particularly intense when only two bidders compete in a single auction. Based on data from a laboratory experiment, the authors report that bidders experience higher levels of self-report arousal and place higher bids in high rivalry treatments, i.e. when bidders face one single opponent in comparison to facing eight other individuals. Thus, so the authors conclude, rivalry and arousal seem to be higher with few rather than with many bidders.

These observations seem to be contradictory to the statement above that rivalry increases *ceteris paribus* with the number of bidders. However, when taking interdependent utilities into account, one may conjecture an interaction between the degree of utility interdependencies and the number of bidders.

Research Questions on Interdependent Utilities

As outlined above, interdependent utilities (IU) seem to play an important role in auction fever. In particular, we identify the following research questions concerning interdependent utilities:

IU1: To what degree does the phenomenon of auction fever depend on interdependencies between bidders' utility functions?

IU2: To what extent does the degree of interdependent utilities depend on the number of active bidders?

IU3: How do audience and co-action effects affect the degree of interdependent utilities?

Further, the existence of interdependent utilities and the general phenomenon of auction fever also seems to depend on the commodity for sale. Product characteristics and their influence on auction fever will be discussed in the following section.

3.2 Product Characteristics

Ariely and Simonson (2003) argue that the occurrence and degree of auction fever is subject to the specific characteristics of the auctioned item, e.g. *"whether the product offered is such that the allure of its low starting price has the potential to generate emotional involvement."* At this stage, there has been little research on how the phenomenon of auction fever depends on product characteristics. Nevertheless, this research question is important, because the literature on auction fever analyzes auctions ranging from retail products such as electronic equipment to collectibles as one-cent coins and fiberglass cows (cf. Ku et al., 2005; Lucking-Reiley et al., 2007).

The conjecture that characteristics of the auctioned commodity have an impact on the degree of auction fever is supported by the observation of Lee and Malmendier (2010). The authors report that the amount of overbidding in eBay auctions depends on the product category, with proportions of overbidding ranging *"between 30% and 60% for most categories."* The authors define overbidding with respect to simultaneouly listed ficed price offers on the same platform. However, the authors do not address *which* characteristics of the commodity are responsible for this observation.

Product Value, Scarcity, and Public Interest

We conjecture that in particular the product's value, scarcity, and public interest play an important role for the occurrence of auction fever.

First, if the value of the item is comparatively high, this affects bidder's individual involvement and, thus, arousal. For instance, Ku et al. (2008) report that bidding behavior is more aggressive when stakes are high by manipulating conversion rates. The perceived loss of the current high bidder in the event of being outbidded is probably higher when stakes are high. Second, Smith (1990) argues that bidders are often uncertain about their own product valuation. In this respect, Lucking-Reiley (1999) notes that this uncertainty inherently increases in Internet auctions, where bidders' information regarding product quality and seller reliability is rather limited and biased.

Third, product scarcity affects rivalry among bidders. For instance, Hou (2007) argue that a long auction duration only then positively affects the endogenous number of bidders, if scarcity is sufficiently high and bidders do not have *"more options at any point of time."* Beyond that, Lynn (1992) report that an item becomes more desirable for consumers if it is scarce. Peters and Bodkin (2007) observe that eBay bidders derive *"joy in finding rare or unusual items."* Finally, a high public interest can presumably increase a bidder's prestige when obtaining the auctioned item, e.g. a charity auction or a unique collectible. Ku et al. (2005) observe charity auctions and conjecture that the intense media attention may also have *"increased arousal and facilitated higher bidding."*

Research Questions on Product Characteristics

As outlined above, product characteristics (PC) of the auction commodity seem to play an important role in auction fever. In particular, we identify the following research questions concerning product characteristics:

PC1: What is the impact of a product's value, scarcity, and public interest on bidding fever?

PC2: Which features of a product are responsible for inducing psychological attachment in auctions, in particular with respect to perceived ownership?

PC3: To what extent does the degree of interdependent utilities depend on product characteristics?

4 Discussion on Methodological Approaches

The last section discussed two main challenges for auction fever research. In particular, interpersonal utilities and product characteristics have been identified as important influencing factors for auction fever. In this section we will now discuss different methodological approaches for analyzing auction fever in economic laboratory experiments.

4.1 Participant Deception

The literature on auction fever frequently conducts laboratory experiments in which participants are intentionally deceived in order *"not to disturb the emergence of auction fever"* (Ockenfels et al., 2006). In particular, participants are told that they (1) bid against other human individuals, while they are actually competing with computerized agents (e.g. Häubl and Popkowski Leszczyc, 2004; Ku et al., 2008), and (2) that their payment is performance depending although every participant eventually receives the same payoff (e.g. Ku et al., 2008). While deception of participants has turned out to be common practice in experimental psychology, it violates established paradigms of experimental economics (cf. Guala, 2005).

With respect to auction fever experiments, Ockenfels et al. (2006) criticize that it remains unclear to what extent participants *"will actually believe any part of the information they are given,"* if the subject pool has been exposed to deception in experiments before. Following this reasoning, the deception of participants turns out to be an inappropriate methodological approach for auction fever experiments.

4.2 Physioeconomics

Hagenau et al. (2007) and Adam et al. (2009) propose a methodology denoted as *"physioeconomics"* for measuring the impact of emotions in electronic auctions. Physioeconomics, so Adam et al. (2009), *"extends existing methods of experimental economics by measuring autonomic nervous system activity using well-established psychophysiological methodology, in order to gain a deep understanding of the dynamic process of human economic decision-making."*

A subject's heart rate and skin conductivity are well established parameters in psychophysiology for assessing her emotional processing. In particular, the *(tonic)* skin conductance level and the *phasic* amplitude of skin conductance responses are sensitive indexes for the general level of arousal and the degree of arousal associated with a single auction event, respectively. Phasic heart rate, on the other hand, allows for evaluating the perceived valence of a certain stimulus with negative stimuli typically eliciting decelatory responses and positive stimuli relative heart rate accelerations.

Physioeconomics allows for identifying the intensity of immediate and anticipated emotions, as well as for assessing a subject's current emotional state. Therefore, it turns out to be a complementary methodological approach for investigating auction fever in particular and the interactions outlined in the framework for emotional bidding in general. While a lot of studies on auction fever *conjecture* an interaction between emotional processing and bidding behavior, physioeconomics allows for actually *measuring* this interaction.

4.3 Human or Computerized Competitors

As depicted in Figure 3, the immediate emotions upon winning and losing an auction can be distinguished into (1) emotions regarding the monetary payoff and (2) emotions regarding the social competition.[5] Both categories of emotions play an important role for human decision-making in auctions (e.g. Delgado et al., 2008; Engelbrecht-Wiggans and Katok, 2008). However, the phenomenon of auction fever

---

[5] Recall that interdependent utilities are an inherent characteristic of the social competition.

seems to be particularly depending on emotions regarding the social competition. For instance, Häubl and Popkowski Leszczyc (2004) argue that for the experience of auction fever, it is a necessary condition *"that an auction participant competes directly with other human bidders."* Heyman et al. (2004) refer to this phenomenon as the *"opponent effect"* and Delgado et al. (2008) argue that actually the *"fear of losing the social competition"* inherent in auctions is responsible for overbidding.

Engelbrecht-Wiggans and Katok (2008) intentionally exclude emotions regarding the social competition by letting subjects compete with computerized agents. In contrast to the studies addressed in Section 4.1, subjects are explicitly told that they compete against computerized agents. Engelbrecht-Wiggans and Katok argue that *"theories [of spitefulness] require inter-personal comparisons and, therefore, cannot explain similar behavior by subjects who were bidding against computerized rather than human competitors."* Following this reasoning, the experimenter can investigate the impact emotions originated in interdependent utilities, by benchmarking human behavior when bidding against computerized agents with bidding against human individuals. This seems to be a promising approach for investigating the significance of interdependent utilities for auction fever. The actual intensity difference of emotional processing can then be simultaneously assessed with physiological parameters and the methodology of physioeconomics.

4.4 Induced Values vs. Real Goods

One major paradigm of experimental economics is the *induced value theory* introduced in the seminal work of Smith (1976). The induced value theory states that in order to observe realistic behavior in laboratory experiments subjects need to be properly incentivized through a proper reward medium that has to fulfill the requirements of monotonicity, salience, and dominance.[6] Typically, experimenters choose real money as the reward medium and provide a performance depending payment scheme to incentivize human behavior in the context of an artificial economic institution.

In contrast, a series of studies on auction fever rewards subjects with a fixed lump sum, which does not allow for performance depending gains or losses (Heyman et al., 2004; Wolf et al., 2005).[7] Particularly with respect to Figure 3, it remains totally unclear to what extent emotions elicited by monetary payoffs are reflected in bidding behavior, if there are neither *actual* nor *potential* monetary gains and losses. Further, is important to keep in mind that the expected utility from winning

---

[6] For a comprehensive survey on the methodology of experimental economics please refer to Guala (2005).

[7] In these studies, subjects are *explicitly* told that they will receive a fixed show-up fee. In contrast, the literature addressed in Section 4.1 pretends a performance depending payment scheme, although all subjects eventually receive the same amount of money.

an auction is the actual reason for bidders to participate. If this utility is zero by construction, the explanatory power of such studies seems rather small.[8]

Another approach is auctioning off real world commodities, or *"real goods,"* in laboratory experiments (Kahneman et al., 1990). While the theory of induced values is a well-established methodological approach to induce real world behavior, one can also directly auction off real goods. Kahneman et al. (1990) conduct a now famous auction experiment in which participants can place bids on coffee mugs.[9] In another well-known auction experiment comprising real goods, Lucking-Reiley (1999) conducts a controlled field experiment on eBay. In particular, the authors auction off collector cards. Ehrhart et al. (2010) conduct a laboratory experiment comprising real goods to investigate the effect of perceived ownership on bidding behavior, by auctioning off USB mass storage devices. The authors argue that it is particularly important to properly choose the auctioned commodity when conducting economic experiments with real goods. Therefore, before running the laboratory experiment, Ehrhart et al. initially conduct a survey study to assess which objects are actually appropriate.

One main advantage, so Ehrhart et al. (2010), for using real goods in auction fever experiments is that subjects can actually develop a psychological attachment with an object, which is not or not to this extent the case for money.[10] Going one step further, it would now be particularly interesting to use real world commodities for identifying those product characteristics which actually mediate psychological attachment. Therefore, we believe that using real world commodities is a promising approach for investigating auction fever. Once again, the actual elicited emotional state can be assessed with physiological parameters and the methodology of physioeconomics.

5 Conclusion

In this paper we focused on the question of how to systematically investigate auction fever and its impact on electronic auctions. Emotions have turned out to be a quality characteristic of Internet consumer auctions. Therefore, it is vital to know how electronic auctions can trigger emotions, and, perhaps even more importantly, how the triggered emotions affect the auction outcome. Following this reasoning, a deep understanding of how cognitive reasoning and emotional processing are reflected in bidding behavior is of high relevance for the market engineer.

---

[8] Recall that the non-monetary component of the joy of winning is most likely intertwined with the phenomenon of auction fever. Therefore, this utility, and particularly its anticipation, arises only during the dynamic process of an auction.

[9] Kahneman et al. (1990) analyze the endowment effect, i.e. effect of actual ownership, by endowing coffee mugs to one half of the participants (sellers), while the other half (buyers) receives no coffee mugs. Sellers and buyers can then exchange the coffee mugs through a double-sided auction. The authors report that the average price a seller is willing to accept (WTA) for a coffee mug is significantly larger than the average price a buyer is willing to pay (WTP).

[10] This is in line with the observation of Wolf et al. (2008), who find that even the time a bidder has for observing the item plays an important role for developing her attachment.

Auction fever literature identified in particular perceived competition, previous investments, and perceived ownership as elicitors of auction fever. Further, in Internet auctions the elicitation of auction fever is mediated through the user interface design of the auction system. Additionally, we identified in particular product characteristics and interdependent utilities as important influencing factors which have often been neglected in auction fever literature, or only gained little attention. Although interdependent utilities are an influencing factor for rivalry, and therefore, for perceived competition, we believe it is important to focus on how such interdependencies arise and how they interact with other facets of auction fever.

Summarizing the methodological discussion, one can conclude that applying physiological measurements in economic laboratory experiments and auctioning real world commodities are promising approaches, which are complementary to traditional methodologies in experimental economics. Further, utilizing computerized agents seems to be an adequate approach for assessing the significance of interdependent utilities for auction fever. In contrast, although a substantial part of auction fever literature is based on deception of participants and hypothetical auction scenarios, one has to consider fundamental drawbacks of these approaches. Therefore, the explanatory power of these approaches seems at least questionable.

References

Adam, M. T. P., M. Gamer, and C. Weinhardt (2009): "Measuring the impact of emotions in electronic auctions: A physioeconomic approach," *Working Paper, Karlsruhe Institute of Technology (KIT)*, pp. 1–26.

Adam, M. T. P., J. Krämer, C. Jähnig, S. Seifert, and C. Weinhardt (2010): "Emotions in electronic auctions: Insights from a literature review," *Working Paper, Karlsruhe Institute of Technology (KIT)*, pp. 1–50.

Andreoni, J., Y.-K. Che, and J. Kim (2007): "Asymmetric information about rivals' types: An experiment," *Games and Economic Behavior*, 59, pp. 240–259.

Ariely, D. and I. Simonson (2003): "Buying, bidding, playing, or competing? Value assessment and decision dynamics in online auctions," *Journal of Consumer Psychology*, 13, pp. 113–123.

Bault, N., G. Coricelle, and A. Rustichini (2008): "Interdependent utilities: How social ranking affects choice behavior," *PLoS ONE*, 3(10), pp. 1–10.

Delgado, M. R., A. Schotter, E. Y. Ozbay, and E. A. Phelps (2008): "Understanding overbidding: Using the neural circuitry of reward to design economic auctions," *Science*, 321(5897), pp. 1849–1852.

Ding, M., J. Eliashberg, J. Huber, and R. Saini (2005): "Emotional bidders: An analytical and experimental examination of consumers' behavior in a priceline-like reverse auction," *Management Science*, 51(3), pp. 352–364.

eBay Inc. (2009): *Annual report 2008*, http://investor.ebay.com/.

Ehrhart, K.-M., L. Goebes, and S. Lotz (2010): "Experimental Analysis of the Pseudo-Endowment Effect with Real Goods," *Working Paper, Karlsruhe Institute of Technology (KIT)*.

Ehrhart, K.-M., M. Ott, and S. Abele (2008): "Auction fever: Theory and experimental evidence," *SFB 504 Discussion Paper Series*, No. 08-27, http://www.sfb504.uni-mannheim.de/publications/dp08-27.pdf.

Engelbrecht-Wiggans, R. (1989): "The effect of regret on optimal bidding in auctions," *Management Science*, 35(6), pp. 685–692.

Engelbrecht-Wiggans, R. and E. Katok (2008): "Regret and feedback information in first-price sealed-bid auctions," *Management Science*, 54(4), pp. 808–819.

Filiz-Ozbay, E. and E. Y. Ozbay (2007): "Auctions with anticipated regret: Theory and experiment," *The American Economic Review*, 97(4), pp. 1407–1418.

Gerrig, R. J. and P. G. Zimbardo (2007): *Psychology and life*, 18th ed edition, Pearson / Allyn and Bacon, Boston, Mass.

Gimpel, H. (2007): *Preferences in negotiations: The attachment effect*, Lecture notes in economics and mathematical systems, Springer, Berlin, Heidelberg.

Glänzer, S. and B. Schäfers (2001): "Dynamic Trading Network und virtuelle Auktionen im Internet: Das Beispiel ricardo.de," in: A. Hermanns and M. Sauter (eds.), *Management-Handbuch Electronic Commerce*, Vahlen, München, pp. 609–616.

Goeree, J. K. and T. Offerman (2003): "Winner's curse without overbidding," *European Economic Review*, 47, pp. 625–644.

Guala, F. (2005): *The methodology of experimental economics*, Cambridge University Press, Cambridge.

Hagenau, M., S. Seifert, and C. Weinhardt (2007): "A primer on physioeconomics," in: G. E. Kersten, J. Rios, and E. Chen (eds.), *Proceedings of the 8th Group Decision and Negotiation Conference (GDN)*, Montreal, Canada, pp. 214–215.

Haruvy, E. and P. T. Popkowski Leszczyc (2009): "The impact of online auction duration," *Decision Analysis*.

Häubl, G. and P. T. Popkowski Leszczyc (2004): "The psychology of auctions: Enriching models of bidder and seller behavior," *Advances in Consumer Research*, 31(1), pp. 91–92.

Heyman, J. E., Y. Orhun, and D. Ariely (2004): "Auction fever: The effect of opponents and quasi-endowment on product valuations," *Journal of Interactive Marketing*, 18(4), pp. 7–21.

Hou, J. (2007): "Price determinants in online auctions: A comparative study of eBay China and US," *Journal of Electronic Commerce Research*, 8(3), pp. 172–183.

Johns, C. L. and J. L. Zaichkowsky (2003): "Bidding behavior at the auction," *Psychology and Marketing*, 20(4), pp. 303–322.

Kahneman, D., J. L. Knetsch, and R. H. Thaler (1990): "Experimental tests of the endowment effect and the Coase theorem," *The Journal of Political Economy*, 98(6), pp. 1325–1348.

Katok, E. and A. M. Kwasnica (2008): "Time is money: The effect of clock speed on seller's revenue in Dutch auctions," *Experimental Economics*, 11(4), pp. 344–357.

Krishna, V. (2002): *Auction theory*, Acad. Press, San Diego, California.

Ku, G. (2008): "Learning to de-escalate: The effects of regret in escalation of commitment," *Organizational Behavior and Human Decision Processes*, 105, pp. 221–232.

Ku, G., A. D. Galinsky, and J. K. Murnighan (2008): "Arousal, interest, and auction bidders," http://ssrn.com/abstract=1298572.

Ku, G., D. Malhotra, and J. K. Murnighan (2005): "Towards a competitive arousal model of decision-making: A study of auction fever in live and Internet auctions," *Organizational Behavior and Human Decision Processes*, 96, pp. 89–103.

Lee, L., O. Amir, and D. Ariely (2009a): "In search of Homo Economicus: Cognitive noise and the role of emotion in preference consistency," *Journal of Consumer Research*, 36, pp. 173–187.

Lee, M.-Y., Y.-K. Kim, and A. Fairhurst (2009b): "Shopping value in online auctions: Their antecendents and outcomes," *Journal of Retailing and Consumer Services*, 16, pp. 75–82.

Lee, Y. H. and U. Malmendier (2010): "The bidder's curse," *The American Economic Review*.

Loewenstein, G. (2000): "Emotions in economic theory and economic behavior," *The American Economic Review*, 90(2), pp. 426–432.

Lucking-Reiley, D. (1999): "Using field experiments to test equivalence between auction formats: Magic on the Internet," *The American Economic Review*, 89(5), pp. 1063–1080.

Lucking-Reiley, D., D. Bryan, N. Prasad, and D. Reeves (2007): "Pennies from eBay: The determinants of price in online auctions," *The Journal of Industrial Economics*, 55(2), pp. 223–233.

Lynn, M. (1992): "Scarcity's enhancement of desirability: The role of naive economic theories," *Basic and Applied Social Psychology*, 13(1), pp. 67–78.

Malhotra, D., G. Ku, and J. K. Murnighan (2008): "When winning is everything," *Harvard Business Review*, 86(5), pp. 78–86.

McAfee, R. P. and J. McMillan (1987): "Auctions and bidding," *Journal of Economic Literature*, 25(2), pp. 699–738.

Möllenberg, A. (2004): "Internet auctions in marketing: The consumer perspective," *Electronic Markets*, 14(4), pp. 360–371.

Morgan, J., K. Steiglitz, and G. Reis (2003): "The spite motive and equilibrium behavior in auctions," *Contributions to Economic Analysis & Policy*, 2(1), pp. 1102–1127.

Murnighan, J. K. (2002): "A very extreme case of the dollar auction," *Journal of Management Education*, 26, pp. 56–69.

Ockenfels, A., D. Reiley, and A. Sadrieh (2006): "Online auctions," in: T. J. Hendershott (ed.), *Economics and information systems, Handbooks in Information Systems*, vol. 1, Elsevier B. V., Amsterdam, The Netherlands, pp. 571–628.

Park, S. C., J. U. Kim, and G. W. Bock (2008): "Understanding a bidder's escalation of commitment in the online C2C auction," in: Z. Irani, S. Sahraoui, A. Ghoneim, J. Sharp, S. Ozkan, M. Ali, and S. Alshawi (eds.), *European Mediterranean Conference on Information Systems (EMCIS)*.

Peters, C. and C. D. Bodkin (2007): "An exploratory investigation of problematic online auction behaviors: Experience of eBay users," *Journal of Retailing and Consumer Services*, 14, pp. 1–16.

Rasmusen, E. (2007): *Games and information: An introduction to game theory*, 4th. ed. edition, Blackwell, Malden, Mass.

Schall, L. D. (1972): "Interdependent utilities and Pareto optimality," *The Quarterly Journal of Economics*, 86(1), pp. 19–24.

Smith, C. W. (1990): *Auctions: The social construction of value*, University of California Press, Berkeley.

Smith, R. H., T. J. Turner, R. Garonzik, C. W. Leach, V. Urch-Druskat, and C. M. Weston (1996): "Envy and Schadenfreude," *Personality and Social Psychology*, 22, pp. 158–168.

Smith, V. L. (1976): "Experimental economics: Induced value theory," *The American Economic Review*, 66(2), pp. 274–279.

Stafford, M. R. and B. Stern (2002): "Consumer bidding behavior on Internet auction sites," *International Journal of Electronic Commerce*, 7(1), pp. 135–150.

Stern, B., M. B. Royne, T. F. Stafford, and C. C. Bienstock (2008): "Consumer acceptance of online auctions: An extension and revision of the TAM," *Psychology and Marketing*, 25(7), pp. 619–636.

Stern, B. and M. R. Stafford (2006): "Individual and social determinants of winning bids in online auctions," *Journal of Consumer Behaviour*, 5(1), pp. 43–55.

Vickrey, W. (1961): "Counterspeculation, auctions, and competitive sealed tenders," *The Journal of Finance*, 16(1), pp. 8–37.

Weinhardt, C., C. Holtmann, and D. Neumann (2003): "Market engineering," *Wirtschaftsinformatik*, 45(6), pp. 635–640.

Wolf, J. R., H. R. Arkes, and W. A. Muhanna (2005): "Do auction bidders really want to win the item, or do they simply want to win?" *Working Paper*, pp. 1–19.

Wolf, J. R., H. R. Arkes, and W. A. Muhanna (2008): "The power of touch: An examination of the effect of duration of physical contact on the valuation of objects," *Judgment and Decision Making*, 3(6), pp. 476–482.

Zajonc, R. B. (1965): "Social facilitation," *Science*, 149, pp. 269–274.

Anticipated Emotions in the Reference-Dependent Valuation of Gains and Losses

Laura Goebes[1], Karl-Martin Ehrhart[1], and Christof Weinhardt[2]

[1] Institute for Economic Theory and Statistics, KIT
   `goebes@wiwi.uni-karlsruhe.de`, `ehrhart@kit.edu`
[2] Institute of Information Systems and Management, KIT
   `weinhardt@kit.edu`

Summary. Standard economic theory offers normative as well as descriptive models to describe and predict human choice behavior. Here, the role of emotion in decision-making has been ignored in the past. To make advantageous decisions, a subject must be able to valuate gains and losses as options to be realized in future outcomes. Additional to standard economic theory it is suggested that decisions are aided by emotions, in the form of somatic states, that are elicited during the deliberation of future consequences and that mark different options for behavior to be advantageous or disadvantageous. To gain insights in how economic decisions are made and what role anticipated emotions play in economic decision-making, the somatic marker hypothesis is applied to several standard economic choice problems. The paper presents an experimental setup to test the role of anticipated emotions in economic decision-making under risk. The proposed experimental design aims at measuring the physiological differences of subjects with high and small probabilities of potential gains and losses in a controlled laboratory experiment with the methodology of physio economics. The authors present an overview of standard economic theory of decision making under risk, a review of the role of emotions in decision-making as well as an introduction into physio economics. The authors further present the design of a laboratory experiment and the hypotheses to be tested within the experiment.

1 Introduction

In economics it is usually assumed that subjects have stable and well-defined preferences and make rational choices according to these preferences. Standard economic theory offers normative as well as descriptive models to describe and predict human choice behavior. Decision-making under risk is usually modeled by a choice problem over a set of lotteries, where a lottery is defined as a (known) distribution of probabilities over a set of outcomes. The standard approach for decision-making under risk is the expected utility theory by von Neumann and Morgenstern (1944). The expected utility theory has dominated the analysis of decision under risk over years and is generally accepted as a normative model. The predictive quality of the expected utility theory as a descriptive model for decisions under risk has often been discussed and criticized, because it is often observed that subjects do not decide as predicted by expected utility theory. With the prospect theory Kahneman and Tversky propose an alternative account of decision under risk. The core idea of the prospect theory is to offer a descriptive model which takes the observed phenomena in human decision-making into account:

- Certain outcomes are overestimated compared to less probable outcomes.
- Gains and losses are weighted differently, that is subjects show risk aversion in the face of gains and risk seeking in the face of losses (except for very small probablities).
- The presentation of a lottery affects subjects preferences.

Standard economic theory ignores the influence of emotions in decision-making. Research in neuroscience suggests that rational decision-making, in fact, depends on prior emotional processing. The somatic marker hypothesis provides a systems-level neuroanatomical and cognitive framework for decision-making and its influence by emotions. The key idea of this hypothesis is that decision-making is a process that is influenced by marker signals, that express themselves in emotions and feelings. The theory suggests that decisions are aided by emotions, in the form of somatic states, that are elicited during the deliberation of future consequences and that mark different options for behavior to be advantageous or disadvantageous. To gain insights in how economic decisions are made and what role anticipated emotions play in economic decision-making, an experimental setup is presented in this paper.

2 Economic Decision-Making under Risk

2.1 Expected Utility Theory

Economic theory usually models decision-making under risk by a choice problem over a set of lotteries, where a lottery is defined as a (known) distribution of probabilities over a set of outcomes. The standard approach for decision-making under risk is the expected utility theory by von Neumann and Morgenstern (1944). In case of discrete outcomes, for example, the expected utility is given by the sum of the probability weighted utilities of the certain (riskless) outcomes. As the name of the expected utility suggests, a subject's decision under risk is based on the comparison of the expected utilities of different lotteries. That is, the subject decides in favor of the lottery which provides the highest expected utility. To be more precise, if the subject faces a binary choice problem of accepting or declining a single lottery, it is assumed that a subject accepts the lottery if the utility, resulting from integrating the lottery with ones endowment, is higher than the utility of his endowment alone. This means that the domain of the utility function is determined by the final endowment, rather than by gains and losses.

A subject is called risk averse if he prefers certain outcomes to risky situations. According to the expected utility theory a subject is risk averse if he prefers the expected value of a lottery to the lottery itself. That is, in case of risk aversion the subject's utility of the expected values is higher than his expected utility of the lottery. The degree of risk aversion is measured by the concavity of the utility function[1]. Note that also with respect to risk aversion, as mentioned before, the expected utility theory does not distinguish between gain risk and loss risk.

The expected utility theory is based on four axioms[2]. A subject is considered as rational if all four axioms are satisfied. In this case, as von Neumann and Morgenstern prove, a subject's preferences can be uniquely and completely described by means of expected utility. Hence, according to von Neumann and Morgenstern, subjects act rational in a way that they maximize their expected utility.

The expected utility theory has dominated the analysis of decision under risk over years and is generally accepted as a normative model. Thus, it describes what a subject should do. However, it is often also applied as a descriptive model, which means it predicts what subjects in fact do. The predictive quality of the expected utility theory as a descriptive model for decisions under risk has often been discussed and criticized, because it is often observed that subjects do not decide as predicted by expected utility theory. As is well known, Allais (1953) presents empirical examples, known as Allais paradox, where systematical violations of the axioms of the expected utility are observed (see next section). These examples and further observations of systematic violation lead to alternative and complementary theories of decision-making under risk, where one of the most famous is the so-called prospect theory by Kahneman and Tversky (1979).

---

[1] More precisely, the (Arrow Pratt) measure of risk-aversion (according to the economists Kenneth Arrow and John W. Pratt) is defined as $r_u(c) = -\frac{u''(c)}{u'(c)}$, where u(c) denotes subject's utility of the certain outcome c and u'(c) and u''(c) the first and second derivative of the utility function u(c).

[2] The 4 axioms of expected utility theory:

- Completeness: For every A and B either $A \succ B$, $A \prec B$ or $A \sim B$ holds.
  Completeness assumes that a subject has well defined preferences to compare and evaluate two alternatives.

- Transitivity: For every A, B and C with $A \succ B$ and $B \succ C$ we must have $A \succ C$.
  Transitivity assumes that, as a subject decides according to the completeness axiom, the subject also decides consistently.

- Independence: Let A and B be two lotteries with $A \succeq B$, and let $t \in (0,1] \Rightarrow tA + (1-t)C \succ tB + (1-t)C$ for all C.
  Independence assumes that the preference order of two lotteries mixed with a third one maintains the same preference order as when the two are mixed independently.

- Continuity: Let A, B and C be lotteries with $A \succ B \succ C \Rightarrow \exists t \in (0,1)$ with $tA + (1-t)C \sim B$.
  Continuity assumes that when there are three lotteries (A, B and C) and the subject prefers A to B and B to C, then there should be a possible combination of A and C in which the subject is then indifferent between this mix and the lottery B.

2.2 Human decision-making in selected choice problems

The application of expected utility theory to choices between lotteries is based on the principles of expectation, endowment integration and risk aversion. In this section, several phenomena that violate these principles are presented and illustrated by examples of empirical tests.

The following observed phenomena systematically occur in human decision behavior.

- Certain outcomes are overestimated compared to less probable outcomes.
- Gains and losses are weighted differently, that is subjects show risk aversion in the face of gains and risk seeking in the face of losses (except for very small probabilities).
- The presentation of a lottery affects subjects preferences.

Examples for these phenomena are presented by a series of choice problems in Table 1 and it is further illustrated where the principles of the expected utility theory are violated.

Expected utility theory predicts that the utilities of outcomes are weighted by their probabilities. Problem 1 to 6 are choice problems that prove as counter-examples to this principle because subject's preferences systematically violate it. Kahneman and Tversky (1979) refer these examples to the certainty effect, because certain outcomes are overestimated. The pair of Problem 1 and 2 is a variation of the well-known and often discussed Allais paradox. As shown in Table 1 in Problem 1 and 2 subjects prefer lottery B over lottery A. In Problem 2 subjects prefer lottery A' over lottery B', which are extensions of Lottery A and B. More precisely, in Lottery A' and B' the common consequence of a 66% chance for winning 0 MU (Monetary Units) has been added. The additional common consequence leads to a shift of preferences as probability is moved from one common consequence to another. It seems that a lottery loses attractivity if gains are not certain anymore. The preference order of Problem 1 (assumed that $u(0) = 0$) implies that $0.34u(2400) > 0.33u(2500)$ while the preference order in Problem 2 implies the opposite. This shift of preferences violates the independence axiom of the expected utility theory.

The same phenomenon of certain outcomes being overweighted is shown in Problem 3 and 4. These examples are also based on an example by Allais. Here most subjects prefer Lottery D over Lottery C but Lottery C' over Lottery D'. This shift of preferences is caused by adding a common ratio to Lottery C and D. That is, Lottery C' can be expressed as (C, 0.25) and lottery D' can be expressed as (D, 0.25). The preference order of Problem 3 (assumed that $u(0) = 0$) implies that $\frac{u(3000)}{u(4000)}$ ¡ $\frac{4}{5}$ while the preference order in Problem 4 implies the opposite. This shift of preferences also violates the independency axiom of the expected utility theory.

Table 1: Example lotteries of the Prospect Theory (Kahneman and Tversky, 1979)
(Number of subjects is denoted by N and the percentage who chose each option is given in [])

Certainty Effect			
Problem 1:	A: (2500, 33%; 2400, 66%; 0, 1%)	¡	B:(2400, 100%)
N = 72	[18]		[82]
Problem 2:	A':(2500, 33%; 0, 67%)	¿	B':(2400, 34%; 0, 66%)
N = 72	[83]		[18]
Problem 3:	C:(4000, 80%)	¡	D:(3000, 100%)
N = 95	[20]		[80]
Problem 4:	C'(4000, 20%)	¿	D'(3000, 25%)
N = 95	[65]		[35]
Possibility			
Problem 5:	E:(6000, 45%)	¡	F:(3000, 90%)
N = 66	[14]		[86]
Problem 6:	E':(6000, 0,1%)	¿	F':(3000, 0,2%)
N = 66	[73]		[27]
Reflection Effect			
Problem 3':	C"(-4000, 80%)	¿	D"(-3000, 100%)
N = 95	[92]		[8]
Problem 4':	C'''(-4000, 20%)	¡	D'''(-3000, 25%)
N = 95	[42]		[58]
Problem 5':	E"(-6000, 45%)	¿	F"(-3000, 90%)
N = 66	[92]		[8]
Problem 6':	E'''(-6000, 0,1%)	¡	F'''(-3000, 0,2%)
N = 66	[30]		[70]
Isolation Effect			
Problem 11:	In the first step it is decided if a subject is rejected with a probability of 75% with an outcome of 0 or with a probability of 25% the subject can can choose between the following lotteries.		
	(4000, 80%)	¡	(3000,100%)
N = 141	[22]		[78]
Problem 12:	In the first step a subject is allocated with 1000. In the second step he has to choose between the following lotteries:		
	(1000, 50%)	¡	(500, 100%)
N = 70	[16]		[84]
Problem 13:	In the first step a subject is allocated with 2000. In the second step he has to choose between the following lotteries:		
	(-1000, 50%)	¿	(-500, 100%)
N = 68	[69]		[31]

The axiom of independence is not only violated if certain outcomes are involved in choice problems. The pair of Problem 5 and 6 illustrates where the independency axiom is violated if the chance for winning is reduced to a *possibility* for winning. If probabilities for winning are very small, most subjects prefer those lotteries with the higher gains, even if the probability for winning is smaller. In Problem 5 most subjects prefer Lottery F over E because the probability for winning is higher. As in Problem 6 the probability for winning is very small but there is still a possibility for winning, subjects prefer Lottery E' over F' because the outcome is higher.

The reflection effect (Problem 3' to 6') describes the phenomenon that preferences for lotteries change when the signs of these lotteries are inverted. Preferences for lotteries with positive outcomes (gains) are contrary to the preferences for lotteries with negative outcomes (losses). As described above, the preference order in Problem 3 and 4 violate the expected utility principle of expectation. Certain outcomes are overestimated which implies risk averse preference to a sure gain over a larger but probable outcome. Subjects' choice in Problem 3' and 4' includes a preference order that implies that certain losses are overestimated, which violates the independency axiom. The shift of preferences in Problem 3' to 4' implies risk seeking preference against a sure loss. This violates the principle of risk aversion of the subjects.

As mentioned in the previous section, the domain of a utility function, as assumed by expected utility theory, is determined by the final endowment rather than by gains and losses. As the before illustrated examples show, certain outcomes are overweighted and subjects are risk averse in the face of gains and risk seeking in the face of losses. In Problem 11 to 13 it is illustrated that subjects preferences shift when, due to another framing of the choice problem, one of these components becomes more obvious. Kahneman and Tversky refer these observations as the isolation effect. In Problem 11, choice between Lottery G and H has to be made before it is decided if the subject is rejected or not. This is the same situation as in Problem 4. However, subjects' preferences are opposite in Problem 11. The first step of the choice problem is not taken into account, the subject only looks at the supposed certain outcome of 3000 MU. Other two-step choice problems are presented in Problem 12 and 13. Both situations are identical with regard to the expected outcome. But the framing of the lotteries is different. Problem 12 is seen as a chance to gain and Problem 13 is seen as a chance to avoid a loss as the reference-point, the subjects endowment, changes. This seems to show, that the basis for the valuation of ones utility is not the final state of endowment but the change of the endowment.

With the prospect theory Kahneman and Tversky propose an alternative account of decision under risk. The core idea of the prospect theory is to offer a descriptive model which takes the observed phenomena in human decision-making into account. That is, the prospect theory includes more degrees of freedom. In general, this does not improve the quality of a model but in this case the explanatory value and predictive quality of the model is increased very much.

Prospect theory differentiates between two phases in decision-making: editing and evaluation. The purpose of the editing phase is to organize and reformulate given lotteries which results in a simpler or better known presentation of lotteries and to set a reference point which defines the domain of gains and losses. Further the edited lotteries are evaluated and the lottery with the highest value is chosen. The overall value of a lottery V is expressed in terms of two scales, Π and v. The first scale Π associates a decision weight to each probability p, that is it reflects the impact of a probability to the overall value of a lottery. The second scale v assigns a number $v(x)$ to each outcome x, which reflects the subjective value of the outcome. As outcomes are defined relative to the reference point, v measures the value of deviations from that reference point (gains and losses). In prospect theory it is differentiated between strictly positive, strictly negative and regular lotteries[3]. For a regular lottery the value of the lottery is given by $V(x, p; y, q) = \Pi(p)v(x) + \Pi(q)v(y)$ with $v(0) = 0$, $\Pi(1) = 1$ and $\Pi(0) = 0$. This value function generalizes expected utility theory by relaxing the expectation principle.

---

[3] A lottery is given in form of: $(x, p; y, q)$. A lottery is strictly positive if $x, y > 0$ and $p + q = 1$, strictly negative if $x, y < 0$ and $p + q = 1$. A lottery is regular if it is neither strictly positive or negative.

For a strictly positive or negative lottery the overall value of the lottery is presented differently: $V(x, p; y, q) = v(y) + \Pi(p)[v(x) - v(y)]$. The value of such a lottery represents the value of the riskless component plus the difference of values between the outcomes multiplied with the weight of the more extreme outcome.

3 Emotions in (economic) decision-making

As mentioned before, in economics it is assumed that subjects have stable and well-defined preferences and make rational choices according to these preferences. Allais described several phenomena that are not consistent with this assumption and Kahneman and Tversky extended the theory of decision-making under risk by integrating these phenomena into their model. It seems that human decision making is influenced by other factors than only rational utility maximization. The psychology and neural processes that underly human behavior in (economic) decision-making is investigated to give answers to the questions about what drives subjects while they valuate gains and losses in order to make advantageous decisions. The role of emotions in economic decision-making is investigated by different disciplines and methods.

3.1 Characteristics of emotions

In the nineteenth century the scientists James (1884), Lange and Kurella (1887) developed a new definition and explanation of the nature of emotions. The James-Lange theory refers to a hypothesis, which states that within subjects, as a response to certain stimuli, the autonomic nervous system creates physiological reactions like muscular tension, a rise in heart rate, perspiration, and dryness of the mouth. Emotions are expressed by feelings which come about as a result of these physiological changes, rather than being their cause. James (1884) explains his concept as:

> "My theory [...] is that the bodily changes follow directly the perception of the exciting fact, and that our feeling of the same changes as they occur is the emotion. Common sense says, we lose our fortune, are sorry and weep; we meet a bear, are frightened and run; we are insulted by a rival, are angry and strike. The hypothesis here to be defended says that this order of sequence is incorrect [...] and that the more rational statement is that we feel sorry because we cry, angry because we strike, afraid because we tremble [...] Without the bodily states following on the perception, the latter would be purely cognitive in form, pale, colorless, destitute of emotional warmth. We might then see the bear, and judge it best to run, receive the insult and deem it right to strike, but we should not actually feel afraid or angry."

According to the James-Lang theory emotions are associated with distinct patterns of somato-visceral activity. There have been conducted several experiments which give evidence for the existence of distinct patterns of peripheral activity associated with basic emotions. Basic emotions are for example happiness, sadness, disgust, anger, surprise and fear. The mentioned experiments investigate response patterns of the autonomic nervous system as a result to different stimuli as for example voluntary facial expression, visual and olfactory stimuli or film clips (see Table 2). Response of the autonomic nervous system is expressed by different physiological reactions. These reactions are for example changes in heart rate, skin conductance, skin temperature, respiration frequency etc. There is also a lot of critiques towards the evidence of distinct response patterns. Cacioppo et al. (2000) state, according to a meta-analysis of the studies investigating the physiological responses observed during basic emotions, that these studies only provide equivocal evidence. Rainville et al. (2006) propose two reasons for the limited result in finding distinctive physiological patterns regarding basic emotions. First, there is inadequate elicitation of the target emotion to be investigated. Second, there is incomplete physiological characterization of the following somatic states. As there is such a controversial discussion about the existence of distinct physiological patterns associated with basic emotions there clearly is the need of further investigation.

Table 2: Selected Literature on Psychophysiological Parameters
(HR = heart rate, SC/SR = skin conductance/resistance, SP = skin potential)
(BP = blood pressure, ST = skin temperature, RF = respiration frequency, MT = muscle tension, P = pulse, PF = blood flow, ECG = electrocardiography)

Author(s)	Published in	HR	SC/SR	SP	BP	ST	RF	MT	P	BF	ECG
Vianna et al. (2009)	International Journal of Psychophysiology, Vol. 72		X								X
Rainville et al. (2006)	International Journal of Psychophysiology, Vol. 61		X				X				X
Christie and Friedman (2004)	International Journal of Psychophysiology, Vol. 51		X		X						X
Vernet-Maury et al. (1999)	Journal of the Autonomic Nervous System, Vol. 75	X	X	X		X	X		X		
Ekman et al. (1983)	Science, Vol. 221	X	X				X				
Averill (1969)	The Society of Psychophysiological Research, Vol. 5, No. 4	X	X			X	X	X			
Collet et al. (1997)	Journal of the Autonomic Nervous System, Vol. 62		X	X		X	X		X		
Levenson et al. (1990)	Psychophysiology, Vol. 27, No. 4	X	X				X				

3.2 Methods on investigating the role of emotions in decision-making

Understanding how the brain deals with uncertainty and how subjective economic preferences are represented neurally are two of the central motivating problems of the emerging discipline of neuroeconomics. Valuation of gains and losses in risky situations play an important role in human decision-making in order to make advantageous decisions. As mentioned before subjects do not maximize their utility by weighting outcomes with probabilities and they would not accept the same amount of money for a good they own that they were willing to pay for the same good. As these irregularities occur systematically the question "Why?" needs to be answered. In recent years the belief came up, that emotional processing plays an important role in decision-making.

There are different methods to investigate the role of emotions in human decision-making and the impact on economics. The underlying neuronal processes of decision-making in different situations within different backgrounds are investigated. Some selected literature on investigating the role of emotions in (economic) decision-making is listed in Table 3. The most common methods on investigating the

Table 3: Selected literature on investigating the role of emotions in (economic) decision-making
(fMRI = functional Magnetic Resonance Imaging, EEG = Electroencephalography, LS = Lesion Study)
(MEG = Magnetoencephalography, PPM = Psychophysiological Methods, TMS = Transcranial Magnet Stimulation)

Author(s)	Published in	fMRI	LS	PPM
D'Acremont et al. (2009)	Neuroimage, Vol. 47	X		
Martino et al. (2009)	The Journal of Neuroscience, Vol.29, No.12	X		
Christakou et al. (2009)	The Journal of Neuroscience, Vol. 29, No. 35	X		
Krajbich et al. (2009)	The Journal of Neuroscience, Vol. 29, No. 7	X		
Bault et al. (2008)	Plos One, Vol. 3, No. 10			X
Xue et al. (2009)	Cerebral Cortex, Vol. 19	X		
Rao et al. (2008)	Neuroimage, Vol. 42	X		
Miu et al. (2008)	Biological Psychology, Vol. 77			X
Clark et al. (2008)	Brain, Vol. 131		X	
D'Argembeau et al. (2008)	Neuroimage, Vol. 40	X		
Tom et al. (2007)	Science, Vol. 315	X		
Berntson et al. (2007)	SCAN		X	
Weller (2007)	Psychological Science, Vol. 18, No. 11		X	
Ben-Shakhar et al. (2007)	Journal of Economic Psychology, Vol. 28			X
Fellows (2006)	Brain, Vol. 129		X	
Van't Wout et al. (2006)	Exp Brain Res, Vol. 169			X
Huettel et al. (2006)	Neuron, Vol. 49	X		
Denburg et al. (2006)	International Journal of Psychophysiology, Vol. 61			X
Hsu et al. (2005)	Science, Vol. 310	X		
Oya et al. (2005)	PNAS, Vol. 102, No. 23		X	X
Shiv et al. (2005a)	Cognitive Brain Research, Vol. 23		X	
Shiv et al. (2005b)	Psychological Science, Vol. 16, No. 6		X	
Bechara et al. (2005)	Games and Economic Behavior, Vol. 52		X	X
Smith and Dickhaut (2005)	Games and Economic Behavior, Vol. 52			X
Leland and Grafman (2005)	Games and Economic Behavior, Vol. 52		X	
Houser et al. (2005)	Games and Economic Behavior, Vol. 52		X	
Crone et al. (2004)	Psychophysiology, Vol.41			X
Maia and McClelland (2004)	PNAS, Vol. 101, No. 45			X
Sanfey et al. (2003)	Science, Vol. 300	X		
Lo and Repin (2002)	Journal of Cognitive Neuroscience, Vol. 14, No. 3			X
Breiter et al. (2001)	Neuron, Vol. 30	X		
Bechara et al. (1999)	The Journal of Neuroscience, Vol.19, No. 13		X	X
Bechara et al. (1997)	Science, Vol. 275		X	X
Bechara et al. (1994)	Cognition, Vol. 50		X	

role of emotions in human decision-making are lesion studies, psychophysiological measures and functional magnetic resonance imaging (fMRI).

Early investigation on the role of emotional processing in human decision-making consider patients with lesions in different regions of the brain to compare their behavior with healthy subjects or with their behavior before the lesion. One of the most famous studies in brain lesions is the case of Phineas Gage. Damasio (1994) tells the story of Phineas and conducts similar studies with patients with several different lesions. This lets him draw conclusions which part of the brain is responsible for decision-making and how stimuli are processed in order to make decisions. Bechara et al. (1994) develop the so-called Iowa-Gambling task to investigate human decision-making under uncertainty by comparing patients' with healthy subjects' behavior in conducting the Gambling-Task. Bechara et al. (1997) and Bechara et al. (1999) extend their investigation by measuring psychophysiological responses of the subjects to draw conclusions of emotional processing in human decision-making. Damasio (1994) develops the somatic marker hypothesis, a neuroanatomical and cognitive framework for decision-making and its influence by emotion. Bechara et al. (2005) develop a neuroeconomic model within the somatic marker hypothesis.

The method of fMRI is applied to identify the neural process underlying the process of valuation of uncertain decisions. This valuation includes the value of the different options as well as the associated risk level. Xue et al. (2009) show that the dorsal and ventral medial prefrontal cortex convey different decision signals, where the relative strengths of these signals determine behavioral decisions involving risk and uncertainty. Additional to the investigation of the involved brain regions in risky decisions, an interesting question to answer is how the human brain learns which decisions are risky. D'Acremont et al. (2009) use four different versions of the Iowa gambling task to investigate this question. It has often been assumed that decision-making under ambiguity is a special, more complex form of decision-making under risk. Huettel et al. (2006) show that decisions under risk and ambiguity are supported by different distinct mechanisms. It is well know that gains and losses are valuated differently while decision-making. Tom et al. (2007) investigate the neural basis of loss aversion. They find that there is increasing activity in several brain regions if potential gains increase but there is decreasing activity in the same brain regions when potential losses are taken into account.

The method of fMRI is not very practicable to combine with the methods of standard economic research, as for example controlled laboratory experiments. As mentioned in the last section, emotions are associated to distinct patterns of physiological states. By measuring different psychophysiological parameters while decision-making one can identify those patterns and draw conclusions from the processes of the brain while decision-making. This methodology, further referred to as physio economics, can easily be combined with standard economic laboratory experiments and is described in detail in the next paragraph.

3.3 Physio economic methodology

The methodology of physio economics suggests that the responses of skin conductance and heart rate can be considered as a good proxy for emotional processing influencing the economic decision-making of subjects (Adam et al., 2009). Physio economic measurement has some advantages compared to the before mentioned neuroscientific methodologies. The measurement complexity to obtain skin conductance and heart rate is relatively low compared to standard economic laboratory experiments. The interest of research of physio economics can be described by the following framework (see Figure 1. The framework was developed by Adam et al. (2009) to describe the decision-cycle in an auction based situation. The cycle is generally applicable for decision situations. The framework describes the relations between expertise and personality of a subject with respect to environment, strategy, events and outcome of a decision situation. The research field of physio economics aims at investigating the role of experienced as well as anticipated emotions and their impact on economic decision making.

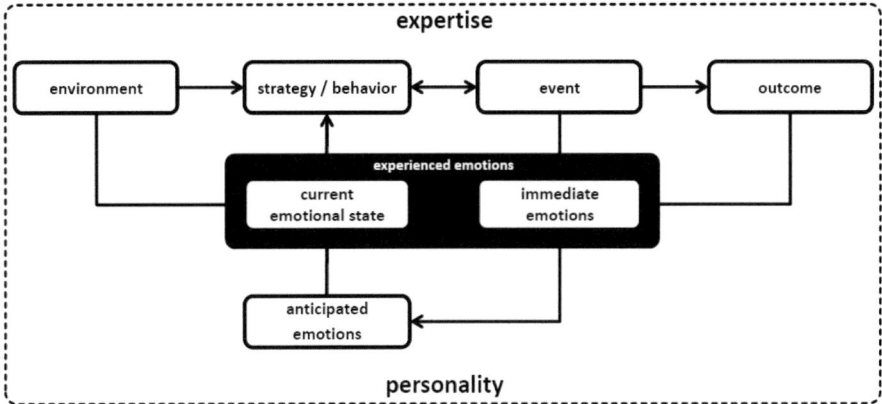

Figure 1: Basic Framework

4 An experimental approach to anticipated emotions in the valuation of gains and losses

Research in neuroscience suggests that rational decision-making depends on prior emotional processing. The somatic marker hypothesis provides a systems-level neuroanatomical and cognitive framework for decision-making under risk and its influence by emotion. The key idea of this hypothesis is that decision-making is a process that is influenced by marker signals, that express themselves in emotions and feelings (Bechara et al., 2005). According to the authors, an emotion is defined as follows:

> An emotion is defined as a collection of changes in body and brain states triggered by a dedicated brain system that responds to specific contents of ones perceptions, actual or recalled, relative to a particular object or event.

The event that predictably causes an emotion is an emotionally-competent stimulus. The body responses referred to the stimulus result in a specific somatic state, that includes physiological reactions. These reactions are for example, as described before, changes in heart rate, skin conductance, respiration etc. A stimulus can be a primary or secondary inducer. In the investment world, primary inducers are reactions to market events, secondary inducers are for example thoughts about what to do next or about consequences of a decision. Primary inducers result in experienced emotions while secondary inducers result in anticipated emotions.

The observations of Kahneman and Tversky captured aspects of human economic choice that were contrary to standard economic theory. However, the prospect theory does not explain why humans choose the way they do.

4.1 Anticipated emotions in the valuation of gains and losses

According to the somatic marker hypothesis subjects decisions are driven by somatic reactions. Hereby you can differentiate between positive and negative somatic reactions, whereas positive somatic reactions serve as a *start-signal* for a decision and negative somatic reactions serve as a *warning-signal* against a decision. What the common economic models of decision-making under risk, as mentioned before, do not explain is: Why do subjects evaluate gains other than losses, for example: Why are subjects risk averse facing gains and risk seeking facing losses? Why do states of optimism lead to different choices than states of pessimism? Why, when the market is crashing everyone rushes to sell, and when it is growing, everyone rushes to buy? To answer these questions, it is suggested that prior to every cognitive processing there is an unconscious valuation of possible outcomes by somatic markers. This unconscious preparing by the body may help to identify which alternatives are advantageous and which are not. In other words, prior to every decision there is an unconscious valuation of different alternatives. The valuation results in physiological reactions, like for example changes in heart rate or skin resistance. This means, the body enters different somatic states confronted with different decision situations. These somatic states are reactions to the anticipated outcome of different alternatives and guide the subject to advantageous decisions.

4.2 Hypotheses

The idea of research in the presented experimental setup is to apply the somatic marker hypothesis to economic choice problems such as presented in the prospect theory to gain insights in emotional processing of decisions. As mentioned above, in human decision making there are observed several effects e.g. the certainty effect and the reflection effect. This means people tend to overweight sure outcomes compared to less probable alternatives. More precisely sure gains are preferred and sure losses are avoided. This is expressed by a different risk attitude towards gains and losses. People are risk averse in the face of gains and risk seeking in the face of losses. We expect that different valuation of gains and losses as well as different valuation of probabilities is associated to prior emotional processing expressed by different emotional states. Further we expect that subjects' risk attitude changes depending on previous gains and losses, as the current emotional state changes and thus the expectations on future outcomes. The hypotheses to be tested in the experiment are described as follows:

> *Hypothesis 1: Subjects show different patterns of physiological states (e.g. higher amplitude of skin conductance) towards sure alternatives of a lottery and less probable alternatives.*

Hypothesis 2a: Subjects perceive gain risk other than loss risk.
Hypothesis 2b: There are different patterns of physiological states towards anticipated positive and negative consequences.

Hypothesis 3a: The valuation of advantageous decisions is associated to prior emotional processing.
Hypothesis 3b: The characteristics of the patterns of physiological states (e.g. amplitude of skin conductance) are associated to the subjects' choice and risk attitude.

Hypothesis 4a: Subjects' risk attitude changes with previous experiences.
Hypothesis 4b: Subjects' physiological reactions differ with respect to the order of positive and negative outcomes.

Hypothesis 5: The impact of a previous decision on the current emotional state is stronger if the outcome of the previous decision is presented to the subject immediately after the choice was made.

4.3 Experimental design

In the beginning of the experiment, the subjects take a seat at their computer terminal and are connected to the measurement system. After a calibration phase to adjust the measurement system and an explanation of the experiment's rules, the participants are assigned to one of four different treatments. Physiological measurement of skin conductance and heart rate allows to test the subjects perceiving of risk related to the decision between different lotteries. In each treatment subjects have to make ten independent risky decisions. Each decision is presented as a lottery, containing two alternatives with different outcomes with different probabilities. For instance, in each period the subjects are presented with two alternatives to chose between. Each component (i.e. alternatives) of a decision is presented sequentially on the computer screen with a delay of 5 seconds. When both alternatives are fully displayed the subjects have to chose between the two alternatives by clicking the referred button. Each alternative contains different possible outcomes given in monetary units, realized with different probabilities. The outcome can be positive, negative or zero. The probabilities range from 100 percent to 1 percent. In every treatment the realized outcomes of three experiment rounds are chosen by chance to be payed to the subjects additional to a show-up fee in the end of the experiment. To control for the effects related to the subjects personal risk attitude, subjects have to fill out a questionnaire and a risk-aversion test, which is based on Holt and Laury (2002).

The treatments differ by the order in which the decisions are presented to the subject and the presentation of the results of the decisions. The decisions to be made by the subjects in the experiment are presented in Table 4 and Table 5. In Table 4 it is shown that in the first six periods, the possible realizations of the lotteries do not contain any negative outcomes, while in the last four periods the possible realizations of the lotteries do not contain any positive outcomes. In the following description of the treatments this order of decisions is referred to as Order 1.

Table 4: Experiment Decisions (Order 1)

Decision	Alternative 1	Alternative 2
1	(2500 MU, 33%; 2400 MU, 66%; 0, 1%)	(2400 MU, 100%)
2	(2500 MU, 33%; 0 MU, 67%)	(2400 MU, 34%; 0, 66%)
3	(4000 MU, 80%; 0 MU, 20%)	(3000 MU, 100%)
4	(4000 MU, 20%; 0 MU, 80%)	(3000 MU, 25%; 0 , 75%)
5	(6000 MU, 45%; 0 MU, 55%)	(3000 MU, 90%; 0 MU, 10%)
6	(6000 MU, 1%; 0 MU, 99%)	(3000 MU, 2%; 0 MU, 98%)
7	(-4000 MU, 80%; 0 MU, 20%)	(-3000 MU, 100%)
8	(-4000 MU, 20%; 0 MU, 80%)	(-3000 MU, 25%; 0 MU, 75%)
9	(-6000 MU, 45%; 0 MU, 55%)	(-3000 MU, 90%; 0 MU, 10%)
10	(-6000 MU, 1%; 0 MU, 99%)	(-3000 MU, 2%; 0 MU, 98%)

Table 5: Experiment Decisions (Order 2)

Decision	Alternative 1	Alternative 2
1	(-4000 MU, 80%; 0 MU, 20%)	(-3000 MU, 100%)
2	(-4000 MU, 20%; 0 MU, 80%)	(-3000 MU, 25%; 0 MU, 75%)
3	(-6000 MU, 45%; 0 MU, 55%)	(-3000 MU, 90%; 0 MU, 10%)
4	(-6000 MU, 1%; 0 MU, 99%)	(-3000 MU, 2%; 0 MU, 98%)
5	(2500 MU, 33%; 2400 MU, 66%; 0, 1%)	(2400 MU, 100%)
6	(2500 MU, 33%; 0 MU, 67%)	(2400 MU, 34%; 0, 66%)
7	(4000 MU, 80%; 0 MU, 20%)	(3000 MU, 100%)
8	(4000 MU, 20%; 0 MU, 80%)	(3000 MU, 25%; 0 , 75%)
9	(6000 MU, 45%; 0 MU, 55%)	(3000 MU, 90%; 0 MU, 10%)
10	(6000 MU, 1%; 0 MU, 99%)	(3000 MU, 2%; 0 MU, 98%)

In Table 5 it is shown that the decisions are presented the other way round. In the following description of the treatments this order of decisions is referred to as Order 2. Figure 2 to Figure 5 give a graphical illustration of the structure of each treatment.

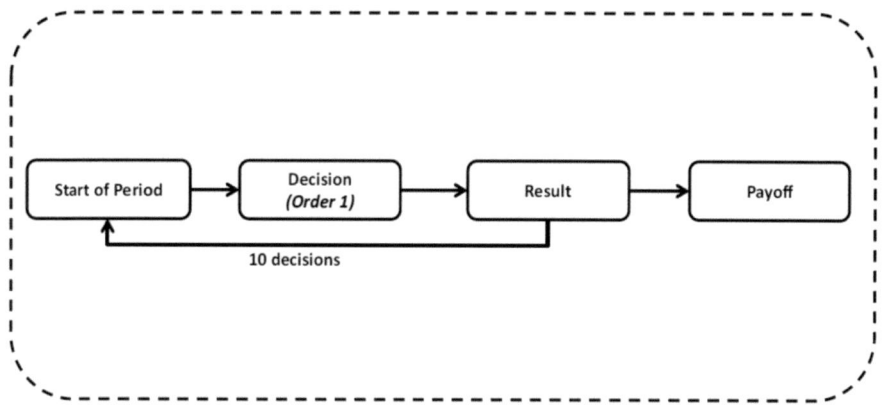

Figure 2: Treatment 1

In Treatment 1 (Figure 2) and Treatment 2 (Figure 3), the order of the decisions corresponds to Order 1. We expect that there might be a difference in risk attitude if previous decisions and realizations are taken into account for future decisions as there might be a change in the current emotional state (Hypotheses 4a and 4b). For this reason, we change the order of decisions in Treatment 3 (Figure 4) and Treatment 4 (Figure 5) to Order 2. The result of each decision is displayed immediately in the end of each period in Treatment 1 and 3. We hypothesize that the presentation of the result has an impact on the intensity of the change of the current emotional state (Hypothesis 5) and therefore on the subjects risk attitude.

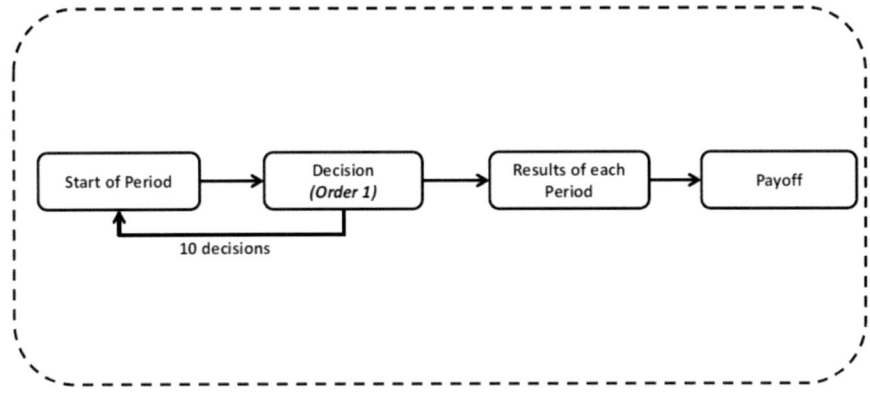

Figure 3: Treatment 2

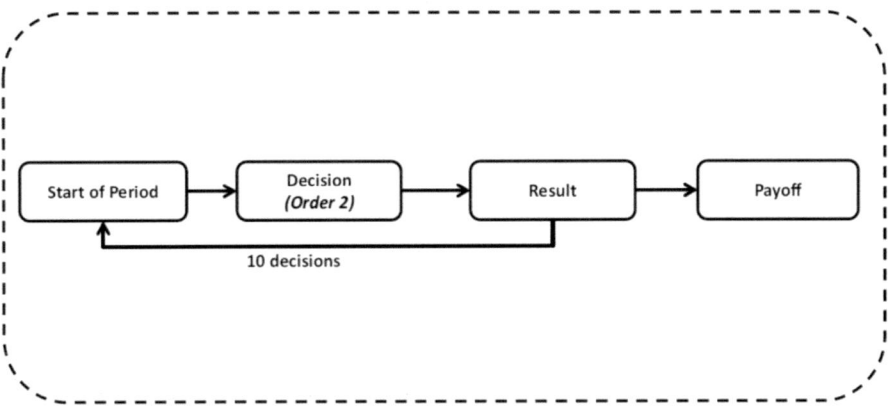

Figure 4: Treatment 3

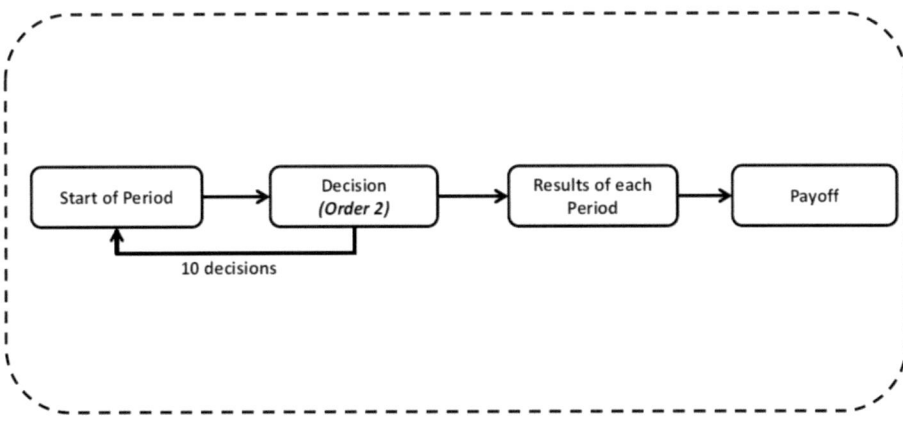

Figure 5: Treatment 4

To control for these effects, in Treatment 2 and 4 the results of each decision are only displayed in the end of the experiment.

The physio economic decision cycle for this experiment is shown in Figure 6. We expect that the different treatments have a different impact on the evaluation of the presented lotteries because of different emotional processing (Hypotheses 3a and 3b) and different emotional states. We assume that according to the current emotional state the risk attitude of the subjects changes. The evaluation of a lottery by a subject is conscious as well as unconscious. Deciding conscious means that a subject actively thinks about the possible outcomes of a lottery and calculates the risk. We assume, however, that decisions are aided by emotions, elicited during the deliberation of the possible outcomes, that mark the different options as advantageous or unadvantageous. This emotional deliberation during decision-making is unconscious. We expect that the confrontation with a decision elicits immediate emotions as a direct reaction to this event but also elicits anticipated emotions. Anticipated emotions express, by imagining future outcomes, how it would feel like to receive a future gain or loss. Emotional reactions towards sure alternatives might be stronger than towards less probable alternatives. Further, we hypothesize that physiological patterns of anticipated emotions towards certain outcomes or less probable outcomes are different (Hypothesis 1) as well as physiological patterns of anticipated emotions towards gains or losses are different (Hypotheses 2a and 2b). Immediate emotions as well as anticipated emotions have an impact on the current emotional state, which changes the subjects' risk attitude. We expect that in Treatment 3 and Treatment 4 the subjects are in a different current emotional state than the subjects in Treatment 1 and Treatment 2. If the result of a decision is displayed immediately, there is an impact on the immediate as well as the anticipated emotions. This again leads to a different current emotional state, as we expect that there is a difference in Treatment 1 and 3 and Treatment 2 and 4.

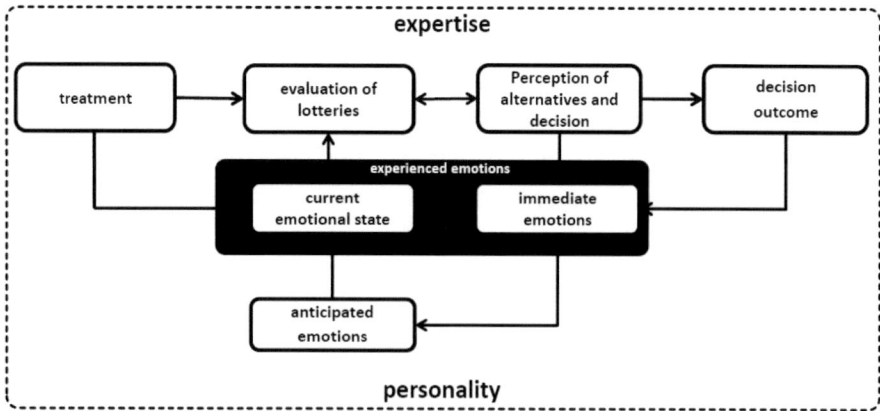

Figure 6: Experimental Framework

5 Conclusion and Outlook

The presented experimental design contributes in special to gain insight into the subjects' valuation of gains and losses dependent on the associated probabilities. With the methodology of physio-economics the role of (anticipated) emotions is investigated to draw conclusions from the impact of prior emotional processing on economical decisions. As Kahneman and Tversky point out in their prospect theory, subjects valuate gains and losses related to a reference-point. The reference-point assigns what is seen as gain or loss individually to a subject. As losses are valuated differently compared to gains, subjects' risk attitude and therefore decisions depend on where the reference-point is set. It is assumed that the reference-point is not only set according to the status quo but also according to expected future gains and losses. In future research, based on the results of the present experimental setup, the impact of the current emotional state on the calculation and shifts of the reference-point will be investigated. The shift of reference-point might cause different effects in decision-making. The so-called pseudo-endowment effect, as one possible approach to explain the so-called auction-fever, is caused by a shift of reference-point resulting in higher willingness to pay. Auction-fever combines different approaches to explain effects on the development of prices in auctions. Insights from the proposed experiment and further research can contribute to extensions of the classical economic theories and models where descriptions and explanations are not conform with actual observations of human behavior.

References

Adam, M. T. P., M. Gamer, and C. Weinhardt (2009): "Measuring the impact of emotions in electronic auctions: a physioeconomic approach." Working paper, Karlsruhe Institute of Technology (KIT).

Allais, M. (1953): "Le Comportement de l'Homme Rationnel devant le Risque: Critique des Postulats et Axiomes de l'Ecole," *Econometrica*, 21(4), pp. 503–546.

Averill, J. R. (1969): "Autonomic Response Patterns During Sadness and Mirth," *Psychophysiology*, 5(4), pp. 399–414.

Bault, N., G. Coricelli, and A. Rustichini (2008): "Interdependent Utilities: How Social Ranking Affects Choice Behavior," *PLoS ONE*, 3(10), p. e3477.

Bechara, A., H. Damasio, A. R. Damasio, and S. W. Anderson (1994): "Insensitivity to future consequences following damage to human prefrontal cortex," *Cognition*, 50, pp. 7–15.

Bechara, A., H. Damasio, A. R. Damasio, and G. P. Lee (1999): "Different Contributions of the Human Amygdala and ventromedial prefrontal cortex to decision making," *The Journal of Neuroscience*, 19(13), pp. 5473–5481.

Bechara, A., H. Damasio, D. Tranel, and A. Damasio (2005): "The Iowa Gambling Task and the somatic marker hypothesis: some questions and answers," *Trends in Cognitive Sciences*, 9(4), pp. 159 – 162.

Bechara, A., H. Damasio, D. Tranel, and A. R. Damasio (1997): "Deciding advantageously before knowing the advantageous strategy," *Science*, 275, pp. 1293–1295.

Ben-Shakhar, G., G. Bornstein, A. Hopfensitz, and F. van Winden (2007): "Reciprocity and emotions in bargaining using physiological and self-report measures," *Journal of Economic Psychology*, 28(3), pp. 314 – 323.

Berntson, G. G., A. Bechara, H. Damasio, D. Tranel, and J. T. Cacioppo (2007): "Amygdala Contribution to selective dimensions of emotion," *SCAN*, 1, pp. 1–7.

Breiter, H. C., I. Aharon, D. Kahneman, A. Dale, and P. Shizgal (2001): "Functional Imaging of Neural responses to Expectancy and Experience of Monetary Gains and Losses," *Neuron*, 30, pp. 619–639.

Cacioppo, J. T., G. G. Berntson, J. T. Larsen, K. M. Poehlmann, and T. A. Ito (2000): "The Psychophysiology of Emotion," *Biological and Neurophysiological approaches*, pp. 173–191.

Christakou, A., M. Brammer, V. Giampietro, and K. Rubia (2009): "Right Ventromedial and Dorsolateral Prefrontal Cortices Mediate Adaptive Decisions under Ambiguity by Integrating Choice Utility and Outcome Evaluation," *J. Neurosci.*, 29(35), pp. 11020–11028.

Christie, I. C. and B. Friedman (2004): "Autonomic specificity of discrete emotion and dimensions of affective space: a multivariate approach," *International Journal of Psychophysiology*, 51, pp. 143–153.

Clark, L., A. Bechara, H. Damasio, M. Aitken, B. J. Sahakian, and T. Robbons (2008): "Differential effects of insular and ventromedial prefrontal cortex lesions on risky decision-making," *Brain*, 131, pp. 1311 – 1322.

Collet, C., E. Vernet-Maury, G. Delhomme, and A. Dittmar (1997): "Autonomic nervous system response patterns specificity to basic emotions," *Journal of the Autonomic Nervous System*, 62, pp. 45–57.

Crone, E. A., R. J. M. Somsen, B. van Beek, and M. W. V. D. Molen (2004): "Heart Rate and skin conductance analysis of antecendents and consequences of decision-making," *Psychophsiology*, 15(4), pp. 316–324.

D'Acremont, M., Z.-L. Lu, X. Li, M. V. der Linden, and A. Bechara (2009): "Neural correlates of risk prediction error during reinforcement learning in humans," *NeuroImage*, 47(4), pp. 1929 – 1939.

Damasio, A. R. (1994): *Descartes Error: Emotion, Reason and the Human Brain*, G P Putnams Sons.

D'Argembeau, A., G. Xue, Z.-L. Lu, M. V. der Linden, and A. Bechara (2008): "Neural Correlates of envisioning emotional events in the near and far future," *NeuroImage*, 40, pp. 398–407.

Denburg, N. L., E. C. Recknor, A. Bechara, and D. Tranel (2006): "Psychophysiological anticipation of positive outcomes promotes advantageous decision-making in normal older persons," *International Journal of Psychophysiology*, 61(1), pp. 19 – 25.

Ekman, P., R. W. Levenson, and W. V. Friesen (1983): "Autonomic Nervous System Activity Distinguishes Among Emotions," *Science*, 221, pp. 1208–1210.

Fellows, L. K. (2006): "Deciding how to decide: ventromedial frontal lobe damage affects information acquisition in multi-attribute decision making," *Brain*, 129, pp. 944–952(9).

Holt, C. and S. Laury (2002): "Risk aversion and incentive effects," *The american economic review*, 92(5), pp. 1644–1655.

Houser, D., A. Bechara, M. Keane, K. McCabe, and V. Smith (2005): "Identifying individual differences: An algorithm with application to Phineas Gage," *Games and Economic Behavior*, 52(2), pp. 373 – 385.

Hsu, M., M. Bhatt, R. Adolphs, D. Tranel, and C. F. Camerer (2005): "Neural Systems Responding to Degrees of Uncertainty in Human Decision-Making," *Science*, 310, pp. 1680–1683.

Huettel, S. A., C. J. Stowe, E. M. Gordon, B. T. Warner, and M. L. Platt (2006): "Neural Signatures of Economic Preferences for Risk and Ambiguity," *Neuron*, 49(5), pp. 765 – 775.

James, W. (1884): "What is an Emotion?" *Mind*, 9(34), pp. 188–205.

Kahneman, D. and A. Tversky (1979): "Prospect Theory: An Analysis of Decision under risk," *Econometrica*, 47(2), pp. 263–291.

Krajbich, I., R. Adolphs, D. Tranel, N. Denburg, and C. Camerer (2009): "Economic Games Quantify Diminished Sense of Guilt in Patients with Damage to the Prefrontal Cortex," *J. Neurosci.*, 29(7), pp. 2188–2192.

Lange, C. G. and H. Kurella (1887): *Ueber Gemüthsbewegungen: Eine Psycho-physiologische Studie*, T. Thomas.

Leland, J. W. and J. Grafman (2005): "Experimental tests of the Somatic Marker hypothesis," *Games and Economic Behavior*, 52(2), pp. 386 – 409.

Levenson, R. W., P. Ekman, and W. V. Friesen (1990): "Voluntary facial action generates emotion-specific autonomic nervous system activity," *Psychophysiology*, 27(4), pp. 363–384.

Lo, A. W. and D. V. Repin (2002): "The Psychophysiology of real-time financial risk processing," *Journal of cognitive Neuroscience*, 14(3), pp. 323–339.

Maia, T. V. and J. L. McClelland (2004): "A reexamination of the evidence for the somatic marker hypothesis: What participants really know in the Iowa gambling task," *PNAS*, 101(45), pp. 16075–16080.

Martino, B. D., D. Kumaran, B. Holt, and R. J. Dolan (2009): "The Neurobiology of Reference-Dependent Value Computation," *The Journal of Neuroscience*, 29(12), pp. 3833–3842.

Miu, A. C., R. M. Heilman, and D. Houser (2008): "Anxiety impairs decision-making: Psychophysiological evidence from the Iowa Gambling Task," *Biological Psychology*, 77, pp. 353–358.

Oya, H., R. Adolphs, H. Kawasaki, A. Bechara, A. Damasio, and I. Howard, Matthew A. (2005): "Psychophysiological anticipation of positive outcomes promotes advantageous decision-making in normal older persons," *Proceedings of the National Academy of Sciences of the United States of America*, 102(23), pp. 8351–8356.

Rainville, P., A. Bechara, N. Naqvi, and A. R. Damasio (2006): "Basic emotions are associated with distinct patterns of cardiorespiratory activity," *International Journal of Psychophysiology*, 61, pp. 5–18.

Rao, H., M. Korczykowski, J. Pluta, A. Hoang, and J. A. Detre (2008): "Neural correlates of voluntary and involuntary risk taking in the human brain: An fMRI Study of the Balloon Analog Risk Task (BART)," *NeuroImage*, 42(2), pp. 902 – 910.

Sanfey, A. G., J. K. Rilling, J. A. Aronson, L. E. Nystrom, and J. D. Cohen (2003): "The neural basis of decision-making in the ultimatum game," *Science*, 300, pp. 1755–1758.

Shiv, B., G. Loewenstein, and A. Bechara (2005a): "The dark side of emotion in decision-making: When individuals with decreased emotional reactions make more advantageous decisions," *Cognitive Brain Research*, 23(1), pp. 85 – 92.

Shiv, B., G. Loewenstein, A. Bechara, H. Damasio, and A. R. Damasio (2005b): "Investment Behavior and the Negative Side of Emotion," *Psychological Sience*, 16(6), pp. 435–439.

Smith, K. and J. Dickhaut (2005): "Economics and emotion: Institutions matter," *Games and Economic Behavior*, 52(2), pp. 316 – 335.

Tom, S. M., C. R. Fox, C. Trepel, and R. A. Poldrack (2007): "The Neural Basis of Loss Aversion in Decision-Making Under Risk," *Science*, 315(5811), pp. 515–518.

Van't Wout, M., R. S. Kahn, A. G. Sanfey, and A. Aleman (2006): "Affective state and decision-making in the Ultimatum Game," *Experimental brain research*, 129, pp. 564–568.

Vernet-Maury, E., O. Alaoui-Ismili, A. Dittmar, G. Delhomme, and J. Chanel (1999): "Basic Emotions induced by odorant: a new approach based on autonomic pattern results," *Journal of autonomic nervous system*, 75, pp. 176–183.

Vianna, E. P. M., N. Naqvi, A. Bechara, and D. Tranel (2009): "Does vivid emotional imagery depend on body signals?" *International Journal of Psychophysiology*, 72, pp. 46–50.

von Neumann, J. and O. Morgenstern (1944): *Theory of Games and Economic Behavior*, Princeton University Press.

Weller, J. A. (2007): "Neural Correlates of Adaptive Decision Making for Risky Gains and Losses," *Psychological Science*, 18, pp. 958–964(7).

Xue, G., Z. Lu, I. P. Levin, J. A. Weller, X. Li, and A. Bechara (2009): "Functional Dissociations of Risk and Reward Processing in the Medial Prefrontal Cortex," *Cerebral Cortex*, 19, pp. 1019–1027.

Consumer Perception of Time-Based Pricing

Lukas Wiewiorra[1], Jan Krämer[1], Christof Weinhardt[1], and Karl-Martin Ehrhart[2]

[1] Institute of Information Systems and Management, KIT
{wiewiorra, kraemer, weinhardt}@kit.edu
[2] Institute of Economic Theory and Statistics, KIT
ehrhart@kit.edu

Summary. The introduction of new mobile phone tariffs with cost caps raises some interesting questions about consumer perception of additional flat rate value components, especially the so called taxi meter effect. The paper presents a seminal experimental setup to test if consumers feel negatively if costs are realized per unit of time. Additionally the design allows to assess the interplay of the so called insurance and taxi meter effect. With this results an even better understanding of cost cap tariffs and potential tariff switching behavior in mobile telecommunications would be possible. In contrast to a flat rate pricing, the cost cap tariff allows for cost insurance, while maintaining the taximeter property as long as the cost cap is not reached. The proposed experimental design aims at measuring the physiological differences of participants with a flat rate tariff in comparison to a pay-per-use and a cost cap tariff in a controlled laboratory experiment with the methodology of physio economics. The authors present a brief summary of the literature about tariff bias research, a review of the related methodology as well as an introduction into physio economics. It follows an outline of the laboratory experiment and the hypotheses that can be tested with this experimental setup.

1 Introduction

Nowadays consumers face a sheer endless variety of tariff alternatives when deciding for a telecommunication or information service. Competing firms engage in price competition, since there is not much scope for quality differentiation. In the early days of mobile telecommunication services in Germany consumers could not opt for a flat rate plan. Network providers offered usage based tariffs with a fixed fee per billing period. Prices per minute were usually higher at daytime, since network providers established tariffs similar to the peak load pricing scheme in classic network industries. Additionally users were charged comparably high rates for calls terminated into a concurring networks.

1.1 Tariffing Mobile Telecommunication

So called "Two-part tariffs" have a long tradition in telephony (Littlechild, 1975). Their popularity stems from the fact that a large portion of the provider's costs are fixed costs related to the build up, maintenance and operation of the network infrastructure, which can be recovered by the fixed component of the two-part tariff (Valletti, 2003). On the contrary, the marginal costs of calling, which are constituted through switching or interconnection fees, for example, are relatively small and can be recovered by the variable component of the two-part tariff. In fact, if the telephony provider holds a monopoly, which has been the case for the fixed-line providers for most of the twentieth century, two-part tariffs can even achieve to extract customer rent completely, comparably to perfect price discrimination (Oi, 1971).

Later on the network providers focused almost simultaneously on three part tariffs witch are defined by a usage allowance, a corresponding access price and a marginal price for any usage in excess of the allowance. This innovation allows them to price discriminate between consumers based on the expected amount of usage. Therefore providers discriminate not solely over the average usage, but also over variation of usage (Lambrecht et al., 2007). A clever design of the set of offered allowances can exploit consumer uncertainty of future demand and lurks them more likely into more expensive tariffs with a higher amount of included minutes. Obviously this pricing scheme is not linear since the average price per minute in different combinations of allowance and access price can vary. It is not surprising that network providers were enthusiastic about this form of price discrimination. Despite the intensive marketing campaigns consumers did not fully accept this tariff scheme until now.

Following the decision of E-Plus (KPN) to grant mobile discounters access to their network, the other operators[1] jumped on the bandwagon soon. Competition led to an enormous variety of tariffs in the market and prices for mobile telecommunication services dropped rapidly. Today every network provider offers all-net flat rates, defined by a fixed price for all calls originated and terminated inside Germany.[2]

Since a few months a new tariff model changes the market again. A new innovative cost cap tariff has been introduced to the German mobile market in 2009 by o2 (Telefonica).[3] The cost cap tariff is a new type of two-part tariff that constitutes a hybrid between a pay-per-use and a flat rate. It is a pure uniform pay-per-use tariff until the total costs exceed a predefined cost cap, at which the tariff effectively becomes a flat rate. o2 claims that the cost cap tariff is a great success and has significantly contributed to attracting new customers (Briegleb, 2009). Since the current cost cap equals the actual market price for an all-net flatrate this tariff obviously became a weakly dominated alternative.

---

[1] T-Mobile, Vodafone and o2 (Telefonica)

[2] Except for all premium- and international calls, roaming, all forms of data connections as well as short- and multimedia messaging.

[3] The tariff, which is called "o2 o", has officially been released on May 5, 2009.

1.2 Flatrate and Pay-per-use Bias

Economic theory assumes that consumers, independent of the tariff alternatives and characteristics, maximize their utility when selecting a pricing scheme for telecommunication or information services. Therefore a chosen tariff usually should lead to the lowest possible bill given the anticipated usage volume of a service. Economically this corresponds to a maximization of the consumer rent. In reality people often behave differently from what theory suggests. Existing research shows that consumers are often biased in favor of flat rate tariffs (e.g. Nunes, 2000; Miravete, 2003; Lambrecht and Skiera, 2006a; Gerpott, 2009; Grubb, 2009). The so called "flat rate bias" describes the phenomenon that consumers tend to choose a flat rate even if a pay-per-use pricing scheme would be cheaper with regard to their usage volume. This behavior has been shown in context with all-you-can-eat buffets (Just and Wansink, 2008), gym subscriptions (Della Vigna and Malmendier, 2006), Internet access plans (e.g. Train et al., 1989; Kridel et al., 1993; Lambrecht and Skiera, 2006a) and mobile calling plans (e.g. Mitomo et al., 2007; Gerpott, 2009). Flexibility is the core property of pay-per-use tariffs. A so called "pay-per-use bias" could be identified in a few studies (e.g. Kridel et al., 1993; Prelec and Loewenstein, 1998; Miravete, 2003; Schulze and Gedenk, 2005). Consumers value the option of consuming less in one billing period without being committed to a high fixed fee. This can sometimes result in decisions for a usage based pricing scheme, even if a flat rate would be cheaper in the long run. Nevertheless this phenomenon seems to be far less widespread than the flat rate bias. With respect to information and communication services, the literature has identified four distinctive effects that are supposed to drive the flat rate bias:

Effects causing a Flat rate Bias

According to the *insurance effect* risk-averse consumers who cannot predict their future demand correctly choose a flat-rate to insure against the risk of high costs in periods of higher than average usage. The *convenience effect* may stem from consumers who want to avoid the effort of finding an alternative tariff. Telecommunications companies try to leverage this effect by offering dominated tariff alternatives. Consumers with potentially high search costs or a high degree of convenience end up with such a dominated tariff more likely. Due to incorrect anticipation of future demand consumers may tend to *overestimation* of service usage and therefore choose a flat-rate more frequently. If consumers enjoy the usage of a telecommunication service more if they use a flat-rate this is called the *taxi meter effect*. The intuition behind the taxi meter effect is borrowed from the analogy of using a cab in a foreign city. It is commonly described as the reduced joy of consuming one unit of the service because of the immediately perceived cost of consumption due to the taxi meter. Since a flat rate has marginal costs of zero per unit of time the joy of consumption is higher. This prevention of immediate cost reception is interpreted as one component of additional value, favoring the decision for a flat rate. The taxi meter effect can be explained by the theory of mental accounting (Thaler, 1985, 1999). Consumers assign costs to different mental accounts, dependent on the time of cost realization. The price of a flat rate is accounted in the beginning of a billing period, since it is comparable to sunk costs. Therefore usage is perceived as costless or free. In contrast to that a usage based tariff is perceived differently, since costs are realized per time unit. This immediate accounting of costs reduces the joy of every consumed unit. Lambrecht and Skiera (2006b) are the first controlling for all four different effects supposed to cause the total flat-rate bias and point out the importance of measuring all effects simultaneously. This paper tries to shed light on two effects that are assumed to lead to biased decisions. The authors propose an experimental design to test isolated for this effects which can be interpreted as additional value components of a flat rate tariff.

2 The methodology of tariff choice bias analysis

The literature about tariff biases is best categorized by the methodology that has been used to conduct the economic analysis itself, but also by the type of underlying theoretical model.

Econometric analysis based on historical usage data identifies ex-post suboptimal tariff decisions as biased. Every consumer who could have saved money in another but his own tariff is labeled as potentially biased. In contrast to this approach of mapping ex-post usage data on different ex-ante tariff alternatives, choice models are designed to capture the decision process of consumers itself. Those econometric models incorporate various independent variables like price and amount of usage to estimate the given tariff decision of a consumer. A tariff bias is incorporated into the model as a unique tariff inherent variable. If such a variable turns out to be significant a tariff decision is assumed to be influenced at least to some degree by other than rational parameters.

Nevertheless many of those classic econometric analyses propose only intuitions and guesses for the biases found in the data. The predominant explanation is the inability of consumers to anticipate their own amount of usage correctly in given period of time. This leads to the methodological discussion of how to analyze the phenomenon. Econometric analysis of usage data appears to be the right tool if one tries to confirm the mere existence of such biases and perhaps to quantify the extent. It seems more challenging to identify and confirm influence factors witch lead to such biases. Since the necessary information cannot be derived by analyzing usage data, researchers have to rely on other methodological tools. Questionnaires are one source of data to identify the influence factors of tariff decisions. Some authors conduct so called "quasi experiments". As an extension of a classic questionnaire they formulate hypothetical situations and induce a usage level to measure how subjects think they would behave in the given situations. This quasi experimental methods obviously lack the controlled environment, as well as the direct monetary incentives that are provided in a classic economical laboratory experiment.

3 An experimental approach to the taxi meter effect

The introduction of new mobile phone tariffs with cost caps raises some interesting questions about consumer perception of additional flat rate value components, especially the taxi meter effect. In telecommunications the best analogy to a costly taxi ride, as described in section 1.2, might be a service hotline call where consumers usually have to pay a higher than usual fee and have to wait in a queue before they receive service. The question arises if consumers experience the taxi meter effect even if they are insured against high costs and how this affects their perceived feelings during the consumption as well as the tariff selection process itself. In contrast to a flat rate pricing scheme, cost cap tariffs allow for cost insurance, while maintaining the taximeter property as long as the cost cap is not reached. Therefore this pricing scheme allows the experimenter to control for the interdependency of this two effects. The experimental design proposed in this article aims at measuring the physiological differences of participants with a flat rate tariff in comparison to a pay-per-use and a cost cap tariff in a controlled laboratory experiment with the methodology of physio economics. Especially the existence of the taxi meter effect has never been verified and examined in an experimental setup. Krämer and Wiewiorra (2010) already showed in a seminal study of end user cost cap tariffs that consumers seem to perceive the taxi meter property differently under a cost cap and a pay-per-use tariff. The following experimental setup will propose several design parameters to isolate the tariff properties driving the taxi meter effect.

3.1 Physio economic measurement

Human decision-making is not a purely cognitive driven maximization of utility. Human behavior is to some extent influenced by emotions and perceived feelings (Loewenstein, 2000). The field of psychophysiology focuses on the relationship of cognitive and emotional processes, physiological states and the human behavior itself. The methodology of physio economics in particular suggests that the responses of heart rate and skin conductance can be considered as a good proxy for emotional processes influencing the economic decision making of human beings (Adam et al., 2009). This approach has several advantages in comparison to the quasi experimental methodology mentioned in section 2. Questionnaire data in general deal with the severe problem of social desirability (Crowne and Marlowe, 1960). Respondents tend to answer questions in a way they assume to appear as socially suitable. Physiological parameters instead measure the activation of the autonomic nervous system and therefore cannot directly be influenced by free will. Physio economic methods add to the field by obtaining objective data not relying on self reported information. Furthermore the measurement complexity to obtain heart rate and skin conductance in relation to standard computer based laboratory experiments is relatively low.

3.2 Isolation of tariff inherent properties

The authors intend to compare pay-per-use, cost cap and flat rate tariffs with each other. Therefore the theoretical differences between them have to be outlined first. Table 1 shows the identified effects and their impact on the the two fundamental pricing schemes and the hybrid cost cap tariff. In a controlled laboratory environment convenience of participants can be ruled out as a possible effect favoring a flat rate tariff, in particular because there are no additional search costs involved and the complexity of the presented information will be low due to the simplified experimental design. Overestimation can be ruled out if the experimenter decides beforehand to inform the participants about the maximum time of one experimental run. Therefore only the remaining effects influence the taxi meter property and a potential switching decision of the participants.

The flexibility effect can't be fully ruled out in the lab without violating the insurance property. If one would announce the exact duration of one run beforehand there is no longer any need for insurance, but also no desire to remain flexible in the cost dimension. The insurance, as well as the flexibility property on the one hand is incorporated by two of the three tariff schemes, the cost cap and flat rate tariff and the cost cap and pay-per-use tariff respectively. The taxi meter property on the other hand is not eliminated by the pay-per-use and the cost cap tariff. Therefore this particular design and the right set of presented information can rule out all effects except for the insurance and flexibility effect potentially influencing the physiological reactions to the taxi meter property.

Table 1: Potential effects on the choice of different tariff schemes

	Pay-per-use (PPU)	Cost Cap (CC)	Flatrate (FR)
Insurance	-	+	+
Convenience	-	?	+
Overestimation	-	+	+
Taximeter	-	?	+
Flexibility	+	+	-

3.3 Basic experimental design

Physiological measurement of skin conductance and phasic heart rate allow the experimenter to test whether consumers feel negatively if costs are realized per unit of time or not. Participants have to accomplish a simple, but time consuming task in the laboratory. For instance they have to listen to a sound recording and are advised to stop the playback the moment they can answer a question which answer is presented somewhere during the record. At the beginning of the experiment all participants get a basic amount of experimental monetary units and will be connected to the physiological measurement equipment. After a calibration phase to adjust the measurement devices and a standardized explanation of the experimental setup the participants are assigned to one of the following tariff schemes:

- Pay-per-use
- Cost Cap
- Flat rate

The first computer screen explains the pricing procedure to the participants. While flat rate users pay the costs for the flat rate at the end of one experimental run, participants in the other groups pay for each time unit immediately and can monitor the duration as well as the cumulating costs on the screen. Additionally it is possible to signal every new time unit with an audio sound. This feature is implemented into some mobile phones, but almost vanished from the market.[4] For traceability the maximum costs under a cost cap tariff equals the price for a flat rate and the price per time unit has to be chosen in direct relation to the duration of one experimental run. Therefore all participants should end up with the same costs for one run. With a classic pay-per-use tariff consumers are not insured against high costs and therefore one expects to measure the pure taxi meter property in this group. Flexibility can only have an effect on a potential tariff switching decision, not on the perception of the taxi meter property itself, because flexibility is ensured by both the classic pay-per-use and the hybrid cost cap tariff. Therefore the treatment as shown in figure 1 is analogous to a taxi ride with a taxi meter directly visible to the customer. Under a cost cap tariff participants know ex-ante the maximum

Figure 1: Treatment - Pay-per-use

amount of experimental monetary units they can loose in one run. In this setting one measures the physiological reactions to the taxi meter property under insurance against high costs. In an additional treatment one can eliminate the taxi meter property completely by introducing a classic flat rate tariff, as shown in figure 3. With this setup one measures the effect of insurance without the taxi meter property. The price of the flat rat, as well as the remaining part of the endowment is presented on the computer screen, but during the experiment participants occur no additional costs. As already mentioned in section 1 compared to a cost cap tariff an equally

---

[4] If there is a significant physiological reaction to additional audio signals this might be a reason why mobile telecommunication operators intervened to abolish this feature.

Figure 2: Treatment - Cost cap

priced flat rate is a weakly dominated alternative. Nevertheless this benchmark treatment allows us to check whether the mental accounting of cost caps results in similar physiological responses as to a pay-per-use pricing or more like to a flat rate. To control for the effects related to the personal usage behavior outside the

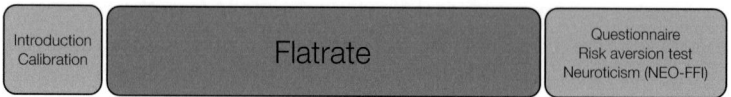

Figure 3: Treatment - Flatrate

laboratory participants have to fill out an additional computer based questionnaire as shown in figure 1, 2 and 3 based on the survey design already successfully used in Krämer and Wiewiorra (2010).[5] To further assess if risk-aversion has an influence on physiological reactions a risk aversion test based on Holt and Laury (2002) will be conducted at the end of all treatments along with the computer based questionnaire. Participants will be paid immediately by the experimenter to obtain reliable data. To control especially for Neuroticism, the experience of negative emotions and environmental stress, one of the "big five" factors of personality[6], the respective questions of the short version of the revised NEO personality inventory, namely "NEO-Five Factor Inventory" (NEO-FFI), will be presented to the participants in a computer based version after the risk aversion test. As mentioned before, there are several parameters that can be modified to gain deeper insights into the taxi meter property. One can aggravate the per unit cost signal by an audio sound. Therefore the immediate cost perception is increased. Another important parameter is the cost per minute. It has to be tested, if an increase of the costs per minute relate to the physiological responses of the participants.

Hypotheses - Basic Experimental Design

Hypothesis 1

Participants under a pay-per-use tariff show a significantly higher amplitude of skin conductance and a relative deceleration of the heart rate in response to the discrete events of interval based costs presentation.

---

[5] The questionnaire collects data on the respondents' actual mobile telephony tariff characteristics (such as contract duration, tariff model, average monthly bill, maximum bill, price per minute etc.). Participants will be explicitly notified that from this point on, they are asked about their real actual mobile phone usage.

[6] Extraversion, Agreeableness, Conscientiousness, Neuroticism, and Openness to Experience

Hypothesis 1b -The physiological responses to the discrete events of interval based costs presentation is significantly higher, if the signaling of costs is not only visual, but audio-visual.

Hypothesis 1c -The physiological responses to the discrete events of interval based costs presentation is significantly higher, if the costs per unit of time are increased.

Hypothesis 2

The average physiological response to the discrete events of interval based costs presentation under a cost cap tariff is significantly lower compared to the average physiological response under a pay-per-use tariff.

Hypothesis 2b - The individual physiological responses to the discrete events of interval based costs presentation under a cost cap tariff depend significantly on the individual mental accounting of the cost cap. (i.e. sunk-costs or insurance)

Hypothesis 3

Participants under a flat rate tariff show no significant physiological response to the discrete presentation of elapsed time units.

3.4 Extended experimental design

The basic experimental design presented so far aims at validating the mere existence of the taxi meter effect and the identification of influence factors on its magnitude. However it remains unclear whether the taxi meter effect has also a significant effect on the tariff switching behavior of consumers. Besides that, consumers could experience the taxi meter property differently dependent on their old tariff scheme. Especially the perception of cost caps might be influenced to some extend by a "mental accounting habit". One can assume that consumers switching from a flat rate to a cost cap tariff are already used to account costs as sunk and therefore show lower physiological responses to the discrete events of interval based costs presentation compared to consumers switching from a classic pay-per-use tariff to a cost cap tariff. To answer this questions a switching decision has to be implemented in the experimental design as shown in figure 4. Again participants in the pay-per-use group pay each time unit immediately and can monitor the duration as well as the cumulating costs on the screen, while flat rate users pay the fixed fee at the end of one run. Initially participants are assigned to one of the three available tariff schemes. After the first run all participants can switch the pricing scheme. The general procedure is identical to the basic experimental design as described in section 3.3.

Hypotheses - Extended Experimental Design

Hypothesis 4

Participants under a pay-per-use tariff in the first run with high physiological responses to the discrete events of interval based costs presentation are significantly more likely to switch the tariff scheme.

Hypothesis 4b - Participants under a cost cap tariff in the first run with high physiological responses to the discrete events of interval based costs presentation are significantly more likely to switch to a flat rate tariff.

Hypothesis 4c - Participants under a cost cap tariff in the first run with high physiological responses to the discrete events of interval based costs presentation are significantly less likely to switch to a flat rate tariff in the second run, than participants under a pay-per-use tariff in the first run with high physiological responses to the discrete events of interval based costs presentation.

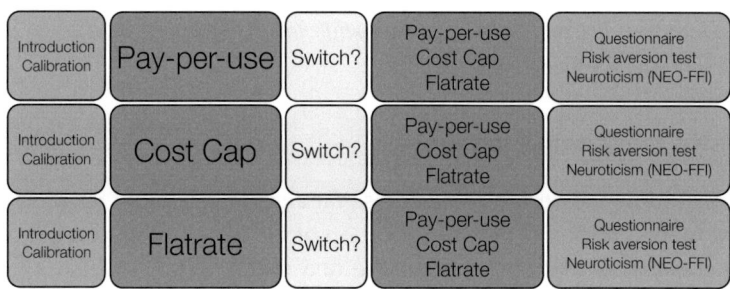

Figure 4: Treatment - Switching

4 Conclusion and Outlook

The presented experimental design contributes to gain insight into newly intro-duced cost cap tariffs and allows for a deeper understanding of the flat rate bias. In general the experiment adds to the field of consumer perception of time-based pricing schemes. Even though the current framing aims at mobile tariffing the results can be generalized to other industries as well. While mobile operators are interested in higher revenues through increased demand, regulators and politicians are sometimes interested in lowering demand or in protecting consumers against unintended high costs. The former could be relevant in electricity markets where smart metering is about to be introduced. Therefore a more immediate cost percep-tion might have beneficial effects on energy consumption. The latter has already be implemented by a regulatory rule to cap data-roaming costs for all mobile telephony customers in the European Union (Labs, 2010). If consumers indeed experience a lower disutility of the taxi meter property due to the insurance effect, a cost cap on data-roaming could even increase demand without any changes in the price per unit of service. The same intuition holds for cost cap tariffs in general. Therefore the open question remains whether cost caps have an indirect effect on demand too. If consumers are more relaxed and unsolicitous due to the insurance property, this could cause an increase of service usage even without reaching the cost cap. Consumers could end up paying more on average compared to a classic pay-per-use tariff even if the cost cap never becomes binding.

References

Adam, M. T. P., M. Gamer, and C. Weinhardt (2009): "Measuring the impact of emotions in electronic auctions: A physioeconomic approach." *Working Paper, Karlsruhe Institute of Technology (KIT)*.

Briegleb, V. (2009): "O2 mit mehr Kunden und Gewinn," http://www.heise.de/mobil/meldung/O2-mit-mehr-Kunden-und-Gewinn-857876.html, heise Newsmeldung.

Crowne, D. and D. Marlowe (1960): "A new scale of social desirability independent of psychopathology." *Journal of consulting psychology*, 24(4), pp. 349–354.

Della Vigna, S. and U. Malmendier (2006): "Paying not to go to the gym," *American Economic Review*, 96(3), pp. 694–719.

Gerpott, T. J. (2009): "Biased choice of a mobile telephony tari type: Exploring usage boundary perceptions as a cognitive cause in choosing between a use-based or a at rate plan," *Telematics and Informatics*, 26, pp. 167–179.

Grubb, M. D. (2009): "Selling to Overconfident Consumers," *American Economic Review*, 99(5), pp. 1770–1807.

Holt, C. and S. Laury (2002): "Risk aversion and incentive effects," *The American Economic Review*, 92(5), pp. 1644–1655.

Just, D. and B. Wansink (2008): "The Fixed Price Paradox: Conflicting Effects of All-You-Can-EatPricing," *Working Manuscript*.

Kridel, D. J., D. E. Lehman, and D. L. Weisman (1993): "Option Value, Telecommunication Demand, and Policy," *Information Economics and Policy*, 5, pp. 125–44.

Krämer, J. and L. Wiewiorra (2010): "Consumer Perception of Mobile Telephony Tariffs with Cost Caps," *Working Paper, Karlsruhe Institute of Technology (KIT)*.

Labs, L. (2010): "Mehr Sicherheit beim EU-Daten-Roaming," http://www.heise.de/newsticker/meldung/Mehr-Sicherheit-beim-EU-Daten-Roaming-943000.html, heise Newsmeldung.

Lambrecht, A., K. Seim, and B. Skiera (2007): "Does Uncertainty Matter? Consumer Behavior Under Three-Part Tariffs," *Marketing Science*, 26(5).

Lambrecht, A. and B. Skiera (2006a): "Paying Too Much and Being Happy About It: Existence, Causes and Consequences of Tariff-Choice Biases," *Journal of Marketing Research*, (May).

Lambrecht, A. and B. Skiera (2006b): "Ursachen eines Flatrate-Bias, Systematisierung und Messung der Einflussfaktoren," *Schmalenbachs Zeitschrift für betriebswirtschaftliche Forschung*, 58, pp. 588–617.

Littlechild, S. (1975): "Two-part tariffs and consumption externalities," *The Bell Journal of Economics*, 6(2), pp. 661–670.

Loewenstein, G. (2000): "Emotions in economic theory and economic behavior," *American Economic Review*, 90(2), pp. 426–432.

Miravete, E. J. (2003): "Choosing the Wrong Calling Plan? Ignorance and Learning," *American Economic Review*, 93, pp. 297–310.

Mitomo, H., T. Otsuka, and K. Nakaba (2007): "A Behavioral Economic Interpretation of the Preference for Flat Rates: A Case of Post-Paid Mobile Phone Services," in: *18th European Regional ITS Conference, International Telecommunications Society, Istanbul*, Springer.

Nunes, J. (2000): "A Cognitive Model of People's Usage Estimations," *Journal of Marketing Research*, 37, pp. 397–409.

Oi, W. (1971): "A Disneyland dilemma: Two-part tariffs for a Mickey Mouse monopoly," *The Quarterly Journal of Economics*, 85(1), pp. 77–96.

Prelec, D. and G. Loewenstein (1998): "The Red and the Black: Mental Accouting of Savings and Debt," *Marketing Science*, 17(1), pp. 4–28.

Schulze, T. and K. Gedenk (2005): "Segmentspezifische Schätzung von Zahlungsbereitschaftsfunktionen 1," *Seminar*, 57(August), pp. 401–422.

Thaler, R. H. (1985): "Mental Accounting and Consumer Choice," *Marketing Science*, 4(3), pp. 199–214.

Thaler, R. H. (1999): "Mental accounting matters," *Journal of Behavioral Decision Making*, 12(3), pp. 183–206.

Train, K. E., M. Ben-akiva, and T. Atherton (1989): "Consumption Patterns and Self-Selecting Tariffs," *Review of Economic and Statistics*, 1, pp. 62–73.

Valletti, T. (2003): "The theory of access pricing and its linkage with investment incentives," *Telecommunications Policy*, 27(10-11), pp. 659–675.

Trading Development Rights: A Laboratory Assessment

Jens E. Müller[1], Stefan Seifert[1], and Karl-Martin Ehrhart[2]

[1] Institute of Information Systems and Management, KIT
   {j.mueller@kit.edu, seifert@kit.edu}
[2] Institute for Economic Theory and Statistics, KIT
   ehrhart@kit.edu

Summary. Within its Strategy for Sustainability, the German Federal Government aims to reduce the land utilization to a maximum of 30 hectare per day in 2020. From an economic perspective, market-based-instruments such as cap-and-trade schemes are promising policy mechanisms to achieve this goal efficiently. Market-based instruments are relatively new mechanisms for the management of natural resources and the environment, for which regulatory approaches have largely failed. First field experiments have revealed that the implementation of a cap-and-trade scheme to limit the land utilization is very complex.

Based on the results of a field experiment, we conducted a lab experiment with different student groups, who played the role of municipalities, and analyzed the effect of framing the task. The study reveals that the total incomes of the municipalities for reaching the target can be higher in the cap-and-trade system than in a comparable command-and-control system. Concerning the framing, we could not observe any impact on the market outcome. However, the spatial planning students were further away from the theoretical optimum than the economics student group. As in the field experiment, the complexity of the trading system and the design of decision support tools are linked to a higher market outcome in the economics student group. As a result, an extensive preparatory phase for practical decision makers in municipal administrations might be necessary in order to assure sufficient competence and acceptance for the new instrument.

1 Introduction

In Germany, there is an ongoing conversion of agricultural land into residential and commercial uses. Negative ecological and economic consequences related to this trend compromise the ecological function of space as a resource for humans, animals, and plants. One of the reasons for the continuous consumption of land is the tight financial situation of many municipalities (Jörissen and Coenen, 2007). At first glance, the development of new areas in the outer area appears attractive because it is often cost neutral or even linked with proceeds from selling land. Moreover, a larger estate per capita ratio is expected to attract the settlement of young families with a positive impact on the redistribution of income taxes. However, the urban sprawl also increases the long term costs of the public infrastructure and, thus, amplifies the financial burden in the long run (e.g. Gutsche, 2006; Preuß, 2009; Siedentop, 2007).

Another challenge is the large number of protagonists, who are involved in the process of land utilization, and the reconciliation of their interests. The Federal Government and the Federal State provide an economic and legal framework but cannot directly control the land consumption. The municipalities are responsible for spatial planning and are allowed to draw up their own spatial development plans. Thereby, the local municipalities have almost full planning sovereignty within their territory. Still, decisions result from a complex interaction between planning and political bodies of the municipalities as well as investors and conservationists.

The above described situation in Germany give rise to a discussion about innovative planning approaches and new policy instruments. The present land use planning policy has only been partially successful in limiting land consumption and urban sprawl. Within this context, the Strategy for Sustainability of the Federal Government states the intention to develop a practical programme for housing and transport-related land utilization while considering ecological, social, and economic objectives (Bundesregierung, 2002, 2004). Furthermore, the Federal Government has set an ambitious 30 ha per day goal in its 2002 Strategy for Sustainability to reduce the usage of new areas by 2020. In this programme, land-related financial, fiscal and development policy instruments will be examined to minimise the urban sprawl, the fragmentation of the countryside and the loss of natural habitat.

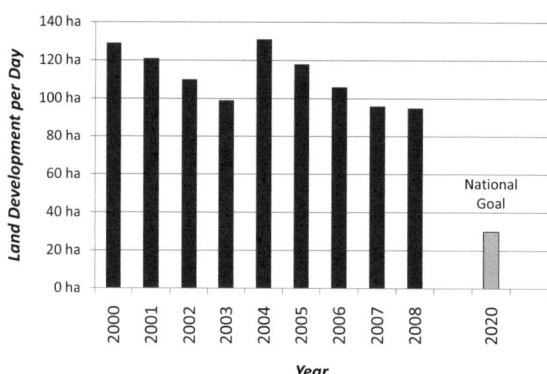

Figure 1: Land Development in Germany

During the last years, the development of new areas has slightly declined, but there is still a big gap between the current development of 113 hectare per day and the national objective of 30 hectare per day in 2020 (Figure 1). Von Haaren and Michaelis (2005) argue that previous legal adjustments of the German planning policies had only little impact on the current land development and are not sufficient to assure a sustainable development in Germany. It seems to be necessary that the Federal Government implements an effective medium- and long-term policy for a sustainable development on the basis of new economic instruments, as legal instruments alone are apparently not sufficient to reduce land consumption (Bundesregierung, 2004):

"Subsidies, taxes, duties and development programs need to be examined with respect to their potential contribution to land consumption reduction. To that end, social, economic and financial effects must also be considered."

In addition to the examination of other land-related financial, fiscal and development policy instruments, the Strategy for Sustainability of the Federal Government focused its attention on inter-disciplinary methods to achieve a stronger link between the existing ecological and planning approaches.

2 Tradable Development Rights in Germany

Market-based instruments (MBIs) are relatively new economic instruments for the management of natural resources and the environment (Whitten et al., 2003). Compared to other regulatory approaches, MBIs ensure that any improvement of environmental protection and quality is reached at the lowest overall costs. In addition, a cap-and-trade system specifies in advance a precise target for environmental protection and the system ensures that the target is reached. Thus, a cap-and-trade system is not only efficient in economic terms; it is also effective with respect to environmental protection. MBIs have been gaining more and more acceptance as policy mechanisms in different areas and have already been applied to different environmental issues. Cap-and-trade systems have become a leading policy option in controlling air emissions and are also being used in fisheries regulation (e.g. EU CO_2 Emission Trading Scheme).

The use of tradable development rights (TDRs) under a cap for land development is considered as a promising policy instrument to reduce the development of new settlement and commercial areas in Germany (Rolfe and Windle, 2006; Henderson and Wang, 2007). Within such a scheme, the right of a local authority to develop new areas would require to submit a certificate for cancelation. By restricting the total number of permits, the extension of new areas is limited in advance. The certificates can be freely traded between municipalities. If a local authority wants to develop a new area and does not have sufficient certificates, it has to buy them on a market. Alternatively, a municipality with a surplus of certificates can sell them. The actual price of the certificates is then determined by supply and demand.

Example: Instead of developing a new area with 5 ha associated floor-space, a city could provide an appropriate site in the inner zone by converting a fallow. In the former case, the proceeds of selling the real estate would cover all costs of the development, but the city would have to submit corresponding development rights for cancellation. In the later case, the infill development is more cost-intensive, but the city could sell (or would not have to buy) development rights on the market.

A system with tradable development rights is quite similar to an emission trading system (e.g. EU ETS). Table 1 summarizes the main characteristics of the Development Rights Trading and compares the trading rules with the Emission Trading Mechanism. In emissions schemes companies are the participants that have to realize a total cap (emitted emission permits) at minimal costs. The goal is to reduce the CO_2-emissions by using alternative fuels or by increasing the energy efficiency of installations. In contrast, in a system with development rights the municipalities would be the participants and the main goal is the reduction of land use. The municipalities should be able to provide the floor space by closing gaps in the inner areas of a city to achieve a total reduction goal, which is determined by the total amount of emitted certificates.

Table 1: Emission Trading vs. Trading Development Rights

Characteristics	Emission Trading	Development Rights Trading
Participants	Companies	Municipalities / Local authorities
Goal	Reduction of CO_2 emissions	Reduction of new land use
Certificates	Emission permit (1 ton CO_2)	TDR (development of 1 hectare area of settlement)
Objective	Realizing total cap (CO_2 emissions) at minimal cost	Realizing total cap (development of new land) at minimal cost
Constraints	Production of given output (electricity, heat, concrete)	Provision of floor space (residential, commercial)
Reduction	Alternative fuels, increasing energy efficiency installations	Closing gaps, conversion of fallows, smaller/denser development areas

However, a system of Tradable Development Rights (TDRs) can give rise to hosts of constitutional and planning policy concerns (e.g. Bovet, 2006; Schläpfer, 2007; Süss and Gmünder, 2005). For instance, when using the certificates the existing planning guidelines have to be considered. In the fields of spatial planning, construction planning law, nature conservation and specialized planning law many legal and planning instruments to protect the open space and to assure a sustainable urban development already exist. As mentioned above, the biggest problem might to be the planning sovereignty of the municipalities, which is guaranteed by the German constitution. Therefore, it is difficult for the Federal Government to set tight limits on the quota for developing new areas in a system with TDRs. Thus, TDRs must be considered as a supplement to the system of existing planning instruments.

Unfortunately, recent case studies have revealed that the design and implementation of a cap-and-trade scheme in land development is complex (Radermacher, 2004; Henger and Schröter-Schlaack, 2008; Walz and Ostertag, 2007). Experiences with existing schemes have also shown some practical difficulties, which implementations must take into consideration (Schleich et al., 2006). Thus, new planning instruments should be carefully investigated before actually applying them in practice. Alongside theoretical analysis, it is important that supplementary areas of research also include numerous practical projects and research programs before continuing to pursue some of these approaches in real practice. Results of pilot projects, which currently run in some municipalities, should be evaluated, and discussed with the potential market participants. With respect to the use of land, exemplary projects and case studies have been already conducted at the national level (e.g. Gutsche, 2007; Preuß, 2006; Walz, 2005). In the future, more simulations and regional reference cases should be pursued.

Experience with cap-and-trade systems has led to a rich empirical and experimental academic literature on the subject. Focusing on the market design, the theoretical literature allows to make predictions about the market outcomes of different designs in particular situations (Roth, 1988; Smith, 1994). Empirical experience with real-world environmental markets give evidence of how well the theory fits with actual results. Another way to do that, is to test and refine environmental markets in the laboratory - the so-called test bedding method (Plott and Porter, 1996; Plott and Cook, 2005). For evaluating environmental policy instruments, different experimental methods have been recently used (Shogren, 2005). In the laboratory, a group of human participants are sitting in front of a set of computers and are linked with each other by specialized software. The participants have to cope with decision tasks, which include carefully controlled incentives, choices, information, and other characteristics. By varying one design parameter between different experimental sessions, while holding all other factors constant, the experimentalists can test how that treatment variable affects the market outcome. Typically, students are recruited for the experiments. They receive a payment based on their performance in the experiment. These economics experiments are increasingly used for investigating public policy and economic theories.

Ostertag et al. (2009) have investigated a potential TDR system in a controlled field experiment with actual German municipalities based on real data. They find that such a system may be well suited to effectively reduce the use of land. While the total cost of the society are lower than under a command-and-control benchmark, the participants failed to reach the efficiency gains that would have been possible in theory. Possibly, the participants in the field study did not perfectly align their actions to the respective monetary valuation. Against this background, this study uses a lab experiment to investigate whether the particular context of trading development rights rather than other economic goods impacts the observed behavior. Moreover, we analyse whether municipal planners behave differently than more economically trained subjects. Thus, the following questions are addressed:

- Do planning experts behave less efficiently than economic experts?

- Is it relevant for the development of a strategy, for the efficiency, and for the scheme design, if participants are trading with rights for land development instead of neutral goods?

Experimental economic research usually abstracts from a particular context and confronts subjects in the lab with a stylized model of a decision making situation (Evans et al., 2008). The underlying assumption is that fundamental principles can be investigated by a context-free design. However, this leads to an abstraction of context-dependent effects. Furthermore, the standard subject pool in experimental economic research are students. Due to the fact that students represent only a small group of the population, results from experiments with students cannot always be transferred to other groups of the society (e.g. Henrich, 2001). Therefore, experts or students from specific fields have been recruited in recent experimental economic research, because they are already experienced in a certain field of application (Carpenter et al., 2005).

3 Experimental Design

The above mentioned field study Ostertag et al. (2009) was clearly framed in a land development context and the subjects were experts in this field. In order to test whether the background of the participants and the framing of the context related to the deviation from the theoretical prediction, we conducted a respective control experiment in the laboratory. The experiment applied a balanced 2x2 design of two treatments and two subject pools. In the treatment "FR" the decision situation was framed with full context information: Participants made decisions over development projects and traded development rights. In the treatment "NE" participants decided over investment projects that required some certificates. Instructions were given in an abstract and neutral language.

Both treatments were conducted with two subject pools, students from the Karlsruhe Institute of Technology ("KA") and students from the University of Applied Sciences for Economics and Environment in Nürtingen-Geislingen ("NU"). The participants from Karlsruhe were mainly recruited from economics study programs. Consequently, a basic knowledge in economics can be assumed. The students from Nürtingen have a background in spatial planning and landscaping and acted as planning experts. Both treatments were run with both groups and two sessions for each combination. The following four working hypotheses guided the design:

Efficiency I The description of the context negatively influences the efficiency of trading.

Efficiency II Economic experts behave more rational (in economic terms) than planning experts, i.e. they achieve the required reduction of land use at lower cost.

Price Discovery I The description of the context negatively influences the price discovery process.

Price Discovery II Prices in the sessions with the economic experts are closer to the theoretical prices than with the planning experts.

The sessions with the students from Nürtingen-Geislingen were conducted in January 2009. A mobile computer lab from the the Karlsruhe Institute of Technology was used for this purpose in order to have the same environmental conditions in Nürtingen and in Karlsruhe. Subsequently, the remaining sessions were conducted in the computer lab at the Karlsruhe Institute of Technology. All students received a financial compensation for their participation in the experiment that depended on individual results. The payments ranged from 6.30 euros up to 20.80 euros with an average of 14.30 euros.

3.1 Rules

In the laboratory experiment we simplified the rules of the field experiment and run each experimental session within a time slot of around 90 minutes. In a session, eight students participated and acted on behalf of one municipality each. One session was divided into seven planning periods. Additionally, two test runs were carried out at the start of a session, to allow the participants to get used to the handling of the software. The participants had the task to develop settlement and commercial areas in each planning period to provide additional space for living and business.

At the beginning of each period the participants were able to sell or buy certificates on a market place. Then, they had to select one of 14 development projects, of which seven were inner-city projects and the other seven involved new land use in the outer area. The inner-city development projected incurred costs that differed from project to project and from municipality to municipality. Overall costs ranged between 27 and 968 monetary units. However, these options did not require development rights, since these areas are already inner-city settlement and transport areas. As an alternative, a participant could develop 2 ha of new settlement area. This areas was assumed to be cost-neutral which means it did not generates expenses for the municipality. This works on the assumption that a municipality can pass the development cost of a new settlement area to the property owner. Due to the fact, that one development rights certificate legitimized the conversion of 1 hectare forest area or agricultural land into new settlement and transport areas, two development rights certificates were needed to develop a new settlement area. The development implementation generated income regardless of the type of development option. Each participant received 1,000 monetary units income for carrying out a development option.

At the beginning of a planning period, each participant received one certificate. The totally emitted development rights allowed the participants to implement on average half of their outer-city projects. If one development option was carried out in a planning period, it could not be used again in the following periods. Each municipality was able to sell its certificate or buy a second certificate on the market. In case a participant developed a new settlement area without having the necessary certificates, sanction payments for each missing certificate were done. The validity of the certificates was limited to one planning period in order to avoid hoarding of certificates. Hence, supplementary certificates expired at the end of a planning period. By this design option, the participants were required to submit limit orders to avoid expired certificates or sanctions. After the collection of the limit orders the platform calculated the market price by means of the principle of largest, best execution. Then, the certificates were transferred between the municipalities and the participants could select a development option.

4 Results

In the following, the results of the different treatments are presented and evaluated with respect to the overall economic efficiency and the strategies of the participants. In order to calculate the achieved cost savings and the efficiency of the trading system we compare the observed costs generated by the municipalities in the simulation runs with the theoretical optimum (cost minimum).[1]

4.1 Monetary Consideration and Efficiency

Figure 2 contrasts the aggregated simulation results and the optimum scenario including trade (OIT) and the optimum scenario excluding trade (OET). The game results represent the sum of the final accounts and comprise costs and returns of the actions, sanction payments, revenues and expenditures from certificate buying and selling, as well as interest payments. In the optimum trading scenario, four certificates should be traded in each planning period. In this case, the municipalities are able to develop in total four new settlement areas and four inner areas per round without the payment of sanctions or the expiration of certificates. Due to the positive interest rate, municipalities choose the cheapest inner-city developments in the optimum scenario first. In the optimum scenario without trade, it is assumed that all municipalities choose inner-city developments in each planning period and that all certificates expire. Similar to the optimum trade solution, the cheapest inner development options are chosen first. So, the scenario which includes trade is the best-case scenario, and the excluding trade scenario is the worst-case scenario. These scenarios benchmark for the results of the laboratory experiment.

The average result of all runs amounts to 56,707 mu, which is 10.8% less than the result of the optimum scenario with trade (63,624 mu). Remarkably, the result of the

---

[1] The following abbreviations are used: The abbreviation "NE" comprises all four neutral runs (hence two runs in Karlsruhe and two runs in Nürtingen). "FR" includes the corresponding runs of the development context. In contrast, the abbreviations "NU" (for Nürtingen) and "KA" (for Karlsruhe) sum up the results of the runs for the respective student group.

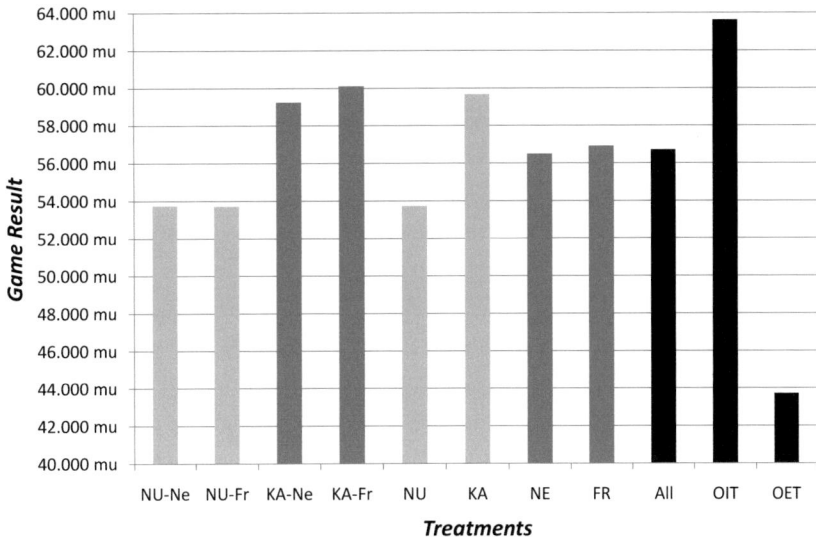

Figure 2: Simulation Results

students from Karlsruhe (59,683 mu) is 11% higher than the result of the students from Nürtingen (53,732 mu). More precisely, the efficiency rate

$$Efficiency = \frac{Optimum\ Excluding\ Trade - Simulation\ Result}{Optimum\ Including\ Trade}$$

shows how much of the cost savings potential of the optimum including trade has been realized compared to the optimum excluding trade. Table 2 summarizes the efficiency rates of the sessions in Nürtingen and Karlsruhe, and in a framed and neutral treatment.

Table 2: Efficiency Rates

	NU-Ne	NU-Fr	All
Nürtingen (NU)	50.43%	50.25%	50.34%
Karlsruhe (KA)	78.06%	82.37%	80.22%
All	64.24%	66.31%	65.28%

The table shows that the available potential was not completely utilized taking into account the theoretical possibilities. The efficiency rate of the students from Karlsruhe (80.22%) is about is about 60% higher than the efficiency rate of the spatial planning students (50.34%). The statistical evaluation of the simulation results reveals significant differences between the two student groups.[2] Consequently, the economic experts achieve the reduction goal at lower costs. However, the

---

[2] Student's *t*-test for paired samples: n = 32, t = 2,686, *p*-value = 0.012.

efficiency rates of the neutral treatment and the framed treatment with 64.24% and 66.31%, respectively, are almost at the same level. No significant differences can be observed.[3] Therefore, the way of describing of the actual situation has not significantly influenced the efficiency of the trading system.

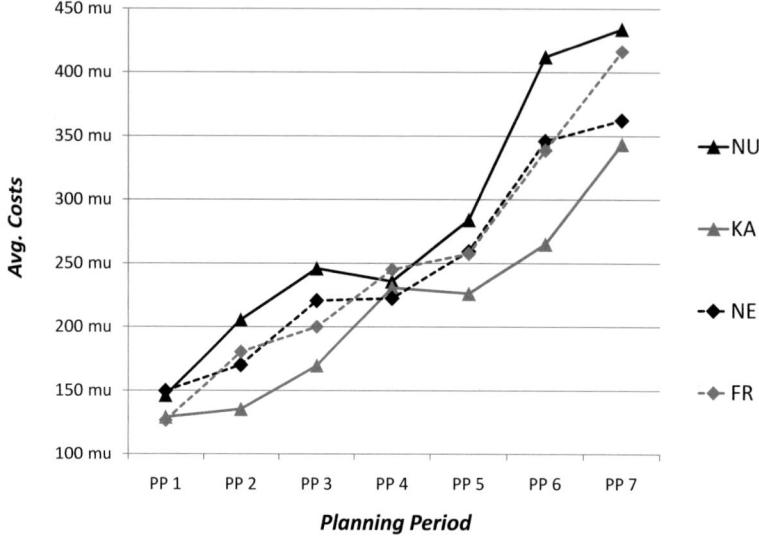

Figure 3: Average Cost of Inner-City Developments

In each round, the average costs of the students from Karlsruhe are below those of the group from Nürtingen. On average, the costs are 22% lower - with the highest difference in round six (36%). Considering the aggregated values of the framed and the unframed treatment, there are no significant differences between the average costs, except for round six. However, the average costs for land recycling increase over the course of the simulation. Sanction payments arose only in the second run for the students from Nürtingen and in the second run for the students from Karlsruhe. No sanctions were paid in the neutral treatments. Overall, the sanctions have little influence on the simulation results. Comparing the total costs, the costs in the Nürtingen sessions are 49.8% higher than the comparative value of the students from Karlsruhe. Some of the cheapest inner-city options remained unused in the group from Nürtingen. The results of the framed runs are 7.1% higher than the results of the context-free runs. Therefore, the description of the actual situation and the related recycling costs have fewer impact on the choice of development options than the knowledge of the experts, or respectively the background of the participants.

---

[3] Student's *t*-test for paired samples: n = 32, t = 0.183, *p*-value = 0.856.

4.2 Trade and Price Discovery

The price curve in Figure 4 shows that the price of the certificates in each planning period is above the theoretical market price. The market price for development rights is also increasing significantly within the course of the simulation run.[4] However, the difference between the theoretical market price and the price in the sessions of the economic experts is decreasing over the course of the simulation and is reaching its minimum with 150 mu in the last round. This reduction of deviation could result from learning effects over the course of the experiment.

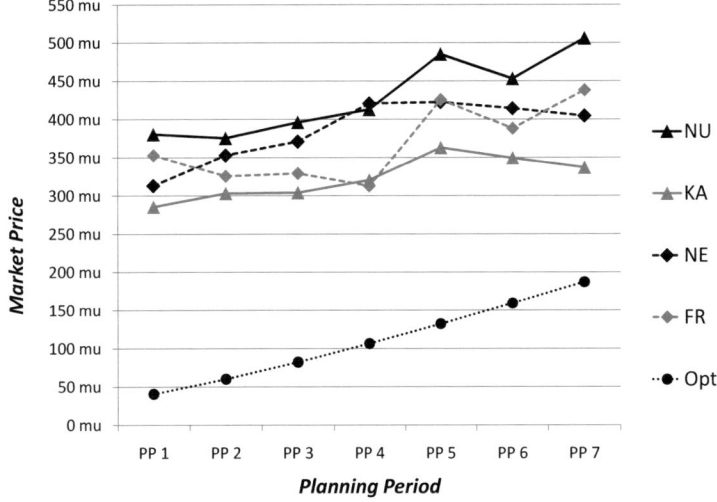

Figure 4: Development of the Market Price

The market prices of the planning experts are on average 350 mu above the price of the theoretical optimum, without converging to the theoretical solution. The Nürtingen groups' market prices for certificates are in each round above the respective prices of the groups from Karlsruhe. Hence, the certificate prices of the groups from Nürtingen are further away from the reference price than the certificate prices of the groups from Karlsruhe. The development of the market price is more closely correlated with the price of the previous rounds ($r_{KA} = 0.802$, $r_{NU} = 0.626$) than with the average costs accrued in a period ($r_{KA} = 0.485$, $r_{NU} = 0.341$). However, differences between trading with development rights and trading with neutral goods cannot be identified.

Figure 5 contrasts the traded volume of the different treatments with the minimum trading volume. The minimum trading volume is the amount of certificates (in ha) that has to be traded in order to achieve the cost optimal result. The reference scenario has a minimum trading volume of 28 ha certificates. With 22.5 ha (KA-NE)

---

[4] Page trend test: n = 7, c = 8, L = 1005, *p*-value ≤ 0.001.

and 21.5 ha (KA-FR), the results of the students from Karlsruhe are closer to the theoretical reference value than the students from Nürtingen with trade volumes of 18.5 ha (NU-NE) and 16.5 ha (NU-FR). Regarding the trade volume, there are no important differences between trading with development rights and trading with neutral goods either. Because of the small trading volume, efficient development option activation was not feasible, as inner-city development potentials could not be chosen where they would have been most favorable from an overall perspective. A further implication of the small trading volume directly results from the experimental design: If an insufficient number of certificates is traded, in tendency, more certificates expire unused. If a municipality only holds one certificate, it has to choose inner-city developments in order to avoid sanctions. Because of the banking restrictions, the certificate would expire at the end of the round as it cannot be transferred to the next round.

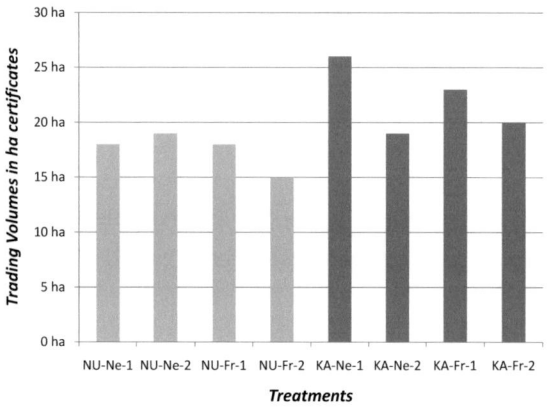

Figure 5: Trading Volume

The planning experts representatives have designated fewer new areas than the economic experts representatives. Two reasons are possible: On the one hand, the efficient use of development rights requires an adequate trade volume in order to be able to select the appropriated inner- and outer-developments. On the other hand, a participant could have decided to choose, for instance, an inner-city development at the beginning of the trading phase and realized it independently from the certificate stock. In this case, the ex-ante decision to definitely carry out land recycling in combination with a too aggressive ask price of the corresponding sell, could be the cause for inefficient results. Sell and buy orders, as well as associated ex-post decisions (after trade) regarding the selection of development options, enhance the probability of an efficient result.

The experimental design and the inter-temporal decision making of the participants influence the use of certificates and the development of new areas (see Figure 6). The decision making of the participants (before or after the trading

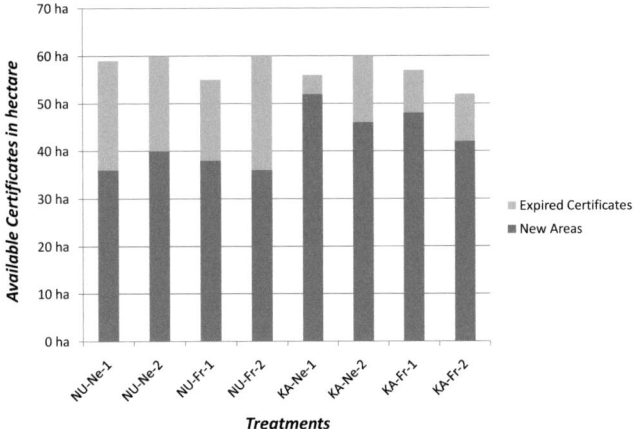

Figure 6: Use of Certificates per Simulation Run

phase) directly influences the trade volume, because accordingly fewer orders are registered. Due to the experimental design, the trade volume influences the number of settlement areas: The more certificates were traded, the more areas could be developed and the less certificates expired at the end of one planning period.

4.3 Analysis of Limit Prices

At the beginning of each planning period, all participants were able to quote a sell price for their own certificates and a buy price for additional certificates. Since at the beginning of a round each participant had only one certificate, it was necessary to buy an additional certificate for an outer-development. The development of the averaged limit prices of the participants during the experiment are demonstrated in Figure 7. During the actual experiment, average limit prices are increasing.[5] The average limit price for a buy order amounted to 288 mu in the first round. Within the course of the experiment, the average price increased to 421 mu (+46.4%) in round seven. The limit prices of the students from Nürtingen (379 mu) are on average 20.7% above the values of the students from Karlsruhe (314 mu).

Figure 8 illustrates the development of the average sell orders. The limit prices of the sell orders increase relatively slightly compared to the buy orders and range between 400 mu and 500 mu. Nonetheless, there is an upward trend.[6] The limit prices of the last round (450 mu) are on average 12,6% higher than in round one (399 mu). Similar to the buy orders, the prices of the planning experts are above the limit prices of the economic experts. The differences between the two groups are even more evident comparing the sell orders. The average limit price of the economic students from Karlsruhe amounts to 359 mu. The prices of the planning experts from Nürtingen (518 mu) are on average 46.6% higher.

---

[5] Page trend test: n = 7, c = 8, L = 1020, p-value $\leq$ 0.001.
[6] Page trend test: n = 7, c = 8, L = 947, p-value $\leq$ 0.01.

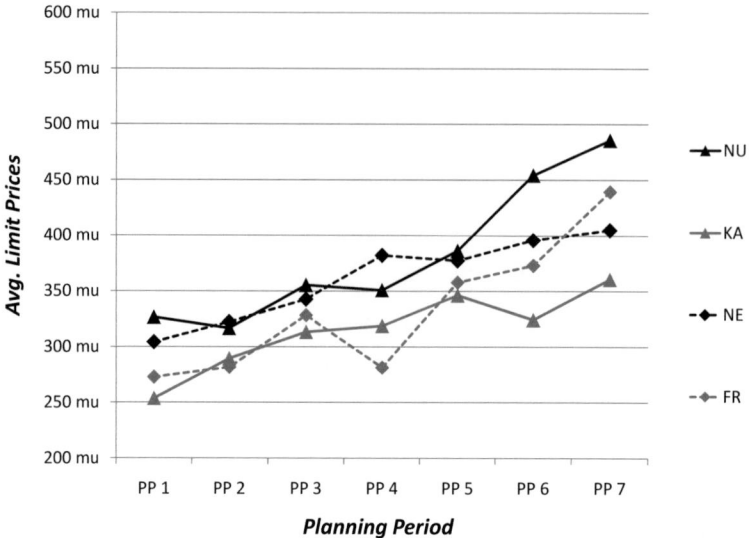

Figure 7: Buy Orders

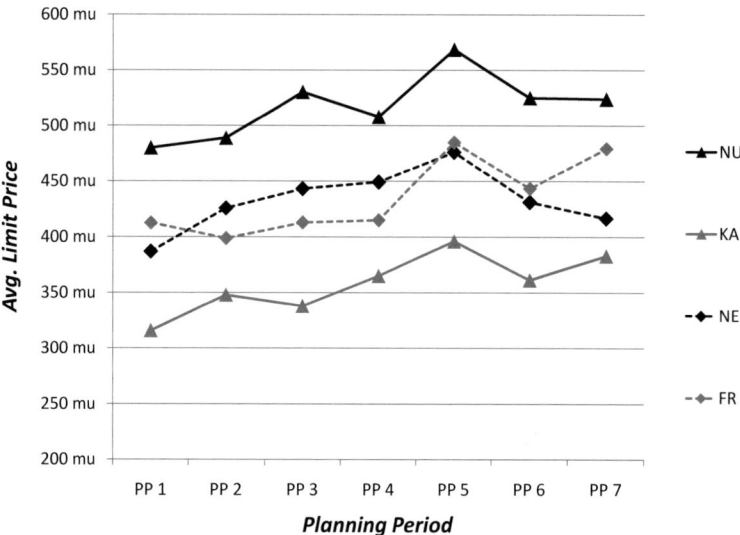

Figure 8: Sell Orders

5 Conclusion

In this article, we presented the results of a laboratory experiment, which was conducted as a complement to the field study by Ostertag et al. (2009). Within the laboratory experiment, city planning development was simulated with eight decision makers over seven planning periods. In contrast to the field experiment, the laboratory experiment was based on virtual data. In order to address specific research questions, a simplified scheme for trading development rights in the laboratory experiment was developed. Thereby, the influence of external factors was minimized. Still, the experimental design and the given data reflects the principal mechanism of development rights trading and allows the test of the hypotheses.

Achieving an ecological, quantitative reduction goal was not the focus of the laboratory experiment. However, the given overall reduction goal was met and even surpassed. Similar to the field experiment, the theoretical potential to minimize costs while providing the required floor space was not completely taking into account. Furthermore, the cheaper development actions were carried out first and the increasing market prices reflected the increasing abatement costs. The results underpin the findings of the field experiment and the results of economic and planning experts differ significantly regarding the efficiency rates and the price discovery process. The difference to the theoretical optimum of the economic experts was smaller than the difference of the planning experts, which means that the economic experts achieved the reduction goal at lower costs due to more efficient abatement strategies. High sell orders in the group Nürtingen, driven by an endowment effect, led to a higher price level in this sessions. Therefore, working hypotheses Efficiency II and Price Discovery II were confirmed. Against this, the description of the actual situation did not influence the efficiency of the trading system. Within the scope of the laboratory experiment, it did not matter whether it was dealt with development rights or with neutral goods. Hence, the working hypotheses Efficiency I and Price Discovery I are not supported.

Some results of our experiment suggest that a trading system will not automatically result in the expected cost savings and efficiency gains. In all simulation runs including the field and the lab experiments, the overall incomes were lower than expected and we observed a gap between actual and optimal prices. According to economic theory, the primary allocation of the certificates should not affect the efficiency of the trading system. If the initial allocation is inefficient, the secondary market should correct this situation by reallocating the certificates to the "right" municipalities. How fast the market can achieve a constellation, where no pareto-efficient transactions are possible, depends on the design and the trading rules of the secondary market as well as on the trading behavior of the participants. Wrongly chosen development options, as observed in the planning experts groups including field and lab sessions, may support high market prices, slow down the price discovery process and may reduce the efficiency of the trading system. Furthermore, the participants' lack of experience with this new instrument stresses the need for the local authorities to acquaint themselves with the rules and the range of possible strategies in a system with TDRs as a supplement to the existing planning regulation systems. It is necessary to consider these factors along with the institutional and legal requirements when choosing a market design for tradable development rights in Germany. For this reason, we suggest to conduct additional surveys and field studies which focus on the mentioned observations and to investigate and test a market for Tradable Development Rights and new decision support tools in other planning simulations.

References

Bovet, J. (2006): "Handelbare Flächenausweisungsrechte als Steuerungsinstrument zur Reduzierung der Flächeninanspruchnahme," *Natur und Recht*, 8, pp. 473–479.

Bundesregierung (2002): "Perspektiven für Deutschland: Unsere Strategie für eine nachhaltige Entwicklung," `http://www.bundesregierung.de/Content/DE/__Anlagen/2006-2007/perspektiven-fuer-deutschland-langfassung.html`.

Bundesregierung (2004): "Nationale Nachhaltigkeitsstrategie der Bundesregierung: Schwerpunktthema Verminderung der Flächeninanspruchnahme," `http://www.bmvbs.de/Anlage/original_22293/Verminderung-der-Flaecheninanspruch-nahme.pdf`.

Carpenter, J. P., G. W. Harrison, and J. A. List (2005): "Field experiments in economics," *Research in Experimental Economics*, 10, pp. 1–16.

Evans, M., S. M. Gilpatric, M. McKee, and C. A. Vossler (2008): "Managerial incentives for compliance with environmental information disclosure programs," in: T. Cherry, S. Kroll, and J. F. Shogren (eds.), *Environmental economics, experimental methods*, Routledge, pp. 243–260.

Gutsche, J.-M. (2006): *Kurz-, mittel- und langfristige Kosten der Baulanderschließung für die öffentliche Hand, die Grundstücksbesitzer und die Allgemeinheit*, Forschungsvorhaben im Auftrag des Ministeriums für Landwirtschaft, Umwelt und ländliche Räume des Landes Schleswig-Holstein, Hamburg.

Gutsche, J.-M. (2007): *Von der Außen- zur Innenentwicklung in Städten und Gemeinden: Erarbeitung von Handlungsvorschlägen sowie Analysen der ökologischen, ökonomischen und sozialen Wirkungen einer Neuorientierung der Siedlungspolitik – Das Kostenparadoxon der Baulandentwicklung*, Forschungsvorhaben im Auftrag des Umweltbundesamtes, Dresden/ Hamburg.

Henderson, J. V. and H. G. Wang (2007): "Urbanization and city growth: The role of institutions," *Regional Science and Urban Economics*, 37(3), pp. 283–313.

Henger, R. and C. Schröter-Schlaack (2008): "Designoptionen für den Handel mit Flächenausweisungsrechten in Deutschland: Ökonomie und Planung der Flächennutzung," Land Use Economics and Planning - Working Paper Series, 08-02.

Henrich, J. (2001): "Challenges for everyone - Real people, deception, one-shot games, social learning, and computers," *Behavioral and Brain Sciences*, 24(3), pp. 414–415.

Jörissen, J. and R. Coenen (2007): *Sparsame und schonende Flächennutzung: Entwicklung und Steuerbarkeit des Flächenverbrauchs*, Edition Sigma, Berlin.

Ostertag, K., J. Müller, and S. Seifert (2009): "Neue Instrumente zur Verringerung des Flächenverbrauchs." *Ökologisches Wirtschaften*, 3, pp. 30–34.

Plott, C. R. and J. P. Cook (2005): "Congestion at locks on inland waterways: An experimental testbed of a policy of tradable priority permits for lock access," Working Papers 1240, California Institute of Technology, Division of the Humanities and Social Sciences.

Plott, C. R. and D. P. Porter (1996): "Market architectures and institutional testbedding: An experiment with space station pricing policies," *Journal of Economic Behavior & Organization*, 31(2), pp. 237–272.

Preuß, T. (2006): *Flächenkreislaufwirtschaft BAND 1. Theoretische Grundlagen und Planspielkonzeption: Kreislaufwirtschaft in der städtischen/ stadtregionalen Flächennutzung. Ein ExWoSt-Forschungsfeld*, Bundesamt für Bauwesen und Raumordnung (BBR).

Preuß, T. (2009): *Folgekosten der Siedlungsentwicklung: Bewertungsansätze, Modelle und Werkzeuge der Kosten-Nutzen-Betrachtung, Reihe REFINA*, vol. 3, DiFU, Berlin.

Radermacher, F. J. (2004): "Neue Wege zu einem nachhaltigen Flächenmanagement in Baden-Württemberg: Sondergutachten," Stuttgart.

Rolfe, J. and J. Windle (2006): "Using field experiments to explore the use of multiple bidding rounds in conservation auctions: International association of agricultural economists (IAAE)," .

Roth, A. E. (1988): "Laboratory experimentation in economics: A methodological overview," *The Economic Journal*, 98(393), pp. 974–1031.

Schläpfer, F. (2007): "Marktwirtschaftliche Instrumente in der Raumplanung: Reaktion auf den Schwerpunkt 'Flächeninanspruchnahme'," *GAIA*, 17(3), pp. 170–175.

Schleich, J., K. M. Ehrhart, C. Hoppe, and S. Seifert (2006): "Banning banking in EU emissions trading?" *Energy Policy*, 1(34), pp. 112–120.

Shogren, J. F. (2005): "Experimental Methods and Valuation," in: K. G. Mäler and J. R. Vincent (eds.), *Handbook of Environmental Economics*, 2 edition, chapter 19, Elsevier, pp. 969–1027.

Siedentop, S. (2007): *Nachhaltigkeitsbarometer Fläche: Regionale Schlüsselindikatoren nachhaltiger Flächennutzung für Fortschrittsberichte der nationalen Nachhaltigkeitsstrategie - Flächenziele*, Forschungen / Bundesministerium für Verkehr, Bau und Stadtentwicklung, Selbstverlag des Bundesamtes für Bauwesen und Raumordnung, Bonn.

Smith, V. L. (1994): "Economics in the laboratory," *The Journal of Economic Perspectives*, 8(1), pp. 113–131.

Süss, A. and M. Gmünder (2005): "Weniger Zersiedlung durch handelbare Flächennutzungszertifikate?" *DISP 160 - Urban Sprawl*, 41(1).

Von Haaren, C. and P. Michaelis (2005): "Handelbare Flächenausweisungsrechte und Planung," *Informationen zur Raumentwicklung*, 4/5.

Walz, R. (2005): *Handelbare Flächenausweisungskontingente zur Begrenzung des Flächenverbrauchs: Ansätze für Baden-Württemberg*, Fraunhofer IRB Verlag.

Walz, R. and K. Ostertag (2007): "Der Fläche einen Wert geben," *Umwelt Magazin*, 7/8, pp. 45–46.

Whitten, S., S. Salzman, D. Shelton, and W. Proctor (2003): "Markets for ecosystem services: Applying the concepts," Paper presented of the 47th Annual Conference of the Australian Agricultural and Resource Economics Society.

Part IV

Electronic Market Regulation

Electronic Markets and their Mechanisms as Intellectual Property

Tim Klümper and Thomas Dreier

Institute of Information and Economic Law, KIT
{kluemper, dreier}@kit.edu

Summary. An Electronic Market is the result of a market designing process. Due to the complexity of this process, electronic markets are major financial investments for their operators. The development of electronic markets is often based on innovative and creative work. However, an electronic market as such is not protected as intellectual property (IP). In this article, the protection of single electronic market elements, especially the protection of the central market element, the economic mechanism, is questioned, if not denoted otherwise according to German law. The criteria which determine the existence of IP will be presented. Using these criteria, it will be shown whether single market elements can be expected to be classified as IP at present and where further approaches can be found.

1 Motivation

Market engineering deals among other things with the creation (the designing) and advancement of electronic markets. Core area of such markets is the elaborated allocation design, using a mechanism, which leads the junction of supply and demand. The economic term "mechanism" here describes any process that takes as inputs the bids and produces as its output the decision as to which bidder receives the item and how much any of the bidders will be required to pay[1].

The development of electronic markets as a whole platform, as well as the development of its inner economic design, happen innovatively and often need major investments.

In order to foster innovation in the area of electronic markets, financial benefits for the innovator have to be secured. This may be achieved by restricting the competitors' possibility to copy single market elements or even a whole market concept. The whole structure of an electronic market and its elements, from single basic ideas to the whole system which contains rules and software, are in legal terms intangible items. To restrain the possibility to copy intangible goods, intellectual property rights are used.

The question is whether electronic markets, as results of a market designing process, are subject to the legal protection of intellectual property rights. To answer

---

[1] *McAfee, McMillan* in: Journal of Economic Literature, Vol. 25, No. 2. (Jun., 1987), p. 699.

this question, the definitions of electronic markets and mechanisms will be analyzed with respect to their fulfillment of the legal conditions of IP: The analysis starts by determining whether electronic markets and mechanisms qualify as intangible good and continues by examining elements of statutory definitions of certain protective laws because of which those intangible goods intensify to IP.

For all kinds of IP protection, there are additional conditions besides the kind of IP like newness, level of creativity, distinguishability, etc. This article contains the examination of the applicability of certain protection rights. To simplify matters it is assumed that these additional conditions are fulfilled by the objects of investigation, if not explicitly stated otherwise.

2 Electronic Markets and their Mechanisms

There are different opinions about the exact definitions of electronic markets[2]. All definitions have in common that electronic markets are inter-organizational information systems used by actors in defined roles with a specific mechanisms to trade products and services. The actors can participate using the roles of suppliers, consumers, or brokers[3].

Schmid[4] shows the following characteristics of electronic markets:

- Electronic assistance of the coordinating mechanisms of a market. That results in appearance of complete electronic coordination (e.g. pricing) or of simple coordination assistance (e.g. price information).
- Simplification of the acts of information search and information analysis. The information asymmetry between market participants should be lowered by a higher degree of market transparency.
- Decrease of the spatiotemporal distance. The disappearance of spatiotemporal frontiers allows for a spontaneous market participation of the actors, independent of their particular time and location.
- Equality of the market partners. This should be achieved through the voluntary participation of the partners in market action and the openness of the market access.
- Participants in electronic markets are human actors. Accordingly, the market action is influenced by human interpretation of the market situation.

To achieve the goals that are pursued by a specific electronic market, market designers may design various market elements. From an economic point of view, the central design element is the economic mechanism.

---

[2] *Schoder* in: Kurbel/Becker/Gronau/Sinz/Suhl, Enzyklopädie der Wirtschaftsinformatik-Online-Lexikon, keyword "Elektronischer Marktplatz" - http://www.enzyklopaedie-der-wirtschaftsinformatik.de - in the version of 01/13/2010 10.55 pm.
[3] *Kollmann*, E-Business, 2nd edition Wiesbaden 2007, p. 390.
[4] *Schmid*, Elektronische Märkte - in: Wirtschaftsinformatik 35 (1993), no. 5, p. 465.

3 Electronic Markets and Their Mechanisms as Intangible Items

In search of the answer to the question, if and how far electronic markets in general, and economic mechanisms in particular within the scope of IP are legally protected, one has to ascertain that electronic markets, respectively economic mechanisms, are intangible items which possibly intensify to IP.

3.1 "Intangible Items"

Intangible items or intangible assets are immaterial economic goods[5]. These goods can be subject of protection intensified to industrial property rights or copyright but also mere ideas, goodwill or know-how[6]. Intangible goods are all immaterial items, independent of their legal protection, as long as the item is the result of an innovative and commercial-mental act of creation[7]. The attribute of being an economically tradable good does not account for also being legally protected. For instance know-how very often is traded, but it is not legally protected by the rules of IP by implication.

3.2 Electronic Markets as Intangible Items

Electronic markets are intangible items. They consist of a multitude of elements[8], whose combination makes the market design. Electronic markets are results of market designing processes with the objectives that have been discussed above, namely creating market transparency, lowering the transaction costs and influencing the bidder's behavior[9]. The specification of the market design may include pure economical but also political parameters[10]. The implementation of the specification is an innovative act that resorts to scientific disciplines like mathematics, economics, psychology, computer science and even cultural sciences. Therefore, electronic markets as result of an innovative commercial-mental creation are immaterial goods. That classification is independent of the legal protectability of the goods and their potential intensifying to IP.

3.3 Economic Mechanisms as Intangible Items

Designing electronic markets requires in the first instance the design of a mechanism which influences the buyers' and bidders' behavior. The design of the economic

---

[5] *Putzo* in: Palandt - Kommentar zum Bürgerlichen Gesetzbuch, 68th edition München 2009, § 453 ref. 9.

[6] *Westermann* in: Münchener Kommentar zum BGB, 5th edition München 2008, § 433 ref. 16 f.

[7] textitAxter/Schütze in: Loewenheim/Meessen/Riesenkampff Kartellrecht, 2nd edition München 2009, Europäisches Recht (Art. 81-86) 3. Teil ref. 1.

[8] In detail vide infra.

[9] The influence to the bidder's behavior is not necessarily centered to profit maximization. Multitude of auction theoretical approaches aim to the target of achieving economically worthwhile ("efficient") prices and avoiding ruinous bidder's competition - cf. Berninghaus/Erhart/Güth, Strategische Spiele, 2nd edition Berlin 2005, p. 556 ff.

[10] E.g. state auctions of transmitter frequencies, mining rights or oil production rights.

mechanism as a single market element is like the design of the whole market result of an innovative commercial creation. Therefore, the designed mechanisms are also intangible items.

4 Intellectual Property on Electronic Markets and Their Mechanisms

4.1 "Intellectual Property"

According to civil law the term intellectual property or IP describes the perpetuation of a right of factual and lawful dominant behavior over an intangible item[11]. Intangible items as such are not subjects of rights. Furthermore, intangible items differ from immovable and movable objects ("chattels"). The specific characteristic of intangible items is their ubiquitary and non-rivaling usability: Intangible items can be used in different places during the same time without mutual exclusion[12].

Offhand there cannot be ownership of "mere" immaterial goods in terms of perpetuation of a lawful dominant behavior; even if a person exercises actual physical authority over such an immaterial good, e.g. through nondisclosure of know-how. Therefore, strengthening or intensifying of immaterial goods to IP is needed. This intensification which is called a lawful autonomisation does not arise from the BGB (Bürgerliches Gesetzbuch - German Civil Code)[13]. The lawful autonomisation of immaterial goods to the absolute right of IP is primary legislated by the (special) statutes of industrial property and copyright[14].

The term intellectual property (IP) therefore represents absolute subjective rights (rights entitled to one person with legal effect against everybody) over autonomized immaterial goods. Therefore, intellectual property in German is also called "Immaterialgüterrecht" (intangible property right)[15]. IP underlies the numerus clausus ("Typenzwang") and the principle of certainty. That means that IP is limited to the rights given by the legislator. The law has to define exactly the purpose of the particular intangible property right[16].

In German law literature, the term "intellectual property" is disputed[17]. As far as the intellectual property only refers to the incorporeal nature of a legal issue, it conforms to the term immaterial property right. If intellectual property in contrast

---

[11] *Bassenge* in: Palandt - Kommentar zum Bürgerlichen Gesetzbuch, 68th edition München 2009, Überbl. v. § 903, ref. 1.

[12] *Dreier* in: Dreier/Schulze UrhG, 3rd edition München 2008, Einl. ref. 14.

[13] *Jauernig*, BGB, 13th edition München 2009, Vorbem. zu §§ 903-1011 ref. 7.

[14] *Ohly* JZ 2003, 545; Götting GRUR 2006, 353.

[15] *Creifelds*, Rechtswörterbuch, 19th edition München 2007, keywords "Immaterialgüterrechte" and "Geistiges Eigentum".

[16] *Ohly* in: Festschrift Schricker, 2005, p. 105-121; declining the terms "numerus clausus" and "Typenzwang" but agreeing with regard to the contents: *Kraßer*, Patentrecht, 6. edition München 2009, 1. Kapitel § 2 I. Nr. 4.

[17] Cf. *Ohly* JZ 2003, 545 ff; Götting GRUR 2006, 353 ff.

means that the legal issue is created by human mind, it only covers a part of immaterial property rights. Trade mark rights and rights of company symbols as well as some of the "neighboring rights" codified in the UrhG (Urheberrechtsgesetz - German Copyright Act) are not accorded due to human intellectual activity but due to entrepreneurial effort[18]. This distinction must not conceal the danger of confusion between the similar terms of intangible goods (= incorporeal items) and intangible property rights (= legally protected interest = IP). This distinction is often blured, especially in English, where occasionally the terms IP and intangible goods are often used interchangeably, which is dogmatically incorrect.

According to legal traditions of continental Europe, IP is divided in results of commercial innovation on the one hand and artistic-literary innovation on the other hand. The distinction is reflected in the two fields of law: intellectual property rights and copy right. The term intellectual property consolidates both fields of law. This consolidation became internationally accepted[19]. In its official definition of IP the World Property Organization (WIPO) adheres to the bisection[20]

> "Intellectual property (IP) refers to creations of the mind: inventions, literary and artistic works, and symbols, names, images, and designs used in commerce. Intellectual property is divided into two categories: Industrial property, which includes inventions (patents), trademarks, industrial designs, and geographic indications of source; and Copyright, which includes literary and artistic works such as novels, poems and plays, films, musical works, artistic works such as drawings, paintings, photographs and sculptures, and architectural designs. Rights related to copyright include those of performing artists in their performances, producers of phonograms in their recordings, and those of broadcasters in their radio and television programs."

In the context of intellectual property, procurable rights are copyrights, patents, Geschmacksmusterrecht (design law), Gebrauchsmuster (utility patent), trademarks, etc. Those rights are partially comparable to ownership rights. They are temporary, exclusive rights and entitle their holder to parry the use of his work by a third party. A major difference between intellectual property and ownership rights is the temporal limitation. German patent rights are temporary limited up to 20 years after the application day (§ 16 sec. 1 sentence 1 PatG - Patentgesetz - German patent law); copyrights are temporary limited up to 70 years post mortem auctoris (§ 64 UrhG). There is an exception for trade mark rights that can be renewed without any temporal limitation.

---

[18] *Kraßer*, 1. Kapitel § 2 II. Immaterialgüterrecht. Geistiges Eigentum (cf. footnote no.16).
[19] *Sambuc* in: Harte-Bavendamm/Henning-Bodewig UWG, 2nd edition München 2009, ref. 180.
[20] http://www.wipo.int/about-ip/en/ - in the version of 12/30/2009 4.00 pm.

Historic Development[21]

From the beginning of human creativity limitation of knowledge was considered. The very thought of limitation was originated not only from the idea to give the creator authority over his work but also from the aspect to grant the creator monetary advantages. The problem here is the unlimited existence of IP after it was created (vide supra).

Already in the ancient world and later in the Middle Ages there were temporal and spatial limited rights of utilization in particular cultures, e.g. in the guild system or for recipes.

These ideas were only rudimentary approaches to the idea of IP. Usually the protection of works was achieved by concealing the work, by only transfering it to followers or offspring, or by recording it in writings which were not readable for most people at that time. In that period it was for example legal to copy each book to which one could get access by transcribing it. Due to the considerable effort which was needed for obtaining such a copy and due to the small number of people that were able to write, there was no need for legal protection to control reproduction.

Furthermore, there was no need for authors to gain monetary outcome by trading licenses or rights. Authors were financed by monasteries, of which they where members, or by patrons, often profane monarchs, that engaged academics. The need for IP protection changed with the invention of letterpress printing in 1452/54 and the spread of the procedure. Well known philosophers like Pufendorf, Fichte, and Kant argued for the protection of mental works and justified their idea of intellectual property with a natural justice basis[22].

The first patent law was established in Venice in 1474; early legal norms about the relationship of authors and publishers can be found in the Allgemeines Preußisches Landrecht (ALR - General state laws for the Prussian states) from 1784. The development of the legal norms continued until today's status quo. In 1965 the copyright law was comprehensively recodified in the Federal Republic of Germany for the first time after World War II and was changed several times since then. The last changes were introduced by the so called "Dritter Korb" 2008 and consider the difficulties arising from progressive digitalization[23].

Today's Reasons for Protection of Intellectual Property

Today the following reasons motivate the protection of intellectual property[24].

Competitiveness is supported by the protection from imitation, the assurance of the pioneers' earnings and the initiation of cooperation or licensing. In this context, intellectual property is condition to take actions against product piracy. By

---

[21] *Ahrens*, Gewerblicher Rechtsschutz, Tübingen 2008, p. 38 f.
[22] *Dreier*, Einl. ref. 54 (cf. footnote no. 12).
[23] Cf. *Dreier*, Einl. ref. 23 ff (cf. footnote no. 12).
[24] *Rebel*, Gewerbliche Schutzrechte, 5th edition Köln 2007, p. 1 ff.

application of regististration rights[25], the subjects of protection are presented to the public, advancing aspects such as deterrence of imitators, gaining of company reputation and promotion.

Market members can read up on registered rights, publicity is generated. Where licenses for existing proprietary rights are accessible one can safe on nonneeded research and development costs. Registered rights initiate new product inventions, problem solutions and avoid risks of collision with existing rights.

Employee invention law and its codified duty to register work-related inventions prevent overreaching the employees and create an incentive for being innovative at the same time. These targets are achieved with very low costs for the registry compared to the high expenditure for research and development, manifacturing preperations, advertising, sales launching, etc. Beyond that the legal protection mechanisms enable a much cheaper opening up of new markets and market development: Costs for market development of protected products are lower, because the launch of protected products is easier, and therewith, cheaper than of non-protected products.

These targets are archieved by the rights of intellectual properties: By excluding third parties from using protected goods (absolute rights), intellectual property rights generate man-made shortage of infinitely available goods. So the marketability of the product is created. This is the only means of creating economic benefits for the creator. The economic benefit is incentive for innovation, investment, and creation of new immaterial goods.

What is regarded as Intellectual Property?

The precise subject of protection is defined by the relevant protection laws' area of application[26]. Intellectual property in the form of copyright contains not only the protection of personal mental creations in the field of literature, science and art, but also the protection of certain mental works that are no creations[27]. Furthermore, computer programs are protected through copy rights for historical reasons[28] (vide infra).

The most famous of the traditional commercially used industrial property rights are patent rights for technical inventions that are new, beyond the state of the art, and results of an inventive step. Further industrial property rights include

---

[25] Registration rights need application and recordation in a register to become valid. Mostly relevant is the application of patents. On the contrary copy rights arise contemporanous to the act of creating and need no application or recordation. Besides copy rights only special rules of the German Trademark Act and the Gemeinschaftsgeschmacksmusterrecht (design protection rules of the Europian Union) need no application process.

[26] *Ilzhöfer*, Patent-, Marken- und Urheberrecht, 7th edition München 2007, ref. 12.

[27] That does not regard new creations but the (re-)discovery of existing incorporal goods, their rendering and realization. Beneath this there are scientific editions, interpretations of an executive artist, wors of photography and achievment of sound carrier producers, film producers, broadcasting companies and databank producers.

[28] Dreier, Einl. ref. 27 (cf. footnote no. 12).

trademark law for the protection of trademarks, company symbols, and geographical indication of source labels, the Geschmacksmusterrecht (German design law) which protects aesthetical arranged forms like patterns of cloth, pieces of jewelry, vases, etc., and other rights that are not relevant in the present context, like plant variety protection rights that protect new species of plants, or topography protection rights for three-dimensional structures of microelectronic semi-conductor circuits[29].

4.2 Intellectual Property in Electronic Markets

There is no legally normed protection right that protects electronic markets as a whole. Since intellectual property rights are subjects of numerus clausus (vide supra) there is no possibility of "creating" new protection rights through further development of the law. Thus, an electronic market as such is not protectable.

The integrated concept of an electronic market can be perceived as an idea. However, there is no possibility to protect pure ideas[30]. Consequently a protection of electronic markets can only be considered by protecting the sum of its single elements. The protectability of single electronic market elements has to be examined individually.

4.3 Intellectual Property in Single Electronic Market Elements

The outer appearance of an electronic market consists of several elements. Every element can be separately protected as IP. Such elements are the name of the market place provider (e.g. "eBay Inc."), the name of the market place (e.g. "eBay"), its internet domain (e.g. http://ebay.com), the logo of the marketplace, its slogan (e.g. "Buy it, sell it, love it"), or the design of the internet presence. While elements of the outer appearance of the market can be assigned relatively easy to existing protection rules (the name of the market place as commercial firm name according to § 37 sec. 1 HGB[31] - Handelsgesetzbuch or German Commercial Code; name and logo of the market place according the German Trademark Act; also the domain according to the German Trademark Act or by registration at the responsible domain registrar[32]; the slogan according to the Trademark Act or under certain circumstances according to the Copyright Act; the internet presence design according to the Copyright Act) the question is considerably more complex for the protection of elements of the inner structure of an electronic market.

The inner structure of the electronic market place represents the real result of the market designing process. It contains the technical, legal, and economic

---

[29] *Götting,* Gewerblicher Rechtsschutz, 9.Aufl. München 2007, § 1 Rn. 7 ff.

[30] Cf. § 1 para. 3 no. 3 PatG; for the protection of ideas in the context of copyright vide infra.

[31] § 37 sec. 1 HGB "Wer eine nach den Vorschriften dieses Abschnitts ihm nicht zustehende Firma gebraucht, ist von dem Registergericht zur Unterlassung des Gebrauchs der Firma durch Festsetzung von Ordnungsgeld anzuhalten.".

[32] DENIC (Deutsches Network Information Center) for domains under the top level doman (TLD) ".de", VeriSign Inc. for domains under the TLD ".com", etc.

implementation of the market place design. While the economic market design represents the functional core of the market place, the legal framework is the verbalization of the economic design parameters, as well as the technical framework is the realization of the functionality of the online software application.

The technical implementation is protected as software according to the § 69a UrhG[33]. That protection only covers a specific programming solution. According to the copyright, there is no protection of the idea behind the software.

The copyright also protects the database which may be part of the technical framework as a database work. The paragraphs to be considered are §§ 4 sec. 2 and 87a ff UrhG that are independent with regard to their contents. § 4 sec. 2 UrhG protects the creative selection and arrangement of a database work, § 87a ff UrhG protects the investment of a database maker in assembling the data[34]. In this respect, both rules are independently applicable for a database behind an electronic market place. While § 4 sec. 2 UrhG requires a personal mental creation, §§ 87a ff UrhG protects databases that are no personal mental creation, as far as these comply with the requirements of the § 87a UrhG. Namely, these requirements are a collection of works, data or other independent elements arranged in a systematic or methodical way, whose elements are individually accessible either by electronic or by other means, and whose obtaining, verification or presentation requires a qualitatively or quantitatively substantial investment.

The legal framework for the particular allocation or pricing mechanism describes the action alternatives and rules for persons acting on the market place. That legal framework is agreed upon by the market place provider and the other acting persons[35]. The rules representing the legal framework are drafted for multiple usages from the provider party and usually the other party has no possibility to negotiate the conditions. So the rules have to be qualified as AGB (Allgemeine Geschäftsbedingungen - general terms and conditions)[36]. Terms and conditions can be subject of copyrights if they fulfill certain conditions - e.g. if the wording is remarkably better than standard phrases or if the terms and conditions are based on a special mental concept or an extraordinary structure[37]. Again, the protection refers to the "construction" of the terms and conditions - not to the represented content.

Therefore, a legal protection of the elements representing the economic design is possible. This protection refers only to the implementation of the design, in particular the software framework, the aligning database, and the legal framework.

---

[33] Cf. in detail *Karl* Der urheberrechtliche Schutzbereich von Computerprogrammen, München 2009, p. 189.

[34] *Dreier*, Vor §§ 87a ff ref. 1 (cf. footnote no. 12).

[35] That agreement and the imperatively resulting disclosure of the rules for the participation on the market place allow inferences of the participant about the design of the pricing mechanism. That is the main reason for the impossibility to protect the inner market design by nondisclosure. So without legal protection the participants can use that knowledge anywhere.

[36] Cf. § 305 sec. 1 BGB.

[37] LG (regional court) München I GRUR 1991, 50, 51 - *Geschäftsbedingungen*.

The idea of the design per se is not protected. So the protection of the economic design per se is still to be examined.

Besides the regulations concerning the market participants (e.g. restrictions because of the professionalism of the participants - b2b, b2c or c2c market places), the customers' structure (e.g. "PowerSeller", closed, membership-based or open market platforms), and often confidence-building systems (e.g. rating systems[38]), economic market design contains most importantly the economic mechanism. The economic mechanism - in most cases of current market platforms in the shape of an auction design[39] - is the real inner core of an electronic market. Using game and auction theoretical findings the mechanism is adjusted to the needs of the particular market place. The practical implementations underlie pre-existing scientific findings as well as extensive models and experiments that are partially tailored to the particular use case[40], and that partially can also be used in other cases.

4.4 Intellectual Property in Economic Mechanisms

A mechanism describes a market economic ruling automatism that regulates the pricing by co-operation of supply and demand. By pricing the production factors are conducted to the location of most efficient usage and goods are conducted to the location of best provision of benefits (optimal allocation of resources). Through this the efficiency of the political economy is achieved[41].

Economic mechanisms may occur for example in the form of a specific auction design or in the form of a simple salesroom. A pricing or allocation mechanism can develop spontaneously. An example could be the development of a black market under an inefficient planned economy. The creation of such mechanisms in the case of electronic markets often is result of innovative action, as in the example which is presented and discussed in here.

Economic mechanisms are results of creative and constructive acting; independent of whether they were developed from a combination of coincidence and empiricism, or from pure innovatively created. As such they are incorporeal goods. Only the protectability in terms of IP is problematic (vide supra).

To examine if and how far a legal protection for mechanisms exists, the first step consists in determining into which protection laws' scope economic mechanisms fall. Every protection law defines its own legal scope. Candidates in the present case are the protection of economic mechanisms as technical findings - therefore the extent of protection of (utility) patent law is affected[42]. Furthermore, the protection

---

[38] About third party rating systems cf. *Balboni*, Trustmarks in E-Commerce, Den Hague 2009, S. 26 ff.

[39] The term "auction" in this context means the economic definition of a pricing by bidding independent how the winner is identified contrary to the legal sense of the term "auction" where a knocking down in the end is mandatory, § 156 BGB and § 34b GewO (Gewerbeordnung - German Trade, Commerce an Industry Regulation Act) - cf. BGH (Bundesgerichtshof - German Federal Court of Justice) CR 2002, 213.

[40] *Berninghaus et al.*, p. 413 ff (cf. footnote no. 9 in the end).

[41] *Roth*, VWL für Einsteiger, Stuttgart 2006, p. 19.

[42] Cf. § 1 PatG; § 1 GebrMG.

can be seen as a work of language or as an illustration of a scientific or technical nature - therefore the protection of copyright is extended[43]. The application of both of the named scopes of protection is imaginable under certain conditions.

Technical Invention

If a protection is aspired in combination with an implementation in a technical (computer) system the scope of (utility) patent law is affected[44]. Conditions for that protection are newness, technical character ("Technizität"), involvement of an inventive step, and commercial usability. While most of the conditions do not cause any problems, proving the technical character of software-referred inventions often is a challenge. Even though in the last years a liberalization of the traditional perception, according to which software is only a behavior guideline and not a technical invention, can be observed, a separate checkup is still required concerning the technical character of the software-related invention. That checkup consists of two steps. First, the connection of the underlying algorithm of the program to a conventional technical area (physics, chemistry, biology, engineering science) is questioned. If the connection exists, the technical character will be assumed. If the algorithm has no technical character other characteristics are required that legitimate a patent protection considering objective target of German patent law[45]. Usually this is the case if the software is solving technical tasks[46].

As an example for the protection of allocation mechanisms by patent law and utility patent law the utility patent for a computer system of the UBS AG to carry out financial transactions[47] shall be named here. The system is protected as a whole including the functionality of the underlieing algorithm, but only in combination with the technical arrangement including the computer components. That means that the utility patent only is effective as long as the exact combination of allocation algorithm, software and hardware should be protected. In the named case a Computersystem zur Durchführung einer Finanztransaktion (computer system to carry out a financial transaction) is protected, that consists of an Indexdatenbank (index data base), a Postendatenbank (entry data base) and a Transaktionseinheit (transaction unit). Already a comparatively small change of the setting eliminates the possibility to enforce the patent rights, e.g. the using of a similar working but independently programmed software running on another computer system than the one described in the patent. The patent protection only is efficient against a one-to-one copy of the whole system. A similar protection problem exists for other trading systems like XETRA or Eurex[48].

---

[43] Cf. § 2 sec. 1 UrhG.

[44] Cf. Gebrauchsmusterschrift (utility patent specification) DE 200 20 859 U1 of the DPMA (Deutsches Patent- und Markenamt - German Patent and Trademark Office).

[45] *Ilzhöfer*, Rn. 108 (cf. footnote no. 26).

[46] BGH GRUR 2000, 498 - *Logikverifikation.*

[47] Gebrauchsmusterschrift DE 200 20 589 U1 of the DPMA.

[48] For the functionality of computer stock markets cf. Kümpel, Bank- und Kapitalmarktrecht, Köln 2004, ref. 17.538 ff.

Copyright Protection

Object of investigation of this article is the protectability of the mechanism itself. On its own the economic mechanism is no technical invention. A patent or utility patent protection only is applicable if the economic mechanism - in the shape of software - was implemented in a technical system. That causes, as aforementioned, a very limited protection just only in combination with the technical system, the mechanism was implemented in. A protection of the mechanism itself can be granted by the copyright as long as the mechanism is qualified as work of language or illustration of scientific nature (vide supra).

Thus, the evaluation scheme for copyright[49] is applicable.

First of all, those objects have to be excluded that are not protectable by copyright[50], even though they fall in the scope of copyrights: copyrights are not applicable for mere ideas, themes, or motives for lack of manifestation. Also there is no protection for free research findings (in detail vide infra). For the generally not protectable content a protection of the specific embodiment has to be considered[51]. Methods, styles, (fashion) trends in the spirit of a time are also not protectable. While trends and styles are not protected, the works, that follow or change these trends, are[52]. If the arrangement of a work is predetermined, or simply a technical must, it is also not protected[53]. The arrangement and choice of already known design elements is also not protectable - even though the "Kleine Münze"[54] is fulfilled in this case if the compilation is notably well-arranged[55].

Irrelevant for the identification of existing copyright protection are criteria like expense, costs, or extent of a work[56].

After excluding the non-protectable elements, one has to determine if and how the representational work differs from other works of the same kind. That rating should respect the work as a whole but also the single elements of the work[57].

By judging the example of mechanisms of electronic markets one has to pay much attention to the aspect of differences to former existing markets. It is easily possible that the newness of a platform is only represented by other market elements than the economic mechanism, which may be the same as in some pre-existing platforms. Even pretended new inventions, which are discussed in some disciplines like the

---

[49] *Schulze* in: Dreier/Schulze, UrhG, 3rd edition München 2008, § 2 ref. 36.

[50] *Schulze*, § 2 ref. 36 (cf. footnote 49).

[51] *Schulze*, § 2 ref. 42 (cf. footnote 49).

[52] *Schulze*, § 2 ref. 45 (cf. footnote 49).

[53] *Schulze*, § 2 ref. 47 (cf. footnote 49).

[54] *Kleine Münze* is the lowermost limit of the creative expression that is needed for protectability of a work.

[55] Cf. OLG (Oberlandesgericht - Higher Regional Court) Nürnberg GRUR-RR 1980, 227, 230 - *Dienstanweisung*; LG Köln GRUR 2001, 152 - *multiple-choice-Klausuren*.

[56] *Schulze*, § 2 ref. 53 ff (cf. footnote 49).

[57] Cf. *Schulze* GRUR 1984, 400, 402 ff.

legal estimation of internet auctions some years ago[58], are no creative improvements from an economic point of view.

Nevertheless, especially in the field of strategic games new economic mechanisms are invented, based on knowledge from models, experiments, and empirical research.

After the differentness and newness of the work is ascertained, it has to be determined which kind of work named in the Copy Right Act is appropriate for the specific work in question. However, the Copy Right Act enumeration is non-exhaustive[59].

The assignment of the work to a certain kind of work is meaningful if the kind of work requires special rules for application. Different kinds of works that have to be considered are named in § 2 sec. 2 no. 1-7 UrhG. The named kinds of works have in common that they require the existence of a personal mental creation for protection[60]. In the case of designed markets, the classification as work of language or as illustration of scientific nature comes in to consideration.

Work of Language

The protection of works of language implies the protection of the self-created illustration in the first place. The self-created relevance is easier to achieve for the author of an imaginary work like a poem or a novel than for example for the originator of a scientific work which is limited in phrasing and structure by the scientific context[61]. Anyhow the protection of a work of language also involves the protection of the content[62]. But in the first place, the protection concerns the specific linguistic arrangement.

For the illustration of an economic mechanism, linguistic methods and descriptive methods of mathematics are used. In principle, both illustration methods have the protectability as a work of language in common. This protectability does not depend on the kind of language that is used in the description. However, the strictly formal mathematical description of a scientific finding does not allow for creative arrangements. Therefore, a copyright protection for mathematical descriptions will hardly be achievable[63].

Even if one uses the possibilities of mere descriptive linguistic methods to illustrate scientific findings, the scope of creativity is more limited because of the obligatory use of technical terminology than it would be the case writing a prose

---

[58] Cf. BGH CR 2005, 53 - eBay auctions are no auctions with respect to the legal definition.

[59] *Schulze*, § 2 ref. 78 (cf. footnote 49).

[60] Cf. therefore *Loewenheim* in: Schricker, Urheberrecht, 3rd edition 2006, § 2 ref. 4 f.; *v. Moltke*, Das Urheberrecht an den Werken der Wissenschaft, 1992.

[61] *Schulze*, § 2 ref. 83 ff (cf. footnote 49).

[62] Fabelschutz ("protection of the tale" = protection of the story/content) cf. *Oechsler* GRUR 2009, 1101, 1104.

[63] *Schulze*, § 2 ref. 93 (cf. footnote 49).

text. So it is nearly impossible to achieve a copyright protection for scientifically characterized works of language[64].

Illustration of Scientific or Technical Nature

The protection of illustrations of scientific or technical nature covers only form and arrangement[65]. Scientific cognition, doctrines, and theories are not protected with regard to the content[66]. The reason therefore is that they are not created by scientists or researchers. They are not result of a creative act but they already existed, and have only to be revealed or "simply" be found[67]. Scientific findings belong to cultural public property which every creator builds on and which shall be common knowledge[68]. Scientific doctrines shall be free and public domain[69]. This strong opinion is based on the ideal of freedom of science and free access to scientific findings, even if in practice the existence of that ideal is more and more doubted[70].

The argumentation that scientific findings are not based on creative but empirical action seems to apply to natural sciences at first sight. But already when looking at applied sciences, one becomes aware that scientific knowledge is also used for problem solving as a creative act. An example is the usage of scientific findings taken from game theoretical research to create an allocation mechanism[71]. The mechanism design is a creative act that falls under the scope of protection of illustrations of scientific nature.

Even in the stage of acquiring scientific knowledge - in the above-mentioned example during the gaining of insights about the behavior of players in specific situations - models and experiments are used that emulate reality, but simplified through certain hypotheses[72]. The setting of such models or such experiments is a creative act on its own. That creativity to configure the experimental parameters affects the results and is reason for some misinterpretation[73]. It remains arguable, whether the described creativity in setting and configuration of the measurement method really leads directly to a creative result. The opinion that creatively chosen measurement methods do not lead to a creative result but still to an empiric finding - independent of its defectiveness, reduction or shorting caused by the chosen method - is justifiable.

---

[64] Analyzing the legal situation identical, but critical: *Haberstumpf* ZUM 2001, 819, 821.
[65] BGHZ 39, 306, 311 - *Rechenschieber*; BGH GRUR 1981, 352, 353 - *Examensarbeit*.
[66] *Schulze*, § 2 ref. 41, 93 ff (cf. footnote 49).
[67] *Schulze*, § 2 ref. 41 with further cit. (cf. footnote 49).
[68] BG GRUR 1981, 352, 353 - *Examensarbeit*.
[69] BGHZ 39, 306, 311 - *Rechenschieber*.
[70] *Hilty* GRUR 2009, 633-644, 635.
[71] *Berninghaus et. al.*, (cf. footnote no. 9 in the end). p. 86 ff.
[72] *Brodbeck* in: Baudson/Dresler, Kreativität und Innovation, Stuttgart 2008, p. 16.
[73] *Berninghaus* et. al., (cf. footnote no. 9 in the end). p. 86 ff; p. 414; with the extensive result to deny economics their scientific status: *Brodbeck* (cf. footnote 72), p. 16.

The reason for the very common point of view, science is no matter of creativity, perhaps arises from the effort of especially empiric scientific disciplines to delete all hints of creativity in their methods before publishing[74].

Considering the above discussion and all the presented arguments, the prevailing view is that only the representation of the findings, and not for the content itself, is protectable[75]. The precise illustration can be protected, if it is adequately individual, e.g. if it is extremely understandable or if it is explained in a different, not pre-given way[76]. Problematic here is the borderline between not yet protected content and the protected precise illustration. This problematic borderline is very obvious in cases where courts use content criteria to affirm individuality of the illustration[77].

In these cases, the borderline between content and illustration is crossed. Main argument of critics of this judicature is a very formal one. They point to Art. 9 sec. 2 TRIPS[78]:

"Copyright protection shall extend to expressions and not to ideas, proce-dures, methods of operation or mathematical concepts as such."

The applicability of that rule in national German right is controversial[79] and in all probability has to be seen as a declaration of political intent[80]. At least that argument cannot set strong priorities against the habit of high courts in Germany to verify the individual illustration using the content. But nevertheless, the usage of the content to test the criteria of individuality does not create protection for the content. To recapitulate copyright protection of a pricing or allocation mechanism is possible as illustration of technical nature. This protection indeed only covers the form of the illustration, not the mechanism itself. Currently, mechanisms are seen as mere ideas that are not protectable in themselves.

Board Games as Example for Protection of mere Ideas

The refusal of the protection of scientific findings and in particular of ideas has to be questioned dogmatically. The protection situation of electronic markets and their mechanisms is comparable to the (not approved) protection of board games that is

---

[74] *Joerges* Zeitschrift für allgemeine Wissenschaftstheorie 1977, p. 383.

[75] *Schulze*, § 2 ref. 43 (cf. footnote 49).

[76] BGH GRUR 1986, 739, 741 - *Anwaltsschriftsatz*; LG München I GRUR 1991, 50, 51 - *Geschäftsbedingungen*.

[77] Cf. overview of such cases in: *Oechsler* (cf. footnote no. 62), p. 1103.

[78] TRIPS - Agreement on Trade-Related Aspects of Intellectual Property Rights.

[79] Again a systematic argument argues against the direct application. In Art. 9 sec. 1 S. 1 TRIPS the Art. 1 - 21 of the RBÜ (Revidiertes Berner Übereinkommen - "revised accommodation of Bern") are declared applicable. That means that for member states of TRIPS that were members of the RBÜ before Art. 9 sec. 2 TRIPS cannot limit the binding effect of the RBÜ. That is the case for the Federal Republic of Germany.

[80] Cf. *Oechsler* (cf. footnote no. 62), p. 1103 with further cit.

subject of the current legal discussion[81]. The discussion already started with the introduction of the German copy right, but currently revived[82].

The analogy arises from the similar construction of board games and electronic market places. While in the case of electronic markets the economic market design and especially the mechanism find their representation in the form of the programmed market place software and the terms and conditions, the game idea underlying a board game is represented in the game articles (boards, figures, cards, etc.) and the rules of the game. In analogy to the protection situation for electronic markets and games shown above, the protection is not applicable to the rules and ideas of board games with regard to the content, but only to the illustration of the rules if they are individual enough[83]. This opinion is based on the opinion that board games are neither works of language, nor literature, nor illustrations of scientific or technical nature regarding to the German UrhG[84]. These grounds are unpersuadable, because of the non-terminal character of the legal enumeration of kinds of works in § 2 sec. 2 UrhG. Other discussants justify their point of view with the argument that game rules are only information and ideas that could not be protected[85].

The differentiation between precise (and possibly protectable) illustration of a board game and the idea behind it is one, that is also applicable to electronic markets. In the field of board games, opinions arise that doubt the general refusal of the protection of mere ideas - at least if these ideas were manifested[86]. After the manifestation within a certain work an idea has to be protected formally and with regard to the content as essential component of the protected work. The coverage of that protection depends on the affected work. However, the discussions about the technical and scientific relevant arrangement have to distinguish between economic mechanisms and board game ideas. But one can find arguments making worth considering a more detailed examination of the flat negation of a copyright protection for ideas.

5 Conclusion

The constraint of the protection of economic mechanisms only indirectly using the illustrating form of its scientific or lingual representation or respectively in combination with a technical implementation as (utility) patent is dissatisfying.

---

[81] Substitutional for the current discussion: *Oechsler* (cf. footnote no. 62), 1101; *Risthaus* WRP 2009, 698; *Schricker* GRUR Int. 2008, 200.

[82] Starting with a judgement of the BGH GRUR 1962, 51 and renewed because of LG Mannheim NJOZ 2008, 3351.

[83] *Ulmer*, Urheber- und Verlagsrecht, 3rd edition Berlin 1980, p. 132; *Schulze* (cf. footnote no. 49), § 2 Rn. 104.

[84] *Ulmer* (cf. footnote No. 83), p. 132.

[85] *Schack*, Urheber- und Urhebervertragsrecht, 4th edition Tübingen 2007, p. 168.

[86] Schricker (cf. footnote no. 81), 203 with further cit.

This is especially true with respect to creativity, invention, and investment that are inherent in economic mechanisms.

It has to be kept in mind that economic mechanisms are, despite the afore-mentioned efforts during their creation, only one element of technical systems respectively of electronic markets. The mechanism itself is "just" a scientific finding or an idea, which cannot be protected by itself according to the presently prevailing view.

If a protection of the mechanism is aspired at present, one has to use the indirectly operating protection rights.

References

Ahrens (2008): *Gewerblicher Rechtsschutz.*

Axter and Schütze (2009): *Kartellrecht*, 2 edition.

Balboni (2009): *Trustmarks in E-Commerce.*

Bassenge (2009): *Kommentar zum BGB*, 68 edition.

Berninghaus/Erhart/Güth (2005): *Strategische Spiele*, 2 edition.

Brodbeck (2008): *Kreativität und Innovation*, Baudson/Dresler.

Creifelds (2007): *Rechtswörterbuch*, 19 edition.

Dreier (2008): *Urheberrechtsgesetz*, 3 edition.

Götting (2006): "Der Begriff des Geistigen Eigentums," *Gewerblicher Rechtsschutz und Urheberrecht (GRUR)*, p. 353.

Götting (2007): *Gewerblicher Rechtsschutz*, 9 edition.

Haberstumpf (2001): "Wem gehören Forschungsergebnisse," *Zeitschrift für Urheber- und Medienrecht (ZUM)*, p. 819.

Hilty (2009): "Renaissance der Zwangslizenzen im Urheberrecht? Gedanken zu Ungereimtheiten auf der urheberrechtlichen Wertschöpfungskette," *Gewerblicher Rechtsschutz und Urheberrecht (GRUR)*, p. 633.

Ilzhöfer (2007): *Patent-, Marken- und Urheberrecht.*

Jauernig (2009): *BGB*, 13 edition.

Joerges (1977): "Wissenschaftliche Kreativität - Empirische und wissenschaftsprak-tische Hinweise," *Zeitschrift für allgemeine Wissenstheorie*, p. 383.

Karl (2009): *Der urheberrechtliche Schutzbereich von Computerprogrammen*, Ph.D. thesis.

Kümpel (2004): *Bank- und Kapitalmarktrecht.*

Kollmann (2008): *E-Business: Grundlagen elektronischer Geschäftsprozesse in der Net Economy.*

Kraßer (2009): *Patentrecht.*

Loewenheim (2006): *Urheberrecht*, 3 edition.

McAfee and McMillan (1987): "Auctions and Bidding," *Journal of Economic Literature*, 25(2), p. 699.

Oechsler (2009): "Die Idee als persönliche geistige Schöpfung - Von Fichtes Lehre vom Gedankeneigentum zum Schutz von Spielideen," *Gewerblicher Rechtsschutz und Urheberrecht (GRUR)*, p. 1101.

Ohly (2003): "Geistiges Eigentum?" *Juristen Zeitung (JZ)*, p. 545.

Ohly (2005): "Gibt es einen Numerus clausus der Immaterialgüterrechte?" in: *Perspektiven des geistigen Eigentums und Wettbewerbsrecht. Festschrift für Gerhard Schricker zum 70. Geburtstag*, Ohly/Bodewig/Dreier/Götting/Haedicke/Lehmann.

Putzo (2009): *Kommentar zum BGB*, 68 edition.

Rebel (2007): *Gewerbliche Schutzrechte*, 5 edition.

Risthaus (2003): "Spiele und Spielregeln im Urheberrecht – Rien ne va plus?" *Wettbewerb in Recht und Praxis (WRP)*, p. 698.

Roth (2006): *VWL für Einsteiger*.

Sambuc (2009): *UWG*, 2 edition.

Schack (3007): *Urheber- und Urhebervertragsrecht*, 4 edition.

Schmid (1993): "Elektronische Märkte," *Wirtschaftsinformatik*, 5(35), p. 465.

Schoder (2010): *Enzyklopädie der Wirtschaftsinformatik-Online-Lexikon*, chapter Elektronischer Marktplatz, Kurbel and Becker and Gronau and Sinz andSuhl, http://www.enzyklopaedie-der-wirtschaftsinformatik.de.

Schulze (2008): *Urheberrechtsgesetz*.

Ulmer (1980): *Urheber- und Verlagsrecht*, 3 edition.

v. Moltke (2006): *Das Urheberrecht an Werken der Wissenschaft*.

Westermann (2008): *Münchener Kommentar zum BGB*, 5 edition.

Municipal Information – Amounts of Data but no Structure? An outline over Legal Aspects of Informational Technologies Within Public Entities

Simone Traub and Indra Spiecker gen. Döhmann

Institute of Information and Economic Law, KIT {simone.traub, spiecker}@kit.edu

1 Introduction

The half-life period of knowledge becomes shorter and shorter. This does not only affect private companies but also the state and its entities. Particularly municipalities with their immediate relations to citizens are continuously facing public tasks connected with lots of information and the need for accurate and quickly accessible knowledge such as economical or environmental data (e.g. concentration of air pollutants) or similar parameters. The necessity of faster and more flexible reactions on the part of the state demands an intelligent generation, collection and management of information. Such information management consists of operative and strategic action on a higher hierarchical level, oriented at the aims of the organization and focused on the planning and controlling of information and information processes within the organization extending to its external communication.[1] Information management provides for the allocation of information infrastructure serving the capture, generation, consolidation, saving and transfer of information. It aims at utilizing knowledge that diffusely exists but has not been established yet in a useful way. Hereby, the decision making of both central and peripheral entities shall be supported.[2]

What does that mean for the information management of municipalities and their supervisory authority? The supervisory agency represents a focal point of information as it controls the municipalities. Therefore it needs information. At the same time, the supervisory agency controls many different municipalities, so it also handles superior knowledge in comparison to the single municipality. Experience teaches that there is an information asymmetry between the single municipality and the supervisory authority. The supervisory authority has available more personnel

---

[1] Compare Sigrid Schaefer, Controlling und Informationsmanagement in Strategischen Unternehmensnetzwerken: Multiperspektivische Modellierung und interorganisationale Vernetzung von Informationsprozessen, Wiesbaden 2009, p. 94; compare Vladislav Rajkovic/Blaz Zupan, Knowledge Management as a Challenge for Public Administration Reengineering, in: Joze Florjancic/Karl Pütz (Eds.), Informatics and Management, Frankfurt/Main 2004, p. 129 (129).

[2] Compare Schaefer, see above note 1, p. 94; compare Rajkovic/Zupan, see above note 1, p. 129.

know-how than the single municipality and in addition it can resort to the above-mentioned experience of other municipalities by its control activity. To reduce this problem, the supervisory authority can provide information by means of databases. From the normative/legal point of view it is questionable whether there are rights of the municipalities or third parties that are opposed to the distribution of municipal data by a database. One of these rights might be Art. 28 sect. 2 German Basic Law (Grundgesetz). In other words: Is the supervisory authority subject of obligations of secrecy, which debar it from providing such data within a database?

The following contribution examines the conditions and limitations of the distribution of municipal data by the supervisory authority. As such a distribution of data is often called for, it is important to demonstrate which rights and obligations have to be considered. The legislature has so far exercised restraint in this field and the upcoming debate is expected to expose interesting developments. Therefore this contribution wants to raise some general questions in order to fuel the discourse without attempting to give conclusive answers.

2 Visiting the field of information - the duties of municipalities

To examine the above-mentioned questions appropriately it is necessary to know which kind of information is generated, collected and distributed by the municipalities that is of interest for a database. In other words, the territory of municipal activity has to be set out. What is the municipalities´ character and how can their position within the state organization be described?

2.1 The competence of municipalities

Municipalities perform two different tasks within the state organization. On the one hand they take care of all activities rooted within the municipal community. Municipal administration concerns people in a very immediate way. Everybody of us is living in a municipality and takes advantage of it. The tasks of a municipality are not limited, not strictly listed.[3] On the contrary, everything which concerns the municipality is the duty of the municipality (so-called principle of universality[4]).[5] If problems arise, they are firstly perceived on the administrative grassroot level, and they call for a solution which must first and foremost be provided by the municipality. According to the principle of subsidiarity only in case of the municipalities´ overload with a specific task or if superior aspects and interests call for a more extensive or more standardized solution, then the Länder or the Federal Government are competent for the administration within the municipalities.[6] These

---

[3] Compare the German Constitutional Court Decision, BVerfGE 79, 127 (127).

[4] E. g. § 1 sect. 3 BauGB: "The municipalities are obliged to construct the local building plans..."

[5] Compare the German Constitutional Court (Bundesverfassungsgericht) in its ground-breaking decision of 1958, BVerfGE 8, 122 (134).

[6] German Constitutional Court Decision, BVerfGE 79, 127 (127).

duties, as described in the following, and connected to the local community, are called both "autonomous tasks" or "tasks within the jurisdiction of an autonomous municipal administration".[7]

On the other hand they also perform administrative tasks that fall into the area of responsibility of a higher level, that means the Länder or the Federal Government. They are doing this by executing the corresponding laws of the Länder and the Federal State. These duties are transferred to the municipalities for reasons of expedience. Therefore they have to be controlled by a higher authority to establish equivalent living conditions throughout the federal territory and to maintain legal or economic unity in the national interest.[8] The municipalities fulfill these duties because they work and act close to the citizens and therefore close to the problem. Moreover they can react more flexible to local specifics than a federal government can. This is why the Länder or the Federal Government transfer a designated part of their duties to the municipalities. In other words, the Länder make use of the advantages of a locally situated, close to the problem working apparatus while at the same time retaining the control and possibility of intervention.

After all, one can differentiate between two fields of municipal duties: There are the autonomous tasks and the transferred duties.[9] The distinction between these two types of duties is not always easy. This distinction is, however, important for the question to what extent the municipality can act autonomously while performing its tasks, and to what extent the state authorities have the competence to instruct and direct. For the data questions of interest here, this means: Who "owns" the data – is the municipality owner of its data or is it the supervisory authority and what rights can be claimed by the municipality?

2.2 The role of the municipalities within the state framework

a Municipalities - integral part of the state but yet independent entities

After having described the tasks of municipalities, their position within the state framework has to be considered to elaborate possible municipal rights that are opposed to the distribution of data by the supervisory authority.

To properly sort the municipalities and the municipal self-administration into the state framework, one has to consider two aspects often opposed to each other. From the viewpoint of polity, municipalities have to be classed with the Federal States. That means that the municipalities are not a "third level" besides the Federal State and the Länder with own sovereignty. This structure can be derived – inter alia – from the fact that according to Art. 106 sect. 9 German Basic Law (the German Constitution, Grundgesetz), revenues and expenditures shall be deemed to be revenues and expenditures of the federal states.[10] For this reason municipal tasks

---

[7] Diana Zacharias, Nordrhein-Westfälisches Kommunalrecht, Thüngersheim/Frankfurt a. M. 2004, p. 58f.

[8] Compare the rule of Art. 72 sect. 2 German Basic Law.

[9] Zacharias, see above note 7, p. 57.

[10] Zacharias, see above note 7, p. 25.

are essentially defined by the field of duties of the Federal States. The municipalities are part of the state administration and thereby executing state sovereignty.

On the other hand, the municipal entity is built on democratic elements – compare § 1 of the Local Government Law of Baden-Wuerttemberg (Gemeindeordnung Baden-Württemberg) – and is a paragon of civil self-administration. Also historically, the tasks of government were first and foremost lodged with the local community. It is not surprising, that Art. 28 sect. 2 German Basic Law and § 2 of the Local Government Law of Baden-Wuerttemberg guarantee to municipalities the right to regulate all local affairs on their own responsibility, within the limits prescribed by the laws.

b Municipal Supervision

To ensure the lawfulness of municipal acts – both in the field of self administration as well as if they act as a part of the state administration municipalities must be supervised by state authorities. Municipal supervision is the downside of the municipal autonomy[11]: The considerable independence of local authorities is counter-balanced by a strict control of the legality (and more) of their actions. Municipalities shall not become autonomous entities in the sense that they may act free of legal bounds, and therefore, they need control.

According to a more modern understanding however, the supervisory authority is a partner of the municipality and has the duty to support the municipality by practicing its self-administration (e.g. § 118 III Local Government Law of Baden-Wuerttemberg, § 11 Local Government Law of North Rhine-Westphalia, Art. 108 Local Government Law of Bavaria). The structural inability of municipalities to adopt a highly professional organization providing highly professional services calls for support by an institution that is able to provide exactly that.

In order to achieve the goal of legal and efficient dealings on the municipal level, municipal supervision is granted a wide array of potential means to assist and control the municipalities.

Among these different means, the informational means are of high relevance. In most cases they are of a preventive nature. Preventive in this context means, that the supervising authority becomes involved before the legally binding act of an autonomous body[12]. Typical is the instrument of "prevent consulting" by the supervising authority. Preventive Consulting is supposed to guarantee (or at least to allow) lawful administration from the very beginning and prevent later possibly more invasive action of the authority.[13] Consulting also allows for considerable discretion rather than the invasive, publicised measures. Consulting is therefore generally in the interest of both involved actors. The supervising authorities have

---

[11] German Constitutional Court Decision, BVerfGE 6, 104 (118).

[12] Compare Christoph Gröpl/Arnold W. Sonntag, Zeitschrift für Landes- und Kommunalrecht Hessen - Rheinland-Pfalz - Saarland (LKRZ) 2009, 326(326).

[13] Winfried Kluth, in Hans J. Wolff/Otto Bachof/Rolf Stober, Verwaltungsrecht Band 3, 5th Ed., § 94, n. 137.

the advantage that they are able to concentrate and to coordinate special knowledge that could not be provided by the individual municipalities.[14] Legally, the necessity of this method is construed as follows: By providing information to the municipalities, the right of self-administration according to Art. 28 sect. 2 German Basic Law (Grundgesetz) is preserved because the municipalities are not forced to accept the opinion of the supervisory authority, but rather have their discretion in decision-making preserved.

Complementary to the consultative rights of the single corporation, the supervising authorities have information rights: Only they allow for the supervisor to know the relevant facts and to decide whether consultation (or more) is necessary. Therefore, the supervisory authority is entitled to get information concerning specific matters of the municipality. Examples of the exercise of these rights are: written questions, access to files or other enquiries addressed towards the municipalities. The authority can also conduct on-site inspections of the municipal administration or convene the municipal council or the mayor.[15]

In summary: The relationship between the supervisory authority and municipality is characterized by consultancy and inspection.

The emphasis of this contribution shall be on possibilities of the supervisory authorities to provide information – that would not be available otherwise – to their subordinate, supervised municipalities. Some of the technical possibilities will be demonstrated first before the technical and particularly the legal limitations will be examined.

3 Collection and distribution of information - devices and process

The 16 different local government laws of the Länder (Gemeindeordnungen) constitute, that the supervisory authorities provide advice to the municipalities concerning their tasks to support their constitutionally guaranteed self-administration. This rule affects not only the functional supervision but also the legal supervision. The advice can concern legal, personnel, economic or technical matters. In many cases the authority provides specific information to help the municipalities in their decision making process. An example for this can be the management of private public partnerships. Therefore, the supervisory authority is challenged to gain and to distribute information effectively. Appropriate information in good time can prevent many inconveniences and invasive procedures to correct serious mistakes by the municipal administration.

Within the field of the innumerous municipal competence areas, a number of cases arise that require special expert knowledge. For example, when the municipality takes on new tasks or if it plans to introduce new operating procedures like the integration of specific permission proceedings to one central procedure. Attending to

---

[14] Kluth, see above note 13, § 94, n. 137.
[15] Kluth, see above note 13, § 94, n. 142.

such innovations, a municipality can conclude private consulting contracts. But the law provides for the opportunity to gain knowledge within the state system: It can address the supervisory authority and ask for their experiences, their knowledge, their qualification.

In case the supervisory authority processes information and provides consultancy, it has to find instruments to do this effectively. These instruments differ according to the type of knowledge processed.[16] As far as so-called "tacit knowledge"[17] is concerned, a continuous dialogue between the supervisory and the supervised authority is irreplaceable. Tacit knowledge is knowledge that is difficult to make explicit by means of writing it down or verbalizing it and to transfer it to another person.[18] Things are different if they concern explicit knowledge. This is the type of knowledge that has been or can be articulated, codified, and stored in certain media.[19] As far as this kind of knowledge is concerned – in other words the actual facts –, the straight implementation of offered technical solutions to simplify the procedure is conceivable. To some degree, the municipal authority can act like the top level management of a private company and introduce new procedures in a strictly hierarchical manner. But in other respects it is to a certain extent restricted because it is bound to the rules of public law, for example by the principle of proportionality, which runs like a golden thread through the public law.
This contribution especially seeks to analyze local databases as a means of providing information by the supervisory authority.

3.1 Technical aspects

For the sake of illustration, it shall be assumed that a supervisory authority es-tablishes a database containing information on all the private public partnership projects of its supervised municipalities. Access to that database is available only to the municipal administrations supervised by that specific authority. The database covers details about the legal design, the financial scale, the public task of that project etc. The technical frame of this device can be described as follows:
Access to information is marked by online access – for the sake of currentness –, thus independent of distance, time and hierarchy for all the concerned participants. The outreach of a single actor is significantly enlarged. The municipality can re-trieve information about and interact with partners within and beyond the borders of its territory by using electronic information and transaction possibilities. This

---

[16] Compare Indra Spiecker gen. Döhmann, Informationsgewinnung im dezentralen Mehrebenensys-tem, in: Jan-Bern Oebbecke (Ed.), Nicht-Normative Steuerung in dezentralen Systemen, Stuttgart 2005, p. 253, (259f).

[17] Jennifer E. Rowley/Richard Hartley, Organizing Knowledge: An Introduction to managing access to information, 4th. ed., Hampshire (GB), Burlington (USA) 2008, p. 7.

[18] Compare Rowley/Hartley, see above note 17, p. 7.

[19] Compare only Rowley/Hartley, see above note 17, p. 7; fundamentally to the differentiation between tacit and explicit knowledge: Ikujiro Nonaka/Hirotaka Takeuchi, The knowledge creating company – how Japanese companies create the dynamics of innovation, New York et al. 1995.

potential of interactivity was essentially facilitated by the introduction and common acceptance of the Internet protocol IP (Internet Protocol) standard. Electronic communication between persons, data, processes and objects is managed by shaping contents into IP-standardized data packages and exchanging them between senders and receivers. Therefore, a major part of vendor-dependant incompatibilities of various technical devices designed to manage information is eliminated. The described conditions are the ground which makes IT-data bases possible.

There exist one not to be underestimated consequence for the digitalization of interaction between municipalities and their supervising authorities: Crucial elements of information management in a supervisory process now can be implemented into complete solutions provided by the supervisory authority including all the necessary data, linkages, interfaces, processes and objects[20]. A system can work by searching the internet sites of the municipalities every day. The single municipality can chose the deepness of the search and can define the prioritization system of the search results. The responsible civil servant is enabled to have a direct access to the requested site and does not depend on the complicate system of postal requests for information or research projects. In addition data bases of private parties that are already existing and made public could be used.

3.2 Normative aspects

After having described the potential technical background of such an information system, this contribution now turns to the legal questions that are linked to such a device.

a Requirement to establish data base information system?

The first question arising is that whether there exists a legal obligation for the introduction of such databases.

aa Efficiency and effectiveness requirements

It could be obligatory for the reason of economy. The principle of cost-effectiveness and thrift according to § 7 Federal Budget Code (Bundeshaushaltsordnung) is a general principle for all public entities and thus also applies to municipalities and their supervisory agencies. This rule is a consequence of the principle of proportionality as state-spent money originates from taxpayers who must not be unnecessarily charged. The principle of cost-effectiveness and thrift contains two aspects: First the aspect of applying small means aiming at a certain desired result (principle of minimality) and secondly, the aspect of getting the best result possible by applying a certain amount of means (principle of productiveness). What are the consequences

---

[20] Heinrich Reinermann, Elektronisierung des staatlichen und kommunalen Leistungsverkehrs, in: Wolfgang Büchner/Alfred Büllesbach (Eds.), E-Government - Staatliches Handeln in der Informationsgesellschaft, Köln 2003, p. 143 (145).

of these principles for the application of databases? The establishment of a database as described could take the place of an individual, time-consuming one-on-one consultation. Rather than having to consult with each municipality interested in a Public Private Partnership, the authority could first refer the interested party to this database for primary information. The authority could then restrict itself to particular information that is not generally available or tacit knowledge. This is particularly time-saving for the authority, as it can concentrate on the difficult questions of consulting that need human, especially legal knowledge.

If the necessary budget of a public procurement project such as a Public Private Partnership reaches or exceeds specific values, it has to be licensed by the supervisory authority. Therefore there are mandatory consultations between the municipality and its supervising authority in advance. Without an electronic database, the responsible civil servant of the supervisory authority would have to look for reference data of other municipalities and their experiences with such projects in regard to costs and the different legal arrangements. In time-consuming elaborate correspondence the responsible civil servant would have to explain the different legal models of Public Private Partnership and the associated advantages and disadvantages.

bb Expedience

In addition to the above mentioned cost-effectiveness, there is expedience, which as a principle also binds public activity. Expedience means, that administration has to omit all unnecessary means that are not appropriate to the affected interests.[21] The increase of information that has to be elaborated within the municipalities demands the ability to access data from databases. It is not necessarily the supervisory authority who provides the data but the principle of expedience suggests this kind of solution because it is the supervisory authority that has the human resources and material to manage such a project.

cc Summary

There are some legal reasons that suggest the obligation of electronic online data bases but these arguments have to be balanced against counter-arguments like the costs connected with such a device, for example the maintenance charges.

b Restrictions on establishment of data based information system

At a first glance, providing data by using databases seems to serve important legal interests and appears to have significant advantages – which could not be drafted here in full extent. However, there are some implicit restrictions for the legal validity and factual success of this procedure.

---

[21] Ferdinand Kopp/Ulrich Ramsauer, Verwaltungsverfahrensgesetz, Kommentar, 10th Ed., München 2008, § 10, n. 16.

aa Acceptance, legitimization and technical restrictions

On the factual side, an important issue is the necessity of confidence in new media which needs to be built on both sides: on the part of the municipalities as well as on the part of the supervisory authorities.[22] The supervisory authority must create the interfaces to enable it to accept reports in digital format. The municipality on its part has to trust provision of consultation and to regard it as equal to a personal contact.

While picturing the single municipalities to build up and work with the databases, another condition comes into play. It is the uniformity of technical systems and applications. Within a company, this might be easily realized but looking at the number of municipalities things appear quite different. Without a preparing process the supervisory authority will not be able to collect data by using just one system for every municipality because of the diversity of different existing systems and their incompatibility. The autonomy of the municipalities resulted and results in technical infrastructures built up independently of each other. The only link – in other words the common denominator – are some rules provided by data protection and privacy law.

In order to gain the ability of using information effectively, a stronger intercommunication in this field is necessary. In addition, standards have to be developed and accepted to reach an overall satisfying performance.[23] Relevant questions in this context are those of security, storage and especially access security.

bb Standard setting and Art. 28 sect. 2 German Basic Law

The legal problem with the requirement of identical or similar standards touches on Art. 28 sect. 2 German Basic Law (Grundgesetz) and its guarantee of self administration. This right can be described as the general clause for municipal independence and freedom of action concerning their area of competence. In this field, state authorities are not allowed to control and to regulate municipalities without a normative grounding. Therefore municipalities cannot be obliged to use one certain IT-standard (e.g. set by the district government) if only their genuine tasks (Selbstverwaltungsaufgaben) are affected, because the supervision is restricted to a legal supervision in this field. Binding standards concerning the concrete conduction are unlawful. Even if only tasks are concerned where the municipalities perform for the Länder or the Federal Government, the obligation of a certain standard is problematic. In early decisions, courts ruling on the question of identical procedural standards required by the supervisory agencies, partly held, that in the field of these transferred tasks the supervisory authority has an unlimited right of instruction[24]. But today, most lawyers claim the limitation of the right

---

[22] Dirk Hoffmann, Kommunen im E-Government - Einblicke in die aktuelle Situation, in: Wolfgang Büchner/Alfred Büllesbach (Eds.), E-Government - Staatliches Handeln in der Informationsgesellschaft, Köln 2003, p. 157 (161).

[23] Hoffmann, see above note 22, p. 161.

[24] See Bavarian Administrative Court, Bayerische Verwaltungsblätter (BayVBl.) 1977, 152 (153); Ernst Forsthoff Lehrbuch des Verwaltungsrechts, Vol. 1, 10th Ed. München 1973, p. 479.

of instruction to the subject-matter-field. In personnel and organizational aspects, the municipalities must retain their power to decide.[25] But bearing in mind that databases provide a certain level of administration quality, the determination of a uniform IT-format concerns subject matter and expedience. It is therefore a question of functional supervision in which the supervisory authority is competent to define a certain standard.

cc "Cost-benefit-analysis"

Another legal restriction – due to § 7 Federal Budget Code (Bundeshaushaltsordnung) – arises in the conduct of a cost-value-weighting before building up a database. The relevant factors within such an analysis are not only monetary figures. Saving on money, personal cost and organizational structures is in general regarded as a valid benefit but also factors such as time, acceleration and transparency have to be taken into account. On the other hand saving time does not necessarily mean cost reduction, for example if a database is only used a very limited number of times each year. Another issue is the elimination of errors to guarantee lawfulness of public acts. Here, a lot of questions still remain to be resolved.

4 Opposing Rights

After having examined the provision of information by IT-databases and arguments against such a line of action, this paper will analyze relevant legal arguments pertaining to the single municipalities. Although the supervisory authority can be described as a partner of the municipality, municipalities often hesitate to pass on information about their concerns to the supervisory authority. What are the reasons for such a thinking? Legal arguments can be procedural rules which bind the supervisory authority or subjective rights of the municipality. For this purpose it should be distinguished between the generation of information and the provision of information to other municipalities.

4.1 Generation of information

One of the first questions of the supervisory authorities, that want to introduce a data base must be the method of generating information. Although the 16 Länder have some differences in their local government laws, the relation between the supervisory authorities and the single municipalities is construed quite similar. According to most of the local government laws (e.g. § 120 Local Government Law Baden-Wuerttemberg, § 129 Abs. 1 Local Self-Administration-Code of the Saarland, Art. 111 Bavarian Local Government Law), the supervisory authority is allowed to request information about any municipal matter if it is necessary to fulfill its

---

[25] Eberhard Schmidt-Aßmann, in: id. (Ed.), Besonderes Verwaltungsrecht, 12th Ed., Berlin, New York 2003, section 1, n. 44.

supervising tasks. Supervisory authorities are authorized to visit and inspect on-site, to demand oral and written reports and to access records and other documents.

Notwithstanding, it is necessary that the supervisory authority claims a specific cause for its information request. This does not extend to the necessity of a special suspicion concerning a specific unlawful act of the municipality. The request of information is a normal act of supervision and therefore does not need a reason of justification on the same level like a state intervention in fundamental rights would require. Nevertheless, an all-encompassing inquiry would be unlawful because of its disproportionality[26].

Therefore, the request for information is primarily a question of discretionary power. This means that there seems to be no limitation of the actual scope of information requests aside from restrictions of discretion.

In general, a request for information will be covered by the supervisory competence. A limit must, however, be assumed, if the information request turns out to be vexatious.[27] This is the case for instance, if – without any concrete indication of an unlawful municipal act and without any specific legal refrence – information is demanded, which cannot be provided without tedious efforts.[28] This would violate the right of self-administration of the municipalities according to Art. 28 sect. 2 German Basic Law (Grundgesetz) and could be contested in administrative court.[29]

Furthermore, in case that personal data are concerned the generation of municipal data is also restricted by § 4 ff. of the Federal Data Protection Act.

As a result, one could argue, that for the information request mainly a limitation of chicanery exists. A request must not be obviously and far beyond the scope necessary for an ordinary supervision.

4.2 The distribution of data

If the supervisory authority provides the collected information to other autonomous municipalities, the state no longer acts as a safe institution for information but rather as a distributor within its administrative competence.[30] Therefore, the next step of the legal test would be to check for potential obstacles to the distribution of data.

---

[26] Gröpl/Sonntag, see above note 12, p. 327.
[27] Gröpl/Sonntag, see above note 12, p.327.
[28] Martin Bauer/Thomas Böhle/Gerhard Ecker, Bayerische Kommunalgesetze - Kommentar, 4th. Ed., München updated: 09/2009, Art. 111 BayGO n. 2.
[29] Compare Franz-Ludwig Knemeyer, in Bayerische Verwaltungsblätter (BayVBl.) 1977, p. 129 (129).
[30] For the public sphere compare Indra Spiecker gen. Döhmann, Protection of Confidential Business Data in the Age of Convergence, in: Stefan Seifert/Jan Krämer (Eds.), International Workshop on Communication Regulation in the Age of Digital Convergence: Legal and Economic Perspectives, Karlsruhe 2009, p. 29 (35).

a Right of self administration according to Art. 28 sect. 2 German Basic Law

The right of self administration according to Art. 28 sect. 2 German Basic Law could be an obstacle to data generation and distribution by the supervisory authority. Municipalities are endowed with the right to regulate all local affairs on their own responsibility, within the limits prescribed by the laws.[31] Claiming the right from Art. 28 sect. 2 German Basic Law (Grundgesetz) to prevent the distribution of data would be possible, if hereby the autonomous fulfillment of its tasks would be endangered. In general, this would not apply for administrative procedures that are already settled. In procedures that are still going on, the competence of independent decision makings could be excessively restricted.

b Secrecy/ Data Protection

Concerning the information that the supervisory authority gets from its supervised municipalities it is bound to the same rules of secrecy and data protection as the municipalities.[32] File contents that concern third parties, (e.g. prospective constructors applying for a building permit) could not be published within databases designed to support municipal planning procedures. Concerning personal data, the limitations of the Federal Data Protection Act have to be observed. In addition, the secrecy in tax matters according to § 30 General Tax Code (Abgabenordnung) must be complied with although it has to be considered that this rule is only applicable for concrete personal data and not for details that are made anonymous for statistical purposes.

Here, a constructive view on databases could consider procedures of pseudonymity or anonymity, as for other municipalities, the exact information might not be necessary.

c Art. 12, 14 German Basic Law for Municipal Enterprises

Substantially more extensive are obligations of secrecy, if data of municipal enterprises are affected. Opposing rights can particularly emerge concerning commercial data, if a municipality acts as a public company. It is a consequence of Art. 19 sect. 3 German Basic Law, that the company can claim the right of protected ownership from Art. 14 German Basic Law if the influence of the municipality is not dominating. In these cases commercial and business secrets, which are protected under Art. 14 German Basic Law constitute the limitation for the distribution of municipal data in databases that are accessible for other municipalities.

---

[31] According to the prevailing opinion, the right of self administration is neither a fundamental right nor similar to a fundamental right. Nevertheless, it is a subjective right with a scope of protection directly derived from the constitution, compare Michael Nierhaus, in Michael Sachs, Grundgesetz, 3rd Ed. München 2003, Art. 28 n. 34.

[32] Richard Kunze/Otto Bronner/Alfred Katz, Gemeindeordnung für Baden-Württemberg - Kommentar, 4. Ed. Stuttgart, updated: 07/2008; § 120 n. 12.

5 Conclusive Remarks

To keep the municipalities empowered to fulfill their original and delegated tasks, a well-organized supervision is necessary. This supervision does not only have the competence of legal and functional control, but additionally has to provide consultation to its supervised municipalities. Information plays a central role in fulfilling these various tasks in a communicative structure between municipalities and supervising authority. The law has so far neglected implications for the generation and the transfer of information gathered in the course of this relationship. One of the ways of making use of technical possibilities and enhancing the quality of control, consultation and supervision is the establishment of a database accessible by municipalities. Its advantages are obvious: More efficiency, less double information, quicker access – and the use of well-established instruments from electronic markets. These advantages might even call for databases as a legal obligation. But there are some downsides to be considered, as well. The implementation of such data bases for the purpose of information generation and distribution faces actual and legal difficulties. Particularly monetary reasons but also duties of secrecy binding the supervisory authority can act as limitations to such a provision of information.

References

Bauer, M., T. Böhle, and G. Ecker (updated: 09/2009): *Bayerische Kommunalgesetze - Kommentar*, 4th edition, München.

Forsthoff, E. (1973): *Lehrbuch des Verwaltungsrechts*, vol. 1, 10th edition, München.

Gröpl, C. and A. W. Sonntag (2009): "Informationsbefugnis der Kommunalaufsicht und ihre Durchsetzung," in: *Zeitschrift für Landes- und Kommunalrecht Hessen - Rheinland-Pfalz - Saarland (LKRZ)*, p. 326 ff.

Hoffmann, D. (2003): "Kommunen im E-Government - Einblicke in die aktuelle Situation," in: W. Büchner and A. Büllesbach (eds.), *E-Government - Staatliches Handeln in der Informationsgesellschaft*, Köln, p. 157 ff.

Knemeyer, F.-L. (1977): "Verwaltungsgerichtliche Überprüfung von Maßnahmen der Kommunalaufsicht," in: *Bayerische Verwaltungsblätter (BayVBl.)*, p. 129 ff.

Kopp, F. and U. Ramsauer (2008): *Verwaltungsverfahrensgesetz, Kommentar*, 10th edition, München.

Kunze, R., O. Bronner, and A. Katz (updated: 07/2008): *Gemeindeordnung für Baden-Württemberg - Kommentar*, 4th edition, Stuttgart.

Nonaka, I. and H. Takeuchi (1995): *The knowledge creating company - how Japanese companies create the dynamics of innovation*, New York.

Rajkovic, V. and B. Zupan (2004): "Knowledge Management as a Challenge for Public Administration Reengineering," *Informatics and Management*, p. 129.

Reinermann, H. (2003): "Elektronisierung des staatlichen und kommunalen Leistungsverkehrs," in: W. Büchner and A. Büllesbach (eds.), *E-Government - Staatliches Handeln in der Informationsgesellschaft*, Köln, p. 143 ff.

Rowley, J. E. and R. Hartley (2008): *Organizing Knowledge: An Introduction to managing access to information*, 4th edition, Hampshire (GB), Burlington (USA).

Sachs, M. (2003): *Grundgesetz*, 3rd edition, München.

Schaefer, S. (2009): *Controlling und Informationsmanagement in Strategischen Unternehmensnetzwerken: Multiperspektivische Modellierung und interorganisationale Vernetzungvon Informationsprozessen*, Wiesbaden.

Schmidt-Aßmann, E. (2003): *Besonderes Verwaltungsrecht*, 12th edition, Berlin, New York.

Spiecker gen. Döhmann, I. (2005): "Informationsgewinnung im dezentralen Mehrebenensystem," in: J.-B. Oebbecke (ed.), *Nicht-Normative Steuerung in dezentralen Systemen*, Stuttgart, p. 253 ff.

Spiecker gen. Döhmann, I. (2009): "Protection of Confidential Business Data in the Age of Convergence," in: S. Seifert and J. Krämer (eds.), *International Workshop on Communication Regulation in the Age of Digital Convergence: Legal and Economic Perspectives*, Karlsruhe, p. 29 ff.

Wolff, H. J., O. Bachof, and R. Stober (2004): *Verwaltungsrecht Band 3*, 5th edition, München.

Zacharias, D. (2004): *Nordrhein-Westfälisches Kommunalrecht*, Thüngersheim/Frankfurt a. M.

How Design Principles can Govern the Knowledge Commons: Elinor Ostrom and the Case of Wikipedia

Kathrin Noack[1], Christof Weinhardt[2], and Thomas Dreier[1]

[1] Institute of Information and Economic Law, KIT
    {kathrin.noack, dreier}@kit.edu
[2] Institute of Information Systems and Management, KIT
    weinhardt@kit.edu

Summary. Through the internet, information and knowledge in general have become easily accessible for many people. The free encyclopaedia Wikipedia is a prime example for the assembling and sharing of knowledge. In her research on collective action regimes governing common limited resources, Elinor Ostrom found out that groups or communities successfully organising their use of a common resource over long time periods tend to display similar characteristics irrespective to the nature of the resource. She summarizes these characteristics into eight design principles for successful regimes governing physical common pool resources. In her later work she discusses the possible application of her model for governing the knowledge commons, which, as an immaterial good, will not be depleted when used. This article follows up on this idea and compares Ostrom's design principles to the case of Wikipedia and in particular the counter-vandalism policy to act against deliberate attempts to place false information into the online encyclopaedia. The thesis will be that Ostrom's design principle can be used as a valid framework to analyse the case of Wikipedia as outlined here and that these principles can provide useful parameters for other online communities dealing with the knowledge commons.

1 Introduction

Information and knowledge have become far more accessible in the digital age. Knowledge is considered a public good and, thanks to the internet, it is easily available for many. In this way, knowledge can be considered as a commons. Therefore it is reasonable to assume that characteristics of self-organised communities using the traditional commons might also be applicable to, or at least interesting for understanding, virtual groups organizing knowledge on the internet. One of the most prominent examples in this respect is the online encyclopaedia Wikipedia, where many individuals work and operate together to create, deliver and archive information and build one of the most considerable and accessible knowledge resources in the world.

Elinor Ostrom's focus of research lies on the organization of the usage of the commons in communities. The nature of the commons analyzed by her was originally grounded to limited natural resources. In her research based on various case studies, she forms a theoretical approach on collective actions and social rules in communities using common goods. (Ostrom, 1990, 2000) She found certain design principles for common action that indicate that some aspects of organisation are more effective than others for the long-term perspective on the efficient and sustainable use of the commons.[1]

Together with Charlotte Hess, Ostrom later widens the scope of the commons also to the realm of knowledge. She claims that there is a possibility to adapt the design principles developed for natural resource commons to the collective action of creating, organizing and archiving knowledge. Knowledge is a public good, as it is cumulative and potentially everyone can access it. As such it can be analysed on the aspects of traditional forms of commons. (Hess and Ostrom, 2007, pp.3-14)

The design principles of collective action shall in the following be compared to the example of Wikipedia. Specifically they are to be analysed using the example of the English Wikipedia policy on how to deal with 'vandalism', the deliberate attempt to disrupt the integrity of Wikipedia, for example by placing false information with malicious intention into articles. This specific set of procedures was chosen because it demonstrates the way the community protects the resource knowledge, as any information displayed in the articles of the online encyclopaedia should be as accurate as possible. Without safeguards to protect the knowledge, the existence of the encyclopaedia would be at risk, because too many disruptions in the articles would make any information within Wikipedia too unreliable to use.

This article will attempt to follow Ostrom's call for further research into how the design principles can be analysed in the knowledge commons. The thesis followed here is that Wikipedia's anti-vandalism policy shows characteristics comparable to the design principles Ostrom found for long term resource regimes in the traditional commons. It will be shown that there are other general characteristics displayed in Wikipedia's organisational structure which can be interpreted by using the design principles as well.

Wikipedia can be interpreted as a system of collective action to govern the knowledge commons. As such rules and decision making processes needed to evolve to back the community of users upholding the online encyclopaedia. Specifically, the intent of this article is to verify if Elinor Ostrom's findings are applicable to the case of Wikipedia and therefore valid as parameters to research and explain the way Wikipedia's community governs itself and the knowledge commons. Following up on these thoughts, one could argue that according to Ostrom's theory the features of Wikipedia which are reflected by the design principles support the longevity of the community.

Concerning the studying of Wikipedia and collective action in the internet, there is much research in progress. Stegbauer's detailed study of the German Wikipedia using empirical methods and network analysis models holds very useful insights

---

[1] Special thanks to Ernst Nordtveit, University of Bergen, for providing valuable insight into Elinor Ostrom's theories and helpful advice.

in regards to the structures and rules of Wikipedia (Stegbauer, 2009). Koniecny wrote an article about whether there are oligarchic tendencies to be found in the community of the online encyclopaedia (Konieczny, 2009). The 'International Symposium on Wikis and Collaboration Systems' is an annual conference taking place since 2005.[2] Here, the internal development of Wikipedia is also often a topic of discussion. The conference is open to participants from various scientific disciplines.[3] The possibilities of Wikipedia's success for new economic models has been discussed in Tapscott's and Williams' book 'Wikinomics' (Tapscott and Williams, 2007). These are just some of the more recent examples on research in the field.

First, in the theoretical part of this article, Ostrom's thoughts on collective action and the evolution of rules and norms for common-pool regimes will be discussed. This will be accompanied with a short discourse on rivalrous and nonrivalrous resources, as Ostrom's original model was derived from regimes on limited forms of commons and will be used on the unlimited resource knowledge. Then Ostrom's design principles on long term self-organised regimes will be explained in detail. As a practical application of the theory the case of the Wikipedia user structure and the basic forms of arbitration will be described in the following. Further on they will be put into context with the English Wikipedia's anti-vandalism policy. Finally, the design principles will be analysed for the case of the Wikipedia policy and Wikipedia's user structure, as far as it is outlined here. It will be discussed in how far they are suitable for researching the case of the online encyclopaedia.

2 Elinor Ostrom's Findings on Collective Action

2.1 Collective Action and the Evolution of Social Norms

Elinor Ostrom's contribution to the research of collective action and the efficient and non-detrimental usage of the commons among her other work has earned her the Nobel Prize in 2009. In 2000, she wrote a paper on the collective action and the evolution of social norms in which she outlines the theoretical, experimental and empirical background of the research of collective action explained on the background of evolutionary theories on social norms. These ideas she expands to the resource of knowledge in her and Charlotte Hess' book on the "Understanding of Knowledge as a Commons" (Hess and Ostrom, 2007).

Ostrom asks why voluntary organisations and adherence to social rules and norms work in general, even if traditional economic theory tends to understand that rational individuals tend not to act for common interests if it negates their personal gains (Ostrom, 2000, p.137). Her research is based on an experimental approach founded on game theory as well as on field studies on smaller communities using common natural resources. On this background, Ostrom derives several design

---

[2] See (WikiSym, 2010; WikiSym '09, 2010).
[3] Compare (Suh et al., 2009).

principles on self-organized resource regimes which have the potential to survive for long time periods (Ostrom, 2000). According to her, these principles hold certain possibilities to be compared to regimes trying to coordinate the resource of knowledge (Hess and Ostrom, 2007, p.7).

Within the game theoretical approach, Ostrom found in controlled experimental conditions that the players tended to behave more cooperatively if they developed their own strategy rather than when a cooperative strategy was imposed upon them from outside and then taken away. When the players were able to communicate directly, cooperative strategies occurred more often than in anonymous games. Some players would choose to reward cooperative strategies and sanction uncooperative behaviour in others. These results were then compared to real world examples on the evolution of rules and norms in communities collectively managing limited natural resources. (Ostrom, 2000, p.145ff)

In the field research, there are many contextual variables to be considered from case to case, ranging from the type of resource disputed to the leadership model used to the heterogeneity of the group. Other variable elements could be the scarcity of the good, the level of cooperation, the possible financial benefits, the history of the group or the cultural background, among others. Many of these aspects varied in the groups researched. However, Ostrom found certain consistencies when comparing differing kinds of various field studies on communities organising common-pool resources. In those systems it was found that communities who develop and enforce norms and rules within their group have a higher probability to use the resource in a sustainable and efficient way for long time periods than communities where the rules were imposed externally. (Ostrom, 2000, p.148)

As common-pool resources Ostrom understands natural or artificial systems where benefits are created up to the limit set by the amount of the resource. This means a participant's consumption reduces the resource and it is often hard to keep beneficiaries away from the resource (Ostrom, 2000, p.148). Therefore she uses the term 'commons' for the resource knowledge later in her work, as it more generally fits the unlimited character of this good (Hess and Ostrom, 2007, p.5).

2.2 Design Principles for Long-term Resource Regimes

Ostrom understands the emergence of rules and norms for self-organised collective actions on a basis of evolutionary theories, where reciprocity plays an important role in forming the behaviour of at least some individuals (Ostrom, 2000, p.149). Collective action, according to Ostrom, is when two or more individuals cooperate to achieve a certain outcome (Hess and Ostrom, 2007, p.5). Members of a group are likely to restrict their own use of the given resource as long as other members in the group are willing to do so as well. This behaviour has a high probability to result in a process of cooperation. When the group has relatively clear conditions on membership and the group boundaries are definable, the trust among the members and the incentives for cooperation will most likely rise. As a consequence, some individuals within the group might take greater responsibility and initiate improvements for the effective use of the resource (Ostrom, 2000, p.149).

Basing on these underlying thoughts Ostrom proposes eight design principles for long-term resource regimes organised through the collective action of their members (Ostrom, 1990). The first design principle is the presence of group boundaries that are accepted by the members and effective externally. "If a group of users can determine its own membership - including those who agree to use the recourse according to their agreed-upon rules and excluding those who do not agree to these rules - the group has made an important first step toward the development of greater trust and reciprocity." (Ostrom, 2000, p.149) This means that within the community, boundaries can serve to maintain trust and reciprocity which are essential for the members to work efficiently together to govern the commons they collectively use. Externally, the boundaries will work as a defining factor on who belongs to the community and who does not.

The second principle is about the rules that actually restrict, organise or manage the resource that is to be used by the collective action. This principle is based on the fairness of the sharing system. (Ostrom, 2000, pp.149f) In the case of the knowledge commons, it could be adapted to the rules that actually manage the gathering, creating, archiving or maintaining the information resources as well as organising the work and input of the members of the group to do so in an efficient way.

The third design principle refers to the ability of the individuals partaking in the collective action to jointly create and modify the rules and norms they wish all the members to adhere to. In various field studies concerning the natural common-pool resources, it was found that the members were more willing to follow rules developed within their group than to adhere to rules at least partially set from outside forces such as elites or government institutions independent from the group using the resource. Rules derived from within the group are also often perceived as more fair. (Ostrom, 2000, p.150)

Norms can only be complied with for long time periods if there are certain enforcement mechanisms in place and the members are aware of the consequences for not following them. Consequently, the fourth design principle describes that the groups select monitors, either accountable to the members or participants themselves, to check on the resource conditions and the usage behaviour of the individual members. The fifths design principle is related to this and says that there should be an enforcement mechanism with graduated sanctions based on how serious the community perceives an offence to be. The community legitimates the monitors who can point out a case of possible sanctioning and enforce it. The initial sanctions are often a form of warning and not necessarily on the same level as the occurred loss. (Ostrom, 2000, p.151) In a sense they work as an educational system for the rules within the community.

The sixth design principle demonstrates the need to have efficient, easily to enter, low cost arenas where disputes among the members and with external actors can be settled. These arbitration forums must be transparent to the community and equally accessible. Within them, the rules and norms themselves can also be discussed and adjusted if necessary. This leads to the seventh design principle on the decision making procedures on rule making mechanisms. Many common-pool resources in the physical world in local arenas rely on unanimous decision, according to Ostrom. However, the consequences of this are high transactions costs on the decision making processes, paid for either in the members' time and effort. This can lead to a situation where norms are not adjusted and improved in time. These processes do not have to be backed by official institutions such as governmental bodies. As long as the members of a community accept them, they are functioning. For large common-pool regimes, Ostrom also recognizes an eighth design principle that allows different groups dealing with differing functionalities to be nested within the greater structure of the collective action in question. (Ostrom, 2000, pp.153f)

These basic design principles can be found in variations in most common-pool resource regimes in the physical world. It can be argued that they are inherent in all forms of democratic organisations. Yet, democracy is not an easy term to define. In political terms it includes broad concepts such as equality, liberty and human rights. The communities researched by Ostrom were often organised on local levels and therefore limited in the number of members. She sees these principles as possible guidelines on how collective actions concerning the commons can be efficient for long time periods. The combining factor is that the members of these communities organised themselves and their actions this way, irrespective of the systems surrounding them, for example the governing structures or the legal frameworks of states.

Ostrom also points out certain threats to the long term viability of such regimes. These threats maybe indigenous or exogenous and can affect the trust and reciprocity within the groups. A major threat is the migration into or out of the community, which can change the balance by either influencing the effectiveness of a community when it loses members or when too many new participants join who do not know or wish to adhere to the norms already established and cannot create an equivalent system balancing the members' interests. Other threats occur when official institutions impose rules where they had not before concerning the general dealing with the resource. (Ostrom, 2000, pp.153f)

The term 'rule' needs more explanation in regards to Ostrom's design principles on self-organised resource regimes. Defining the meaning of 'rule' is a matter of many discussions, so the article will follow her ideas on what a rule may be from one of her earlier works. (Ostrom, 1986) There, she defines rules as prescription which are created and adhered to by a group of participants in order to serve as a framework for their relationships. Within this framework certain actions must be taken, are allowed or can be prohibited. These prescriptions are the implicit or explicitly set rules by individuals who need to organise their actions within their group and create a predictable environment. They do so by: "(1) creating positions (e.g., member, convener, agent, etc.); (2) stating how participants enter or leave positions; (3) stating which actions participants in these positions are required, permitted, or forbidden to take; and (4) stating which outcome participants are required, permitted, or forbidden to affect." (Ostrom, 1986, p.5) Therefore the rules can be adapted, discarded or changed by the majority of individuals within the group or by external entities.

Rules emerging in groups can also be explained through the emergence of social structures. According to a social science definition by Stegbauer, social structures emerge within the complex interaction of differing actors with each other (Stegbauer and Rausch, 2006, p.19). Have these interactions been well established through the course of history, they are largely defining what we understand as social structures. They are made up of interconnections and within them norms are formed and gradually accepted as the usual behaviour within a group. Norms correspond to the expected behaviour and conduct of individuals within the group and will be mirrored in the rules which the members are supposed to follow. Within virtual groups existing in the internet, often certain positions or roles are formed which constitute the social structure. As in real life, their functionality could possibly lead to hierarchies, as often some participants within a group are more experienced than others exercising certain functions. (Stegbauer and Rausch, 2006, pp.59-61)

Stegbauer's theoretical explanation to the norm building aspect within groups in the virtual as well as the natural world is similar to Ostrom's understanding how rules evolve. According to this line of thought, rules and norms emerge within groups parallel to their establishment. For a group to survive, it needs certain aspects which make it distinguishable to other groups, which means there must be at least certain understandings in place who belongs to the group and who does not, which essentially establish the boundaries of the group. Ostrom sees this as the starting point for self-organised collective action which has the potential to be continued for a long time within the community committed to it.

2.3 Rivalrous and Nonrivalrous Commons

As mentioned above, Ostrom's design principles relate to the collective action of the physical forms of commons, which are limited in nature. Yet she also writes about the possibility to adapt them to the knowledge commons. These have changed drastically through the emergence of the internet. Knowledge becomes far more accessible and can also be spread at far lower cost as it was possible before the new technologies allowed information to be distributed globally (Hess and Ostrom, 2007, p.9). Lawrence Lessig also discusses the new way to access and distribute immaterial forms of commons digitally (Lessig, 2002).

Lessig focuses on the idea of the internet as a commons, independent from which form of digital content and as a scarcely limited resource. He defines the possible circumstances on usage on the internet as a commons in terms of an "opportunity for individuals to draw upon resources without connections, permission, or access granted by others. They are environments that commit themselves to being open." (Lessig, 2002, p.85)

At this point Lessig points out two important differences between rivalrous and nonrivalrous resources. The term nonrivalrous was already used by Thomas Jefferson in respect to the resource of ideas, which are in themselves not depleted by another's use, as Lessig elaborates. Is the resource rivalrous it calls for a control mechanism that prevents the overuse of the good while ensuring that is it produced at the same time. If the resource is nonrivalrous, then only the creation of the resource has to be guaranteed and maintained, as nonrivalrous resources are unlimited to use. Lessig refers this to Ostrom's understanding of a provisioning problem. (Lessig, 2002, pp.94f) His interpretation of a nonrivalrous resource might fit the broader concept of the intellectual good knowledge well. This shall be used here as a definition of the knowledge commons.

In the case of Wikipedia, the resource knowledge is the one distributed and managed. The main concern of Wikipedia is not the space needed to hold that much data, as this is technically possible at relatively low cost, but rather the organisation needed to archive and sort out what knowledge is to be maintained and delivered. The organisation and the people involved in it are the scarce resource which Wikipedia needs for its survival. While the knowledge is freely available in general, the effort needed to archive and maintain the knowledge is not and comes at the cost of time and work of the members.

This factor changes also the main dilemma Ostrom discusses. In the case of physical resources the use of the resource will deplete it. That means it is in the interest of each participant that the other participants involved restrain their use. At the same time, like in the gaming situation mentioned, their immediate outcome is often the highest when not cooperating in the beginning. In the case of Wikipedia the most probable dilemma is free riding, as it is much easier to just access the knowledge displayed than actively contributing. Most people will access the information on the online encyclopaedia and not add to it. However, when people lose interest in spending time and effort to write articles, correct mistakes and keep the information up to date, then the point of Wikipedia as a reliable knowledge base becomes more and more obsolete. It is not necessary for the majority of readers of Wikipedia pages to become involved, but a certain amount of people will be necessary to uphold the system. There are no numbers which point out how many members need to work on the information exactly, but a loss of editors is of great concern for the longevity of the project as a whole (Angwin and Fowler, 2009). Therefore, free riding can become a problem if it leads to dwindling numbers of editors to the point where the information in Wikipedia cannot be updated and archived properly.

Another variation of the commons of knowledge being undermined is the possible sabotage and misuse of the common good for purposes other than the ones originally benefitting the community. Sabotage is not part of the tragedy of the commons in Hardin's sense (Hardin, 1968), but a disruption to the successful workings of a community using a common good, though this problem is certainly not specific to those. In the case of Wikipedia, the knowledge displayed in the articles is meant to be as accurate as possible and should be able to be referred to valid sources. To use Wikipedia for other means to intentionally spread personal opinions or propaganda; or to discredit and insult individuals, for example, is contrary to the original aim of the community. This goal has remained unchanged as it would diminish the worth of the encyclopaedia. Therefore policies and internal rules exist to weed out disruptions placed in bad faith to the validity of the information displayed. The counter-vandalism policy, which will be discussed in detail below, is one such tool. As Ostrom's design principles focus on the outline of governing common resources successfully, measures against sabotage are also a means to ensure the longevity of the collective action. Consequently it will be discussed in the following how Ostrom's ideas can be applied as an analytical framework to the practical example of Wikipedia.

3 The Example of Wikipedia

3.1 Access Levels of Users in the English Wikipedia

Several characteristics of Wikipedia have to be described to outline how the community upholding the online encyclopaedia works against the posting of content it does not find suitable to its goals. First of all, the official positions of participants within Wikipedia will be lined out by describing the access levels they hold within the online encyclopaedia. Then a general definition of what is understood by 'vandalism' in Wikipedia will be given followed by the measures and processes to react upon it. This article looks at the policy and access levels for users of the English Wikipedia version.

The English Wikipedia was launched in January 2001 by Jimmy Wales and Larry Sanger. With the help of thousands of participants willing to post articles and correct the content it became the most widespread, accessible and miscellaneous source of knowledge in the world with 14 million articles (3.1 million in English) in various languages. (Wikipedia: About, 2010)

The visitors and participants of Wikipedia, who read, create, add on and correct content are distinguished through the access levels they receive which vary in the degree of the change they are allow to exert on the Wikipedia pages. According to their access levels they take certain official responsibilities within Wikipedia. The main difference between the positions lies between normal users and the more influential roles of so-called 'administrators', 'bureaucrats' and 'stewards'. (Wikipedia: User access levels, 2010)

There are four types of regular users. Anonymous users do not hold an account, can read all regular Wikipedia pages and edit pages which are not protected in any way. While they can create 'talk'-pages where they can discuss and write comments, they cannot upload files or images. They must make themselves known as human beings and not computers by answering a Captcha, a picture test using deformed numbers and letters which cannot be recognized automatically. New users have their own account and can start new pages and fill them with content, yet cannot upload files either. Autoconfirmed users are generally recognized by the Wikipedia software as users who have upheld their account for four days and made 10 edits. They can then also edit semi-protected pages, move pages and upload files or pictures. They are no longer required to pass the Captcha test in most cases. Confirmed users have the same rights as autoconfirmed users, but are granted their status manually by administrators. (Wikipedia: User access levels, 2010)

To become an administrator in the English Wikipedia, the community must confirm this right to the user requesting it. There must be a discussion taking place among fellow editors about the contributions of the applying individual. Seven days into the discussion a 'bureaucrat' will decide upon the consensus reached for granting administrator rights to do so. Generally, 70% to 80% of the comments in the discussion should be in favour of the promotion of the applicant, which means there is not a clear vote or numerical measurement involved. (Wikipedia: Administrators, 2010) Only then does the new administrator gain control over certain tools and special functions in Wikipedia. For example, they can delete, protect, block or release pages. An administrator can remove or grant rights to users and can access and modify protected pages and the Wikipedia interface. They are also called 'sysops', standing for system operators. (Wikipedia: User access levels, 2010)

'Bureaucrat' rights are granted by the community and are allowed certain actions on other users' accounts, for example handing out administrator rights. 'Stewards' are the highest rank within the Wikipedia network itself. They are elected globally and can evoke and renounce the rights of individuals in the groups below them. They can hand out the special rights to exercise the control mechanisms of 'Oversight' and 'CheckUser' to other users and implement them themselves. (Wikipedia: User access levels, 2010) These functions are mentioned here as they have the highest enforcement level. 'Oversight' means that the user exerting this right can hide revisions of all other users from pages permanently. This tool is among the highest control instruments. (Wikipedia: Oversight, 2010) 'CheckUser' enables the holder to view the IP addresses of user accounts in case of infringements. These rights are only granted to those who have identified themselves to the Wikimedia Foundation and are at least 18 years of age. (Wikipedia: Checkuser, 2010)

If disputes arise among the members of the community, about the communication between members and about the handling of the content, there is the possibility to create 'talk' pages concerning the single articles. These are the most basic level forums. If disputes cannot be settled, they can be brought towards the Mediation Committee, whose solutions are not binding but rather suggestions. New members to the Mediation Committee are selected by the Mediation Committee itself. An open discussion by members of the Mediation Committee and non-members alike will take place beforehand. The Mediation Committee was established next to the highest ranking Arbitration Committee by Jimmy Wales in 2004 to create bodies that can settle disputes. (Wikipedia: Mediation Committee, 2010)

The Arbitration Committee is elected and can enforce rules and decisions when disputes cannot be settled otherwise. It will only get involved if the Mediation Committee could not resolve the issue. Its members are elected in an open vote throughout the community. After a certain time period of open discussion about the nominees the vote will take place yearly. Apart from settling disputes and handing out major sanctions the Arbitration Committee also can decide upon which members hold the 'Oversight' and 'CheckUser' abilities mentioned above. (Wikipedia: Arbitration, 2010; Wikipedia: Arbitration/Policy, 2010; Wikipedia: Arbitration Committee/Procedures, 2010) Election modes in Wikipedia vary according to the decision made. Often the simple majority of participants will be sufficient. However, only users with an account can vote. In most cases, the users eligible to vote must have a certain number of edits within a specified time frame, so that they can be accepted as active editors. This was the case when a discussion took place about the Wikipedia content to be migrated to another licence and a vote was held on the issue. Content in the free encyclopaedia was originally placed under the GNU Free Documentation Licence (GFDL). Now the Creative Commons Attribution-ShareAlike 3.0 Unported Licence was approved of additionally to the GFDL for the text base, since the majority of the eligible users agreed to the migration by vote in 2009. (Wikipedia: Licensing Update, 2010)

Wikipedia is supported through the Wikimedia Foundation, Inc., which gains its financial needs through donations. Some language versions of Wikipedia, like the German one, have their own version of the Wikimedia setup.[4] Wikimedia is lead by a board of trustees, currently nine persons who are financed by the donations as well. It also supports the other aligned Wiki projects, like, among others, Wikisource for free source documents, Commons for free media files, Wiktionary for dictionaries or Wikiversity for free learning tools. (Wikimedia Foundation Inc., 2010)

These are only the basic access levels on the English Wikipedia. It already shows that there are many differing roles and functions recognized users can hold within the system. Looking at what the holders of these positions can do within the Wikipedia community, one can certify a certain regime of rules, positions and enforcement procedures which controls the process of the creation of content in Wikipedia. It allows members of the community special forms of access to the part of the knowledge commons within the encyclopaedia.

3.2 The Counter-Vandalism Policy of the English Wikipedia

Elinor Ostrom's design principles will be compared here to a special process in Wikipedia, when the community encounters disruption and has to deal with it to maintain itself. The example of 'vandalism' in Wikipedia is chosen because it illustrates well how the community wishes to protect its way of creating the resource knowledge in Wikipedia. 'Vandalism in Wikipedia "is any addition, removal, or

---

[4] Wikimedia Deutschland is legally organized as an incorporated association (Wikimedia Deutschland e.V., 2010).

change of content made in a deliberate attempt to compromise the integrity of Wikipedia." (Wikipedia: Vandalism, 2010) Examples for that could be the placement of ill-considered humour, the blanking of articles or inserting intentionally false and misleading information. There are many types of vandalism, but the defining characteristic is that it is not done in good-faith. Any attempt to improve the online encyclopaedia, even by accidentally placing false information, is not considered as such. Therefore, there is a fine line to decide if something counts as deliberately disruptive behaviour or not. Any user who finds an article being vandalized can revert it into the previous state and warn the user, who they can identify under their alias or IP in the edit page. However, these warnings should be done carefully and there are special guidelines on when and how to issue them. When a user is found to committing vandalism regularly, he or she can be reported to the administrators, who are able to block users for some time or protect the article in question to a certain degree. (Wikipedia: Vandalism, 2010)

4 Ostrom's Design Principles and Wikipedia

As already explained above, Ostrom derived the design principles for self-organised regimes on common pool resources from her research of the traditional physical commons schemes. They can be summarized as follows: (1) Defined boundaries are needed. (2) Rules are in place accepted by the community and adapted to the circumstances. (3) Those people affected by the rules have the possibility to participate in the modification of said rules. (4) External bodies respect the communities' members to create their own rules. (5) A recognized system is effective to self-monitor the members' behaviour. (6) There is a sanctioning system for the enforcement of the rules in place with graduated sanctions. (7) All members have the possibility to access an easily available conflict-resolution tool. (8) In larger systems nested structures exit within the main frame for the single governance mechanisms. (Hess and Ostrom, 2007, p.7)

The first design principle refers to the boundaries of the regime. In knowledge commons, where the resource is nonrivalrous, the quantity of the resource does not play a role. However, there is a discussion about whether Wikipedia is finally reaching its growth limit, as most of the more easily achievable knowledge has already been inserted into the encyclopaedia. (Suh et al., 2009) Some sources also say that there are less editors active than before (Angwin and Fowler, 2009). In case of the users and participants of Wikipedia the boundaries are more recognizable. Though there are no real restrictions in place on who can access the wiki, everyone who does and especially everyone who edits something will leave a mark which can be traced at least on a digital level through the IP addresses or directly through their account if they created one. Therefore, there are certain boundaries in place through the fact that people actively decide which roles and responsibilities they take through their involvement as users of the encyclopaedia. They follow the rules of the community and therefore one can argue that they accept the boundaries set in place of the group.

The second principle states that the members of the community have developed certain accepted behaviours which they see as commonly accepted rules. They can exist as common practices or in written form. These rules should be adaptable to the special situation of the regime. In case of Wikipedia, there are many policies dealing with what is perceived to be good or bad behaviour within the community. The case of the counter-vandalism policy of Wikipedia is in itself an example for a rule in place to organize the resource, more specifically to protect it. For the encyclopaedia to be working effectively and to be useful, its content needs to be as accurate as possible and cannot be altered for the sake of individuals not interested in correct articles but deliberately using them for other means, like promoting false information or spreading insults. Such actions would go against the purpose of the Wikipedia project as a whole and undermine its effectiveness, therefore lessen the value of the knowledge commons contained within, whose main characteristic has to be a high degree of reliability.

The rules are most effective, according to Ostrom, when they derive from the community itself. Within Wikipedia, this third design principle is generally true. However, because of the large amounts of participants it is not always easy for single voices to be heard. Also, it is more likely that participants with high seniority can initiate discussions on the policies themselves than new users could. Yet, in the case of the anti-vandalism policy possibilities like talk pages exist to discuss the policy. The policy page itself cannot be edited by normal users, as this would be considered too much disruption and the rules need to be reliable until a majority within the community attempts for their change.

This point goes along with Stegbauer's analysis of the German Wikipedia, where he found that the positions held previously do have an influence on the levels of power single users can exert (Stegbauer, 2009, p.154). In his research, Stegbauer analysed the German Wikipedia using network analysis models and positional theories (Stegbauer, 2009). The later are linked to the position which individuals can occupy in a social setting and are akin to sociological models about identities and roles individuals can hold. The position within the setting can in turn influence the individual to fulfil certain prerequisites, for example successfully accomplishing certain tasks or acting in a certain way. What the position inclines is always bound to the expectation other individuals have, who in turn derive their expectations from their role, e.g. in a teacher-student relation. These relations are not static and are bound within processes. (Stegbauer, 2009, pp.35f)

When analysing the reactions of individuals to certain kinds of vandalism, Stegbauer finds his positional model verified in that different members of the community act according to certain roles or positions, for example the perpetrators and the hunters of creating a self-enforcing system that draws on peer supervision (Stegbauer, 2009, pp.155-161). However, he realizes differences between the user levels concerning their interactions and cooperation tendencies. On the level of administrators a relatively strong internal cohesion exists. The lower the level of users the degree of heterogeneity increases. This might not necessarily be considered surprising, as users with higher access levels in Wikipedia should be expected to have more experience in cooperation and more connections with other users, which is natural because the number of individuals within that group is also smaller. Yet it might make it more difficult for someone on a lower level to exert influence within the system and be acknowledged on the higher levels. (Stegbauer, 2009, p.154)

This does not lead inevitably to a form of oligarchy, as Piotr Konieczny observes in his research on governance and democratic tendencies in Wikipedia (Konieczny, 2009). He sees many possibilities for individuals in Wikipedia to influence its rules and policies. At the same time communication is facilitated both through its digital character and the many opportunities to edit and comment on the content. The Wikipedia community shares a dedication to its main goal, the creation of a reliable online encyclopaedia, which is generally supported. Unlike Stegbauer's indication, Konieczny does not think that Wikipedia demonstrates significant power distances and therefore can keep bureaucracy balanced to the open character in general. Still, he does not negate that oligarchic tendencies could take over in the future if the aforementioned characteristics change (Konieczny, 2009, p.189). This could happen if the group of administrators exerted increasing control over the majority of users of lower access levels and overrode their opinions, for example.

Back to the question at hand though, the tendencies for oligarchic behaviour might counter Ostrom's third design principle for long term self-organised regimes. As she states that rules are most effective when derived and adapted by the members of a regime itself, the dominance of a group of members over the others might prove fatal to the long term reliability of the collective action. If that would be the case, it could lead to a form of migration from one project to another. As knowledge is a nonrivalrous resource and the Wikipedia community works on voluntary basis, there are no restrictions on the creation of possible competitive projects. This actually happened to Wikipedia when Larry Sanger, the co-founder of Wikipedia next to Jimmy Wales, decided that he would create a fork to Wikipedia, the online encyclopaedia "Citizendium". He felt the current Wikipedia community did not work as efficiently as they used to and the policies are not as openly discussed as he wished. He also felt that the maintaining of the quality standards of articles needed improvement. His project did not yet become as successful in terms of the numbers of users and articles. (Deterding, 2007) This could be due to the fact that not a large number of users of the original Wikipedia migrated to the new platform. It might also be the case that because of the increased expectations on the quality standards the initial threshold for participation is higher.

In the fourth design principle Ostrom states that external authorities should accept the community's rules. Considering the global nature of the internet, there are little restrictions in place by outside authorities on the Wikipedia's internal rules. The anti-vandalism policy refers directly to matters within the workings of the community, and as such is not bound by external regulations. In general, though, there are areas where the laws and regulations of the different states have an impact, such as the author's rights and influences on the licensing regime of Wikipedia. Also, the personality rights of living persons and their biographies on Wikipedia are specially protected by internal rules, (Wikipedia: Biographies of living persons, 2010) which in itself are not necessarily because of external pressure, though personality rights are also part of external legal frameworks. In states where censorship exists, the access to Wikipedia might be limited for political reasons.

In case of Wikipedia in general, it basically survives on peer review. Only by the correction of the content by the users is the encyclopaedia able to create reliable knowledge. Therefore self-monitoring as the fifth design principle is an integral part of the system as a whole. In case of the anti-vandalism policy, all users should be aware of possible disruptive behaviour and have the possibility to warn perpetrators according to guidelines which are expected to be used. In case the vandalism needs to be stopped by actually blocking the trespassing individual's account or protecting the article in question, an administrator is at least needed to enforce this. In the English Wikipedia there is even a group of members who see their main responsibility within the system to counter vandalism. They do not hold special rights other than the ability to edit articles that basically any user can gain. Yet they still can issue warnings or convey the problem to an administrator if nothing else works (Wikipedia: Counter-Vandalism Unit, 2010).

As to the sixth principle, the sanctions for causing vandalism are gradually increased. Possible first sanctions are rather seen as a reminder or a slight warning. Considering the anti-vandalism policy itself, which considers only deliberate acts of vandalism as such, it is not always easy to tell if someone acted intentionally in a disruptive way or not, therefore the sanctions need to be low in the beginning. The sanctions can reach much more severe levels than a posted reminder, though, as has been described above with the 'CheckUser' or 'Oversight' abilities, which normally are only exerted after discussion and wielded only by very high ranking members.

Any system where disputes can arise and where disruptive behaviour is sanctioned needs certain possibilities for arbitration, Ostrom states as the seventh design principle. As already described above, the English Wikipedia has both a Mediation Committee and an Arbitration Committee, which can settle disputes at the highest level. Requests for arbitration can be entered through the Wikipedia system and are generally open to all users. Discussants on lower levels can create pages to the articles to communicate about diverting opinions.

The eighth design principle underlines the possibility of nested structures within the whole framework of the community. In larger successful systems using the commons, Ostrom often observes "the presence of governance activities organized in multiple layers of nested enterprises" (Ostrom, 2000, p.152). Enterprises in this case are understood as organised forms of collective action. Within Wikipedia, there are many projects where many users participate. The general access levels and major rules are the same throughout the system, but an inherent characteristic of subsidiarity can be observed, meaning that problems are to be solved at the lowest levels if possible. Users can warn other users of their infringements, talk pages allow users to communicate over disputes on the content of articles, for example. Arbitration should come only into play at the last possible level. Therefore one can say that many projects within Wikipedia are nested in the overall structure.

5 Conclusion

On the whole, the case of the anti-vandalism policy and many traits of Wikipedia hold structures and processes that can be considered applicable to the design principles Elinor Ostrom set out for long term self-organized regimes for traditional common pool resources. Even in the case of Wikipedia, where the resource in question is knowledge, which is nonrivalrous and where possibly everyone can access it through the internet, the principles are adaptable or their main characteristics can be found. Therefore Ostrom's model could set valuable parameters for new studies on other forms of knowledge or information commons in the digital world.

One of the major factors in deciding if the design principles reflect successful collective action regimes is the longevity of them. In case of Wikipedia, the system has been functioning since 2001, which can be considered a long timeframe in internet history. It also shows that the community has proven resilient to major disruptions so far. An indicator for this is the amount of knowledge bundled in Wikipedia. Following Ostrom's indications one can argue, that a possible reason for this might be based on the dispute settlement and arbitration system and the fact it has so far managed to resolve conflicts within the community successfully.

There are many forms of collaborative actions in the virtual sphere of the internet, which could be of interest for future research. Apart from wikis for all kinds of topics, there are other collaborative actions such as Open Source projects and other virtual communities sharing and creating intellectual goods. Some of them are closely linked with commercial interests, something also often happening with Open Source Software, or by the advertising marked they provide. These influences could also change the dynamics for collective action within some groups. It would open up questions on how Ostrom's understanding of the commons can be adapted to other virtual communities as well. It might also be worth comparing the parameters singled out by Ostrom to communities which have not explicitly evolved around one form of content, such as social community websites, which still need to organise their members' interactions through rule settings and guidelines.

References

Angwin, J. and G. A. Fowler (2009): "Volunteers Log Off as Wikipedia Ages," *The Wall Street Journal*, (27 Nov 2009), online available at: `http://online.wsj.com/article/SB125893981183759969.html`; accessed 18 Jan 2010.

Deterding, S. (2007): "Next Wikipedia, take a right. Wikipedia, Citizendium, and the politics of knowledge: An interview with Larry Sanger," *Bundeszentrale für politische Bildung*, (Dossier Open Source. 08 Jan 2007), online available at: http://www.bpb.de/themen/KD5Y51.html; accessed 18 Jan 2010.

Hardin, G. (1968): "The Tragedy of the Commons," *Science*, 162(3859), pp. 1243–1248.

Hess, C. and E. Ostrom (2007): *Understanding Knowledge as a Commons: From Theory to Practice*, The MIT Press, Cambridge, London.

Konieczny, P. (2009): "Governance, Organization, and Democracy on the Internet: The Iron Law and the Evolution of Wikipedia," *Sociological Forum*, 24(1), pp. 162–192.

Lessig, L. (2002): *The Future of Ideas. The Fate of the Commons in a Connected World*, 2nd; first published 2001, new york: random house, inc. edition, Vintage Books Edition, New York.

Ostrom, E. (1986): "An Agenda for the Study of Institutions," *Public Choice*, 48(1), pp. 3–25.

Ostrom, E. (1990): *Governing the Commons: The Evolution of Institutions for Collective Action*, Cambridge University Press, New York.

Ostrom, E. (2000): "Action and the Evolution of Social Norms," *The Journal of Economic Perspectives*, 14(3), pp. 137–158.

Stegbauer, C. (2009): *Wikipedia. Das Rätsel der Kooperation*, VS Verlag für Sozialwissenschaften, Wiesbaden.

Stegbauer, C. and A. Rausch (2006): *Strukturalistische Internetforschung. Netzwerkanalysen internetbasierter Kommunikationsräume*, VS Verlag für Sozialwissenschaften, Wiesbaden.

Suh, B., G. Convertino, E. Chi, and P. Pirolli (2009): "The Singularity is Not Near: Slowing Growth of Wikipedia," *WikiSym '09*, (25-27 Oct 2009, Orlando, Florida), online available at: http://www-users.cs.umn.edu/~echi/papers/2009-WikiSym/wikipedia-slow-growth-ASC-PARC.pdf; accessed 18 Jan 2010.

Tapscott, D. and A. D. Williams (2007): *Wikinomics. Die Revolution im Netz*, Carl Hanser Verlag München.

Wikimedia Deutschland e.V. (2010): *Wikimedia Deutschland e.V.: Satzung*, online available at: http://wikimedia.de/index.php?id=9; accessed 06 Feb 2010.

Wikimedia Foundation Inc. (2010): *Wikimedia Foundation: Home*, online available at: http://wikimediafoundation.org/wiki/Home; accessed 14 Jan 2010.

Wikipedia: About (2010): Wikipedia: The Free Encyclopedia, online available at: http://en.wikipedia.org/w/index.php?title=Wikipedia&oldid=341846856; accessed 04 Feb 2010.

Wikipedia: Administrators (2010): Wikipedia: The Free Encyclopedia, online available at: http://en.wikipedia.org/w/index.php?title=Wikipedia:Administrators&oldid=341141411; accessed 04 Feb 2010.

Wikipedia: Arbitration (2010): Wikipedia: The Free Encyclopedia, online available at: `http://en.wikipedia.org/w/index.php?title=Wikipedia:`
`Arbitration\&oldid=339214493`; accessed 04 Feb 2010.

Wikipedia: Arbitration Committee/Procedures (2010): Wikipedia: The Free Encyclopedia, online available at: `http://en.wikipedia.org/w/index.php?title=`
`Wikipedia:Arbitration_Committee/Procedures&oldid=340711791`; accessed 04
Feb 2010.

Wikipedia: Arbitration/Policy (2010): Wikipedia: The Free Encyclopedia, online available at: `http://en.wikipedia.org/w/index.php?title=Wikipedia:`
`Arbitration/Policy&oldid=332115367`; accessed 04 Feb 2010.

Wikipedia: Biographies of living persons (2010): Wikipedia: The Free Encyclopedia,
online available at: `http://en.wikipedia.org/w/index.php?title=Wikipedia:`
`Biographies_of_living_persons&oldid=341835264`; accessed 04 Feb 2010.

Wikipedia: Checkuser (2010): Wikipedia: The Free Encyclopedia, online available at: `http://en.wikipedia.org/w/index.php?title=Wikipedia:`
`CheckUser&oldid=341431596`; accessed 04 Feb 2010.

Wikipedia: Counter-Vandalism Unit (2010): Wikipedia: The Free Encyclopedia,
online available at: `http://en.wikipedia.org/w/index.php?title=Wikipedia:`
`Counter-Vandalism_Unit\&oldid=329944176`; accessed 04 Feb 2010.

Wikipedia: Licensing Update (2010): Wikipedia: The Free Encyclopedia, online available at: `http://en.wikipedia.org/w/index.php?title=Wikipedia:Licensing_`
`update&oldid=335720750`; accessed 04 Feb 2010.

Wikipedia: Mediation Committee (2010): Wikipedia: The Free Encyclopedia,
online available at: `http://en.wikipedia.org/w/index.php?title=Wikipedia:`
`Mediation_Committee&oldid=336793986`; accessed 04 Feb 2010.

Wikipedia: Oversight (2010): Wikipedia: The Free Encyclopedia, online available at: `http://en.wikipedia.org/w/index.php?title=Wikipedia:`
`Oversight&oldid=341614245`; accessed 04 Feb 2010.

Wikipedia: User access levels (2010): Wikipedia: The Free Encyclopedia, online
available at: `http://en.wikipedia.org/w/index.php?title=Wikipedia:User_`
`access_levels&oldid=339364994`; accessed 04 Feb 2010.

Wikipedia: Vandalism (2010): Wikipedia: The Free Encyclopedia, online available at: `http://en.wikipedia.org/w/index.php?title=Wikipedia:`
`Vandalism&oldid=341625714`; accessed 04 Feb 2010.

WikiSym (2010): "About WikiSym," *The International Symposium on Wikis and Open
Collaboration*, online available at: `http://www.wikisym.org/about/`; accessed 17
Feb 2010.

WikiSym '09 (2010): "WikiSym 2009 Program and Schedule," *The International Symposium on Wikis and Open Collaboration*, online available at: `http://www.wikisym.`
`org/ws2009/tiki-index.php?page=Program`; accessed 17 Feb 2010.